An Illustrated History of
Modern Britain
1783-1964

By Denis Richards

AN ILLUSTRATED HISTORY OF MODERN EUROPE,
1789–1945

AN ILLUSTRATED HISTORY OF MODERN BRITAIN,
1783–1964
Denis Richards and J. W. Hunt

A HISTORY OF BRITAIN

Vol I   BRITAIN AND THE ANCIENT WORLD
James A. Bolton and Denis Richards

Vol II MEDIEVAL BRITAIN
Denis Richards and Arnold D. Ellis

Vol III BRITAIN UNDER THE TUDORS AND STUARTS
Denis Richards

Vol IV BRITAIN 1714–1851
Denis Richards and Anthony Quick

Vol V   BRITAIN 1851–1945
Denis Richards and Anthony Quick

Vol VI TWENTIETH CENTURY BRITAIN
Denis Richards and Anthony Quick

Vol VII BRITAIN 1714–1960
A Shorter Narrative

ROYAL AIR FORCE, 1935–45
A history in three volumes
Denis Richards and Hilary St George Saunders

OFFSPRING OF THE 'VIC'
A history of Morley College

An Illustrated History of

MODERN BRITAIN
1783-1964

Denis Richards M.A.

FORMERLY SENIOR HISTORY AND ENGLISH MASTER, BRADFIELD
COLLEGE, AND SCHOLAR OF TRINITY HALL, CAMBRIDGE

J. W. Hunt M.A.

FORMERLY SENIOR HISTORY MASTER, CITY OF LONDON SCHOOL, AND
SCHOLAR OF PETERHOUSE, CAMBRIDGE

Longman

LONGMAN GROUP LIMITED
London

*Associated companies, branches, and representatives
throughout the world*

First published 1950
Twelfth impression 1963
Second edition 1965
Eighth impression 1977

ISBN 0 582 31486 0

Permission has been given for this book
to be transcribed into Braille

*Printed in Hong Kong by
Yu Luen Offset Printing Factory Ltd*

Preface to the Second Edition

The book has been thoroughly revised in the Second Edition. There has been some rearrangement of material and the period after 1900 has been given fuller treatment. Two chapters have been added and other chapters extended to cover the period from 1945 to 1964. The maps have been re-drawn.

All too often the young student carries away false impressions of events in history, not because the statements he has read are untrue, but because the demands of compression have left too much to his imagination. In this book we have therefore aimed at length rather than brevity, details rather than generalizations, the concrete rather than the abstract.

On the other hand, a wealth of detail may cause the reader to lose sight of the wood in contemplating the trees. We trust that the detail we have introduced will illuminate rather than obscure the main themes of modern British history—notably the transfer of political power to the people, the improvement of social conditions, the development of science and its application to industry, the evolution of the Commonwealth, and the great external struggles against France, Russia and Germany. If this is to be so, however, we must appeal for the co-operation of the teacher in one respect: because certain facts may throw light on an important personality or event, or arouse interest by adding colour, it does not follow that the pupil should be expected to learn them by heart. We have, to take an extreme example, given the details of a meal consumed by Palmerston at an advanced age; we should expect the pupil to remember from this, not the sequence of the courses, but the fact that Palmerston was something of a 'card'. In other words, it would greatly help our intention if the teacher, when he sets a passage of the book for private study, would call attention in advance to salient points which he wishes memorized.

In view of the importance of the subject, we have included a chapter on the history of science. To do this we have had to sacrifice a chapter on the arts. We console ourselves with the thought that scientific developments can be 'explained' better than beauty.

We hope our use of the term 'Britain' will not be considered unscholarly. To use 'England' is to invite criticism from north of the border; 'Great Britain' still excludes Ireland; and within the limits of our period the country had three different official titles.

D. R.
J. W. H.

Contents

List of Maps

Introduction

In 1783 George III had just lost a bitter struggle against an important section of his subjects on each side of the Atlantic. The American colonists, aided alike by the skill of George Washington and the incompetence of Lord North, had gained their independence; and the King's attempt to assert decisive influence through subservient ministers and the use of patronage had collapsed in the general debacle. Henceforward genuine parliamentary government—democratic in America, at first far from democratic here—was assured of two strongholds in the world.

This was the dominant political fact of the moment in 1783. Equally important for the future, however, were the economic changes which the country was undergoing. The enclosure of the old open fields and commons was resulting in a more efficient agriculture and a better food supply; while the change from hand-work in the home to machine-work in the factory, which goes by the name of the Industrial Revolution, was beginning to create fresh sources of wealth and a greater volume of goods. With more food and more goods Britain could support great increases in her population—increases which had arisen, in the first place, from improved medical knowledge and a lower death rate.[1]

But the population was not only increasing in size; it was also changing in character. The enclosures were enriching great landowners on the one hand, and producing landless agricultural labourers on the other. With the development of trade and transport and towns there was growing up a powerful and prosperous middle class, together with a large working class to whom at least the prospects of advancement were open. As the nineteenth century wore on, each of these classes in turn—first the urban middle class, then the urban working class, and finally the agricultural labourer—was to make good its claim to have some effective say in the destinies of nation and city and parish. Before the onslaught of these new forces the old aristocratic monopoly of privilege was to be swept away, but only the wealthier middle

[1] The population of England and Wales was about 5½ millions in 1700, 9 millions in 1800, and 36 millions in 1900.

class, with its great industrial and commercial power, was to penetrate to the political centres of control—Parliament and Corporation—before 1900. If the eighteenth century may be called the Century of the Aristocracy, the nineteenth may thus be termed the Century of the Middle Class; and our own times may well have some title to be known as the Century of the Working Class.

The changes in almost every sphere of life which have occurred since 1783 make it difficult for the modern man to realize the links which bind him to his ancestors. From a Britain of aeroplanes and atom bombs, film stars and football pools, trade unions and trousers, he looks back on a Britain of coaches and cudgels, piquet and port, pocket boroughs and knee-breeches. His house, his hobbies, his livelihood probably bear little resemblance to those of his forebears; and even the things which retain the same name, such as beer or boxing, have mostly undergone profound changes of character.

Yet for all its strangeness today, the Britain of 1783—where domestic servants were plentiful at £10 a year, and the most popular sporting spectacle was a public execution, and the chief danger to pedestrians was the slops from the upper windows— was already part of the Modern Age. For the distinctive feature of modern times is man's increased control over his physical environment; and from the perfection of an efficient steam-engine in the eighteenth century until today this control has been continuously developed at a pace unknown in any previous period of history. The material basis of civilization is power, and with the steam-engine the old dependence of man on the power of the human body, assisted by beasts of burden and a limited use of wind and water, was ended. Thenceforward material civilization was to rest increasingly on the power of the machine; and in this sense the nineteenth century is the Century of Steam, or Coal, just as surely as it is the Century of the Middle Class, and just as surely as the twenty-first century—if there is one—will be the Century of Atomic Energy.

From the stage-coach to the stratoliner, from Burke's Bill for the reduction of sinecures to Shinwell's Bill for the nationalization of the mines, there are thus two clear and closely related lines of development. One is the growth of mechanical power, the other the transference of political and economic power from the fortunate few to the broad mass of the community. These at least are continuous threads in the tangled skein of Modern History.

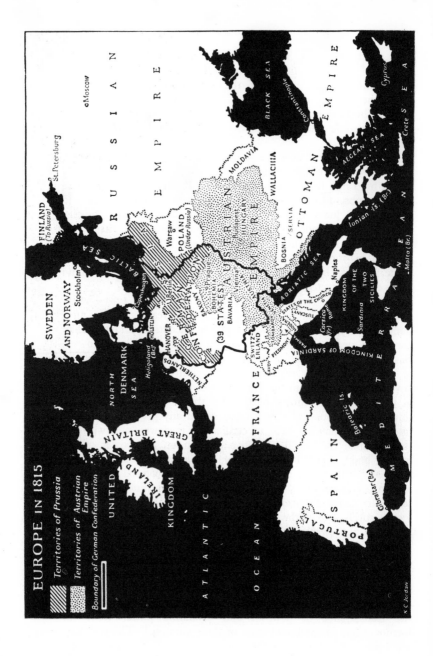

EUROPE IN 1815

Territories of Prussia
Territories of Austrian Empire
Boundary of German Confederation

GREAT BRITAIN
IRELAND
UNITED KINGDOM

ATLANTIC OCEAN

FRANCE

SPAIN
PORTUGAL
Balearic Is.
Gibraltar (Br.)

SWEDEN AND NORWAY
Stockholm

FINLAND (To Russia)
St. Petersburg

RUSSIAN EMPIRE

Moscow

DENMARK
Copenhagen
Heligoland (Br.)
HANOVER
HOLSTEIN
NETHERLANDS
GERMAN CONFEDERATION (39 STATES)
BERLIN
SAXONY
BOHEMIA
Prague
BAVARIA
Vienna
SWITZERLAND
SAVOY
PIEDMONT
LOMBARDY
PARMA
TUSCANY
STATES OF THE CHURCH
ROME (Fr.)
Corsica (Fr.)
KINGDOM OF SARDINIA
Sardinia
KINGDOM OF THE TWO SICILIES
Naples
Sicily
Malta (Br.)

WARSAW
POLAND (Under Russia)

AUSTRIAN EMPIRE
Budapest
HUNGARY

MOLDAVIA
WALLACHIA
SERVIA
BOSNIA

OTTOMAN EMPIRE

Constantinople

BLACK SEA

AEGEAN SEA
Ionian Is. (Br.)
ADRIATIC SEA
MEDITERRANEAN

Crete
Cyprus

BALTIC SEA
NORTH SEA

K. Jordan

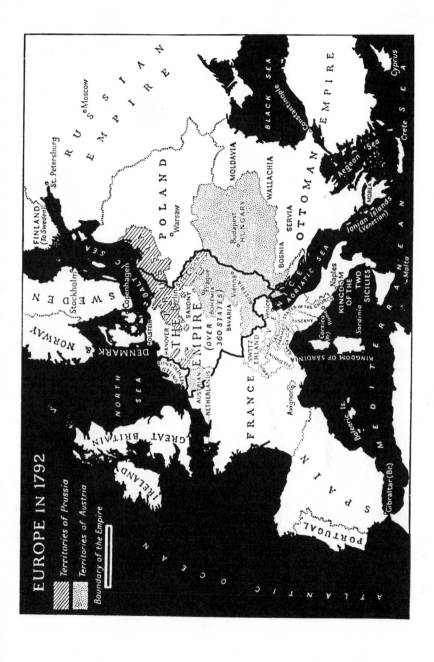

EUROPE IN 1792

Territories of Prussia
Territories of Austria
Boundary of the Empire

RUSSIAN EMPIRE

o Moscow

o St. Petersburg

FINLAND
(To Sweden)

NORWAY

SWEDEN

Stockholm o

BALTIC SEA

Copenhagen o

DENMARK & HOLSTEIN

NORTH SEA

GREAT BRITAIN

IRELAND

ATLANTIC OCEAN

HANOVER

UNITED NETHERLANDS

AUSTRIAN NETHERLANDS

THE EMPIRE (OVER 360 STATES)

Berlin o

SILESIA

SAXONY

BOHEMIA

Prague o

BAVARIA

Vienna o

AUSTRIA

SWITZERLAND

FRANCE

Avignon o

PORTUGAL

SPAIN

Balearic Is.

Gibraltar (Br.)

MEDITERRANEAN SEA

KINGDOM OF SARDINIA

Corsica (Fr.)

PIEDMONT

SAVOY

NICE

Sardinia

TUSCANY

STATES OF THE CHURCH

Rome o

Naples o

KINGDOM OF THE TWO SICILIES

Venice o

ADRIATIC SEA

POLAND

Warsaw o

HUNGARY

Budapest o

BOSNIA

SERVIA

WALLACHIA

MOLDAVIA

OTTOMAN EMPIRE

Constantinople o

BLACK SEA

AEGEAN SEA

Ionian Islands (Venetian)

MOREA

Crete

Cyprus

Malta

1. The Agrarian Revolution

During the eighteenth century English agriculture was revolu- The motive forces
tionized and the English countryside transformed. Two basic
forces, one conscious, the other unconscious, were responsible
for this. The first was the normal human desire to get rich, the
second the increase in population. For as more mouths were born,
they clamoured for more food; as more food was demanded, so
its price rose, and as the price of food rose, so enterprising
gentlemen determined to make their land yield its utmost.

At the beginning of the eighteenth century nearly two-thirds of The old system
English ploughland was still under the age-old open-field system,
with its scattered strips and its wheat—barley (or oats)—fallow
rotation. Implements had scarcely improved for hundreds of
years, and the method of sowing—'broadcasting' by hand—had
been inherited without a break from biblical days. From time
immemorial, too, the villagers had enjoyed certain rights on the
common pasture and waste, though legally this belonged to the
lord of the manor: rights such as cutting peat from bog, collecting
sticks and felling trees, turning pigs into the woods for acorns,
grazing cattle on the heath, or letting them crop the stubble
in the great fields after harvest. Even the 'squatters', who
owned no strips and had no legal standing, availed themselves
of most of these rights, for custom often permitted what the law
denied.

The widespread (but by no means universal) existence of an Defects of the old system
open-field system had more or less answered England's needs
for many centuries. But when the population began to rise so
sharply and the need for increased food production was felt,
many landowners became acutely conscious of its defects. In the
first place it entailed great waste of land, since under this system
one-third was usually fallow. Secondly, there was great waste of
time and labour, since each man's strips were widely scattered.
Thirdly, it was impossible to rear good cattle, partly because there
were no hedges to give them shelter, partly because the diseased
mingled freely with the rest, partly because there was insufficient
winter food in the way of root crops—a deficiency responsible for
the custom of slaughtering most of the beasts at Martinmas and

I

salting down the carcasses.[1] Poor cattle were, indeed, a very prominent feature of the old agriculture, and a typical Warwickshire sheep of the early eighteenth century was thus described:

> His frame large and loose, his bones heavy, his legs long and thick, his chine as well as his rump as sharp as a hatchet, his skin rattling on his ribs like a skeleton covered with parchment.

There was one other great disadvantage of the old open-field system. To apply fresh practices to unenclosed land was virtually impossible. The small size of the strips and the limited equipment of their holders made it out of the question to work each strip individually, and the system depended on mutual help at times of ploughing and harvest. Any proposed change would thus have to command general assent before it could be carried out. Moreover, there was a definite bar to experiment in the habit of allowing the cattle to graze on the stubble after harvest. This custom ruled out experiment with crops which ripened later than the general crop of the field since, given a choice, even cattle would prefer the experimental crop to the stubble. Thus, taken all in all, the defects of the open-field system were very great, and the first step to all agricultural improvement was obviously to consolidate and enclose each man's holdings.

Jethro Tull and hoeing

Once this had been done, there were many improvements that could be carried out. The first was the elimination of much fallow. Jethro Tull (1674–1741) had already proclaimed in the *New Horse-hoeing Husbandry* that if land were well and truly hoed, the fallow year would be unnecessary. This had scarcely been practicable while the strip system was persisted in, since the strips were too narrow for effective cross-hoeing, but if the farms were made compact it could be widely applied. And it was worth applying, for the use of the hoe in combination with a seed-drill of his own invention had enabled Tull to grow crops twice as heavy as before, using only one-third of the seed.

'Turnip' Townshend and the 'Norfolk rotation'

A more general solution to the fallow problem, however, was available in the new rotation of crops first popularized during the 1730s by Lord Townshend in Norfolk. Between 1709 and 1711 Townshend had been ambassador to the Netherlands, where he

---

[1] Hence (1) the physical value of the Catholic custom of eating fish on Fridays, since too much salt meat leads to scurvy, and (2) the importance of spice, which was badly needed to disguise the flavour of the Salt Beef of Old England.

had picked up valuable ideas which he put into practice on his own estates at Raynham. The central feature of these was the elimination of fallow, after a preparatory use of manure and marl, by growing root crops or grasses between the years of corn crops.

(James Gillray, 1793, from a print in the British Museum)

The war against France brought a call for recruits. In the absence of proper provision for dependants or the disabled, it was a rash man who volunteered.

    1. 'John Bull, Happy.'   2. 'John Bull going to the Wars.'
    3. 'John Bull's Property in Danger' [his wife is forced to pawn it].
    4. 'John Bull's glorious Return.'

'Turnip' Townshend, as he came to be known, and the 'Norfolk rotation' in fact revolutionized English agriculture. In place of the three-year sequence of wheat—barley (or oats)—fallow, a four-year cycle of wheat—turnips—barley (or oats)—clover was introduced. Both the turnips and the clover had the effect of introducing nitrogen, a great fertilizer, into the soil.

Robert Bakewell and stock-breeding

The widespread adoption of root-crops could offer another important advantage in providing winter food for the cattle. With this, and the new hedges for shelter, it was now possible to sustain large herds throughout the winter—herds which would no longer be contaminated by mixing on the common. Scientific stock-breeding was thus beginning, a pioneer in this direction being Robert Bakewell (1725–1795) of Dishley in Leicestershire, a grand John Bull figure who entertained prodigiously and threw his farm open for others to study his methods. By breeding from selected beasts to produce special characteristics he vastly improved the quality of English stock; his 'New Leicester' sheep and 'Leicester Longhorn' cattle were to become famous the world over, and English herds came into great demand, especially when the huge grazing areas of the Argentine had to be stocked. The work of Bakewell and his followers (notably the brothers Robert and Charles Colling, of Durham, who developed the Shorthorn breed of cattle) finally transformed English beasts from tough, scraggy and diseased specimens into fat meat-producing creatures whose carcases for the first time now became more valuable than their skins. On the average, beasts at the end of the eighteenth century weighed anything from two to three times as much as their forerunners a hundred years earlier.

George III, 'Coke of Holkham' and the model farm

These were the main innovations which stimulated and accompanied enclosure, but there were a host of others, from better implements to improved methods of draining, fertilizing and ploughing. Many of these were popularized by the reigning monarch, George III ('Farmer George'), who took great pride in his model farms at Windsor. Another notable farmer was Thomas Coke of Holkham, in Norfolk. Leading gentry from all over the country came every year to the great show on his estates where he offered prizes to local farmers for new ideas, new seeds and so on, as well as for their skill in such matters as sheep-shearing or handling a plough. When he took over these estates in 1776 it was remarked that they produced 'but one blade of grass, and two rabbits fighting for it', but when he died in 1842 this erstwhile sandy waste had been converted into one of the finest properties in the kingdom.

Arthur Young and the spread of information

Agricultural education on an even wider scale was undertaken by Arthur Young (1741–1820), who travelled the country noting improvements, spreading information, and constantly urging farmers to support enclosure as the foundation of all agricultural progress. The fact that he had himself failed as a practical farmer, even paying someone £100 to take off his hands a farm of 300 acres which later proved perfectly profitable, did not stop his being a magnificent propagandist. Constantly active, he gave the results of his surveys to the nation in such works as *The Farmer's Letters to the People of England*, *The Management of Hogs*, *Travels in France, Italy and Spain* and *An Essay on Manures*. These works were widely read, and many were translated into French, German and Russian. But though his work in spreading knowledge of the new processes was invaluable, he lived to doubt whether enclosure had proved to be quite the blessing he had thought.

Enclosure as a movement went on in one way and another for many centuries, but it was at its height from 1760 to 1820. Between these dates something like 4,000 Enclosure Acts were passed, and over 5 million acres of open field and common disappeared. Enclosure was at first carried out by private arrangement, but since a few objectors could hold up the whole scheme this method soon exhausted itself, and as the eighteenth century wore on, the accepted way of enclosing a village came to be by means of a special Act of Parliament. *The new system —enclosure*

Under this procedure, advocates of the scheme—usually two or three of the greatest local landowners—promoted a Bill in Parliament to carry out enclosure in their particular village, and Parliament normally assented if the local lord of the manor, the tithe owners and the owners of four-fifths of the strips were in favour. But the owners of four-fifths of the strips might amount to a mere three or four men, while a hundred or more held the remaining fifth. The enclosure petitions were in consequence often highly unpopular. Once the Enclosure Bill was passed, however—and objectors were for the most part far too poor or powerless to organize strong opposition—everyone in the village was compelled to come into the scheme. Parliament then appointed Commissioners to investigate all claims and re-allot the land in compact holdings, and ultimately a map of the new arrangement, with its big enclosed farms instead of open scattered strips, was drawn up. In 1801 the whole process was speeded up by a General Enclosure Act, rendering a special Act for each village unnecessary. *The Enclosure Acts*

There was great room for unfairness in this method of settling claims; all too often the lord, or one of his agents or friends, was allowed to sit as a Commissioner—an abuse which persisted for over fifty years before it was checked by Parliament. But perhaps *Unfairness of the enclosure procedure* the most important source of hardship was that the lord's legal right to the common was enforced. Although the strip holders were given a little extra land in settlement of their common rights, this was not nearly equal in value to the old extensive privileges, and the villagers usually resented the enclosure of the commons more than any other feature. Thus from the redistribution the richer owners usually came off better than they should have done, the poorer not so well. The most unfortunate of all was the 'squatter', who, having no strips, had no claim, either on paper or by right of custom, to a share in the land; entirely uncompensated, he saw the common which was his livelihood disappear into the lord's estate. This element in enclosure was the cause of much distress, for the few acres of common, if any, that were preserved were quite inadequate to support a single family.

A further source of hardship was the great cost of enclosure. Even the smallest holder had to pay not only the cost of hedging and ditching his own land, which was very great in view of the high standards enforced, but a share towards the surveying, the redistribution and the map-making—to say nothing of hedging and ditching the vicar's land. Together these costs often proved too much for the small man, who was virtually forced to dispose of his property—probably at a very low price—to a larger landowner.

Social results of enclosure

The use that those who sold their land made of the proceeds varied greatly. Many of the small farmers went to towns, set up in business, and became profiting pioneers—or pioneer profiteers —of the Industrial Revolution. Others were not so successful, and sank to be town labourers, as did large numbers of the late squatters. Others still, lacking the imagination or the heart to desert the countryside, often drank away their little capital in the local ale-house, and finished up, like those squatters who remained, in one of the worst-paid occupations of all—that of the landless agricultural labourer.

From one important angle the direct results of the enclosure movement were thus to make ownership of land still more unequal, to drive important rural elements to the towns, thereby speeding on the Industrial Revolution, and in general to make the rich richer and the poor poorer. But the disappearance of the land-holding peasantry, important and tragic though it was, was not the main result of the enclosure movement. The greatest consequence was an increase in the food supply: for after enclosure vital agricultural improvements, mostly worked out many years before by enthusiastic pioneers, could be and were applied by enterprising individuals all over the country to their own farms.

The agrarian changes of the eighteenth century were a turning point in British history, marking off the last of medieval England from the England of the nineteenth century. The open fields and strips gave place to compact farms, neatly hedged and ditched. The land was made to yield more food, the beasts grew fatter, and the growing population could be fed. In the course of this the large class of peasant smallholders disappeared, and the countryside came to know only great landlords, tenant farmers and landless labourers. A drift to the towns set in, and has never ceased. Before the Agrarian Revolution there was inefficiency relieved by peasant independence; afterwards, efficiency blackened by widespread distress. The necessity for enclosure was undeniable, and its purely agricultural results were excellent; but the social consequences of the way in which it was carried out were often deplorable.

2. The Industrial Revolution

1 The Causes of the Industrial Revolution. The Textile Industry

During the nineteenth century Britain became the 'workshop of the world'. Behind every aspect of the Victorian Age, behind the politics, science, art and religion, behind the fortunes of the rich and the misery of the poor, there were the factories, the steam-engines, the foreign trade, the investments, the dividends. But though all this reached its climax in the latter half of the nineteenth century, its beginnings were a hundred years earlier, in the grey dawn of the Industrial Revolution.

Causes of the
Industrial
Revolution

The Industrial Revolution is the name given to the movement, spread over many decades, by which industry was transformed from hand-work at home to machine-work in factories. The primary motive force behind this development was, as with the Agrarian Revolution, the increase of population. Just as the larger population demanded more food, so it also demanded more clothes, more goods, more houses. Equally, as more clothes and goods and houses became obtainable, so it was possible for the country to support a larger population.

Mere pressure of numbers could not, however, produce unaided a movement of this nature. The development of scientific knowledge prompted inventions, like the steam-engine, which in turn were responsible for much of the whole transformation. Further, that scientific development could hardly have occurred except in a country like England, which had enjoyed internal peace for a century, and which was torn neither by political nor religious feuds. England, moreover, already had the nucleus of a vast commercial system capable of dealing with expanding industry—banks, cheques, exchanges and insurance concerns like Lloyd's—while together with Scotland and Wales she made up probably the largest free-trade unit in Europe, completely unhampered by the local tariff systems which paralysed French and German trade. When to all this is added the great improvement in communications by road, river and canal which began about 1760, and the fact that the British Isles contained rich deposits of the coal and iron necessary to make and drive machinery, it becomes apparent why the Industrial Revolution began in Great Britain.

*   *   *   *   *

The Industrial Revolution was a general movement, but its force was first felt in the textile industry. In the seventeenth century this industry was largely a spare-time occupation. The material employed was wool, though there were a few centres of silk manufacture, and flax was used in Ireland; cotton at this stage was comparatively unimportant. The old textile system—

The process of cloth-making began with 'carding', or separating the short 'staples' of wool from the raw mass. This was done by women and children in the home with a pair of 'hand-cards', in appearance rather like hair-brushes. Then followed spinning, or joining these short staples into continuous thread. This again was usually done by the women of the house, with the aid of a spinning-wheel. Finally the continuous thread was woven into cloth—a more difficult and specialized process, usually performed by men. The house might boast a small hand-loom, in which case the process could be completed at home, but a very usual method was for one man in the village to specialize as a weaver and for people to take their thread to him to be made up into cloth. If there was no weaver in the village, a travelling weaver sometimes came round with a portable loom.

As the British had long since found it more profitable to export finished cloth than raw wool, the cloth industry had become organized on a large scale. Great cloth merchants had sprung up —'clothiers' they were called—who encouraged households to produce far more than was necessary for family purposes. Riding round his area of the country with a train of pack-horses, the clothier of the seventeenth and the early eighteenth century would distribute raw wool to peasant households, and return later to collect made-up cloth. It was a system which had the advantages of securing a regular supply of cloth, augmenting the meagre earnings of agricultural life, and allowing work to be done in the free atmosphere of the home. On the other hand it was wasteful in the travelling involved, and often the quantity of finished cloth did not tally with the quantity of wool provided—a possibility for which the clothiers usually catered by paying very little for the work. its advantages and dis-advantages

The main defect in the old methods was that weaving was

many times faster than spinning. A man could weave into cloth in one day the yarn it had taken a woman the best part of a week to produce; for the hand-loom, as a piece of machinery, was far in advance of the spinning-wheel. And this disparity became even more pronounced after the first great textile invention of the eighteenth century—Kay's 'Flying Shuttle'.

The new inventions. Kay's 'Flying Shuttle', 1733

John Kay was a Lancashire man, who in 1733 produced a completely new device for weaving 'broadcloth'. Previously it had been necessary, when 'broadcloth' was being made, for two men to stand side by side at the hand-loom, and pass the shuttle to and fro. The 'Flying Shuttle' was an arrangement by which the shuttle was automatically thrown from one side of the loom to the other, so that one man could weave the widest cloth desired. Moreover, weaving of any sort became faster.

Kay himself did not benefit from his invention. Instead, he suffered much violence from mobs who claimed that he was putting them out of work, and finally he took refuge in France. Nevertheless, his invention lived on, and round about 1760 the 'Flying Shuttle' began to come into fairly general use. As soon as this happened the disparity in speed between weaving and spinning became much worse: the whole textile industry was thrown out of gear by the impossibility of keeping the production of thread up to the level required for Kay's machine, and some new spinning invention became imperative.

Wyatt and Paul, c. 1733

The pioneer work of speeding up spinning was done by John Wyatt and his backer, Lewis Paul. Wyatt's machine, produced in 1733, proved its worth in a small factory operated by ten women and two donkeys, but its inventor had no commercial success; indeed, at one time he was imprisoned for debt. Although the work of Wyatt and Paul was little known, and had no direct effect in the 1740s, it provided Arkwright with the idea for the later 'Water-Frame'.

Hargreaves's 'Spinning Jenny', c. 1765

It was Hargreaves's 'Jenny' which first began really to solve the vital problem of speeding up spinning. James Hargreaves was a Blackburn man, a carpenter and weaver by trade—hence his double interest in machinery and textiles. His invention was a machine in which eight spindles were harnessed to one treadle. The Jenny was thus only a multiplied spinning-wheel, but it was profoundly important, for the multiplication could go on almost indefinitely.

For some years Hargreaves did not make his invention public. When he did, his machines and house were smashed up by mobs and he was swindled by manufacturers. He did not, like Kay and Crompton, die in want, but his fortune was small compared with what he deserved, for Jennies began to spread with amazing speed. By 1788, ten years after his death, there were 20,000 of them varying in size from the original eight-spindle model to others working eighty spindles or more. The small ones became popular in cottages all over the country; the larger ones, needing greater capital, space and motive-power, began to appear in factories. In general, however, the Jenny remained a domestic apparatus, which revolutionized the spinning industry without driving it from the home. One of its main results was to increase the importance of cotton, for which it was invented.

The Jenny had one serious defect. It span a fine, weak yarn suitable for the weft (the 'cross'-thread in the shuttle) but not for the warp (the 'lengthwise' threads on the loom). The strong thread required for the warp had still to be spun on the wheel; and it became very usual to make a cloth of woollen or linen warp and cotton weft. Thus the cotton industry, before it could establish supremacy over wool, needed a thread which, while fine, would yet be strong enough to serve for warp as well as weft. To this ideal Arkwright's Water-Frame was the next step.

Richard Arkwright, the most prominent figure of the Industrial Revolution and an early example of the 'self-made man', was born at Preston. In turn barber, hair-dealer and horse-trader, he had no direct connection with textiles at first, but he more than made up for this by his hard-headed business ability. The machine which made him famous was a device for stretching the thread by drawing it through two pairs of rollers, the second of which revolved faster than the first. Spindles then twisted the stretched thread. The invention was virtually Wyatt and Paul's machine of a generation before, which Arkwright had had an opportunity of studying. It was patented in 1769, and later incorporated other details derived from earlier inventions.

Arkwright's 'Water-Frame', 1769

The effect of this machine, usually known as the Water-Frame since it came to be propelled by water-power, was doubly revolutionary. In the first place it span a yarn which was strong enough to be used for both warp and weft, and which thus made possible the production of satisfactory all-cotton fabric. Secondly, since it required greater motive-power than the hand, it led to the factory system. Arkwright himself showed the way. Financed by some wealthy Nottingham hosiers, he set up a 'mill' at Cromford, near Derby, on the rushing Derwent. Within a short time he was weaving all-cotton fabric and had secured the repeal of an old Act of Parliament which forbade printed cotton goods. Then he established other premises in Derbyshire and Lancashire, though enraged hand-workers burned down his largest mill, near

(*T. Onwyn*, 1840)

CHILDREN IN A COTTON FACTORY
A scene from a Victorian novel

Chorley, and rival manufacturers succeeded in a legal attack on his patent. Arkwright, however, was not the man to succumb before even these setbacks—he simply opened up more mills, drove incessantly and furiously over the North of England from one to another in his coach, took grammar and spelling lessons at the age of fifty, and by the time of his death in 1792 was Sir Richard Arkwright and halfway to being a millionaire.

A further improvement was, however, essential before English cotton goods could rival their Indian originals. Arkwright's yarn was strong but coarse; the Jenny yarn fine but weak. The problem of producing a yarn at once strong and fine was solved by Samuel Crompton, a Bolton spinner and weaver. He combined, some-where about 1779, the principles of Jenny and Water-Frame (the moving carriage and the rollers respectively) into a composite machine, which, as a 'cross-bred', came to be known as a 'Mule'. As such it could not be patented, and Crompton used it at first only in his own tiny workshop. The fineness of his thread, how-ever, aroused the curiosity of neighbours and rivals, and he was so extensively spied on that he decided to make the invention public. He had no business ability, and he was shamefully treated by the local manufacturers, whose promise of a 'public subscrip-tion' brought in only £67 6s. 6d. Eventually he secured another subscription of £500 and a grant of £5,000. But most of this was swallowed up by debts he had now incurred as a manufacturer, and he died practically penniless.

If Crompton's 'Mule' made little money for its inventor, it proved a gold mine to many others. By 1812 it was driving about five million spindles throughout the country. The Jenny was now quite out of date; the spinning industry took its farewell of the cottages, and in the factories the 'Mules' clattered out strong, fine yarn destined to make British cotton goods famous all over the world. And so good was Crompton's work that to this day, in spite of the general use of the modern 'ring-spinning', 'mule-spinning' is still employed when the finest type of cotton thread is required.

The Jenny, the Water-Frame and the Mule between them increased the speed of spinning to such an extent that it was now weaving which lagged behind. For a time this told greatly in favour of the hand-loom weavers, whose services were in great demand, and who might even be seen strolling through the streets of northern towns with £5 notes stuck in their hat-bands. But their heyday was brief; an enterprising clergyman, Edmund Cartwright, soon succeeded in doing what the northern manufac-turers had pronounced to be impossible, and invented a mechan-ically driven loom.

Cartwright, who had been a fellow of Magdalen College,

Crompton's 'Mule'. 1779

Cartwright's power-loom, 1785

Oxford, produced his first machine without ever having seen a weaver working. Within three years he had effected such improvements that it was really practicable. In 1787 he set up a factory with twenty looms, at first using animal power, and then, in 1789, a steam-engine. In 1791 a bigger effort in partnership with a Manchester firm, to run 400 steam-looms, came to grief when the newly erected mills were set on fire by infuriated hand-loom weavers. Cartwright was in desperate straits, but he lived to see the triumph of his invention, though not to grow rich. Within thirty years the power-loom was everywhere winning the fight against the hand-loom, while the once-proud craftsmen of that historic apparatus were sweating their souls out in hovels at starvation wages.

Changes in the woollen industry

Mechanization, then, had triumphed in the cotton industry. It was only a question of time before the same processes would spread to wool. When they did, that part of the country, Yorkshire, which first had the sense to adopt them, gained a long lead. Slow in taking up the new ideas, and then handicapped by their greater distance from the main coalfields, the woollen industries of Somersetshire and East Anglia fell into decay, while the more enterprising Northerners prospered. All the great inventions were ultimately applied to the Yorkshire woollen industry, but the process took at least a generation. This delay occurred partly because the woollen industry was more hampered by ancient legal restrictions, partly because the amount of wool available was very limited until Australian sheep-farming opened up fresh sources of supply.

2 The Iron and Coal Industries. The Results of the Industrial Revolution

The Industrial Revolution would not have gone very far if the methods of producing iron had remained unchanged. At the beginning of the eighteenth century Britain's great natural deposits of iron ore were almost entirely unworked. She was becoming increasingly dependent on iron from Sweden, Germany and Russia, not from lack of native iron, but from lack of fuel to smelt it. For the fuel employed for smelting was charcoal; sufficient charcoal could not be produced without great quantities of timber; and timber depended on the forests, which were

The crisis in the iron industry

rapidly becoming exhausted. So the iron industry, centred then near the wooded areas of the south and south-west, was in a state of crisis, just as the cotton industry had been before the great spinning inventions.

The natural solution to this difficulty was the discovery of some other fuel. Coal had been burned as a household fuel in some parts of the country for centuries, and was already used in many industries; but for long it seemed impossible to employ for the smelting process, since its sulphur compounds, when released by combustion, made the iron brittle and unworkable. After many experimenters had failed the secret of success was hit upon by Abraham Darby, a Quaker iron-master of Coalbrookdale, in Shropshire, about the year 1709. He reduced coal to coke—by which stage it has lost most of its sulphur and become almost pure carbon, like charcoal—and with this he found that good pig-iron could be produced from the rough ore. The process was kept a family secret for some time, being improved by his son, another Abraham Darby, and it was not till the latter part of the century that it became widespread. *Darby's coke-smelting process, c. 1709*

Before the iron industry could expand to any really great dimensions, another invention was necessary. Darby's process of coke-smelting worked well for producing pig-iron suitable for making castings, but it could not make wrought or malleable iron. Henry Cort, a Northerner who had set up as an iron-master in Hampshire, solved this difficulty by the process known as 'pud-dling'. In this, the impure 'pigs' of iron were placed in a vessel heated by a reverberatory furnace—a furnace which allowed no direct contact between the iron and the coke (or later, coal). Iron oxides were mixed with the 'pigs'; and the heat, together with the stirring by long hooks—hence the name 'puddling'— caused the oxygen from these oxides to combine with the remaining carbon in the pigs and come off in the form of gas, thereby leaving the iron freer from carbon, and so less brittle. The iron was then passed between rollers—also invented by Cort—to reduce it from great lumps to bars. This was about fifteen times as quick as the old method of repeatedly heating and hammering, which, though it also ended by expelling the carbon and producing pure iron, was extremely expensive in fuel and labour. Darby's invention had speeded up the production of pig-iron; now Cort had discovered how to turn pig-iron, with equal ease, into bar iron. With timber no longer required, Britain could rely hence-forth on her vast resources of coal. The real 'iron age' had begun. *Cort's 'puddling' process, 1784—* *and rolling-mill*

A great 'iron-master'—Wilkinson

Just as the cotton inventions produced great mill-owners like Arkwright, so the iron inventions produced notable 'iron-masters' with a burning faith in the future of their trade. The best known of these was John Wilkinson, whose most famous ironworks were near Birmingham, though he had extensive interests elsewhere. Like many factory-owners, he issued his own currency, which was generally accepted in the vicinity—tokens bearing his strong features and the plain but proud legend 'WILKINSON, IRONMASTER'. His father had been one of the first to adopt Darby's coke-smelting process; and he himself was one of the first to order a Watt's steam-engine for blast purposes. In association with the second Darby he built the first iron bridge; it spans the Severn at the town called in its honour Ironbridge, and was opened in 1779. Eight years later he confounded the prophets by launching on the same river a boat made of iron plates—a boat which did not sink. Less spectacular but no less important were the cast-iron pipes he made for city water systems—Paris alone bought forty miles of these. And even Watt's steam-engines depended on the accuracy with which men like Wilkinson could turn out metal cylinders.

In the cotton factories the early wooden machines were now replaced by iron ones, far more accurate and durable. Everywhere iron began to take a new place in the national life—a place it has since yielded only to its more aristocratic relation, steel, when the production of that in turn was revolutionized in the later part of the nineteenth century.[1] Wilkinson foresaw, indeed, not only iron ships and iron railroads, but iron houses—and, true to his faith, he was buried in an iron coffin.

Roebuck

A similar figure in Scotland, though one less financially successful, was John Roebuck, who founded the great Carron ironworks in 1760, and who first encouraged and financed James Watt. His most famous productions were great guns, known throughout Europe under the name of 'Carronades'. Thus the iron inventions, like so many other things, were used not only to improve the standard of life but also to deal out cheaper and speedier death.

*　　*　　*　　*　　*

With the exhaustion of the forests and the increased use of coke and coal for iron smelting, the coal-mining industry was not likely to stand still. Coal was already much used as a household

[1] See page 360.

fuel, both in coal-producing districts and in towns easily supplied from Newcastle—in London it was known as 'sea coal', since it was brought down by water. It was also employed in many industries. Thus far, however, coal had been mined only in a primitive fashion from deposits near the surface. The main dangers which confronted deeper working were those of flooding, bad ventilation, explosion and collapsing, while there was also the difficulty of drawing the coal to the surface. These handicaps would have to be overcome before there could be any great increase in coal production. *Problems confronting the coal industry*

Flooding, possibly the greatest problem, was one of the first to be solved. The old method of draining by means of a chain of buckets was no use for anything except the slight floodings associated with shallow workings. A steam-pump had been invented just before the close of the seventeenth century by Thomas Savery, a Cornishman, but it was not fast or powerful enough. It was soon superseded by a more efficient pump, the work of Thomas Newcomen, a Dartmouth locksmith and black-smith. The principle of this was simple—a cylinder was alter-nately subjected to the entry of steam and cooling by cold water poured on the outside. When steam entered, it pushed up a piston in the cylinder—a piston which was attached by means of a beam to a pump. When cold water was poured on the outside of the cylinder, the steam inside condensed, and the decreased atmospheric pressure allowed the piston to sink to the bottom of the cylinder again. These engines, after certain improvements, spread rapidly, both for mines and for water supply. But they, too, had one great drawback—the process of alternately admitting steam and then cooling caused a great waste of heat, and hence of fuel. It was the glory of James Watt to invent a steam-engine which overcame this defect. *Flooding* *Newcomen's 'atmospheric' steam-pump, 1706*

James Watt, a highly intelligent, well-educated and cultured maker of scientific instruments, became particularly interested in the steam-engine when he had occasion to mend a Newcomen model. By 1769 he had patented a steam-engine of his own invention which completely overcame the defects of Newcomen's; instead of cooling the cylinder he let the cooling process take place in a separate compartment known as the 'condenser'. This device avoided the need to keep raising the temperature again within the cylinder, and thus saved fuel. Moreover, Watt made the steam do the direct work of forcing the piston both up and down instead of merely forcing it up and leaving atmospheric *Watt's steam-engine, 1769* pressure to send it down. His engine thus had a vastly more powerful 'drive' than Newcomen's. It remained only for him to harness this new motive-power to a rotary motion—which he soon did (1781)—and the steam-engine could go beyond the old up-and-down pumping, and drive factory machinery of all kinds.

Watt's success in establishing the steam-engine was partly due in the first place to the encouragement of Roebuck, and then subsequently to his partnership with a famous Birmingham manufacturer, Matthew Boulton, who supplied the valuable assets of capital and business organization. Watt also owed not a little to a devoted employee of Boulton's, William Murdock. The latter, a self-taught mechanical genius, helped Watt towards the rotary-motion idea, invented gas-lighting in England (Boulton's factory at Soho, outside Birmingham, was gas-lit by 1803), and was one of the first Englishmen to build a steam locomotive. The perfect co-operation of Watt, Boulton and Murdock secured a regular supply of steam-engines, which by 1800 had proved their worth in many spheres beyond pumping. Meanwhile the main obstacle to improved coal-mining had been triumphantly overcome, for the superior power and fuel economy of Watt's engine enabled it to pump out water from depths never before worked.

It remained to tackle the other drawbacks which were holding up the coal industry. The old means of ventilation was to sink two shafts on different levels, the air being drawn down one and rising in the other. To increase the current a furnace was usually placed at the bottom of the 'up-cast' shaft, which led to an obvious danger of explosion. The system entailed keeping many passages blocked for fear of a draught-circulation in the wrong direction, and to this end small boys and girls were employed to open numbers of trapdoors when trucks were passing, and then close them immediately afterwards. Moreover, an open candle was the usual means of lighting—the mine being unfit to work only when the flame would not burn! In such conditions, coupled with the constant risk of collapse, loss of life was so common that inquests on victims of pit disasters were never held. Less dangerous conditions, however, came at the end of the century with the invention of an exhaust fan by John Buddle, a mining engineer and coal-owner. This sucked foul air out of the up-cast shaft, and thus caused fresh air to rush down the other. Buddle also helped to establish a society for the prevention of accidents in mines, and it was this body which commissioned Sir Humphry

Rotary motion 1781

Watt's helpers

Boulton

Murdock

Ventilation and explosions

Buddle's exhaust fan

Davy to produce a safety lamp. The result, the famous Davy lamp, together with the improved ventilation, greatly reduced the danger of explosion. *Davy's safety lamp, 1815*

Among the other mining problems, pit-propping began to be studied scientifically and some economy was achieved by substituting wooden props for the great pillars of coal which had previously been left uncut. A big advance was also made in colliery transport through the use of rails and locomotives.[1] *Propping* *Colliery transport*

CHILD LABOUR IN A MINE NEAR HALIFAX

A girl draws along a truckload of coal by means of a girdle and chain. The 'beast of burden' is naked, there are no rails for the truck, and some of the passages are no more than 16 to 20 inches high. A sketch reproduced from the *Report of the Children's Employment Commission*, 1842.

The drawing of coal to the surface remained, however, for long an outstanding difficulty. The system of using women and girls to carry it up in baskets by a series of ladders was both slow and barbarous. Watt had already made steam haulage possible by 1783, but the ropes were always breaking, and the old methods remained in favour. Where steam haulage was used the weakness of the rope limited the mine to a comparatively shallow working. About 1840, however, wire ropes were invented, and steam haulage could at last replace hand carrying. Thenceforth mines could go deeper and deeper; the usual two or three hundred feet of the eighteenth century became a thousand feet by 1850, and today there are coal mines at Pendleton, in Lancashire, working at a depth of just on 4,000 feet. *Haulage* *Wire ropes, c. 1840*

The result of all these improvements in mining technique may be seen very simply in the estimated statistics of British coal-production—6 million tons in 1770, 10 million in 1800 and 20

[1] See page 341.

million in 1820. That figure had again nearly doubled by 1840, and progress was fast and furious until in 1913 280 million tons[1] were brought to the surface. This tremendous growth in the output of coal was fundamental to the Industrial Revolution, for without it Watt's steam-engine could never have been applied to drive machinery on a large scale. On the coal industry depended—and still depends—every other industry.

★   ★   ★   ★   ★

The results of the Industrial Revolution

Increased production and British industrial supremacy

The main result of all these innovations in the textile, iron and coal industries—and in many other industries not described—was a vast increase in production, and hence in the national wealth. It was this great industrial expansion which, more than anything, gave Britain her outstanding position in the world. For fifty years at least Britain was almost without competitors as an industrial producer, and only in the latter part of the nineteenth century was her supremacy seriously challenged by younger industrial rivals such as Germany and the United States. Without that industrial supremacy Britain could not have defeated Napoleon or built up her nineteenth-century empire, nor could she have sustained at home a population of increasing size, prosperity and education.

Changes in the distribution of population

Beyond this broad result of increased production—and therefore of increased power—there were many subsidiary results. The centres of population were practically reversed. Whereas the south-east of the country had been the most populous area from the Norman Conquest to 1750, people now began to settle where the new industries were arising—at first where there was water-power, later near the great coalfields. Thus South Wales, the 'Black Country' north of Birmingham, Lancashire, the New-castle area, the Clyde Valley became the great new centres of population. Industry became associated with the Midlands and the north; the south, with the exception of London, became comparatively unimportant. Moreover, apart from changing the distribution of population, the Industrial Revolution actually speeded on its growth. Thousands of articles were at last brought within the reach of poorer people, and greater numbers were thus enabled to subsist not only in Britain but all over the world.

Growth of population

New industries, e.g. engineering

Another important result of the Industrial Revolution was the creation of industries which had never existed before, such as the engineering industry. At first Boulton and Watt relied on

[1] Production for 1962 totalled 197 million tons.

hand-tools to make their steam-engines; gradually, however, there came into being a new industry, that of making machine-tools (i.e. tools operated in a machine), and as soon as this was accomplished standardization of product and increase of output began to be achieved. An engineer like Joseph Bramah, for instance, was a new type. He made machine-tools which in turn made locks, and he placed mankind considerably in his debt by a great trio of inventions depending on the principle of the forcing-pump—the hydraulic press, the pull-over beer-handle and the water-closet. One of his pupils was Henry Maudslay, who invented both the slide-rest and the first screw-cutting lathe (1800). These two inventions constituted the ground-work of mechanical accuracy, thus making possible thousands of future inventions. So the machine-tool industry, itself a new creation, could in turn give rise to many other industries. Such a development was characteristic of the Industrial Revolution.

Bramah

Maudslay

But if the broad results of the Industrial Revolution, such as fresh industries, increased production, and a long-enduring commercial and political supremacy were to Britain's lasting benefit, there was also another side of the story. The face of Britain was disfigured; fair landscapes became grimed with smoke and scarred with slag-heaps. Ugly jerry-built houses sprang up in ugly jerry-built towns, soon to become acres of dreary slums; and thither the population drifted, uprooting itself from the countryside which had been the source of many of the best elements in the national character.

The disfigurement of the countryside

More important still, the life which was led in the new factories and towns was usually one of the utmost hardship. Men and women slaved for fifteen or sixteen hours a day in dangerous, harsh and insanitary conditions; and because of their parents' poverty or lack of feeling, children down to four or even three years of age were often driven to toil from early morn till late at night. Fifty years or more were to elapse before there was much attempt to remedy this blacker side of the new industrial system. Meanwhile, though brutal overseers strapped tiny children unmercifully in the factories, and naked little girls on all fours were harnessed to trucks in the mines, the wheels of industry turned at an ever faster pace. From all the changes, with their incalculable consequences for good and ill, a new Britain was being born —the Britain of world markets, world power, world responsbility.

Harsh working conditions

3. The Younger Pitt: the Years of Peace

Birth and early years While Coke was holding agricultural shows at Holkham and Arkwright was piling up cotton mills and cash in Lancashire, the political destinies of the nation were in the hands of a young man in his twenties.

William Pitt got off to a good start in life. Born in 1759, the 'Year of Victories', he was the second son of the great William Pitt, Earl of Chatham. Frail in health but strong in intellect, he went up to Cambridge at the tender age of fourteen—though he was not, as is sometimes said, escorted there by his nurse. At the University he studied the classics, delighted in the speeches of the great orators, formed a lasting friendship with William Wilberforce, was converted to a belief in freer trade by Adam Smith's *Wealth of Nations*, and got heavily into debt. All these things had their significance for the future.

Entry into Parliament, 1781 From Cambridge, Pitt went to Lincoln's Inn, but he soon felt the family call to politics. Nominated for one of the nine 'pocket boroughs' on the estates of a friend, he was elected without ever having troubled to visit his constituents. In such a way could promising—or even unpromising—young men obtain seats in Parliament in the eighteenth century, provided they knew the right people.

George III, North and the 'King's Friends' When Pitt took his seat, as a Whig, the Government of the country was under the direction, or rather misdirection, of Lord North, an easy-going Tory who was prepared to carry out George III's personal wishes. That monarch, striving to recover some of the control over policy which had been surrendered by the early Hanoverians to their Whig ministers, had driven the Whigs from office; and he had taken back into his own hands the 'power of patronage'—i.e. of granting places, pensions, and sine-cure offices—which the Whigs had consistently used for their own ends. With a fund of this kind at his disposal, George had been able to build up a body of some sixty or seventy M.P.s who could be counted on to vote as he wished. Since 1770 these men—nicknamed 'King's Friends' by the Whigs—had lent their support, on George's orders, to the compliant North and his Tories. But unfortunately for the King's efforts to shape policy, he and North had blundered into war with Britain's American colonies. More unfortunately still, the war had gone badly, and when General Cornwallis had to surrender at Yorktown in 1781 the days of North's Ministry were obviously numbered. The leading Whig orators, Charles James Fox and Edmund Burke, thundered against the Government, and the newly elected Pitt joined his attack to theirs. In 1782, overwhelmed by unpopularity, North insisted on resigning—much to the King's annoyance; for this threw George back on the Whigs. *The War of American Independence*

Resignation of North, 1782

The Whigs in 1782 were by no means a united body. The Rockingham group, led by the elderly and colourless nobleman of that name, comprised most of the great Whig aristocratic families, with the middle-class Irishman Edmund Burke thrown in to supply the talent. It was opposed to the King's American policy and to his assertion of personal influence, but otherwise had few progressive ideas. The Fox group was a more lively affair. Fox himself, the son of Lord Holland, was a reckless and dissolute figure, who at the age of fourteen had been granted by his father a gambling allowance of five guineas a night. An ardent Tory under North in his early youth, he had swung round to complete opposition, demanding the reform of Parliament and in general following a fairly democratic line. Men forgave his immorality and his recklessness (he frequently spent the whole night gambling at Almack's) because of his warm heart, his charm and his great oratorical skill—a skill recently exercised in turning out North. Finally, there was the Shelburne group. Led by a complex character, Lord Shelburne, whom few trusted, their main idea was that of Pitt's great father—to form a more national party than either the Tories, or the King's Friends, or the other Whig groups. Not having succeeded in this, they had merely added to the number of Whig sections. It was naturally to the leadership of Shelburne, representing his late father's policy, that young Pitt, on entering Parliament, attached himself. *The Rockingham Whigs*

The Fox Whigs

The Shelburne Whigs

Pitt's maiden speech in Parliament in 1781 made a great impression, and he early determined that he would 'never accept a subordinate situation'—rare confidence in a young man of twenty-two. True to his word, when George had to accept, on North's resignation, a Whig Ministry led by Rockingham (but including members of the other groups, notably Fox and Shelburne), Pitt refused to occupy the minor post offered him.

The Rockingham
Ministry, 1782
As something of a free-lance during the Rockingham Ministry (March–June 1782), Pitt's voice was frequently raised on the side of reform. He supported the Ministry's most important bill, introduced by Burke—the Economical Reforms Bill, which abolished many of the royal sinecures and thus lessened George III's influence. Further, he himself proposed a Bill for the reform of Parliament, on the ground that the Commons represented, not the people, but only a few individuals.

The need for
parliamentary
reform
Pitt's Bill was defeated, in spite of support from Fox and the great playwright-politician Sheridan, but the truth of his contention was undeniable. Great towns like Manchester and Birmingham had no separate representation, while because Cornwall had been a centre of royalism no less than nineteen of its towns had their own M.P.s. Many boroughs were 'rotten'—i.e. had almost ceased to be inhabited—yet still returned two M.P.s; the classic examples of this were Old Sarum, where the seven voters had to meet under a tree, and Dunwich, which had disappeared beneath the ocean. Altogether fifty-six towns had less than forty voters apiece. 'Pocket-boroughs' under a local grandee's influence were equally common, and it was calculated that 162 landlords could nominate 306 M.P.s, or a majority of the Commons. The only traces of true representation were to be found in a few exceptional boroughs like Preston or Westminster (where all householders had a vote) and in the counties (where the voters consisted of all who possessed freehold land to an annual value of 40s.). These places alone could give any real indication of national feeling, and it was no accident that Fox sat for Westminster.

The Rockingham Ministry had lasted but three months when Rockingham died, and George III was faced with the problem
The Shelburne
Ministry, 1782
of a suitable successor. His choice fell upon the unpopular Shelburne, and this promptly dissolved the momentary union of Whig groups. Fox, Burke and Sheridan all refused to serve under Shelburne, and resigned; whereupon Shelburne offered
Pitt's first
office—the
Exchequer
Pitt the position of Chancellor of the Exchequer. Even Pitt could hardly class this office as a 'subordinate situation', and—at the age of twenty-three—he duly accepted.

The Shelburne Government was weak in Parliament, both because Shelburne was personally disliked, and because it had no majority. Shelburne soon ended the American war by fixing up preliminaries of peace which recognized the independence of the Colonies and arranged a restitution of conquests between Britain, France and Spain. This aroused the wrath of both

Tories and Foxite Whigs, who declared that better terms could be obtained. Shelburne was thus faced by what had seemed impossible, a combination of the two extremes and arch-enemies, Fox and North. They had no common ground at all except a momentary objection to the peace terms, a dislike of Shelburne and a desire to attain office; but their alliance was fatal to Shelburne's Ministry.

The Fox–North coalition

To no one was the prospect of a Fox–North coalition more distasteful than to George III. Of all politicians there was none he detested more than Fox. In vain he strove to detach North from Fox, or even to offer the Premiership to young Pitt, who had no following at all, and who at this juncture could not possibly have formed a Ministry. After threatening to retire to Hanover, George at last gave in, accepted the infamous partnership—and bided his time.

To weaken the Fox–North coalition proved less of a task than the King had feared. Though it commanded a big majority in Parliament, it was unpopular in the country, which was shocked by the strange alliance. George himself cleverly detached many of its supporters by refusing to grant any honours while the coalition was in office, and when Fox and North came to conclude at Versailles the final treaty winding up the American war, they were unable to obtain any better terms than those they had so strongly criticized. The coalition was clearly losing ground.

The Treaty of Versailles, 1783

Before the end of the year, the King had the chance to deliver the *coup de grâce*. In November 1783, Fox introduced his India Bill. What might have been a valuable measure was made suspect by the fact that all the seven Commissioners selected to supervise the political activities of the East India Company were strong partisans of the Fox–North coalition, and that these men would have at their disposal, through the appointment of officials, a power of patronage worth hundreds of thousands of pounds a year. Scenting a Fox entrenched in power for a generation if this went through, the King let it be known that any peer who voted for the measure would be counted as his personal enemy. The Lords thereupon threw out the bill; and the Fox–North coalition, defeated on an important measure, could legitimately be dismissed by the Crown. It promptly was.

The Fox–North India Bill

End of the Fox-North Ministry

Pitt, approached again by the King, now consented to form an administration. He would be confronted by a bitterly hostile majority in the Commons; he could include in his Cabinet practically none of the outstanding figures in either the Whig or

Pitt as Prime Minister, 1783

Tory parties; and he was but twenty-four years of age—

> A sight to make surrounding nations stare
> A Kingdom trusted to a schoolboy's care. . . .

In such circumstances, a lesser man might have thought government impossible. Pitt, however, had carefully studied the reports of election officers. He knew that the trend all over the country

(*Thomas Rowlandson, 1784, from a print in the British Museum*)

The popular view of Fox before the French Revolution. Fox wages a gallant but unequal fight against the hydra of Tyranny, Assumed Prerogative, Corruption, etc.—i.e. the personal influence of George III. He is supported by the Indians, the English (bearing the standard of Universal Liberty) and the Irish. Four gentlemen at the side, possibly foreigners welcoming the divisions in England's ranks, dance round the standard of Sedition.

was setting against the Fox–North coalition. He knew that it was a question, not of defying the electorate, but of defying the House of Commons until the next election, which, with skilful handling, might give him a majority. So he set himself out to win the country's favour—and meantime George could dangle the bait of patronage (though the number of offices in his gift had been much reduced by the Economical Reforms Act) before the weaker members of the Opposition. The contemptuous Fox gave the new government a month to live and nicknamed it 'The Mince-pie Administration', since it was not expected to survive the Christmas holidays. But it became a very stale mince-pie: it lasted for over seventeen years.

With only a minority for him in the Commons, Pitt at first had a very difficult time. His India Bill was rejected, and votes of censure were carried against him; but the obstinate youth refused to resign. An assault on him by hired ruffians only increased his popularity in the country—as did his refusal to earmark any sinecures for himself. Gradually the tide turned. Fox's supporters, influenced partly by public opinion, partly by the blandishments of George, dropped away, and the majorities against Pitt grew smaller. Within less than three months the Fox–North majority had dwindled to one vote; the others had turned towards the rising sun. Pitt saw that the moment had come: Parliament could now be dissolved and a fresh appeal made to the electorate. At the ensuing elections there was a whole-sale turn against Fox and North. About 160 of the coalition supporters lost their seats—'Fox's martyrs', they were jestingly termed—and Pitt was triumphantly returned at the head of a substantial majority. *[margin: Pitt's early difficulties]* *[margin: Pitt's triumph]*

Pitt's majority was a composite affair. It contained neither the great Whig leaders nor the great Tory leaders, but many of the rank and file of both parties. The son of a great Whig, and a Whig in name himself, Pitt had risen to power through the help of the Crown. In the course of the following years, especially after the French Revolution, he drew his support from the Tories, or from Whigs who came over to the Tory position. The true Whigs, progressively few in number after 1789, remained under the spell of Fox. So Pitt's Ministry cut across the old party lines, and the new Prime Minister must be reckoned no longer a Whig but the founder of a reconstituted Tory party.

*   *   *   *   *

The first and most essential need of the country in 1783 was to restore efficiency in finance. The American war under North's bungling direction had left a big legacy of debt, amounting to almost £250,000,000—nothing for these days, but a vast sum for 1783, when the annual revenue was barely more than *[margin: Pitt's financial work]*

£25,000,000. Pitt's solution was partly to improve the system of public borrowing, partly to take long-distance measures to pay off the debt, partly to stop obvious leakages in revenue, and partly to create additional revenue by fresh taxation.

Improved borrowing

In regard to borrowing, Pitt cut out North's system of granting some of the stock cheap to political friends, and instead threw the whole stock open for public competition. His scheme to pay off debt, however, was a more doubtful success. Pitt was greatly captivated by the properties of compound interest, and he proposed to set aside £1,000,000 a year from revenue to form a

Sinking Fund

Sinking Fund. Six commissioners were appointed to purchase national stock with this, and then invest the interest on the stock in the same way. The Fund, accumulating at compound interest, was supposed eventually to catch up with the National Debt, and wipe it out. In actual fact by 1793 Pitt had reduced the National Debt by £10,000,000, but thereafter war sent the debt racing up again to astronomical figures.

Reduction of revenue 'leakages'—e.g. smuggling

Pitt had more success in stopping leakage of revenue. He began by refusing to pocket any undue amount of public money himself. He also restricted the abuse of the parliamentary privilege of sending letters post free—certain members had had standing arrangements with commercial firms to send off all the firms' correspondence under parliamentary franking, in return for a financial 'consideration'. Moreover, he managed to reduce the volume of smuggling by cutting down the excessive duties which had made smuggling worth while. Thus an average duty of 119 per cent of the value on various kinds of tea was reduced, at any rate on the cheaper kinds, to one of 12½ per cent. Thenceforth tea came through the ports instead of entering illegitimately. Other duties were reduced too, and the smuggler's livelihood was never quite the same again. A further measure of distinct benefit to trade was the extension of bonded warehouses.

Taxation

Another success, in general, was the new taxation. Pitt strove to tax luxuries rather than necessities, and in his first budget taxed racehorses, men's hats, gauzes and ribbons. He also taxed, in one budget or another, more essential articles such as bricks, candles, domestic servants and shopkeepers. His most famous innovation in the pre-war period was the Window Tax, on all windows beyond five in any house. This again was designed as a luxury tax, but it had the bad effect of discouraging light and air, and therefore of damaging health. It was not, however, till during the war (1797) that Pitt was driven to impose the soundest of all taxes, an Income Tax. For this idea he was indebted, as for his trading theories, to Adam Smith.

Pitt also tried to apply Smith's economic ideas to commercial treaties with other countries. An effort to achieve free trade with Ireland came to nothing, but in 1786 he concluded a remarkable agreement with France. British ports were all opened to French vessels, and French ports to British. No passport was required by citizens travelling between the two countries. Britons in France and Frenchmen in Britain were to enjoy complete religious liberty. Nearly all tariffs were greatly reduced, that on French wine being lowered to correspond with the favoured terms enjoyed by Portugal. The benefits were largely reaped by British manufacturers who, with their more advanced industrial processes, poured cheap goods into France, thus causing unemployment in French towns and to some extent hastening on the French Revolution. A few more years might have seen both countries deriving equal advantages, but the promising experiment was soon to be crushed by war.

Commercial treaty with France, 1786

Pitt's success in reforming the financial and commercial system of the country was not matched by any corresponding success in regard to the political system. In 1785 he proposed a Reform Bill, which erred, if anything, on the side of moderation. Its main feature would have been to transfer the representation of thirty-six rotten boroughs to more populous areas. But the Bill was heavily defeated and Pitt never again broached the subject of parliamentary reform.

Pitt's Parliamentary Reform Bill, 1785

Another subject over which Pitt received a rebuff was the slave trade. Pitt's friend, Wilberforce, had opened his eyes to the full horrors of the journey from Africa to America. Conditions were, indeed, almost unimaginable. The slaves were herded together on the lower decks, often with so little head-room that they had to crouch the whole five or six weeks of the voyage. Chained to each other, deprived of even a moment's liberty, they were periodically taken on deck for exercise, which consisted of lashing them until they jumped up and down in their fetters. No humane man could know of such conditions and tolerate them, and Pitt's sympathies were here always on the side of reform. He supported a Bill—which was passed—regulating the conditions of the voyage, and he voted, with Fox and Burke, for two Bills of Wilberforce's—which were not passed—aiming at complete abolition of the traffic. Years later, in his second ministry, Pitt was able at least to prohibit the import of slaves

Pitt and the slave trade

into Guiana, but he always refrained from making such subjects a test of loyalty to the government, which indicates that he was not prepared to risk losing office over them.

Pitt's lack of success over parliamentary reform and the slave trade did not stop him achieving at least one admirable measure in another sphere. In 1780, in North's Ministry, a proposal to relieve Catholics of some of the many penal laws against them had occasioned the Gordon Riots, when a crazy nobleman, Lord George Gordon, roused the London mob with the old cry of 'No Popery' and led an armed attack on the Commons—an attack which degenerated into an orgy of drunkenness and plunder. Against such possibilities Pitt had to contend when he took up the cause of Catholic reform. Nevertheless, in this he succeeded, and by 1791 he had secured the passage of a Bill enabling Roman Catholics to exercise their religion freely in Britain.

Shortly before this Pitt had been confronted by the Whig campaign against Warren Hastings, the ex-Governor-General of Bengal.[1] In 1786 Burke demanded that Hastings should be impeached before the House of Lords, alleging that he had been tyrannous, faithless and extortionate in his dealings with the Indian princes and peoples. Impressed with the preliminary evidence, and not sorry to see the Opposition divert its energies to another subject, Pitt allowed the charges to go forward. So in 1788, in Westminster Hall, began the longest trial in English history.

Hastings, who had undoubtedly behaved with great severity in certain cases, was accused of the most extravagant crimes, including the unjust exaction of huge fines and the judicial murder of a hostile witness. In reality he had frequently resisted the pressure of the Company's directors for greater returns of money, and it was only his firm leadership which had saved British India from the ambitions of the French and the Maratha princes. Most of the charges against him arose from the spite of one of the members of his Council, Sir Philip Francis, who, after trying to undermine Hastings's position, had come off second best in a duel and returned to England to spread calumnies against him. Francis, a strong Whig, had had no difficulty in stirring up Burke, Fox and Sheridan, all of whom had a genuine hatred of tyranny; and the Whig leaders now expended their most magnificent eloquence in an effort to secure Hastings's conviction. For seven years the trial dragged on, distracting

Religious toleration for Catholics, 1791

The trial of Warren Hastings, 1788–1795

[1] See page 390.

attention from far more serious events on the Continent, until finally it ended in the complete acquittal—and bankruptcy—of the accused. Monstrously unjust to Hastings as these long and costly proceedings were, they at least established one point firmly —that a Governor-General had responsibilities to the people of India as well as to the East India Company.

The trial of Hastings had barely begun when Pitt ran into another Whig storm over the Regency Bill. The Prince of Wales —the future George IV—was a fat and dissolute figure whose only claim to admiration was his good taste in artistic matters; and even this—like his mistresses—ran him into debt. Politically, he was a friend of Fox and the Whigs; and Carlton House, his residence, was a regular Whig stronghold. All this was very objectionable to his father, George III, who had an equally strong dislike of both immorality and Whiggery. But George III had suddenly lost his reason. The question of a Regency therefore arose; and the Regent could only be the Prince of Wales, whose first move would be to dismiss Pitt and install the Whigs under Fox. Pitt consequently strove to have the Regent's power limited by Parliament, while Fox argued that George had a hereditary right to occupy the Regency with full royal authority— which was hardly good Whig doctrine, though it would certainly have tended to the advantage of the Whigs. The controversy was still raging when the King recovered, the proposed Regency became unnecessary, and the hopes of the Whigs—and the Prince of Wales—were dashed to the ground.

The Regency question, 1788–1789

There was one subject of Pitt's reforming interest, in these years of peace, for which the country was soon to be extremely grateful. In 1783, though Britain had broken the momentary French control of the seas off the American coast, the Royal Navy was in a bad way. According to one admiral there was not a single ship fit for service without repair, while the dockyards were hotbeds of inefficiency and corruption. Pitt's solution was to appoint Admiral Lord Howe as First Lord of the Admiralty. That energetic sailor stopped a great deal of waste, increased the output of the dockyards, and in five years built up a strong fleet of over ninety ships of the line. But little was done to remedy those standing abuses in British naval conditions—brutal discipline, bad food, overdue pay and the press-gang.

Pitt's naval reforms

Pitt's reforming activities were to find yet another outlet in imperial affairs. His solution to the problem of governing British

Pitt's imperial policy

Pitt's India Act,
1784

Pitt's Canada
Act, 1791
India—the India Act of 1784,[1] as amended shortly afterwards
—lasted until the Mutiny of 1857. His Canada Act of 1791,[2]
by which separate Assemblies were set up for Upper and Lower
Canada, while far from perfect, was at least a step in the direction
of self-government; it lasted until the Rebellion of 1837. And
his despatch of an expedition to Australia to form with 700
convicts the first penal settlement in that continent was to lead to
far more important consequences than he ever imagined.[3]

Pitt's foreign
policy
Outside imperial affairs, Pitt's foreign policy before the war
with France was marked by three main incidents. He protected
the independence of the Netherlands by backing Prussia when
The Netherlands
and the Triple
Alliance, 1788
she intervened to suppress a revolt against the House of Orange
—a revolt supported by the French and Austrians; and he
cemented the Anglo-Prussian-Dutch friendship in the Triple
Alliance of 1788. Two years later he made Spain climb down
when she claimed the whole Pacific coast of America and seized
The Nootka
Sound incident,
1790
British ships and settlers at Nootka Sound, Vancouver Island.
And he badly wanted to send a fleet to the Black Sea to make
Catherine of Russia give up the port and fortress of Oczakoff,
The Oczakoff
incident, 1791
which she had seized from the Turks—but Parliament would not
consent. In all, up to 1793, Pitt gave his country ten years of
peace, yet not at the price of neglecting British interests. His work
in the sphere of foreign policy must be accounted as successful
as his financial, commercial and imperial reforms.

The turning-
point—the
French
Revolution
Meanwhile, the French Revolution had broken out in 1789.
Its course soon became so violent, its repercussions so widespread, that all other events, even in Britain, seemed of secondary
importance. Up to this point Pitt's record in office had been
admirable. Now he had to deal with a fresh and highly critical
situation—with the France and the Europe, and not least the
Britain, of the French Revolution. Henceforward he was to be
occupied with the great international struggle, and to lose interest
in the cause of reform. But at all events, Britain was the stronger
for the period of his peace-time stewardship. In the storms and
stresses of the years ahead, Pitt's reorganization of national
finance, of commerce, of the Navy and of the Empire were to
stand his country in good stead.

[1] See page 391.   [2] See page 430.   [3] See page 434.

4. Britain and the French Revolution

When, in 1789, news came that the States-General was to meet after an interval of 175 years, it seemed that France, taking Britain's constitution for a model, was at last pursuing the ways of wisdom. And the attack on the Bastille, though it had an unpleasant flavour of mob action, was in general taken at its face value as a blow against absolutism. Fox, generous soul, thrilled to the news and exclaimed 'How much the greatest event it is that ever happened in the world, and how much the best!' Pitt, more cautious, was less interested and less impressed, but still welcomed the general trend of events. Few indeed were those in Britain who like Burke 'already heard the fall of civilization in the falling stones of the Bastille'. Impact of the opening incidents of the Revolution

Outside Parliament the events of 1789 often made little impression one way or the other, but the Protestant Dissenters, who were officially ineligible for seats in Parliament, were greatly stirred by the news. Despairing of full civic rights under existing conditions the Dissenters had taken up the cause of Parliamentary reform; and as reformers they were prepared to give a warm welcome to developments in any other country which tended to religious or political equality. Their attitude was soon made clear by Dr Price, one of their outstanding ministers, who delivered a remarkable sermon in praise not only of democratic principles but also of the actions of the French National Assembly. When, during the course of 1790, the French went on to destroy the power of the Established Church, the joy of the Dissenters knew no bounds; while they naturally shared the enthusiasm of the Whigs for the new constitution by which Louis XVI was to decline from an absolute to a limited monarch. The effect on the Protestant Dissenters Dr Price

If most of the Whigs welcomed the Revolution, and Pitt was glad of anything which prevented France from being a nuisance to Britain, one man regarded events with unqualified dismay. Burke disagreed profoundly with the popular view, and was horrified by the doctrines of Dr Price's sermon. When that divine delivered another great address on 14 July 1790—the first The attitude of Burke anniversary of the fall of the Bastille—he determined on a public refutation of Price's views. The result was his *Reflections on the Revolution in France*, published in November 1790.

The *Reflections*, 1790

The *Reflections* began with a criticism of Dr Price's sermon. Price had proclaimed that France was in fact imitating Britain, whose king, George III, was 'almost the only lawful king in the world, because the only one who owes his crown to the choice of the people'. This, Burke maintained, was a completely false interpretation of the principles of the Revolution of 1688; for that Revolution had taken place, not to set up a new government of the people's choice, but to stop James II from overturning the ancient laws and religion of the kingdom. Our liberties, according to Burke, were ' . . . an entailed inheritance, derived to us from our forefathers, and to be transmitted to our posterity . . . an inheritable crown, an inheritable peerage, and a House of Commons and a people inheriting privileges, franchises and liberties from a long line of ancestors'. In other words, we had no right to make and unmake systems of government; for our rights were privileges inherited from the past, which it was our duty to pass on intact to the future.

Starting from this gospel of Conservatism, the *Reflections* attacked the French for breaking not only with the traditions of their Monarchy but also with the traditions of their Church. This was the more serious in that, in Burke's view, the Church should naturally be so bound up in the State that the two were inseparable, the Government being consecrated and fortified by its connection with religion. The attack on the property of the Church, too, was an attack on rights inherited from the past. Nor was ecclesiastical property the only form of property to be subject to attack, for the issue of paper *assignats* was forcing a fundamentally worthless currency on the whole French nation.

Burke's prophecies

Burke's conception was thus of liberty as an inheritance from the past, and of society as a mysterious, divinely ordered body linking the past with the future and incapable of being reshaped by any one generation at any one special time. To this abstract doctrine Burke added concrete prophecies. He foretold that the attack on the privileges and property of the Church would lead to the complete abolition of the Christian religion; and his words were remembered when, within three or four years, the rulers of France instituted first the 'Worship of Reason' and then the 'Worship of the Supreme Being'. He prophesied—quite accurately—that *assignats* would rapidly become worthless. He proclaimed that no one would dare to oppose extreme measures, and that everyone would outbid everyone else in the aim of producing 'something more splendidly popular'—a forecast entirely justified when Lafayette went down before the Girondins and the Girondins in turn succumbed to the Jacobins.

This was not all. The new French constitution, Burke prophesied, would be unworkable. It was. Everything would fall into chaos and anarchy. It did. In the effort to preserve authority, irresponsible tribunals for 'crimes against the nation' would behave with the utmost tyranny—the Reign of Terror soon showed how. Finally, from the welter of anarchy and tyranny, only one thing could emerge—the call to a strong man to restore order, and the establishment of military dictatorship. 'In the weakness of one kind of authority, and in the fluctuation of all, some popular general . . . shall draw the eyes of all men upon himself. . . . The moment in which that event shall happen, the person who really commands the army is your master—the master of your king, the master of your assembly, the master of your whole republic.' Words could hardly have foretold more clearly the advent of Napoleon Bonaparte.

The *Reflections* were published in 1790, and it was some time before their author's prophecies were all vindicated. For a year or two, opponents were able to put up a stout contest before public opinion swung irrevocably over to Burke. The impression made by the *Reflections* may be seen by the fact that within a year or so some forty replies were published. The most famous and effective of these were *The Rights of Man* by Tom Paine and *Vindiciae Gallicae* by Sir James Mackintosh. Counterblasts to the *Reflections*

Mackintosh, a prominent Whig, attacked Burke on the ground that he did not realize how far the French had sunk into despotism. The nobility, the priesthood and the judges, argued Mackintosh, were incapable of reform—only revolutionary measures could deal with them. There was no harm in breaking with the past. Men had certain Natural Rights, regardless of whether they had actually managed to secure their recognition, and they were entitled to try to convert these from theory into fact. Mackintosh's own particular prophecy—not a bad one, either—was that if the monarchies of Europe were so rash as to attack France, revolutionary fanaticism would hurl back the invaders, and enthusiasm for liberty would fire Europe like a new crusade. Mackintosh's *Vindiciae Gallicae*, 1791

Mackintosh's work was outrivalled as a popular favourite by

Paine's. Tom Paine, an English Quaker by origin, had been in turn a stay-maker, a sailor, an usher and an exciseman, before he sailed to Philadelphia to make his fortune. In America he had borne arms for the Colonists, and his pamphlets had helped George Washington through many difficulties. Falling out with many of his political friends he had then returned to England, where he was accepted in the Shelburne circle as an advanced thinker, and patronized by leading Whigs who wished to pursue good relations with America. As soon as Burke's criticisms of the French Revolution appeared, Paine, who reckoned that he had 'made' the American Revolution, rushed into print with a reply.

Part I of *The Rights of Man* was much less extreme than Part II, published a year later. Its object was to offer a different set of principles from that continuity with the past which Burke so valued. Each generation, Paine argued, was sufficient to itself— it could either accept the past, or reject the past, but in no case was it bound by the past. The French, then, had a complete right to fashion their government anew, if they chose—and to fashion it in accordance not with tradition, but with reason and the 'Natural Rights' of man. And since the 'Natural Rights' of each man were the same as those of every other man, the only true government was a democracy.

Between the publication of the first and second parts of Paine's work, two tides of opinion began to run strongly in Britain. The upper and most of the middle classes fell in solidly behind Burke. But the educated lower classes, led by some intellectuals and reformers of greater wealth, began an intense campaign for democracy, with *The Rights of Man* as their gospel—a very profitable gospel for its author, whose sales quickly exceeded 200,000 copies. In July 1791 occurred an incident which showed which way the wind was blowing. The friends of France in Birmingham held a dinner to celebrate the second anniversary of the fall of the Bastille. They were promptly set on by the local mob, which was roused by the sermons of the Anglicans against the Dissenters and spurred on by two Justices of the Peace. Everywhere in Birmingham the Dissenters, the main supporters of the Revolution, had their chapels and houses stormed, regardless of whether, as individuals, they had any political views at all. The most famous sufferer was Dr Priestley, whose discovery of oxygen availed him nothing against popular fury. It was enough that he had opposed Burke, and that he had meant to attend the dinner. His house was wrecked, and an attempt was made to fire it by

Tom Paine: his early life

The Rights of Man, Part I, 1791

Opposing tides of opinion— Burke v. Paine

The Birmingham riots, July 1791

means of Priestley's electrical machine—'with that love for the practical application of science which is the source of the greatness of Birmingham'. Gaols were opened, prisoners set free, and the mob practically held the town at its mercy for two days. Ultimately order was restored, three of the rioters were executed, and Priestley received compensation—£2,000 short of what the damage cost him. Three years later he thought it advisable to emigrate to the United States.

(Rowlandson, Dec. 1792, from a print in the British Museum)

By the end of 1792 the British were firmly convinced that French Revolutionary ideas of Liberty were a great deal less attractive than their own.

All these things occurred in England some time before blood became the order of the day in France. Months before France declared war on Austria, and over a year before the massacres of 1792, Burke's eloquence so aroused the fears of the governing classes that they were stirring up mobs against likely reformers. But to stir up mobs was not difficult in the England of 1791. The rougher sections of the urban population were always glad of a little vigorous amusement; and riots were an acceptable diversion in days when there was neither cinema nor television to provide greater thrills at less personal risk.

The Rights of Man, Part II, 1792
During the course of 1791, Paine was as much in France as in England. Then, at the beginning of 1792, when his cause was already unpopular over here, he published Part II of *The Rights of Man*. This applied in detail to his own country the general democratic arguments advanced earlier. Since men were essentially equal in rights, the monarchy and the peerage must be stripped away, and Parliament must become a body genuinely representative of the people. Once a republican and truly representative Parliament was established, it would make an alliance with France, thereby doing away with the need for a large fleet, and so reducing taxation; and it should show itself truly worthy of popular support by introducing family allowances, old age pensions, compulsory free elementary education and a graduated income tax.

Pitt takes action against Paine
All this—and particularly the demand for a republic—was naturally very alarming to Pitt and his colleagues. So the book was suppressed, and Pitt decided to prosecute Paine for a 'scandalous, malicious and seditious libel' on the Lords and the Monarchy. Before the case could be brought to trial Pitt decided to go a step further and arrest Paine. But the latter, urged by the poet Blake—who had a vision that Paine's arrest was impending—had fled the country, escaping the agents of the Government by no more than an hour.

Paine in France
Safe in France, Paine became a member of the Assembly. By now events had taken a far more violent turn. Louis XVI had The crisis of 1792 been forced by his Girondin ministers to declare war on Austria, which was then supported by Prussia; a Catholic rising had broken out in Brittany; and under the stress of the double danger, Louis had been suspended from his royal functions, the Girondins had lost ground to the more extreme Jacobins, and 2,000 Royalist prisoners had been massacred. Paine was all against kings and aristocrats, but he saw no reason to end their lives as well as their power. He therefore protested strongly against the September massacres, and he went on to protest against the proposed execution of the King. This of course earned him a spell in prison, and it was only by a fortunate chance that he escaped the guillotine.

By 1792 Paine had been chased out of Britain, but there were others who took up the burden of the democratic cause. Thomas Hardy, a London shoemaker, founded the most important of all the political societies of the time, the Corresponding Society. Predominantly a working-class society, its object was to discuss political questions by correspondence both among its own members and between the Society and other reformist bodies. It had only two definite points in its programme—Universal Suffrage (a vote for all adult males) and Annual Parliaments. However, it was soon accused of Republicanism, since its members circulated Paine's writings, and were suspected of demanding the vote in order to use it to abolish the monarchy.

Another society founded in 1792 to demand parliamentary reform was the 'Friends of the People'. This had far more aristocratic connections than the Corresponding Society, being under the guidance of Charles Grey, a young Whig nobleman—who, of course, expressly repudiated Paine and Republicanism. The foundation of this society further split the Whigs, since the anti-reform section now followed Burke in working with Pitt and the Tories. Fox, true to his principles, sided with the reformers—a decision which condemned him to spend the rest of his life, except for a few weeks in 1806, out of office.

Neither the Corresponding Society nor the Friends of the People could arrest the flow of public opinion in 1792, which expressed itself in Manchester in riots like those in Birmingham a year before. And when the September massacres occurred, feeling hardened irremediably against the new rulers of France. The British, except for the convinced reformers, had now made up their minds—they wanted no French Revolutions here.

Hardy and the Corresponding Society

Grey and the Friends of the People

The tide sets against the reformers

5. The Revolutionary War

As the French Revolution daily grew more violent, and as British public opinion hardened against France, so the danger of war between the two countries increased. But it was the foreign rather than the domestic policy of France which finally brought about the rupture.

Causes of the war

After the crisis of September 1792, the French beat back their foes, set up a Republic and swept into the Austrian Netherlands. This established a major naval power on what is now the Belgian coastline, and thereby ran counter to a constant object of British foreign policy. Moreover, the French went on to use Antwerp as a naval and trading base, sending warships down to the mouth of the Scheldt, and thus violating Dutch neutrality and the Treaty of Utrecht. When to all this were added the Decrees of November 1792—which promised French help to all peoples desiring to 'recover' their liberty—and the execution of Louis XVI in January 1793, war was certain. The French for their part resented Pitt's refusal to recognize the Republic and his objection to the opening of the Scheldt; and it was they, in the intoxication of success against Austria and Prussia, who finally declared war on Britain.

The First Coalition, 1793–1797

The course of the ensuing struggle certainly surprised Pitt, who expected it to be over in one or two campaigns. Before 1793 had progressed far, republican France was faced with what seemed like an overwhelming combination against her—the monarchies of Austria, Prussia, Great Britain, Holland and Spain. The Coalition began well enough by driving the French from the Austrian Netherlands, but that was the last success for many years. The French reorganized their armies, introduced conscription, made the most of the untrained zeal of their ragged troops by flinging them in great columns against the thin lines of bewigged professionals, and used the threat of the dreaded Revolutionary Tribunal to check wavering morale. To the accompaniment of the butchery of thousands of Royalists in Paris, the

The elimination of Holland, Prussia and Spain

French recovered, recaptured the Austrian Netherlands and overwhelmed Holland. The latter, reshaped into the Batavian Republic, was then made to declare war against Britain. At this

40

stage Prussia found it advisable to transfer her activities to partitioning defenceless Poland, and in 1796 the humbled monarchy of Spain sought an alliance with the republican victor. Thus within three years Austria and Britain alone survived of the Coalition, while Holland and Spain had actually joined their forces to the French.

The process of breaking up the Coalition was carried one step further when the Directory (the new government of France formed in 1795 after the fall of Robespierre and the end of the Terror), despatched Napoleon Bonaparte to conquer the Austrian dominions in Italy. That penniless young Corsican officer had made his mark in expelling British forces from Toulon in 1793 and in rescuing the Directory from a Royalist rising in Paris. Promoted General, he now, in one of the most astonishing campaigns in history, swept the Austrians from Italy, compelling them to give up the struggle and to recognize the French conquests by the treaty of Campo-Formio (1797). The remarkable transformation was thus complete. By 1797 Britain was as isolated as France had been in 1793.

Bonaparte's Italian campaign, 1796; elimination of Austria

Britain's share in these years of catastrophe was hardly brilliant. An expedition sent to the Austrian Netherlands under the Duke of York was chased right into Germany; an effort in 1793 to support a Royalist rising in Toulon collapsed after the town had been held for some months; and an attempt in 1795 to encourage the Catholic Royalists of Brittany against the Republic by landing at Quiberon a force which included several thousand French nobles only met with instant disaster. For these ignominious failures Admiral Howe's victory off Ushant on the 'Glorious First of June', 1794, was small consolation.

Britain's military failures on the Continent

The 'Glorious First'

Military operations on the Continent were, however, in Pitt's eyes the least important part of the war effort. His principles were those of his father—to employ a small force in Europe, to subsidize allies to make good this deficiency, and to devote Britain's main energies to capturing enemy colonies. Of this threefold strategy the first two aims had proved conspicuously unsuccessful. The forces despatched to Europe were too small to be effective, and the subsidies were largely wasted.

Pitt's general strategy

The operations against enemy colonies went rather better, though the conquest of Tobago, Martinique and St Lucia, and the temporary occupation of Haiti were not achieved without great cost. One large fleet was lost in a hurricane; yellow fever, thriving on the habit of performing British drill in British

Operations against enemy colonies

(Gillray, 1797, from a print in the British Museum)

In the critical year 1797 the Bank of England had to suspend payment in gold and the Government ordered the issue of a paper currency. Pitt here offers the new notes, which are readily accepted by John Bull, despite the warnings of Fox (in a French soldier's headdress) in one ear, and Sheridan (in a French 'cap of liberty') in the other.

uniforms at midday in the West Indies, laid low thousands of the troops; and altogether, although action casualties against the small enemy forces were very slight, some 80,000 British soldiers died or became unfit for service. Much more profitable results were obtained after Holland and Spain joined the enemy. Ceylon and the Cape of Good Hope were captured from the Dutch in 1795, Trinidad and Demerara from Spain in 1797.

If the colonial campaigns of 1797 were successful, and the victory of Jervis and Nelson over the Spanish Fleet at Cape St Vincent was at least one crumb of comfort, everything else in that year at first went badly for Britain. The Austrian defeats in Italy meant the loss of the last ally on the Continent; in India the French encouraged Tipu Sahib, the 'Tiger of Mysore', to attack the British; Ireland was on the very verge of revolt and in danger of invasion; the lower classes in England were becoming restive under Pitt's repressive measures, and the harvest prospects were bad; and the Government, its finances shattered by the constant drain of the subsidies, was forced to suspend payments in gold and to institute a paper currency. On top of all, the Navy mutinied, first at Spithead and then at the Nore. The strain on Pitt was immense; and, as though public disasters on all sides were not enough, private misfortune plagued the Prime Minister in the shape of an unhappy love affair and the bailiffs distraining on the furniture at No. 10 Downing Street. *Britain's critical year—1797*

Of all these events, the naval mutinies were the most dangerous, for on the Navy depended Britain's security from invasion and her hold on the colonies. In April 1797 the Channel Fleet, when ordered out from Spithead, refused to put to sea. The main demands of the men—which had been moderately voiced but ignored—were better pay, better provisions (and full weight), better medical services, payment for the wounded, opportunities for leave and the chance to air complaints against brutal officers. They had reason enough for these requests. The salt meat was sometimes years old, and so hard it could be polished like leather. The cheese and ships' biscuits were frequently full of worms, and fresh vegetables so rare that hundreds of men died each year from scurvy. The water was usually slimy and full of growths. The only generous ration was rum—but the punishment for getting drunk was a flogging. As for leave—many a sailor barely off ship was knocked down and brought back by the press-gang, so that men often went without leave for years on end. Pay, too, was an average of a couple of years in arrears. Medical attention *The Mutiny at Spithead* may be judged from the fact that badly shattered men were often thrown overboard alive. With regard to discipline, it was not flogging in itself but the excess of it that angered the men. The official maximum for the cat o' nine tails was a dozen strokes, but in practice anything from two dozen to a hundred was common, while three hundred was not unknown. Flogging on this scale, often for trifling offences such as slowness in coming down the rigging or lowering a boat, frequently killed men outright.

The remarkable points about the Spithead mutiny were the skilful organization of the whole affair by the sailors' delegates and the successful outcome. After trifling for some time the Admiralty at last realized that the men were in earnest and had genuine grievances. Moreover, the contagion began to spread to other fleets, and Pitt and the Admiralty suddenly thought it well to settle grievances at Spithead before every naval station was flying the red flag. The men finally secured better pay, promises of better provisions in port, the dismissal of fifty-nine particularly brutal officers—and a Royal Pardon.

The Mutiny at the Nore

A much less happy conclusion marked the mutiny at the Nore. The fleet at the Nore declined to return to duty when the Spithead mutineers accepted the Admiralty's concessions, partly because they were not entirely covered by the King's Pardon, partly because they had not been relieved of unpopular officers— including the notorious Bligh of the *Bounty*—and partly because they objected to the unfair distribution of prize-money, whereby a Captain often received six thousand times as much as an ordinary seaman. So the mutiny continued, the ships at Yarmouth joining in, until the whole North Sea fleet was affected. Even the popular Admiral Duncan could find only two loyal battleships to continue blockading the Dutch in the Texel— where he confined almost a hundred enemy craft by the bluff of making signals to his non-existent fleet.

The Admiralty, fearing unlimited mutinies ahead, resolved from the first to offer no further concessions to the men at the Nore. Instead they despatched troops to Sheerness, and cut off the mutineers' supplies of food and water. The sailors thereupon resorted to blockading the mouth of the Thames, partly to seize food from merchant vessels, but chiefly to put pressure on the Government. This still brought no concessions, and some of the mutineers began to waver. Finally their 'President', Richard Parker, an ex-midshipman who had suffered terrible conditions on board his own ship, gave an unforgivable order to fire on a defaulting vessel and ordered the fleet out to sea to take refuge elsewhere. The Government, however, had meanwhile removed the buoys, which made the operation of putting to sea perilous, especially in the absence of officers; and most of the men, tired of the mutiny and not prepared to go to such extremes, refused to obey Parker's signal. Eventually the ships sailed one by one up the Thames to give themselves up, under an offer of pardon to

FRENCH-TELEGRAPH making SIGNALS in the Dark.

(Gillray, 1795, from a print in the British Museum)
Fox, an enthusiastic admirer of the French Revolution, signals the French Republican fleet to invade England. (The wooden telegraph was a new invention used to great effect by the French armies.)

all except 'ringleaders'. Twenty-nine of the latter were executed, while many others received sentences of imprisonment or flogging —ranging up to 380 lashes. Parker himself was hanged from the yardarm of his ship, a grandstand being erected on the coast for the better enjoyment of the edifying scene. Doubtless such severity arose because George III and Pitt thought that the mutineers were 'Jacobins', though, in fact, the men throughout protested their loyalty to the Crown, if not to Pitt, whose swinging effigy they used as a shooting target. The true measure of their fidelity was seen three months later, when under Duncan's

Camperdown, 1797

command they smashed the Dutch Fleet at Camperdown and secured Britain from invasion.

The financial recovery; income tax

Thus the year 1797 ended after all in triumph. To improve the situation further, financial recovery set in. At the end of the year Pitt proposed, and carried, a curious form of income tax, by which the amount paid in taxes on houses, windows, servants and some other items rose in accordance with one's income. The tax was unpopular, but it was imposed only for the duration of the war, and in a simpler form it soon did much to restore the national finances.

The strengthening of Pitt's position

Heartened by Camperdown and the financial recovery, and supported by the wit of a young Tory disciple, George Canning, in a new paper known as the *Anti-Jacobin*, Pitt's administration recovered its strength. The Prime Minister's domination became even more unquestioned when, at the end of 1797, Fox and many of the Whigs, despairing of winning Parliament to their opinions, ceased to appear regularly in the House. So the country, menaced by French success, rallied round 'Billy' Pitt, even though the reformers hated his repressive measures, and the upper classes felt equally strongly about his income tax.

* * * * *

The prosecution of reformers: Thomas Hardy

The national recovery and closing of the ranks in 1798 was the more remarkable since for some time Pitt had been taking a strong line against the supporters of parliamentary reform. Paine had saved his life by his inspired flight in 1792, but Government measures soon began to operate against others. In 1794, Thomas Hardy, founder of the London Corresponding Society —which had now no less than seventy branches in the capital— was charged with high treason. But all Hardy had advocated was parliamentary reform—which Pitt himself had proposed in the past, as he was compelled to admit at the trial of one of Hardy's associates—and the Government rightly failed to secure a conviction.

Further measures against reformers

If Hardy and one or two more, such as the 'fighting parson' Horne Tooke, got the better of the Government, a different fate awaited many other reformers. Throughout the years from 1793, the courts witnessed a succession of prosecutions against editors, authors and preachers. To make assurance doubly sure, Pitt suspended the Habeas Corpus Act in 1794, and could thus lodge suspects in prison for long periods without trial. Political societies were now closed down in great numbers, and only in Parliament, where speech was free, was it really safe to proclaim the need for reform. Public meetings without a licence from a magistrate were forbidden, and it was declared treason to correspond with France. In 1798 the whole committee of the London Corresponding Society was lodged in prison, some being kept there three years without trial, while one was eventually executed. The following year all political associations were suppressed. Finally, to complete the destruction of working-class organizations, came the Combination Acts. These forbade any combinations of workmen to act together for higher wages or any of the other normal objects of trade union activity. A similar measure forbade combinations of masters to operate against the workpeople, but this was enacted simply to give a false air of impartiality.

The Combination Acts, 1799

It is easy to criticize Pitt for this crushing legislation and for the entire 'Anti-Jacobin' scare. Having lost his early interest in reform and become convinced of the sanctity of the whole corrupt British Constitution, he suppressed all political liberty in England for years. But his views were shared by the majority. They had seen a movement for orderly reform in France get out of hand, destroy Church and Crown, and spread its ferment through the whole of Europe. It was the Government's duty, Pitt thought, to see that no such thing occurred in Britain. The reformers, too, by adopting the language of the French Revolution or supporting ʀepublicanism, gave the Government a genuine excuse to deal with them. Paine, for example, was quite ready to advise Bonaparte how best to invade England. On the whole, severe as Pitt's code was by the settled standards of the later nineteenth century, it was no more than was to be expected in a nation at war.

Defence of Pitt's attitude

★   ★   ★   ★   ★

For a short time, in spite of Pitt's 'Anti-Jacobin' measures at home, it seemed as though great things would come of the revived confidence of Britain. In 1798 the Directory despatched an expedition under Bonaparte to capture Egypt from the Turks and to damage British trade in the Eastern Mediterranean; while Bonaparte himself nourished grandiose schemes of marching from Egypt into India. The news of the enterprise determined Pitt to send a fleet into the Mediterranean once more, but the French expedition arrived safely in Egypt, where the Turkish forces were soon overwhelmed at the Battle of the Pyramids. At this stage Nelson, who had sailed the length of the Mediterranean and back looking for the expedition, came up and found

Bonaparte's Egyptian expedition, 1798

Aboukir Bay:
the Battle of the
Nile
the French Fleet anchored in Aboukir Bay, at the mouth of the Nile. Within a short time its ships had been scattered, sunk, or captured. This left a large French force locked up in Egypt— though the resourceful Bonaparte now planned to extricate it by conquering Syria and marching home through Asia Minor, Constantinople and the Balkans. However, he was held up at

The defence of
Acre
Acre, where forces were landed by the British Admiral, Sir Sydney Smith, to support the local garrison, and he then turned back to deal with a revolt in Egypt.

The Second
Coalition, 1798
Meanwhile, Pitt had taken advantage of this promising situation to form a second Coalition, consisting of Britain, Austria, Russia and Turkey. This at first met with great success, the Russians and Austrians driving the French from their newly conquered territories in Italy. Learning of these disasters from newspapers thoughtfully conveyed to him by the eccentric Sir Sydney Smith, Bonaparte promptly resolved to return to Europe. Setting off with a few companions he eluded Nelson, landed in the south of France, and within a short time had overthrown the unpopular Directory and set up a new constitution with himself as First Consul. With Bonaparte in charge, the French, already rallying, soon regained the upper hand. Another British expedition to the Netherlands under the Duke of York ended in disaster, Russia quarrelled with Britain about Malta and withdrew from the Coalition, and Austria was heavily defeated. Making peace

The Treaty of
Lunéville, 1801
at Lunéville in 1801, Austria once more retired from the conflict, leaving Britain again to carry on the struggle single-handed.

The situation was the more critical since by now an 'Armed

The 'Armed
Neutrality'
Neutrality' of Russia, Prussia, Sweden and Denmark had taken shape against Britain. As in the American War of Independence, this was aimed against the practice of searching neutral vessels at sea for 'contraband'. The leader was the half-mad Tsar Paul of Russia, who was also incensed by the British occupation of Malta—for he was the Patron of the Knights of St John, who had ruled the island. The danger of this 'Armed Neutrality' lay in its extreme claims—for example, that 'neutral' Russian warships might convoy French merchantmen—and in the probability of its naval forces coming under the direction of France. Moreover it was mainly from these countries that Britain imported naval stores—timber, tar, hemp and pitch. The British reaction was to despatch a fleet against Denmark, which had the strongest navy of the Northern Powers.

The British force was under the direction of Sir Hyde Parker, with Nelson as second in command. The first move of the Danes was to withdraw their ships to the protection of the guns and floating batteries of Copenhagen, and this set the British the difficult task of negotiating a narrow channel to get at the enemy fleet. Three ships ran aground, and though fighting had become general Sir Hyde Parker signalled Nelson to break off the action. It was at this point that Nelson did the famous trick with the telescope, and carried on with the attack. The Danes had to acknowledge defeat and withdrew from the alliance; the Swedes hastily followed suit; and to complete the whole business, just as Nelson was preparing to go on and tackle Russia, news came of the murder of Paul and the accession of Alexander I, who was well disposed to Britain. An awkward situation had thus been firmly handled, and another threat to Britain's security repelled.

Battle of Copenhagen, 1801

Collapse of the 'Armed Neutrality'

*   *   *   *   *

It was during this alarming crisis that Pitt, to the consternation of the country, resigned office. The cause of the difficulty was one which was to trouble many another statesman—Ireland.

Events leading to the resignation of Pitt, 1801: Ireland

The native Irish had for long been abominably treated. The Catholics—the great bulk of the population, except in Ulster—were subject to a savage Penal Code by which they could not keep schools, hold commissions, become barristers, buy land, serve on juries, vote for or sit in Parliament. Everything was run for the benefit of the small Protestant minority, which kept the rest of Ireland in subjection by military force directed from Dublin Castle, the seat of government. But the Parliament at Dublin—though it was both elected by, and consisted of only the Protestants—had since 1782 enjoyed complete independence of Parliament at Westminster, and was by no means always responsive to British direction.

The situation in Ireland became acute when, under the impetus of the French Revolution, a young Belfast lawyer, Wolfe Tone, founded the 'Society of United Irishmen'. Its object was to free Ireland from British control, to reshape the government on a democratic pattern, and to introduce religious equality. Pitt at first met this with a policy of concession. He allowed Catholics the vote, and in 1794 he appointed Lord Fitzwilliam, a great friend of the Catholic cause, to the position of Lord Lieutenant. Fitzwilliam, however, went beyond instructions, and promised Catholic Emancipation, or the admission of Catholics to full civic rights, including that of sitting in the Dublin Parliament—for

Wolfe Tone's 'United Irishmen', 1791

Appointment and dismissal of Lord Fitzwilliam,

which indiscretion he soon ceased to be Lord Lieutenant. After this, the Irish Catholics began to join the 'United Irishmen' in large numbers, but none the less indulged in outrages against the Protestants. The 'United Irishmen' thus ceased to be a link between the two religions, and became instead an anti-British rallying-centre for the Catholics.

Wolfe Tone and French help

Even before the dismissal of Lord Fitzwilliam, Wolfe Tone had taken decisive action. He wrote to the French Government demanding that France should act up to the November Decrees and bring liberty to Ireland. An invading force under Hoche duly set sail from Brittany in 1796, and appeared in Bantry Bay, but it was scattered by a great storm, and failed to make a landing. All through 1797 the danger continued, but Duncan's blockade and defeat of the Dutch Fleet again held up the French plans. The next year the 'United Irishmen', fearing that further delay would be fatal, staked everything on a rising. But the Government seized the ringleaders, and a desperate effort by the rank and file was defeated at Vinegar Hill. Too late to help the Irish rebellion, and too few to do anything by themselves, a party of a thousand French, with Wolfe Tone, now managed to land, and defied capture until opposed by a force ten times its size. Wolfe Tone himself was taken prisoner and sentenced to be hanged, but committed suicide in captivity.

Vinegar Hill, 1798

Pitt's solution

This trouble with the 'United Irishmen' made Pitt even more conscious of the danger of an independent Ireland. He was fully aware that the Irish would never be satisfied until Catholics had equal rights; but at the same time it seemed impossible to allow Catholics to sit in the Irish Parliament, where, with an overwhelming majority, their first act would be to throw off all allegiance to England. Pitt was thus led to the idea of a Parliamentary Union with England, on the lines of the Scottish Union of 1707, coupled with Catholic emancipation as a solace; for however Catholic were the Irish M.P.s, at Westminster they would be swamped by the Protestant English, Scots and Welsh. The Irish Protestant Parliament was naturally not keen on this solution, but pressure from Dublin Castle, combined with a wholesale distribution of honours, places and pensions, soon wrought a change of heart. Moreover, Union was seen to have certain advantages, such as protection against the danger of the French, or of a revived Republican movement. So the Irish Parliament gave way and passed the Act of Union, thereby ending its own life, and the measure was promptly seconded at Westminster.

The Act of Union, 1800

By the Act of Union Great Britain and Ireland were to have a common King, Parliament, Army and Flag. Twenty-eight Irish peers, elected by their fellow-peers, were to sit in the Lords, together with four Irish bishops, while one hundred Irish Members of Parliament were to sit in the Commons. Free Trade was to be established between the two countries, and the Irish were to contribute two-seventeenths of the revenue of the United

(*Rowlandson, 1801, from a print in the British Museum*)
Pitt thinks the Act of Union with Ireland will soon prove a success. St Patrick thinks it a poor kind of union, and foresees further strife.

Kingdom. Such terms were not unfair in themselves, though free trade exposed undeveloped Irish industries to the full blast of English competition.

What was unfair, however, was that Pitt failed to put into effect a number of promised 'compensations' to the Irish. These included relief to Catholics from paying tithes to support the Anglican Church in Ireland, State payment of salaries to the Irish Catholic priesthood, and above all, Catholic emancipation, with its central point of the right of Catholics to sit in Parliament.

George III
forbids Catholic
emancipation

Pitt indeed tried to carry into law this main engagement, but George III—whose views Pitt well knew—here put down his extremely stubborn foot. He insisted that Catholic emancipation would violate the terms of his Coronation Oath, by which he had sworn to maintain intact the privileges of the Anglican Church

Resignation of
Pitt

Pitt and his chief colleagues now felt in honour bound to resign, while George appointed as Prime Minister a less independent character in the person of Addington, the Speaker. George then had another short attack of lunacy, which he ascribed to Pitt's action, and Pitt promised never again to raise the question of Catholic emancipation during the King's lifetime.

*   *   *   *   *

Addington

If the way in which Union had been carried out left Ireland betrayed and resentful, it saddled England with an incompetent Prime Minister. All the leading figures of Pitt's Cabinet refused to serve under Addington, and his position would have been untenable had not Pitt promised George to lend the Ministry his support. Even that, however, could not conceal Addington's mediocrity, which was well expressed in the irrepressible Canning's famous jingle—

> Pitt is to Addington
> As London is to Paddington.

The one outstanding 'achievement' of Addington's Ministry was to bring to a close—a very temporary close—the war with France. Pitt himself supported this policy. It seemed to him, as to many others, that France was invincible on land, Britain on the sea, and that such conditions of stalemate had better be recognized. Preliminaries of peace were agreed on in the autumn of 1801, and after some delay the Treaty of Amiens was signed

The Peace of
Amiens, 1802

in March 1802. By that treaty Britain was to restore all her conquests overseas except Ceylon and Trinidad, while the French were to evacuate Egypt—where they had already been defeated by a British army under Sir Ralph Abercrombie—and the Papal States. Thus while Britain was to give back such valuable acquisitions as the French West Indies, the Cape and Malta, France abandoned practically none of her conquests, and was left in possession of the Austrian Netherlands—the main reason for war in 1793.

So came about what Sheridan termed 'a peace that every man was glad of and no man was proud of'. The populations of both countries, war-weary and anxious to avoid heavy taxation, certainly approved of the move. Festivities ran high in Paris, while in London Bonaparte's first representative had his carriage drawn through the streets by cheering crowds. A vote of thanks was carried in Parliament to Pitt for seeing us through so much of the war, 'Pitt Clubs' were founded in many places and Canning wrote his famous song, *The Pilot that weathered the Storm*. But the rejoicings were short-lived. Little over a year later the two nations were again at each other's throats.

6. The Napoleonic War

The Treaty of Amiens was in effect an experimental truce. Though the French had not been dislodged from the Austrian Netherlands, Britain was tired of fighting and willing to give the new French Government under Napoleon Bonaparte a chance. But the first step taken beyond the bounds of Amiens would mean war again—and war it very soon was.

Causes of renewed war

The break came over Malta. Britain had promised to restore the island to the Knights of St John, but delayed doing so until it was clear that Bonaparte's ambitions were satisfied. When Bonaparte again interfered in Switzerland and Holland, annexed further parts of Italy, and began to think of re-occupying Egypt, Britain decided that the retention of Malta would be a valuable safeguard. Then Bonaparte, already infuriated by British journalists and caricaturists, publicly rebuked His Majesty's Ambassador in Paris; and Britain, determined to allow no time for preparations, in May 1803 declared war.

This crisis found the incapable Addington still at the helm. It was a year before George III could be induced to part with the Prime Minister, whose political outlook and abilities corresponded so well with his own. During this time Pitt was busy as Lord Warden of the Cinque Ports, supervising the development of the Rye–Sandwich military canal, recruiting a Volunteer Corps, and organizing the erection of 'Martello' towers as coastal strongpoints against Bonaparte's threatened invasion. Eventually the reluctant Addington made way. His compensation for a minor position in the new Cabinet was the title of Viscount Sidmouth, under which name he later achieved something like infamy.

Pitt's return to office, 1804

On return to office, Pitt was anxious that his new administration should be truly national. He even strove to include Fox, who was at last beginning to regard Bonaparte as a danger; but George III declared that he would sooner face civil war than admit such a fellow to the Cabinet. Pitt entered the House again as Prime Minister on 18 May 1804, the very day on which Bonaparte reached the height of his ascent to power by proclaiming himself Emperor.

Pitt's first duty as Prime Minister was to take steps against the

54

invasion threat. Napoleon was building troop-transports and massing a great army at Boulogne in the hope of slipping past the Royal Navy on some foggy night. Once ashore, he counted on being welcomed by a popular rising against the Pitt Government. Then the technical problems involved, such as the number of tides required to embark his army, began to dawn on the French Emperor. So the attempt was delayed while Boulogne and the adjacent harbours were enlarged—and even then he felt no more comfortable about the enterprise than a later dictator in a similar situation. Pitt, meanwhile, after having seen that the fleet was in readiness, strove to weaken Napoleon's position elsewhere. His first effort to do this merely added to Britain's foes, for, aware of a secret Franco-Spanish agreement, he ordered the Navy to seize some Spanish treasure ships which might otherwise have come under French control. This, of course, precipitated war with Spain, and enabled Napoleon to count on the use of the Spanish Fleet in the forthcoming venture.

More success attended Pitt's efforts to build up another Coali- tion on the Continent. In early 1805 Russia joined, and in August Austria followed. Both were to draw from the patient British tax-payer £12 10s. annually for every man they put into the field.

While these negotiations were taking place, Napoleon had al- ready begun the campaign which was intended to lead to the inva-sion of Britain, and which ultimately led to Trafalgar. The plan in its final version was for Admiral Villeneuve to get the French Mediterranean Fleet safely out of Toulon past Nelson's blockade, and then pick up the Spanish Fleet at Cadiz. Together the two fleets would then make for the West Indies, where they would be joined by the French Atlantic Fleet—if the latter could evade the British blockade off Brest and Rochefort. Nelson, it was thought, would undoubtedly give chase, and while he was searching for the point of attack in the maze of West Indian islands the three fleets would be gaily sailing back to Europe. With Nelson out of the way, they could then overcome the Channel Fleet and escort the troops at Boulogne across those few miles of water which have so often stood Britain in good stead. Alternatively, if Nelson was not drawn to the West Indies, the French could do great damage to British interests there.

This ingenious scheme broke down on the efficiency of the Royal Navy and the genius of Nelson. Villeneuve began well. He emerged from Toulon, avoided a trap of Nelson's, and gained Cadiz, where he linked up with the Spaniards. Together the two fleets then set off for the West Indies. But the French Atlantic Fleet remained bottled up by the British blockade, and a major element in the plan had gone wrong.

The scheme
breaks down

Meanwhile Nelson, seeking Villeneuve, sailed first east to Sicily, and then west to Portugal. There at last he received reasonably certain information that the enemy had set sail for the West Indies, and thither he followed, a month behind his quarry. Once among the West Indies he began to search for the French Fleet, but quickly realized that Villeneuve—who had heard of Nelson's arrival, and decided not to wait for the Brest contingent—had doubled back towards Europe. So he set off after him, now only four days behind. Moreover, one of his fastest brigs, sent on in advance with despatches, caught up and passed Villeneuve, and duly reported the enemy's position to the Admiralty. The result was that two British Admirals—Cornwallis off Ushant and Calder off Ferrol—were on the alert to intercept the Franco-Spanish force. Villeneuve, his force inadequate in strength and his ships by now in very poor condition, did not even get past the first obstacle; he ran into Calder, and was driven to take refuge in Vigo. Thus at the end of July 1805 Napoleon's great scheme had broken down and Britain was saved from invasion—some months before the Battle of Trafalgar was fought.

While Nelson returned to England for a little well-deserved leave, Napoleon was moving off on another campaign. Seeing his naval plans come to nothing, he resolved to deal with the new Coalition on the Continent. Breaking up his camp at Boulogne, he raced across Europe and dealt a heavy blow to the Austrians at

Ulm, 1805

Ulm. But he could not be everywhere at once; and at sea he might well have been . . . at sea. Two days after his success at Ulm, his remaining hopes of challenging Britain's naval supremacy were shattered at Trafalgar.

Trafalgar,
October 1805

Trafalgar was an action quite needlessly undertaken by the enemy. Villeneuve, after taking refuge in Vigo, had managed to sail along the coast of Spain and put in at Cadiz. When a troop convoy sailed from England, Napoleon ordered Villeneuve out to intercept it. Taunted by the Emperor with cowardice and saddened by his knowledge of British superiority in equipment and seamanship, the gallant French Admiral sailed from Cadiz in a pessimistic frame of mind, though he had twenty-one French and twelve Spanish ships against Nelson's twenty-seven.

21 October 1805 was one of the great days of British history. Nelson's plan was true to his brilliant and daring genius. The

British were to approach (but not attack) the enemy line at right-angles in two columns, the larger led by Collingwood in the *Royal Sovereign*, the smaller by Nelson in the *Victory*. This method of approach would conceal the actual plan of attack for as long as possible. At a given moment Collingwood would then put his

(Gillray, 1805, from a print in the British Museum)

THE PLUMB PUDDING IN DANGER: *or*, STATE EPICURES TAKING UN PETIT SOUPER

Napoleon frenziedly helps himself to the continent of Europe (excluding Scandinavia and Russia). Pitt, watching him with a wary eye, takes an even larger portion—the oceans of the world, including the West Indies.

fifteen ships parallel to the rear twelve of the enemy, and concentrate all efforts on annihilating these. Meanwhile Nelson would make for the enemy's flagship—which he assumed would be somewhere in the middle—and engage the enemy Commander and centre so hotly that they could not turn to the rescue of the rear. The enemy van was to be left alone, Nelson's whole idea being to settle the issue before the leading ships could turn to help their comrades. Collingwood, in other words, would smash the rear with superior force while Nelson held the centre busy; the enemy van would not come into the battle at all until too late; and the British fleet, numerically inferior though it was, would be numerically superior at the decisive points of action. With minor modifications in the heat of conflict the plan was substantially carried out. The Franco-Spanish line was broken at the points of impact of both the *Victory* and the *Royal Sovereign*, and in the end two-thirds of the enemy fleet was destroyed, scuttled or captured. Only the death of Nelson cast a cloud over British rejoicing.

After Trafalgar, British sea power, already supreme, was virtually unchallenged. The disaster at Ulm was forgotten in the glory of Nelson's victory, and at the Lord Mayor's Banquet in November Pitt received an unprecedented ovation. To the toast of the Prime Minister as 'the Saviour of Europe', Pitt replied in his shortest and finest speech, consisting of three sentences—'I return you many thanks for the honour you have done me. But Europe is not to be saved by any single man. England has saved herself by her exertions, and will, as I trust, save Europe by her example.' But before the year was out, heavier tidings were again to be brought to the Prime Minister. In December 1805 Napoleon crushed the Austrian and Russian armies at Austerlitz, and drove Austria from the Third Coalition. A British force, landed on the coast of North Germany to persuade the wavering Prussia into the Coalition, had now to be hastily withdrawn, and all Pitt's schemes were again in ruins.

Austerlitz,
December 1805

From the news of Austerlitz Pitt never recovered. Racked by gout—the legacy of too much port wine—and worn out in the service of his country at the age of forty-six, he died in January 1806, murmuring—according to most authorities—the grief-stricken phrases, 'My country! How I leave my country!'[1]

Death of Pitt,
1806

Pitt was not as great a minister in war as he was in peace. The military expeditions to the Continent which he planned were invariably disastrous. He paid too much attention to the West Indies. His financial policy lacked boldness and resulted in a vast accumulation of debt. He frittered money away on subsidies to inefficient allies, and he tried to oppose the dynamic force of the French revolutionary and national spirit by combinations of outworn monarchies. Yet in spite of his weaknesses, Pitt had at least the elements of greatness. He was the first to have the courage to

Pitt as a war
minister

[1] Disraeli, however, who had the legend from an old waiter at the House of Commons, in later years used to maintain that Pitt's final words were: 'I think I could eat one of Bellamy's veal pies.'

impose that necessary evil, an income tax. His naval policy, though the blockade might have been closer, worked well, and some of his choices for command, such as Nelson, performed outstanding service. His colonial ventures were successful, while in India his Governor-General, Wellesley, overcame Tipu Sahib of Mysore and the Maratha chiefs of Central India.[1] And above all, Pitt had those moral qualities which are indispensable to a great national leader—patience, determination, utter devotion to duty, and unfailing courage.

* * * * *

Bereft of its great leader, Pitt's Cabinet could no longer hold together, and George was driven to accept the services of Fox in a Coalition Ministry comprising the main figures in Parliament, including Sidmouth. This administration, nicknamed at the time 'All-the-Talents', was very short-lived, but before it foundered on the rock of George's prejudices it had put one great measure on the statute book. In 1806, thanks largely to the enthusiasm of Fox, it passed an act abolishing British participation in the slave trade. Before the year was out Fox was dead; and without so gallant a fighter 'All-the-Talents' soon came to grief. Its break-up occurred when George III demanded an undertaking that the Ministry would introduce no concessions to Catholics.

After the fall of 'All-the-Talents' the Foxite Whigs were out of office for over twenty years. Meanwhile the government of the country was conducted largely by Tory mediocrities who nevertheless managed to beat Napoleon. Until 1809 the Prime Minister was the Duke of Portland, an elderly Whig who had deserted Fox and reform as long ago as 1794 and had joined forces with Pitt and the Tories. Next, Spencer Perceval held the reins, until he met his end by the hand of a madman in the lobby of the House of Commons. Then, from 1812 to the end of the war—and far beyond—the Government was led by Lord Liverpool, whose main distinction was the knack of keeping his colleagues from quarrelling. During all these years no measure of home reform was touched, and the Tories concentrated their whole energies on bringing the war to a victorious conclusion.

* * * * *

The military situation in 1806, at the death of Pitt, was by no means promising. Austria had just been beaten out of the

[1] See page 391.

The 'All-the-Talents' Ministry, 1806

Abolition of the slave trade

Death of Fox

Prime Ministers, 1807-15

Third Coalition, while Prussia, bribed by Napoleon's offer of Hanover, was carrying out anti-British measures which led to a few months' war between the two countries. Finding Napoleon an exacting and overbearing ally, Prussia then belatedly turned against the French, only to be promptly and overwhelmingly crushed at Jena. Napoleon next went on to deal with the last continental member of the Coalition, and defeated Russia at Friedland. After this, the Tsar Alexander, meeting the French Emperor at Tilsit, suddenly abandoned his allies, and agreed to help Napoleon defeat Britain by excluding British trade from Russia. Britain once defeated—so ran the vaguer terms of the bargain—Napoleon was to rule an Empire of the West while the Tsar enjoyed an Empire of the East, probably including India. This agreement left Britain once again without an ally.

Without friends on the Continent, Britain had now to rely more than ever on her sea power. Any threat to her maritime supremacy must be dealt with instantly. So when Canning, the energetic Foreign Secretary of the Portland Ministry, scented out from clues picked up by British agents that Napoleon and Alexander had also secretly agreed to make the Scandinavian countries and Portugal close their ports to British vessels and submit their fleets to French direction, he resolved to act speedily. He was responsible for the immediate despatch of a military expedition to Copenhagen bearing the demand that the Danes should hand over their fleet to the British for safe keeping. The Danes were not at war with Britain, and the action was loudly denounced throughout Europe. The Danes gallantly chose to fight, but the British force established a footing and bombarded Copenhagen from the landward side, and the Danish fleet was soon under British control.

The best means of striking a heavy blow at Napoleon which Britain could adopt at this stage was to intensify the trade war. The outstanding landmark in the economic struggle thus far had been the issue of the Berlin Decrees by Napoleon in 1806. These, taken in conjunction with earlier measures and the later Milan Decrees, aimed at establishing a 'Continental System' by which British goods were to be excluded from territory under French control. It was this system which Russia had agreed by the Treaty of Tilsit to enforce in her own extensive domains. Napoleon thus hoped to cripple not only Britain's commerce but her currency also, since she would have to export gold instead of goods to pay for her vital imports. The scheme came near to success, particu-

Jena, 1806

Treaty of Tilsit, 1807

Bombardment of Copenhagen and capture of the Danish Fleet, 1807

Economic warfare

Berlin Decrees, 1806

larly in 1810–11, when British trade was in great difficulties. But economic warfare was a game that two could play. In retaliation, Britain issued a series of Orders in Council, to the effect that she would allow no ships of any other country to enter ports from which British vessels were excluded. This was designed either to force the admission of British ships, or to arouse discontent in countries under French occupation by causing a shortage of goods and hence rising prices. Obviously, however, the Orders in Council would offend neutral powers whose vessels were stopped in the course of trade with France or French-occupied territory, and trouble was to come from this source. *Orders in Council, 1807 onwards*

It was Napoleon's anxiety to extend his 'Continental System' over the whole of Europe which gave Britain the opportunity to strike her next military blow. By 1807 the French Emperor had most of Europe under his control, but he had as yet found no opportunity to bring Portugal into the system—a grave weakness in view of the volume of British trade with Lisbon and the Portuguese colony of Brazil. So he secured permission from Spain to send troops across the Peninsula, and rapidly conquered Lisbon. Then he made a fatal error: he sent more troops into Spain, then used the presence of his forces to bully the Spanish royal family into resigning the Crown to his brother Joseph. This action was bitterly resented by the Spaniards, for the strongly Catholic peasantry were far too backward to welcome Napoleon in the name of the principles of the French Revolution, as many Italians, Germans and Poles had done. Spurred on by their priests, they began a relentless struggle against the infidel Napoleon, who was soon to show himself capable of kidnapping the Pope. Such a situation—a people in revolt—presented a new and obvious opportunity to Britain. *The French in Spain and Portugal*

The British share in the Peninsular War began with an attempt to wrest Portugal from French control. The command of the first small expedition was given to Sir·Arthur Wellesley, who had already gained a great reputation in India.[1] Landing in Portugal in June 1808, Wellesley soon gained the support of the peasantry by the unusual practice of paying for locally requisitioned supplies. After a successful encounter with the French at Vimeiro he was planning the capture of Lisbon when he was frustrated by the arrival of a senior general. This officer preferred not to risk fighting and instead made with the French a curious agreement known as the Convention of Cintra, by which they were to *British landing in Portugal* *Vimeiro, 1808* *The Convention of Cintra, 1808*

[1] See page 391.

evacuate Portugal and be carried back to France in British ships! Wellesley then returned to England, where there was some indignation at this half-success.

Napoleon in
Spain

The loss of Portugal and the eviction of Joseph Bonaparte from Madrid after the success of the Spanish irregulars now drew Napoleon himself to the Peninsula. Within a short time he had restored the French position and reinstated Joseph. As he was preparing to overrun the south of Spain, Sir John Moore, the new British commander in Portugal, advanced into Northern Spain and attacked French communications, drawing upon himself the attentions of Napoleon and the French armies. In overwhelming numbers they promptly chased Moore back to the coast

The retreat to
Corunna, 1808

at Corunna, causing him to lose a large proportion of his army in the cruel winter retreat. The remainder were safely evacuated, though Moore himself was killed in the final rearguard action. It was an heroic episode, and it saved the south of Spain—but the bulk of the British troops had been driven out of the Peninsula, and only 10,000 men, based on Lisbon, remained as the nucleus for further operations.

It was at this stage that Portland's Tory Cabinet—and particularly Canning, the Foreign Secretary, and Lord Castlereagh, the Secretary for War—rendered a great service to the country. Disregarding the Whig clamour for the abandonment of Lisbon and the whole Peninsular campaign, they decided to send out a new

Wellesley's
second expedi-
tion, 1809

expedition under Wellesley. Within a few weeks of arriving at Lisbon Wellesley expelled Soult's forces from Portugal. Then he advanced towards Madrid and defeated Joseph Bonaparte at

Portugal again
liberated.
Talavera, 1809

Talavera, but a threat from Soult to the rear of his army at once forced him to retire back to Portugal. For his success at Talavera he was created Viscount Wellington.

If the events of 1809 were not unfavourable to the British cause in the Peninsula, they were disastrous elsewhere. Austria, who had felt sufficiently encouraged to enter the war once more,

Wagram:
The Austro-
French Alliance

had suffered a further humiliation. Defeated at Wagram, she was compelled to apply the 'Continental System' against Britain and to submit to an alliance with Napoleon. Moreover, calamity had descended on another British venture—the force despatched by Castlereagh to capture Antwerp and the French warships under construction in its dockyards. The expedition, the best equipped that had left these shores, captured Flushing as a preliminary and then settled down on Walcheren to perfect its arrangements for

The Walcheren
expedition, 1809

attacking Antwerp. But Walcheren, a swampy typhoid-ridden

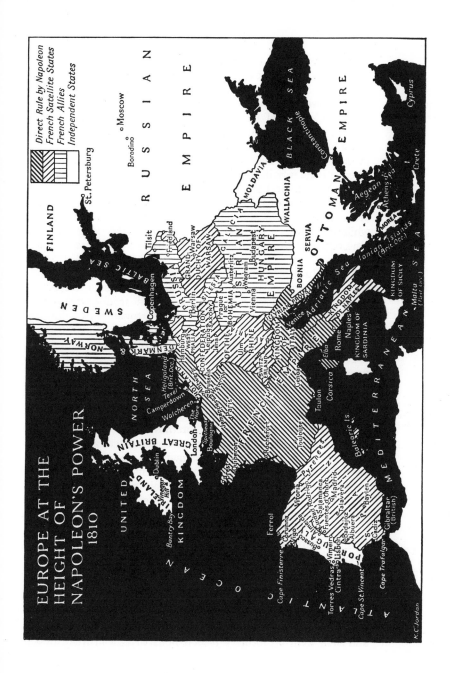

EUROPE AT THE
HEIGHT OF
NAPOLEON'S POWER
1810

Direct Rule by Napoleon
French Satellite States
French Allies
Independent States

FINLAND

RUSSIAN EMPIRE

St. Petersburg

Moscow

Borodino

SWEDEN

NORWAY

BALTIC SEA

Tilsit
Friedland

Copenhagen

DENMARK

GRAND DUCHY OF WARSAW

Warsaw

Berlin

PRUSSIA

NORTH SEA

Hamburg
Heligoland (Brit. Occ.)
Texel
Camperdown
Walcheren

GREAT BRITAIN

UNITED KINGDOM

Dublin

IRELAND

Bantry Bay
Vinegar Hill

London

Spithead
Boulogne

The Hague
Brussels

Jena
Auerstadt

CONFEDERATION OF THE RHINE

Leipzig

SAXONY

SILESIA

GALICIA

MOLDAVIA

WALLACHIA

Prague

BOHEMIA

Austerlitz

AUSTRIAN EMPIRE

Vienna
Wagram

HUNGARY

Budapest

SERVIA

BOSNIA

OTTOMAN EMPIRE

Ulm

SWITZERLAND

FRENCH EMPIRE

Ferrol

Cape Finisterre

Corunna
Vigo
Ciudad Rodrigo
Oporto
Salamanca
Talavera
Fuentes d'Onoro
Vimeiro
Lisbon
Cintra
Torres Vedras

PORTUGAL

Madrid

Badajoz
Albuera

St. Sebastian
Pyrenees

Vitoria

Baylen

Gibraltar (British)

Cadiz

Cape St. Vincent

Cape Trafalgar

Strasbourg

Paris

Rochefort

Toulouse

Toulon

Corsica

Genoa

Venice

Adriatic Sea

Rome

Naples

KINGDOM OF NAPLES

Elba

KINGDOM OF SARDINIA

Sardinia

Balearic Is.

MEDITERRANEAN SEA

KINGDOM OF SICILY

Sicily

Malta (Brit. Occ.)

Ionian Islands (Brit. Occ.)

MOREA

Athens Sea

Aegean Sea

Crete

Cyprus

BLACK SEA

Constantinople

ATLANTIC OCEAN

K. C. Jordan

island, took its toll of the soldiers in thousands, and ultimately
the survivors had to be brought home again with nothing accomplished.

Retirement of
Canning

This fiasco had a further unfortunate consequence in depriving the Cabinet of its two outstanding figures. Canning complained that Castlereagh's Walcheren expedition had made it impossible to send adequate reinforcements to Spain, and urged the
Prime Minister to remove Castlereagh from his post. Castlereagh,
resenting the way in which this was done, challenged Canning to
a duel. With their first shots, both men missed; with their second,
Canning hit one of Castlereagh's buttons and Castlereagh hit one
of Canning's thighs. Both then retired from public affairs for a
while. Castlereagh returned to office before very long but Canning refused to serve with him and remained in eclipse for many
years.

The struggle in
the Peninsula

The failure of the Walcheren expedition meant that Britain
could again concentrate on the war in the Peninsula. Here Wellington had a difficult task, as fresh French troops were poured
into Spain after the defeat of Austria. Fortunately two-thirds of
these were occupied in suppressing the numerous Spanish rebellions inspired by the Juntas, or local 'resistance' committees,
operating under the central Junta at Cadiz. Pursued by French
forces under Masséna, Wellington was compelled to retire almost
to Lisbon in spite of a victorious delaying action at Busaco. On
the Lisbon Peninsula itself, he then constructed the triple posi-

The lines of
Torres Vedras,
1809

tions known as the lines of Torres Vedras. The rearmost of these
covered the harbour, while the foremost was an almost impreg-
nable line based on mountains, earthworks, blocks and floods. To
complete the job Wellington systematically devastated the country beyond the foremost line—and Masséna found that he could
neither pierce the defences nor even maintain his forces in front
of them. After a disastrous winter of disease and starvation, the
French marshal had to retire across the border into Spain.

The following year, 1811, Wellington strove to secure control
over the three great fortresses—Almeida, Ciudad-Rodrigo and

Fuentes
d'Onoro

Badajoz—which dominated the routes between Spain and Portugal. After holding off Masséna at Fuentes d'Onoro, he took

Almeida, 1811

Almeida, but not till the early months of 1812 did the other two

Ciudad-Rodrigo,
Badajoz, 1812

fortresses fall. Then he was in a position to strike well into Spain.
Harassed for a while by Marshal Marmont (who had replaced

Salamanca, 1812

Masséna) he seized a sudden chance to beat him at Salamanca,
and then went on to drive Joseph Bonaparte from Madrid. But

just when things looked set for an advance clean across Spain, Soult from the south linked up with Joseph, and Wellington was compelled to retire right back into Portugal for the winter. The Spaniards, however, could now hold the south in Soult's absence, so the campaign was not profitless, though the decisive victory for which Wellington had hoped was deferred for another year.

The setback in Spain coincided with a fresh complication in the form of a war with the United States of America. The real but unavowed reason for this was the American desire to conquer Canada, but the Americans had ample cause for grievance in the British practice of searching American warships for deserters and the operation of the Orders in Council. Under the latter Britain was trying to exclude American trading vessels from all European ports controlled by Napoleon, and a clash was almost bound to ensue. Eventually, after protests not only from the Americans but from British commercial circles, the U.S.A. was exempted from the Orders, but this was too late to avoid war, which had broken out a week beforehand. In the subsequent hostilities, which lasted for two years before the Treaty of Ghent wound up the struggle without determining the principles at issue, the Americans tried unsuccessfully to invade Canada, British naval pride received a number of unpleasant shocks, and one of the numerous British expeditions burnt all the public buildings in Washington. The whole episode only increased the already strong anti-British sentiment in the United States. <i>War between Britain and U.S.A., 1812 1814</i>

Meanwhile, great things had been happening in the European struggle. In 1811, Alexander, finding that Russian trade was suffering and that Napoleon showed no signs of supporting his ambitions in the East, opened his ports to British goods. Napoleon, unable to tolerate this great gap in the 'Continental System', then embarked on the fatal Moscow campaign. In the result, of 610,000 men, a tattered remnant of 20,000 alone returned to tell the tale of the bloody conflict of Borodino, the flames of Moscow, the interminable harassing by the Russian forces, the ravages of disease and the killing cold. Napoleon deserted his troops once more and sped back to France, for he knew that Europe, encouraged by his disastrous failure, would rise against him. Like the superman he was, within three months he had raised new forces of a quarter of a million men. <i>The Moscow campaign, 1812</i>

The time was ripe for some great new effort by the foes of France. Wellington was ready to play his part, for the French in Spain had been seriously weakened by withdrawals of troops for the Moscow campaign. 'Adieu, Portugal!' he exclaimed as he crossed the frontier—'I shall never see you again.' Within forty days he had advanced across the Peninsula, freed Madrid and driven Joseph headlong before him. As the retreating French neared the Pyrenees, Joseph turned in desperation and was overwhelmed at Vitoria. After this it took the rest of the year and a winter campaign to reduce the last two or three strongholds and to force the enemy across the frontier, but already by July 1813 the issue was settled. The French had lost the Peninsular War

They were also in difficulties elsewhere. In the spring of 1813, before Wellington began his advance, a new Coalition had been formed between Britain, Russia and Prussia. The latter had recovered and indeed increased her strength in a remarkable fashion since Jena; she had abolished serfdom, reformed her army and educational system and breathed a modern spirit into her entire administration. The statesmen responsible for these measures now impelled the Prussian king to place himself at the head of the German nationalist movement, which was slowly forming as a result of the hardships and indignities accompanying Napoleon's otherwise enlightened rule. The Prussians, for all their reforms, were beaten two or three times by Napoleon, but they were soon joined by other allies. First Bernadotte, one of Napoleon's own marshals, who had been installed by his master on the throne of Sweden, revolted against the 'Continental System', declaring that he would not be one of Napoleon's customs officials. Then, on the news of Vitoria, Austria broke from her enforced alliance with France and joined the common cause. The result was that in October 1813 the armies of Russia, Prussia, Sweden and Austria met and overwhelmed Napoleon at Leipzig, in the great 'Battle of the Nations'. After this it was simply a question of chasing the dispirited French across Germany.

At the beginning of 1814 the French were thus on the defensive, both on the Pyrenees and along the Rhine. At this stage Britain's Allies might have been tempted to make peace, but Castlereagh held the Alliance firm and persuaded them to fight for the recapture of the Low Countries. His arguments were assisted by the fact that Napoleon refused to accept even a Rhine frontier. So the Allies renewed their advance and crossed the Rhine, while Wellington forced his way over the Pyrenees into southern France. Still Napoleon continued to fight, conducting an extraordinarily skilful and evasive defence on French soil in the spring of 1814, until the Allies captured Paris and compelled

The advance across the Peninsula

Vitoria, 1813

The Fourth Coalition, 1813

The Battle of Leipzig, 1813

(George Cruikshank, 1815, from a print in the British Museum)

Napoleon escapes from Elba and breaks up the Congress of Vienna, where the kings and diplomats are dividing the cake of Europe. Only Britain (Wellington, on the right, who says nothing but draws his sword) is undismayed!

Abdication of
Napoleon, 1814

Toulouse, 1814
his abdication. A few days later—since the news of peace had not
reached the south—Wellington brought the campaign to a successful conclusion by smashing Soult's army at Toulouse. So
while Napoleon departed to rule the little island of Elba—his
consolation prize—the Allies settled down in congress at Vienna
to reconstruct the map of Europe.

Then ensued some months of wrangling over the spoils of victory. From this degrading spectacle Europe was rescued by the
Napoleon's
escape
news of Napoleon's escape from Elba. Tired of nearly a year's
confinement in his little realm, he had calmly set sail for France
with a handful of supporters. French forces sent to capture him
turned round and fell in behind him, and the restored Bourbon
King, Louis XVIII, was soon in flight. Once more installed as
Emperor, Napoleon offered to accept the losses imposed on
France in 1814, and to live at peace with Europe. But Castlereagh and the British Cabinet were not taking any chances; they
Renewal of the
Coalition
instantly set about reconstructing the Alliance, and pledged
themselves to war until the Emperor was again driven from the
throne.

Wellington was now placed in charge of a motley assembly of
troops in the Low Countries. They comprised 27,000 British
(mostly raw levies, for many of his Peninsula veterans had been
sent off to fight in America) and some 40,000 allied troops,
mainly Dutch and Hanoverians—in all 'an infamous army', as
their commander put it in his own characteristic style. The other
force immediately available was an army of 120,000 Prussians,
under Blücher. The function of the two forces was to contain
Napoleon in France until Austria and Russia could also bring
their troops to bear. Napoleon for his part determined to strike
at the forces on his border before the Austrians and Russians
appeared on the scene. So began the brief campaign which was
decided outside Brussels, on the fields of Waterloo.

The essence of Napoleon's strategy was to smash in the centre
of the allied dispositions, drive Wellington's and Blücher's forces
out of contact with each other, and then finish them off piecemeal.
But his ensuing attacks, though they resulted in the defeat of the
Ligny and
Quatre Bras,
16 June 1815
Prussians at Ligny, separated the two forces by a narrower margin
than he either intended or imagined. For he was too slow in sending detachments after the Prussians, who were thus able to conduct an orderly retreat; while Wellington, after holding his
ground at Quatre Bras till nightfall, played his part by retiring in
conformity. A day of rain and storm then hampered the French

as they followed up Wellington, and by evening the latter was installed in a pre-selected emergency position at Waterloo. By this time Blücher, whose movements were still unknown to Napoleon, had regrouped his forces sufficiently well to be certain of giving Wellington some aid on the following day.

18 June 1815 dawned fine after a night of heavy rain. Confident that he was facing 'bad troops under a bad general', Napoleon very unwisely planned a heavy frontal attack upon Wellington's forces in their carefully chosen defensive line—a sunken road lying just behind a ridge, with a thickset hedge for protection against cavalry, and the fortified farmhouses of Hougomont and La Haye Sainte to harass the flanks of advancing columns. Fortunately Napoleon waited until the afternoon for the ground to dry out under the hot sun, and by this time the Prussians, much to his consternation, were beginning to appear on his right flank. Then followed repeated assaults on Wellington's position, but the 'infamous army' stood firm. It was the column against the line—or the line forming squares to resist cavalry; and the line won. In Wellington's own words, 'the Emperor did not manœuvre at all; he just moved forward in the old style, in columns, and was driven off in the old style'. Waterloo, 18 June 1815

Finally, at sundown, Napoleon flung in against Wellington his last reserve—the Old Guard. They too were repulsed. The Prussians now had a firm hold on the French flank, and the decisive moment had arrived. 'Right ahead, to be sure!' exclaimed Wellington, as he stood in his stirrups and held his hat aloft as the sign to advance. The unwavering lines rose to the opportunity, breasted the ridge and poured after the retreating French down the hill, while the Prussians continued the rout far into the night. The whole French Army dissolved into fragments, and victory was complete. It had been a touch-and-go affair—'a damned nice thing—the nearest run thing you ever saw in your life', as Wellington himself put it. Within a few days Napoleon surrendered to the English as 'the most generous of his foes', and before long was on his way to a safe spot—St Helena, in the South Atlantic. It only remained for the Allies to restore Louis XVIII, and to assemble again at Vienna to continue the process of reshaping Europe. Exile of Napoleon

*　　*　　*　　*　　*

The twenty-two years' struggle against the France of the Revolution and the Empire was at last over, and Britain had played an

Britain's contri-
bution to victory

The exercise of
sea power and
the blockade

unequalled part in securing victory. More than anything, her sea power had proved decisive—through that alone had it been possible to defy invasion, to sweep up enemy colonies, to transport troops to likely jumping-off grounds for attack, to preserve Britain's trade with the other great continents, and to carry out the vast blockade of Napoleon's ports. The blockade alone had the most far-reaching effects, for the economic measures and counter-measures of France and Britain, such as the Berlin Decrees and the Orders in Council, by their grim restrictions on standards of living, helped to bring Russia, Sweden, the Peninsula and most of Germany to the point of revolt against Napoleon.

Economic
strength

The success of Britain's economic measures depended of course not only on her sea power but also on her industrial strength. The war came in that fortunate moment of history when Britain alone was engaged in mass production of iron and textiles and when a supply of cheap British goods was essential to less highly developed countries. This was why Britain could survive on trade with America and the tropics when the 'Continental System' barred her from Europe; and it was because her industry and trade were world necessities that nations rose in arms rather than lose her goods, while even Napoleon had to grant special licences for his armies to be clothed and shod by British products. It was Britain's industrial strength, too, which enabled her to finance repeated coalitions and military expeditions.

Military
campaigns

If sea power and economic warfare were Britain's main contributions tó the allied victory, purely military efforts also had some weight. The earlier military disasters were wiped out in the glories of the Peninsular campaign and Waterloo. Wellington himself, tireless in attention to essential detail, a master of tactics if not of strategy, and commanding the unqualified respect of his men, was a great asset to the allied cause. What the Duke himself was moved to say about Waterloo he might equally well have applied to the Peninsular War—'By God, I don't think it would have done if I had not been there.'

All in all, Britain's effort was fruitful in every sphere, naval, economic and military. Her Navy and her wealth enabled her to hang on until the forces of nationalism which Napoleon had evoked turned against him. Then she could employ effectively the final—the military—factor. Thus her first decisive success was in defeating the enemy's challenge at sea, her second in overcoming the 'Continental System' by the Orders in Council, and her third in liberating Spain and advancing into France. So Britain, more than any other Power, saved Europe from the domination of one man—not for the first time, and not for the last.

7. Castlereagh, Canning and the Congress System

1 The Vienna Settlement

With Napoleon at a safe distance in St Helena, the Great Powers could once more concentrate at Vienna on the business of treaty-making. Many decisions had already been arrived at before the Hundred Days, and others were fixed up in Paris immediately after Waterloo. Taken together, the various agreements provided the most comprehensive settlement of Europe since the Treaty of Utrecht in 1713.

The Paris and Vienna treaties

The main intentions of the treaty-makers in 1814 and 1815 were to reward the victors and prevent further aggression by France. Among the rewards Prussia acquired some Rhineland provinces and much of Saxony, Russia was entrusted with the care of a small Polish Kingdom, and Austrian rule was recognized over most of North Italy. In addition, Sweden received Norway—of which Denmark was relieved as a punishment for deserting Napoleon too late in the day. Great Britain, with her unchallenged sea power, did not need to submit the fate of her overseas conquests to the verdict of the Powers; she contented herself with the Cape of Good Hope, Mauritius, Ceylon, Heligoland, Malta, the Ionian Islands, Trinidad, St Lucia and Tobago.[1] Where no special reward was arranged, the principle followed was usually that of 'legitimacy'—i.e. restoring the family which had ruled before the eruption of France. Thus the French throne went back to the Bourbons in the person of Louis XVIII, while other branches of the same house regained their ancient possessions in Spain and South Italy. Nothing could restore the three-hundred-and-sixty-odd states in Germany which had existed before 1789, so these were now reduced to thirty-nine, and combined for external affairs in a German Confederation.

The victors' rewards

---

[1] Other British conquests, including the Dutch East Indies, were handed back. This led Sir Stamford Raffles, a servant of the East India Company who had acted as Governor of Java during the British occupation, to recommend the purchase of Singapore from the Sultan of Johore.

The prevention of further French aggression was sought partly by territorial arrangements, partly by an alliance. Thus the old Austrian Netherlands went to Holland to form a larger state, supposedly more able to deal on equal terms with France. For the same reason Piedmont, in North Italy, was increased in size, and the German Confederation was reckoned to be more capable of standing up to France than the old Holy Roman Empire had been. In addition, the great Powers, Britain, Austria, Prussia and Russia, renewed their treaty of 1814 and formed a Quadruple Alliance, pledged to resist any attempt by France to overthrow the new settlement. By this treaty the Allies also promised to meet in further congresses to settle other European problems as they might arise.

The prevention of French aggression

The Quadruple Alliance

Much has been written on the follies and vices of the Vienna settlement. It is easy to see that the treaties completely neglected that spirit of nationality which had proved so powerful in defeating Napoleon. Countries and peoples were bandied about regardless of their wishes and feelings as though they were mere counters in the game of power-politics. Trouble was bound to arise, and much of the history of the nineteenth century is concerned with the struggles of Italians, Poles, Belgians, Norwegians, Boers and even Germans to free themselves from alien or despotic rule imposed on them at Vienna.

The neglect of nationalism

But however great the faults of the settlement in its neglect of national and popular factors, in one or two respects at least it showed wisdom. Castlereagh, the chief British representative, determined that France should not be unduly victimized for what were held to be the faults of Napoleon. He thus left her with no great grievance, and at the same time bolstered up her new régime. And a further piece of wisdom—in intention, if not in execution—was the attempt to settle European affairs by meetings in Congress. The history of British foreign policy during the next decade is the history of this well-meant if unfortunate scheme.

The treatment of France

The 'Congress System' largely originated in the mind of Castlereagh. If all heads could be 'put under the same thinking cap' by meeting in Congresses, the Great Powers might gradually learn the meaning of co-operation, and establish a true 'Concert of Europe'. What had been—and was still—a military alliance against France might be expanded into a permanent and bloodless method of settling the affairs of the Continent. This was Castlereagh's vision, and it had something of the same idealism as a later and equally unsuccessful attempt to achieve the same

The Congress System Castlereagh's plan

ends—the League of Nations. The system envisaged was, however, very sketchy compared with that which operated from Geneva after 1919. There was no covenant, no fixed period of assembly, no official building, no staff, no attempt to include more than the four great Powers—or five after the admission of France in 1818. It was, in brief, simply an effort to substitute conferences for wars, instead of having the war first and the conference afterwards.

Often confused with this Quadruple Alliance and Congress System is another product of 1815, the Holy Alliance. The Tsar Alexander at this stage held fairly liberal views; and he was under the influence of an ardently religious woman. With the admirable (but momentary) intention of carrying Christianity into politics, he proposed a league of the sovereigns of Europe, pledged to treat each other and their subjects on Christian principles. As a gesture of goodwill nothing could be said against this, and with three exceptions the crowned heads of Europe appended their signatures. One of the exceptions was George III, who was now completely insane, and confined to Windsor Castle. The Prince Regent—the future George IV—would have been willing to join any group of sovereigns for almost any purpose, but he was not allowed by the Cabinet to sign anything like a treaty on his own account. Moreover, Castlereagh's strong vein of practical sense revolted against so vague and unrealistic a project. He roundly termed it 'a piece of sublime mysticism and nonsense', while Metternich, the Austrian Chancellor, declared that 'the Tsar's mind was quite clearly affected'. After the initial flourish of goodwill, nothing thus came of the Holy Alliance. The Quadruple Alliance and Congress System, however, continued unaffected.

The 'Holy Alliance'

2 The Later Congresses

Congress of Aix-la-Chapelle, 1818

The first European Congress ever to meet except at the end of a war was held at Aix-la-Chapelle in 1818. It was called to consider the future position of France, who had by now paid off her war indemnity. Castlereagh therefore urged—and secured—the withdrawl of the occupying forces. The French were also admitted into the Congress System, and the Quadruple became the Quintuple Alliance.

France admitted to the Quadruple Alliance

The next two or three years brought disturbances all over Europe, organized by liberals and democrats against despotic governments. The major outbreaks occurred in Spain, Portugal, Naples and Piedmont, whose monarchs were all forced to accept some elements of democracy. In Germany, too, discontent was at fever heat. Moreover, the Spanish colonies in South America had for some time refused to recognize the rule of the restored Bourbons in Spain, and persisted in regarding themselves as independent. To consider these and kindred problems, Metternich and Alexander—the latter by now thoroughly scared out of his liberalism—demanded another Congress. Anti-despotic movements in Europe

The Congress of Troppau (and its continuation at Laibach the following year) marked the first stage in the decline of the Congress System. Castlereagh knew that the despotic powers were out to secure a general authority to put down revolutions, and that they would then suppress the popular movements in Spain, Portugal and Naples. For himself, he had no sympathy with popular movements, and every sympathy with suppressing them. But he wished the suppression to be done by and in the name of the power whose interests were actually threatened. Only in the case of a revolution against the Bourbon monarchy in France would he have been prepared to use British troops; otherwise Britain would land herself in continual difficulties, and he would be called upon to face vehement opposition in Parliament. So he refused to send a representative to Troppau or Laibach, and sent instead an 'observer', who duly dissociated himself from any general 'right to intervene'. That, of course, did not stop Austria suppressing the democratic risings in Naples and Piedmont, or clamping down agitation in Germany. Congress of Troppau (and Laibach) Castlereagh welcomes Austrian suppression of the revolution in Naples, but acknowledges no general right of intervention

A further Congress, to give special attention to the problem of Spain and her colonies, had been called for 1822. It duly met at Verona, but by that time two fresh complications had arisen. Another great rebellion had broken out—that of the Greeks against the Turks; and Castlereagh had killed himself. Overwork, bad medical treatment, and sensitiveness to his unpopularity—which had been caused by his support of repressive measures at home—had combined to unhinge his mind. His disappearance from the political scene left Liverpool free to invite his rival Canning to take his place as Foreign Secretary and Leader of the House of Commons. In sentiment Canning was far more liberally inclined than Castlereagh, and the already perceptible movement of Britain away from the Congress System was thus soon quickened. Suicide of Castlereagh; Canning Foreign Secretary

To the new Congress at Verona, Liverpool and Canning despatched Wellington as the British representative. Acting under Congress of Verona, 1822

(Cruikshank, 1823, from a print in the British Museum)

Alexander I of Russia and Francis I of Austria urge Louis XVIII of France to invade Spain and suppress the popular movement. Louis is nothing loath.

Canning's instructions he refused to agree to a scheme for French help to the Spanish King, or to any 'moral support' by the other powers, and returned to England before the end of the Congress. When the French later persisted in invading Spain to restore the King to his 'rightful' position, Canning encouraged the Spaniards to resist. The popular party, however, was easily defeated, and the King restored to full power (1823)—a position in which he re-introduced the Inquisition and executed an extensive selection of his opponents. Two further questions of great moment then arose—would the French and the Spanish monarchists try to take similar steps in Portugal, and, above all, would they try to restore the revolted Spanish colonies of South America to the Spanish Crown? British opposition to intervention in Spain

The question of the colonies was the more important, and it was settled first. Before the colonies had broken away their trade had been largely monopolized by Spain. Since that break their trade with Britain had increased some fourteen times. There were thus important commercial motives for not allowing the colonies to revert to Spanish control; and Britain also held the decisive card in the form of her unrivalled fleet. Canning therefore warned France that any attempt to recover the colonies for Spain would mean war with Britain. Moreover, he negotiated with Monroe, President of the United States, who was very loath to see the great European powers re-establish their influence in America. Monroe thereupon recognized the independence of the South American republics, and proclaimed the 'Monroe Doctrine'— that any attempt by European powers to establish fresh colonies on the American Continent, or to interfere with the liberty of colonies which had declared themselves independent, would be regarded 'as the manifestation of an unfriendly disposition to the United States'. This bold pronouncement—for the diplomatic phrase conveyed a threat to use force—remained the basis of the foreign policy of the United States for over a century. Since it was intended to apply to Britain as well as to other European states, it was by no means the response for which Canning had hoped. And since the force on which the Doctrine relied was really the British Navy and not the then diminutive arms of the United States, a joint declaration would have been more appropriate. However, Canning promptly welcomed the Monroe Doctrine, and before very long recognized the republics of Buenos Aires, Colombia and Mexico as independent states. In this way France and Russia (who was aiming to extend her influence south from The Spanish colonies The 'Monroe Doctrine', 1823 Canning recognizes independence of Spanish colonies

Alaska) were warned off American soil, and British commercial interests were safeguarded.

The whole affair of the Spanish colonies, by separating Britain violently from France and Russia, brought still nearer the final breakdown of the Congress System and the 'Concert of Europe'. Canning himself, justifying the recognition of the republics somewhat later, used his most famous words—'I resolved that if France had Spain, it should not be Spain "with the Indies". I called the New World into existence to redress the balance of the Old.' The use of the personal pronoun explains why fellow-politicians frequently disliked the Foreign Secretary. Incidentally, George IV, that ardent Royalist, so objected to recognizing the republics that he refused to read the royal speech to Parliament announcing the decision. His excuse was that he had lost his false teeth.

Canning's support of the constitutional movement in Portugal

Portugal was the next state to feel the benefit of Canning's policy. The Portuguese King in this case actually proposed to grant a constitution to his own subjects, but was opposed by his younger brother and by Spain. When Spain began to equip an army to suppress the constitutional party in Portugal, Canning sent a fleet and 4,500 troops to Lisbon. Faced with this, Spain gave way, and Portugal too was saved from absolutism. Again, France and the other members of the Alliance could scarcely approve.

Britain's dissociation from the Congress System

Thus far, though Canning's actions and his refusal to take part in any further Congresses had already gravely weakened the 'Concert of Europe', the division was merely of one power—Britain—against four. The system of co-operation begun at Vienna was not to be finally smashed until there was a division of three powers against two. That division now came about as a result of Canning's attitude to the Greek War of Independence.

3 The Greek War of Independence

The Greek revolt, 1821

The 'Eastern Question'

The Greek revolt had already broken out in 1821, and before long it raised in an acute form that nightmare of our ancestors, the 'Eastern Question'. That question, broadly speaking, was—what was to happen to the Turkish Empire, and in particular how much of it was to fall under Russian domination? It was a very important question; for though, when the nineteenth century opened, the Turks were a power in decline, their territory was still extensive. It covered the present Turkey, together with Albania, Serbia (i.e. most of Yugoslavia), Moldavia and Wallachia (i.e. Rumania), Bulgaria and Greece, while outside Europe it included Asia Minor, Syria, Palestine, Egypt and the whole North African coast to Morocco.

The classic British treatment of the Eastern Question had already been laid down by Pitt in the Oczakoff incident.[1] Unwilling to see Russia advance towards Constantinople and the Mediterranean, where British trading interests might be seriously threatened, he had wanted to support the Turks and bottle up Russia in the Black Sea. The same problems arose in connection with the Greek revolt, and with every other revolt against Turkish overlordship. There was always the peril that a weakening of Turkish authority would benefit Russia in some way or other—either in the shape of a direct acquisition of territory or by a newly formed rebel state coming under Russian influence. Broadly speaking, the policy of Pitt, and later of Palmerston and Disraeli—though not of Gladstone—was thus to support Turkey even against her subject races struggling for freedom. In this line of policy, however, the British treatment of the Greek revolt was to some extent an exception. The standard British attitude

The revolt of the Greeks against the Turks differed in British eyes from revolts by Serbs, Bulgars or Rumanians. The study of the Greek classics formed part of the education of a British gentleman; and though the peasants and traders of 1821 might have little in common with Homeric heroes and Platonic philosophers, they still held some lustre from their far-off ancestors. So it came about that before the British Government took up any very definite attitude in the matter, the British public had already made up its mind. Subscriptions to Greek funds poured in, and British volunteers, stirred by Turkish atrocities, gave military assistance. In 1823 the Greeks were lucky enough to attract the sympathy of the poet Lord Byron, the adored and detested leader of the 'Romantic movement'. His journey to Greece and his death at Missolonghi in 1824 still further hallowed the Greek cause. So the 'War of Independence' smouldered on, successfully in many ways, until the arrival of a new and very different figure on the scene. Support of the Greeks by British public opinion Lord Byron

In 1825 there landed in the Morea (Southern Greece) the army of Ibrahim Pasha, son of the Egyptian Pasha, Mehemet Ali. The latter, who in theory ruled Egypt as the representative Ibrahim Pasha in Greece, 1825

[1] See page 32.

of the Sultan of Turkey, had been promised the Morea in return for help against the Greeks. By the summer of 1827 Ibrahim had not only occupied most of the mainland, but was massacring or expelling the entire Greek population. Immediately the outcry in Britain for intervention to support the Greeks became almost irresistible; and Canning, who had earlier declared British neutrality in the struggle, had to think out a fresh policy.

The particular danger of the situation, so far as Britain was concerned, was that by this time nothing could stop Russia helping the Greeks; for Alexander's brother and successor, Nicholas I, was an ardent champion of the Orthodox Church, and was determined to protect his co-religionists. Canning therefore decided that if Russia was going to intervene, Britain had better intervene too. Had the rebels been Serbs or Bulgars, and the Foreign Secretary someone other than Canning, intervention might have taken the form of support for the Turks to counterbalance Russia's support of the Greeks. As it was, British popular sympathy with the Greeks, Canning's reluctance to encourage despotic rule abroad, and the horror aroused by Ibrahim's activities, rendered that course impossible. So Canning instead proposed that Greece should have self-government in practice, while still remaining in theory under Turkish rule, and liable to pay tribute. The Tsar agreed, and Canning then secured the adhesion of France to the proposal.

On the retirement of Liverpool in the spring of 1827, Canning became Prime Minister, and could press his policy to a conclusion. In July 1827 a formal treaty embodying the proposals agreed between Britain, Russia and France was signed in London, and the Turks and Greeks were given a brief time to fix up an armistice. If they did not, the three Powers would make them see reason by joint naval action. From these important decisions Prussia and Austria held firmly aloof, resenting to the last any support of rebels, and bitterly opposed to any foreign influence penetrating the Turkish Empire—except their own.

The naval forces sent out to enforce the armistice were under the command of Admiral Codrington. After a preliminary blockade of the Turkish and Egyptian Fleets, Codrington made up his mind to force Ibrahim out of the Morea. The allied squadrons accordingly sailed into Navarino Bay, where Ibrahim's far larger fleet was drawn up. Codrington then sent a boat to order the removal of a Turkish fire-ship at the entrance of the harbour. Ibrahim fired on the boat, the Allies fired on Ibrahim, and in a

Marginal notes:

Russia determines to support the Greeks

Canning decides to act with Russia, to control her—

—and secures French support

Canning Prime Minister, 1827

Treaty of London, 1827

Navarino Bay, 1827

very short time the Turkish and Egyptian Fleets were at the bottom of the sea. Thus the main danger to the Greeks was effectively removed; for Ibrahim's communications with Egypt were cut, and the Greeks had virtually won their war of independence.

This striking result of his labours Canning himself did not live to see. His premiership had lasted only four months, for he died in office a few weeks before the battle of Navarino. By the beginning of 1828 Wellington was Prime Minister; and Wellington was inclined to repent of destroying a Turkish fleet which might have come in useful one day against Russia. He therefore muddled about in search of a policy, and even apologized for Navarino as an 'untoward event'. The result of this swing towards the Turks was that Russia, deprived of the steadying factor of British support, soon picked a fresh quarrel with Turkey and declared war. To the French, too, fell the honour of finally expelling Ibrahim's army from the Morea. All this proved too much for the Turks, who collapsed before the Russian advance and were compelled to make terms at Adrianople (1829).

At this stage Wellington, convinced by the march of events that Greek freedom must after all come about, sensibly decided that semi-independence would merely give Russia further excuses for interfering in Greek affairs, and that it must be complete independence or nothing. Official recognition and guarantees of the new Greek state were then given by Britain, France and Russia in 1830. Greece, though still confined within unduly narrow boundaries, had thus become independent, and the first great rent had been made in the rotting fabric of the Turkish Empire.

The Greek revolt proved an exception to the normal British policy on the Eastern Question. It also proved the end of the Quintuple Alliance. On the South American and Spanish questions, the line-up had been Britain versus Austria, Prussia, Russia and France. Now, on the Greek question, the new line-up was Britain, Russia and France versus Austria and Prussia. The Congress System, which depended on unanimity, was in fragments, and no further Congresses met. As Canning put it, shortly before his death: 'Things are getting back to a wholesome state again —every nation for itself and God for us all.'

It may seem strange that Canning thus rejoiced in the collapse of one of the first schemes of international co-operation. But, unlike Castlereagh, he had not had practical experience of the

Death of Canning

Wellington Prime Minister, 1828

Russia and France continue to help Greeks

Wellington decides for an independent but small Greece

End of the Quintuple Alliance and Congress System

Canning's motives

benefits of co-operation in the final moves against Napoleon, nor had he any of Castlereagh's 'parent's fondness' for the Congress System. Moreover, he disapproved of the use to which the other powers wished to put the Alliance. He preferred to have his hands free, in the usual tradition of British foreign policy, and not to be bound by international decisions to be for ever suppressing revolutions all over Europe. He did not wish to see the Alliance used to crush popular movements in Spain, Portugal or Greece, or to damage British commercial interests in South America. Loving to pose as a great champion of freedom, he challenged the despots of the Continent, and he addressed his speeches deliberately to public opinion—a new line in the conduct of British foreign policy. But his liberalism can be exaggerated, for he approved the Liverpool Cabinet's measures against agitation at home, such as the Six Acts; and he raised no objection to 'foreign domination' when it was practised by his own country.

Though the first attempt at European organization was partly defeated by a British statesman, that organization had come to stand for the very opposite of freedom, and Europe was the better for its disappearance. At any rate, if some ill-used populace on the Continent felt like rising against misgovernment, it could now revolt without fear of suppression by the combined forces of the European Powers. Such was the curious gift to Europe of Canning and the Tories in the decade after Waterloo.

8. Social Distress and Tory Repression

1 The Causes of Distress

It is part of the good fortune—or merit—of Britain that she has been remarkably free from the extremes of class conflict. Nothing like the savage butchery of the French Revolution, the Russian Revolution or the Spanish Civil War of 1936–39 has sullied our annals in modern times. All the same, there have been periods of great tension and bitterness between the classes, and never more so than in the opening decades of the nineteenth century.

The causes of discontent among the labouring class went wide and deep. In the new industrial towns of the north men and women were toiling up to seventeen hours a day, and were yet reduced to exposing their own little children, perhaps no more than four or five years old, to the danger, weariness and brutality of the cotton mills. In the countryside the enclosures had reduced the smaller peasant-farmers to landless labourers, while the poorer rural homes were suffering both from the general loss of 'common' rights and the decline of domestic textile work. But these were things largely incidental to the great economic changes which had taken place since 1750; in addition, there was all the distress caused by long years of warfare and by harsh or unwise government action.

The effects of the Agrarian and Industrial Revolutions

The Revolutionary and Napoleonic Wars brought misery upon the working classes not by any large demand for fighting men— though to be press-ganged into the Navy was a bad enough fate —but by a great rise in the cost of living. Bread in particular rose in price, for Britain depended on supplementary imports of wheat from Europe in years when the home crop was not at its best, and these were difficult or impossible to obtain during the more critical phases of the conflict. From 46s. a quarter before 1790, wheat rose to an average of 94s. a quarter between 1810 and 1815, with a peak price of 126s. in 1812. But the rise was also general —amounting to about 100 per cent over the whole period of the wars—for the cost of the war compelled the Government to go

The effect of the Wars: higher prices and increased taxation

The BRITISH-BUTCHER,
Supplying JOHN-BULL with a Substitute for BREAD. Vide...

(Gillray, 1795, from a print in the British Museum)

Bad harvests and the war against France brought about a steep rise in the price of wheat and bread. Pitt recommended the consumption of more meat; but this was quite beyond the ordinary labourer's means.

off the gold standard in 1797.[1] Moreover, the war led to increased taxation, which, in spite of the income tax on the wealthier classes, fell heavily on the purses of the poor. Nor was either of these hardships—higher prices or increased taxes—offset by a corresponding rise in wages. While prices doubled, the wages of the agricultural labourer rose only from 9s. to 13s. a week.

As the war drove up the cost of living, more and more districts were compelled to adopt the 'Speenhamland system' of poor relief. First applied in systematic form by the Berkshire justices at Speenhamland in 1795, this supplemented a labourer's wages from the local rates in accordance with the number of his children and the price of bread. Though well-intentioned the practice was in the long run disastrous; for farmers, seeing that their labourers would draw a supplement from the rates, refused to give proper increases of pay, while the parish as a whole was soon faced with higher rates merely to save the pockets of the farmers. Meantime, the labourers were humiliated by receiving as parish 'charity' what they ought to have received in increased wages.

The 'Speenhamland System'

Agricultural labourers were not the only class to suffer from the increased cost of living, though in general their sufferings were the greatest. Skilled artisans in the towns usually got fairer increases in wages, but there were some notable exceptions in special cases affected by machinery, as with the hand-loom weavers in the cotton trade. These men had been greatly in demand in the early days of the Industrial Revolution, when the factories were producing yarn but not cloth. Then the restriction of trade through the Berlin Decrees, the Orders in Council and the war with the United States dealt cotton a heavy blow, while the perfection of the power-loom made the hand-loom unnecessary. Around 1800 the earnings of a hand-loom weaver averaged some 27s. a week; by 1815, about 15s.; and by the early 1820s, not more than 8s. Finally, in the 1830s hand-loom wages sank to the tragic figure of 5s. a week, by which time the craft was on the point of extinction.

The hand-loom weavers

The hand-loom weavers were not alone in resenting the introduction of machinery. Angry mobs, who saw in machinery the cause of low wages or unemployment, were always liable to smash up the new inventions. This 'machine-breaking' was the main

Attacks against machinery:

---

[1] This caused a decline in the value of the currency. The shopkeeper or manufacturer therefore demanded more of it—i.e. higher prices—in exchange for his goods.

The 'Luddite'
Riots, 1811–1812

Nottingham-
shire ('wide'
frames)
feature of the 'Luddite' riots, which began in 1811 in Nottinghamshire. The object of attack in this county was a special type
of 'wide' frame illegitimately used by many masters for making
stockings. The 'wide' frames had been chiefly employed in the
past for making pantaloons, but the main market for these had
disappeared during the war with the closing of the Continent to
British trade. Some masters therefore began to use their 'wide'
frames to produce material which was then cut into the shape of
stockings and stitched up the edges. These 'cut-ups', very inferior
articles compared with real stockings made on a 'narrow' frame,
were bitterly resented by the stocking-workers, who formed a
secret organization directed, it was said, by a certain Ned Ludd,
or 'King Ludd', from Sherwood Forest. The leader may have
been mythical, but the actions of the Luddites were severely practical. They marched in small well-disciplined bodies at dead of
night to a selected village, smashed up the 'wide' frames in the
local mill and burnt any stores of 'cut-ups' they could find. Their
raids were so successful that the real stocking trade soon came
back into its own, and the wages of the operatives rose appreciably.

Lancashire and
Cheshire
(power-looms)
The success of the Nottinghamshire Luddites inspired imitation. In Lancashire and Cheshire power-looms were attacked,
hand-loom weavers taking a leading part. Factories were
stormed, and determined owners often garrisoned them as for a
regular siege. At Middleton a manufacturerer and his bodyguard
killed five of a mob which attacked his power-looms, only to have
his house burnt down by the way of retaliation. Not all machinery,
however, was attacked—only new machinery to which the workers
were unaccustomed.

Government
attitude to
machine-
breaking
The grievances of the Luddites evoked little sympathy in the
governing classes. After the Nottinghamshire riots Liverpool's
Cabinet introduced a bill making machine-breaking punishable
by death—valuing a life 'at something less than the price of a
stocking-frame', as the poet Byron put it in the House of Lords.
But the voices of Byron and of a few others in Parliament were
powerless against the majority, and soon the death penalty was
being put into effect against the Luddites.

The post-war
'slump'
The Luddites of 1812 were simple men, often driven by downright hunger, who aimed direct blows at what they saw was obviously harming them. But the reasons for general distress were
extremely complicated, and became more so in the years which
followed the war. It is easy to see that the increased cost of living
caused by the war was a source of great hardship. What is more

difficult to grasp is that the great fall in prices which took place after the war was to many equally disastrous. But falling prices are generally a sign that the manufacturer cannot sell easily; and as the demand for goods falls off he produces less and dismisses surplus employees. Thus falling prices are good for those workers in stable employment, for they can purchase more with their wages, but they are bad for the manufacturing class and for those who are 'turned off' in consequence of declining trade.

In 1816, after a short-lived boom, prices dropped to a level unknown since the early days of the war. A fall in prices was natural at the end of the war, but it was made sharper by the decision of the Cabinet in 1819 to return to the gold standard.[1] Added to all this, there was the usual end-of-war dislocation— the demobilization of soldiers and sailors (about 200,000 of them), and the withdrawal of government contracts for uniforms, guns, sails and so on. So until manufacturers could get back to peacetime production and more stable prices, there was a great slump and widespread unemployment.

If Liverpool's Government regarded such problems as beyond its power of remedy, at least it was concerned to stop the pricefall in one sphere. Parliament, a body in which the great landowners and country gentry were most strongly represented, was determined that, whatever the situation in industry, the landed classes should not suffer. It thus pressed for special protection for agriculture; and Liverpool's Cabinet, anxious to avoid dependence on foreign foodstuffs, responded by introducing the Corn Law of 1815. There had been other Corn Laws before, and there were other Corn Laws after, but this most memorable of Corn Laws laid down that foreign corn might not be imported until homegrown wheat had reached the price of 80s. a quarter. It was clearly intended to keep prices artificially high in the interests of landowners, while entirely neglecting the need for cheap food on the part of the industrial masses. Thus the Corn Law, too, became a cause of ill-feeling between the classes.

The Corn Law of 1815

Strangely enough the Corn Law of 1815 for all its severity did not ensure prosperity for agriculture. For one thing it did nothing to overcome the low purchasing-power of wages—people remained unable to buy all the food they needed. Moreover, the post-war depression hit the farmers like everyone else, for during the war they had taken into cultivation much soil, such as chalk

[1] The new gold coins issued were 'sovereigns' of twenty shillings value, as opposed to the old 'guinea' of twenty-one shillings.

(Cruikshank, 1815, from a print in the British Museum)

A commentary on the New Corn Law. French traders offer corn cheaply but the English landlords refuse to allow it in. Enraged, the English workman and his hungry family vow to emigrate.

downland, which it was profitable to plough only when the very highest prices for corn could be obtained. After the war it no longer paid to till this soil, yet its full worth as pasture would not be regained for many years to come. As this land went out of cultivation farmhands were dismissed and agricultural unemployment spread. Worst of all, the people who really scored from the Corn Law were not the farmers, but the corn-dealers. These men developed the habit of buying up and holding back sufficient English wheat to tip the price up to 80s., and then rushing in large stocks of foreign corn which they had ready. This resulted in prices fluctuating violently, to the benefit of neither farmer nor labourer.

Yet another cause of the discontent in the years immediately following Waterloo was the Government's handling of taxation. During the war the National Debt had risen enormously, increasing from some £247,000,000 in 1792 to roughly £902,000,000 in 1816. This meant that the annual interest to be paid to debt-holders rose correspondingly from some £9,000,000 to over £31,000,000—a very large amount to find when the whole annual revenue of the Government was no more than £55,000,000. The obvious way to raise such a sum was to increase the income tax. Unfortunately, Parliament had other views. *Finance: abolition of the income tax, increase of indirect taxation*

Income tax had been introduced purely as a wartime measure, and when peace was concluded the tax-paying classes at once set up an irresistible outcry for its repeal. Liverpool's Cabinet thereupon abolished the tax, with the result that duties had to be increased on common articles like tea, sugar, tobacco, beer, paper, soap and candles. The poor were thus taxed to pay interest to the rich—a point which did not escape their attention.

2 The Radical Movement and the Post-War Disturbances

Against all the grievances—low wages, harsh factory conditions, unemployment, heavy indirect taxation, the Corn Law—the working classes naturally agitated. The Government, however, had little more liking for orderly agitation than for actual revolt, and the consequence was a series of clashes and disturbances which set men of property a-tremble for their possessions.

The first of these incidents after the war occurred at the Spa

This Monster was Bred in a PITT Suckled by a FOX christen'd in a Scotch CASTLE Scourge and by a BROOM

Thunderstruck have done at last after many years Deplorable Suffering & to you give him the finishing Blow!

Down Down to h—ll I say Sink thee!!

The DEATH of the PROPERTY TAX !!!
or 37 Mortal Wounds for Ministers & the Inquisitorial Commissioners !!!!!!!!!

(Cruikshank, 1816, from a print in the British Museum)

Helped by the British Lion and a stout supporter wielding petitions from the commercial towns, Brougham inflicts the death-blow (by a parliamentary majority of 37) on the hated hydra of the Property or Income Tax. On the left another of Brougham's supporters, Tierney, helps the long-oppressed Britannia to her feet. Above, the defeated Ministers and the gouty Prince Regent are forced to take the road to Economy.

Fields Meetings of 1816. The big slump of that year had already caused riots, machine-breaking and other demonstrations in various parts of the country. A group of reformers known as the Spencean Philanthropists planned something more systematic. Ardent followers of one Thomas Spence, whose cure for all ills was the nationalization of land and the abolition of all taxes in favour of the income tax, they decided to hold a big meeting in Spa Fields (on the outskirts of the City of London), and then present a great petition to the Prince Regent. For their main speaker they hoped to have Henry Hunt, whose skill in addressing crowds had brought him the nickname of 'Orator'. Hunt, however, would not speak except in favour of the programme of the Radicals, who demanded the vote for all men as the preliminary to all other reform. The result was that *two* meetings were held instead of one—the first run by the Spenceans, and the second by Hunt and the Radicals. The effect of two great political demonstrations on one day was too much for the London mob, who got out of hand, broke into a gunsmith's shop, and marched off in a noisy demonstration towards the City. After a little rioting they were dispersed by a force collected by the Lord Mayor.

This activity, though in reality very little of it was violent, thoroughly alarmed Liverpool's Government. Having lived through the French Revolution, its members feared not only for their own property but for the whole established order of the country. Unfortunately they were liable to see matters out of their true perspective, since the Home Secretary, Lord Sidmouth, employed professional 'informers'. In the absence of any detectives (except the Bow Street Runners, who dealt with highwaymen), or any police except the inefficient town watchmen and parish constables, the employment of informers was natural. The objection to their use was twofold—the normal objection to a sneak, and the fact that the informer, in his anxiety to have something to report to the Government, all too often acted as an *agent provocateur*, stirring on simple men to violent courses which they might otherwise never have adopted. Information from such men, combined with rash words or stupid gestures from some of the crowd at Spa Fields (such as carrying tricolours and 'caps of liberty'), caused Sidmouth and his colleagues in the Cabinet to panic. They promptly suspended Habeas Corpus again (it had been restored to operation in 1815) and passed further laws against seditious meetings.

Agitation persisted throughout 1817, and the Manchester unemployed planned a great march to London, where they hoped
to petition the Regent for reform, relief of distress and the can-
cellation of Sidmouth's recent measures. The marchers were to
carry blankets, in which to sleep *en route*, and from this they
earned the nickname 'Blanketeers'. But their march never really
got going. When a big 'send-off' meeting was held in St Peter's
Fields, Manchester, it was at once broken up by troops, and the
leaders of the march were arrested. A few groups who had already
started were chased and quickly scattered, and only one man got
right through to present his petition. Many were arrested as
vagrants and spent some time in prison without trial—a convenience for which the Government had already catered by suspending Habeas Corpus.

A government that scented danger in the activities of the
Blanketeers would not fail to see red revolution in the Derbyshire
outbreak of the same year. In the spring of 1817 Government
spies began to send in reports of a forthcoming mass revolt in the
north, and Sidmouth, after arresting many Radical leaders, therefore despatched a notorious spy named Oliver to work his way
into the heart of the conspiracy. Oliver went about this task by
travelling the country, urging local Radicals to take up arms and
assuring them that the revolt was already perfectly prepared in
every other district. He had only two successes. At Huddersfield a
few men gathered under arms, but promptly dispersed when they
found that they were unsupported. In Derbyshire, however, some
unemployed textile workers led by one Jeremiah Brandreth set
out to link up with other contingents and capture Nottingham
Castle. The other contingents were a figment of Oliver's imagination; very much more real was the party of troops waiting to capture the marchers. Brandreth and three others were hanged, fourteen were transported, and a few more were imprisoned.

Among many Radical leaders scheduled for arrest in 1817 was
the most famous of all, William Cobbett. Born in Surrey of
peasant stock, Cobbett had become first a solicitor's clerk and
then a soldier. In America he had made a reputation as a journalist and had started a newspaper—*Peter Porcupine's Gazette*—
in which he opposed the influence of Paine and Priestley and of
democratic ideas generally. A man of violent prejudices, his outspoken pen had soon involved him in an action for libel with
heavy damages, and he had left America in disgust. Returning to
England, he had then founded, in 1802, *The Weekly Political*

Register. Hating the new England of enclosure and factory, and sighing for the old 'yeoman' days, Cobbett's sympathy at this stage was with the Tories, and the judicious outlay of the profits of his writings soon enabled him to become a considerable landed proprietor himself. In 1805, however, tired of Tory blindness to the need for reform, Cobbett had changed sides and become a fully fledged Radical. His conversion had been made all the more complete in 1810, when he was sentenced to a fine of £1,000 and two years' imprisonment for criticizing the flogging of British soldiers by German mercenaries. *The Political Register,* now no longer Tory but ardently Radical, was at this stage lending powerful aid to the cause of reform, but at a shilling a copy it was too dear to reach many homes. Moreover, working men who clubbed together to buy it, or met in a public-house to hear it read aloud, had begun to find themselves up against Sidmouth's spy network. Cobbett in 1816 had thereupon taken the bold step of reducing the price of *The Register* to twopence, at once increasing his influence tenfold. So dangerous a man was obviously best, in Sidmouth's eyes, under lock and key, and in 1817 Cobbett decided to decamp to America while the going was good. *The Register,* however, went on, run by a friend under Cobbett's direction. Two years later, when the scare had died down a little, he returned to England, bringing with him as an act of repentance the bones of Tom Paine, whose views he had so violently attacked in the past.

The Political Register

A good harvest and a trade revival in the latter part of 1817 for a while lessened the unrest in the country. During 1819, however, unemployment became rife again, and the working-class demand for relief and parliamentary reform grew more violent. The climax to this agitation, and to the whole system of government repression, came in the August of that year, in the famous 'Manchester Massacre'.

Once again the scene of trouble was St Peter's Fields,[1] Manchester. From all over South Lancashire contingents were to come to a mass meeting to demand reform, the leading speaker being once again 'Orator' Hunt. Everything, the Radical leaders determined, was to be peaceable. No sticks were to be carried, except by the aged; best clothes were to be worn; and women and children were to form part of the processions as a guarantee that only the most orderly demonstration was intended. So the crowds, in a holiday spirit but bearing banners with determined-

'Peterloo', 1819

[1] Later covered by the Free Trade Hall and adjoining buildings.

looking devices such as 'Votes for All' and 'Reform or Death', set off for Manchester. Some found certain roads blocked by the authorities, but they made their way by other routes, and an enormous crowd was eventually permitted to gather at the selected meeting-ground. Here soldiers, including the Manchester Yeomanry, a volunteer body of cavalry, were drawn up in readiness

(*Cruikshank, 1819, from a print in the British Museum*)

A cartoon which appeared very shortly after 'Peterloo'. The Tory Ministers (left to right, Castlereagh, Eldon, and Liverpool, who trips over a pile of money) are thrown into panic by the Radical Movement. This they see as a nightmarish Frenchified monster in the form of a guillotine which pours forth blood and flames. The flight is headed by the Prince Regent, whose face is not shown, but who is recognizable by his plump hindquarters and gouty leg.

for a disturbance. Magistrates, too, were on the scene. Hunt, scenting trouble, offered to give himself up, but the magistrates preferred to let him speak. Then, when he was well into his address, the soldiers were given orders to seize him. The 'Orator' was duly arrested, but the hubbub about him gave the magistrates the impression of opposition, and they foolishly ordered the cavalry to charge. In an instant, men, women and children were being battered and slashed by sabres, or knocked down and trampled underfoot. Altogether eleven people were killed, including two women and a child, and some 400 were seriously injured.

The reaction throughout the country was instantaneous. The Government hastened to congratulate the magistrates on their zeal for public order, and to strengthen their hand against further demonstrations. To this end Sidmouth rushed through Parliament the famous Six Acts, a codification and extension of the laws relating to public order. The Government was in fact by no means sure that the meeting in St Peter's Fields had been illegal, since it was officially for the purpose of presenting a petition: one of the Acts therefore limited meetings for the presentation of petitions to the residents of the parish in which the meeting was held—a drastic restriction of the rights of the subject. Another Act extended the stamp tax on newspapers to all papers and periodical pamphlets of a certain size—a great blow at Radical literature, aimed especially at Cobbett's *Register*. Magistrates were also given wide powers of search for blasphemous and seditious literature—which would include the cheap reprints of Tom Paine then enjoying a wide sale. The other three Acts were measures which any government is entitled to take, prohibiting private military training and the collection of firearms. Magistrates were also given power to try cases previously reserved for judge and jury at the Assizes—another severe blow to Radicalism. Taken together the Six Acts constituted the sharpest attack on the Radical movement yet delivered, outdoing both Sidmouth's own previous measures and the earlier efforts of Pitt.

Results of 'Peterloo'

The Six Acts

Three cheers for the magistrates and Six Acts against the Radicals were not, however, the only results of the 'Massacre'. Most people were horrified at the idea of cavalry charging women and children in a reasonably peaceful meeting. Almost everywhere it was felt that the authorities had gone too far, and that such severity must not be repeated. The popular name given to the incident—'Peterloo'—was a sign of general contempt for the 'victory' of the magistrates.

Unpopularity of authorities

At this stage a change to a less repressive attitude on the part of the Government might have come more quickly, but for a wild conspiracy which was now brought to light. Arthur Thistlewood, a Spencean Philanthropist who had been imprisoned for challenging Sidmouth to a duel had been released in the autumn of 1819. Together with a few associates, who laid their plot in a house in Cato Street, off the Edgware Road, he planned to blow

The Cato Street Conspiracy, 1819

up the entire Cabinet at a 'Grand Cabinet Dinner' and then seize London. Actually, the Cabinet was not in the habit of meeting together for a meal, and the notice of the 'Dinner' had been published by government agents only to tempt the conspirators to action. Thistlewood—who killed one of the force attempting to arrest him—and the other leaders of the conspiracy were duly executed, Thistlewood himself enjoying the distinction of being the last person in England to be beheaded.

The Bonnymuir riot

In Scotland a parallel movement to Thistlewood's conspiracy, aiming at a general strike in Glasgow, broke down after some Scottish miners had taken up arms and come into conflict with the troops at Bonnymuir. This, too, resulted in some executions.

The affair of Queen Caroline, 1820

Such popularity as Liverpool's Government might have gained as a result of the Cato Street and Bonnymuir incidents was rapidly lost over the Queen Caroline affair. The Prince Regent, who had illegally married Mrs Fitzherbert (and then denied the marriage), had committed bigamy ten years later by marrying a German princess, Caroline of Brunswick. He had long ago quarrelled with her, and they lived apart, Caroline wandering round Italy with an extremely disreputable retinue. As early as 1806 he had tried to get rid of her, but a parliamentary enquiry into her conduct proved no serious charge. In 1820 the situation arose in a much more acute form, for George III at last died, and the Regent became King as George IV. This meant that Caroline would become Queen of England, a situation which George was determined to prevent. He therefore forced the Government to introduce a Bill of Pains and Penalties, intended to dissolve the marriage and deprive Caroline of her title. This involved a public enquiry into her conduct, which in turn meant a counter-enquiry into George's.

Radical support for Caroline

All was set for a feast of scandal sufficient to satisfy the most voracious appetite. In the midst of the excitement Caroline, on the advice of Henry Brougham,[1] an extreme Whig, appeared in London. She was given a rousing reception by the populace, who regarded her as a much-wronged woman. For the whole of the autumn of 1820 the monarchy was dragged through the mud while the details of the royal couple's behaviour emerged, and

---

[1] Brougham was one of the founders of the *Edinburgh Review*, a learned journal of strongly Whig views. As a lawyer he had pleaded the cause of the Liverpool merchants against the Orders in Council with great success, and in Parliament he had led the demand for the repeal of the income tax in 1816. His main enthusiasms were legal and parliamentary reform, negro emancipation, education, religious equality and Henry Brougham.

the republican movement flourished as never before in British history. Finally the Lords passed the bill by only nine votes, whereupon Liverpool declined to introduce it into the Commons, much to the fury of George, who threatened to retire to Hanover.

With the situation still not settled, though Caroline lost most of her popularity by accepting a big government pension, George's coronation now took place. Caroline duly appeared and tried to force her way into the Abbey, demanding the right to be crowned. The mob cheered her on, but booed when she eventually gave up the attempt. A month later, to the unspeakable relief of George and the Government, she died. On the whole, the country too had tired of her—a feeling expressed in the pleasant little verse of the time—

> O gracious Queen, we thee implore,
> To go away and sin no more;
> But if that effort be too great,
> To go away at any rate.

The whole affair had been a tragi-comedy, the main results of which were to lower the prestige of the monarchy and to distract attention from more serious matters.

9. The Dawn of Reform

1 The 'Liberal Tories'

Reconstruction of Liverpool's Ministry, 1822

During the years immediately following 'the Queen's Affair' the Radical agitation slackened off a little. The Government took on a less repressive tinge when Canning replaced Castlereagh and Sir Robert Peel replaced Sidmouth in 1822; while about the same time commercial and financial policy came under the wiser direction of 'Prosperity' Robinson as Chancellor of the Exchequer and William Huskisson as President of the Board of Trade. These changes made both for a better atmosphere and for improved trading conditions.

Canning

Canning's achievements in domestic matters were not as important as in foreign affairs. He did not press his own ideas of reform, such as Catholic emancipation, with any great vigour, and he was content to support the repressive measures of his colleagues. He was, however, a man of genius and vision, and his admission into the Cabinet was a sign that the old blind Toryism was at last breaking down. Moreover, his highly successful foreign policy gained Britain the markets of the South American republics, and thus speeded on the return of commercial prosperity. This object was very near his heart, and explains his valuable support of the work of Huskisson, for he hoped that increased trade, and attention to a few outstanding grievances, would gradually kill the demand for Parliamentary Reform. Never really trusted by Liverpool, Wellington, Sidmouth and the 'High Tories', he was popular in the country for his attitude to foreign affairs, and he had a following of younger, more liberal Tories, who knew that the days of unstinted repression must have an end.

Huskisson

William Huskisson, at the Board of Trade, supported by Robinson at the Exchequer, did a really great work in a quiet way. As a youth in France he had witnessed the fall of the Bastille and rescued the Governor of the Tuileries from the Paris mob, but no trace of these exciting events coloured his general interests, which were purely economic. As President of the Board of Trade, Huskisson set about introducing a freer commercial policy, such as the manufacturers of Manchester, London and Glasgow had

THE 'LIBERAL TORIES' 99

long been demanding. Duties on a mass of articles—rum, silk, wool, cotton and linen goods, china, glass, metals, books, paper —were reduced, while the general duty on manufactured goods (other than those with special rates) was lowered from 50 per cent to 20 per cent. Moreover, Huskisson offered 'reciprocity' treaties to foreign powers, by which reductions in their tariffs would be met by corresponding reductions in those imposed by Britain against them. He also relaxed the Navigation Acts, which had restricted colonial trade and the use of foreign vessels. All this unspectacular work was really progressive—a remarkable change for Liverpool's Cabinet.

The new occupant of the Home Office, Sir Robert Peel, also brought a keen and fair mind to bear on old problems. Peel was almost a new type in British politics. His father, a great Lancashire cotton magnate, by name also Sir Robert, had made a fortune out of the usual abominable factory conditions, but had inspired an Act in 1802 improving the lot of pauper apprentices. Later on, in conjunction with Robert Owen,[1] he had also sponsored the Act of 1819, limiting the hours of children's work in cotton mills to twelve a day. Having won his own way to power and reputation, he was extremely anxious that his son should make a great mark in the world. The boy had accordingly been given the best education of the day—Harrow (where he was in the same form as Byron) and Christ Church, Oxford (where he secured a 'double first' in classics and mathematics). Carefully avoiding the family cotton mills he had then entered Parliament at the age of twenty-one, through the influence of his father, who was quite determined to see young Robert finish up as Prime Minister.

Peel's start in political life was promising. After holding a minor office under Perceval, he was promoted by Liverpool to a more difficult and responsible position, that of Chief Secretary in Ireland. In this office, from 1812 to 1818, he was a great success from the Tory point of view, keeping order firmly and opposing all the things, such as Catholic emancipation, which would have made him a success from the Irish point of view. Next he acted as Chairman of the Currency Commission whose report led to the

[1] From small beginnings Owen had become a great cotton manufacturer. His mills at New Lanark, in Scotland, were a model of their kind. Housing and recreational facilities were excellent, adults worked no more than $10\frac{1}{2}$ hours, no children under 10 were employed, and free schooling was provided. Owen later helped to found the Grand National Consolidated Trades Union (see page 120), and he was an early advocate of Socialism.

The marginal note "Peel" appears beside the second paragraph.

return to the gold standard in 1819. Then in 1822 Liverpool persuaded him to take Sidmouth's place in the Cabinet as Home Secretary—a position in which he was soon to become a household name.

Reform of the Penal Code, 1824

The great achievement of Peel as Home Secretary was to make the English Common Law at once more humane and more efficient. Until just before Peel took up the subject men could be executed for an extensive variety of offences, including such curious misdeeds as damaging Westminster Bridge or impersonating a Chelsea Pensioner. Peel was not one whose nature was to take automatically the path of reform. Instead he usually started from the opposite side, but his fair and open mind gradually led him to reforming conclusions. In particular he was convinced by the evidence collected by a Radical lawyer, Sir Samuel Romilly, who for years had manfully introduced bills into Parliament to reform the penal code. Romilly had managed to get pocket-picking removed from the list of capital crimes; and Sir James Mackintosh, the author of *Vindiciae Gallicae*[1]—of which he had long since repented, though he had never ceased to support progressive measures—had later secured the exclusion of a few more offences from the capital list. It was the glory of Peel to follow up these pioneer labours, and to introduce measures which altogether removed about one hundred offences from the list of crimes punishable by death. This was not only desirable from the point of view of humanity, but it also resulted in more certain punishment for criminals, since juries had often acquitted men in face of all the evidence rather than send them to the gallows for trivial offences.

Besides reforming the penal code, Peel greatly improved the state of the larger prisons. The vicious system of compelling prisoners to pay the gaoler's fees was abolished; the larger prisons were henceforth to be inspected; women were to be guarded by female gaolers; and in general several steps were taken in the direction advocated earlier by John Howard, and more recently by Romilly and Elizabeth Fry. Unfortunately no other Home Secretary followed up these efforts for many years, and the state of the smaller prisons, and those for debtors, remained a national disgrace.

Foundation of the Metropolitan Police, 1829

As an essential counterpart to removing death penalties, Peel founded the Metropolitan Police. Like any schoolmaster who knows his job, Peel was aware that offences are checked not by the severity but by the certainty of punishment. But punishment

[1] See page 35.

was not at all certain when there was no regular police system beyond watchmen and parish constables. This arrangement had, indeed, worked reasonably in the old days, but had become hopelessly inefficient after the great movements of population during the Industrial and Agrarian Revolutions; and penalties in the eighteenth century had grown more and more savage largely because criminals were so rarely caught. Moreover, any scheme to establish a regular police had almost invariably been opposed as an attack on the liberty of the subject, for men were justly suspicious of the use to which Sidmouth would put such a force. Peel, however, determined to remedy matters at least in London and the suburbs. The measure he introduced, the Metropolitan Police Act of 1829, established a Commissioner at Scotland Yard, directly under the Home Office, and in control of 3,000 paid constables over a twelve-mile radius from Charing Cross, excluding the historic City. Armed only with staves the constables could not be accused of being a military formation, nor had they the objectionable character of Sidmouth's spy system, which Peel had dropped. They soon won their way to popularity, and their founder was rapidly immortalized in their successive nicknames of 'Peelers', 'Bobbies' and 'Roberts'. Indeed, they were so successful that large numbers of criminals cleared out of London and took refuge in the provinces—a fact which drove other authorities to create police systems modelled on Peel's. A better method of maintaining public order thus spread over the country in the next twenty or thirty years. It could be applied not only to criminals but to open-air public meetings—with what successs may be seen from the fact that there has never been another 'Peterloo'.

The presence of open-minded men like Canning, Huskisson and Peel in the Cabinet was also partly responsible for a surprising reform carried in 1824—the repeal of the Combination Acts. One of the greatest grievances among the working classes was that Pitt's Act of 1799 forbade their combining together for the purpose of raising wages or lowering hours. Many unions had defied this ban, but as soon as they tried to stage a 'strike' they were prosecuted, and their members as often as not imprisoned. It was this state of affairs which a remarkable Radical leader, Francis Place, set himself to remedy.

Born of humble stock, Place had been apprenticed to a leather-breeches maker, and in due course had become a journeyman in the same trade. In 1793 he had organized some strikes, after

Repeal of the Combination Acts, 1824

Francis Place

which he had been refused work by most of the masters in London. However, he had soon set himself up in a tailor's shop at Charing Cross, and this rapidly became a great Radical centre; for Place, a self-educated but widely-read man, had a large library behind the shop in which the leading Radicals studied and foregathered. There the visitor might meet Sir Francis Burdett (a Radical M.P. for whom Place's organization had won an election at Westminster), Joseph Hume (another of the small band of Radical M.P.s—a man with a keen eye for unnecessary government expenditure), or the legal reformer Jeremy Bentham. It was through such men that Place, by furnishing them with arguments, facts, witnesses and general organization, managed to exert his influence.

In 1824 Place persuaded Hume to 'pack' with sympathizers a parliamentary committee appointed to enquire into the Combination Laws. Both he and Hume seem to have believed that trade unions could not really alter economic conditions greatly, but that the working classes would think otherwise until they had their unions and learnt better. Specially selected and most respectable artisans were sent as witnesses before the committee, while over-aggressive trade unionists or hostile employers were carefully kept away. The Committee duly reported in favour of repeal. A Bill repealing the Combination Acts was then rushed through Parliament, Liverpool afterwards making the astonishing confession that he 'had not been aware of its extent, and did not, until it came into operation, know its provisions'.

Spread of trade unions and strikes

Suddenly freed from legal prohibition, a mass of trade unions now either sprang into being or else revealed an existence they had long enjoyed under the disguise of Friendly Societies. A wave of strikes instantly broke out, partly because of the new freedom, partly also because there was a trade boom and the workers were anxious to share in the increased profits. The strikes were intensified when the boom collapsed and the masters tried to cancel improvements in wages that had been granted. Naturally, however, the strikes were all attributed to the repeal of the Combination Laws. Parliament therefore hastily repented of its recent work, and would have re-enacted the old prohibitions but for Place's renewed activity. He produced evidence to point out the relation of the strikes to the boom and slump, and so the Amending Act of 1825 was not as severe as it would otherwise have been. As it was, it took away the complete freedom given to trade unions but still allowed them to exist for bargaining about wages

The Amending Act of 1825

and hours as long as there was no attempt to 'molest' or 'obstruct' either employers or fellow-workmen. This might make it difficult to conduct strikes, but at least trade unions were no longer illegal for their primary purpose, and one great weapon had been placed in the hands of the depressed classes.

2 Catholic Emancipation and the End of Tory Rule

Before they fell from power, the Tories were to be responsible, quite against their wishes, for one more great reform—Catholic emancipation. The way in which this came about was somewhat complicated.

Early in 1827 Lord Liverpool suffered a paralytic seizure and retired from politics. His lack of originality was such, a wit once remarked, that if he had been present at the Creation he would have prayed God not to disturb Chaos; but he had had the invaluable quality of keeping a Cabinet together. Some successor in the Tory ranks had to be found, and the obvious man, clearly marked out by his talents, was George Canning. This raised the old question of Canning's personality—whether he was to be 'trusted', and whether his tactics were quite those of a 'gentleman'. For some of the more hard-and-fast Tories, too, his views were somewhat advanced. So it came about that when Canning became Prime Minister several Tories resigned, including Wellington, who disliked him, and Peel, who was opposed to Catholic emancipation—one of Canning's favourite projects. Canning was thus driven to include a few Whigs in his Cabinet, and the normal party lines were again in confusion. However, he was already a sick man when he became Prime Minister, and he barely had time to settle policy on the Greek Revolt before he died. *(Retirement of Liverpool, 1827 — Canning's Ministry, 1827)*

The direction of affairs was next taken over for a few months by a friend of Canning's, 'Prosperity' Robinson, now Lord Goderich, but he was a pliant character, who could deal neither with the ill-assorted Cabinet nor with the extremely awkward King. At the beginning of 1828 Goderich resigned, and matters were again in confusion. *(Goderich's Ministry)*

At this moment Wellington, always the man for a crisis, stepped to the fore. Assuming the position of Prime Minister, he kept the Canningite Tories in office, but not the four Whigs, and he brought back Peel to his old position of Home Secretary. As *(Wellington's Ministry, 1828–1830)*

Prime Minister, however, Wellington allowed many of the worst points in his character to emerge. He was dictatorial, expected his colleagues to follow him with the same blind obedience as soldiers in battle, and on occasion was positively insulting. He had 'a social contempt for his intellectual equals, and an intellectual contempt for his social equals'. Within a short time he allowed Huskisson to resign over a trifling issue, and Huskisson was followed by the other Canningites. This left Peel as the only talented figure besides Wellington in the Cabinet. Both were known as firm opponents of Catholic emancipation—and both would have to be firm if they were to resist the storms now blowing up from Ireland.

The 'Sliding Scale'

By the end of 1828 the Ministry had, in fact, carried a few small reforms, including a slight improvement in the Corn Laws. This took the form of substituting a sliding scale of duty for the old fixed rate. As English wheat got dearer, so the duty on foreign wheat became less, until at 74s. a quarter entry was quite free. However, the measure still had the unfortunate effect of causing dealers to hold back corn at certain points to bring in foreign corn duty free, and it thus failed to solve the problem of securing stable prices.

Repeal of the Test and Corporation Acts, 1828

Another minor reform introduced into the Commons, although at first opposed by the Ministry, had also reached the statute book. This was the repeal of the Test and Corporation Acts, the measures of Charles II's reign which had closed the great offices of state and the membership of town corporations to all who were not willing to take the Church of England communion. In actual fact many Protestant Dissenters had enjoyed office for years, and had always been exempted from the due penalties by an annual Indemnity Act. Now, on the motion of Lord John Russell, a rising young Whig, their full civic rights were assured by the repeal of the obnoxious Acts. If this reform did not accomplish anything very new, it was at least symbolic of a new spirit—the willingness to cut away dead wood and to make the legal and religious systems of the country correspond more closely to the needs of the time. And, above all, it raised in a more acute form the question of Catholic emancipation.

The demand for Catholic emancipation

English Catholics were comparatively few in number at this date, and the demand for Catholic emancipation had long centred in Ireland. Though George III had baulked the passage of the measure when Pitt promised it in return for the Irish Union, many Whigs and some leading Tories, such as Canning, had remained convinced of its necessity, and the Commons on two or three occasions had come very near to granting it. But the proposal always ran up against the no-popery sentiment of the people, the interests of the Church, the conscience of George III or the prejudice of George IV. It thus never got through the Lords, where the Tory party was very strong as a result of Pitt's new peerages. In 1828, however, Catholic emancipation ceased to be merely a desirable reform and became a matter of life and death to the unity of the British Isles. The reason for this was the activity of Daniel O'Connell in Ireland.

The ultimate object of Daniel O'Connell, an Irish lawyer of good family, was the repeal of the Act of Union, though he did not want complete separation from Great Britain. He envisaged an Ireland linked with Great Britain for some purposes, such as foreign policy, but ruling herself through her own freely-elected Parliament—a Catholic Parliament, far removed from the Protestant assembly which had disappeared at the union. Though land troubles and economic distress were at the root of many of Ireland's grievances, O'Connell did not concern himself directly with them so much as with destroying English Protestant rule. To this end the first step was Catholic emancipation—a measure to which men like Peel were opposed just because they knew so well that it was only a first step. Daniel O'Connell

Since efforts at Catholic Relief were consistently defeated at Westminster, in 1823 O'Connell decided to go in for agitation in a big way, and founded the Catholic Association. This body soon took the step of asking a penny a month contribution from poorer Catholics, and within a short time this 'Catholic Rent' (as it was called) was bringing in £1,000 a week. O'Connell also won over the priesthood to his schemes, and they in turn used their powerful influence with the Irish peasantry. Before very long Ireland was demanding Catholic emancipation in no uncertain tones. 'Catholic Rent

At the elections of 1826 O'Connell then tried out his plan, which was to make the forty-shilling freeholders in Ireland vote against the candidates put up by the great Protestant landlords, a thing they had never previously dared to do. This policy, successful because fear of the priest or of O'Connell's followers was now stronger than fear of the landlord, was next extended to a test case. Although he could not, as a Catholic, sit in Parliament, O'Connell put himself up for election in the County Clare constituency against a very popular Protestant landlord. The Irish leader was returned triumphantly at the head of the poll, and County Clare election, 1828 the demand rang throughout Ireland that he should be accepted at Westminster.

Wellington now became convinced that to refuse O'Connell his seat would be to touch off a civil war in Ireland. O'Connell himself was no believer in violence, but it was by no means certain that he could control the mass enthusiasm his organization had called into being. The great Duke, martinet though he was, had a strong aversion to bloodshed, and most of all to that spilt in civil strife. Accordingly he decided that Catholic emancipation must be introduced as a sheer necessity—though a few months earlier he had turned out of his Cabinet every minister who believed in it. More remarkable still, he decided that he and Peel—who wanted to resign—must be the men to introduce it; for he knew that he and he alone could secure the agreement of George IV, who was secretly very afraid of his 'dear Arthur'. So the unhappy Peel was brought to introduce the Catholic Relief Act into the Commons, where it passed with the help of the Whigs, while Wellington forced its acceptance upon the reluctant Lords and Sovereign. Henceforth Catholics could sit in Parliament, and occupy all great offices except the very highest.

Wellington decides for Catholic emancipation

The Catholic Relief Act, 1829

Wellington, however, was not the man to retreat without striking a blow at the enemy. To offset Catholic emancipation, the Irish forty-shilling freeholders were disfranchised, and the property qualification for voting was fixed at £10 a year, in the vain hope that the Irish electorate would not return men of the O'Connell movement. To this very real grievance Wellington added the minor pinprick of refusing to allow O'Connell to take his seat (on the ground that the Catholic Relief Act had not been in force when he was first elected), until he had fought and won the County Clare election all over again. Thus whatever benefit the measure might have had in winning over Irish opinion was to some extent lost, although the primary object of averting civil war was attained.

The Tory revolt against Wellington

Wellington and Peel now had to face the music at home. The rank and file of the Tories were infuriated at Wellington's disregard for party principles, and smarted for revenge. They had not long to wait. After the success of the orderly and bloodless revolution of July 1830 in Paris, when the absolutist Charles X was deposed in favour of the more liberal Louis Philippe, the parliamentary reform movement gained fresh ground in England. A new motion was introduced into Parliament, and Wellington, in opposing it, stoutly defended the existing system as perfect.

He thereby sealed his own fate. He had offended the liberal Tories by their dismissal in 1828, the High Tories by Catholic emancipation, and the Whigs by opposition to Reform. So the discontented elements in his own party took the next opportunity of combining with the Whigs to vote him out of office. They might be cutting their own throats in the process, but at least they hoped to teach Wellington and Peel to be loyal to party principles. The Whigs, of course, reaped the fruitful harvest of Tory discord. After nearly fifty years of almost unbroken Tory supremacy, they were again in office. The gateway to parliamentary reform —and to many of the other reforms of which Britain had stood so long in need—was at last open.

The Whigs in power, 1830

10. The Great Whig Reforms

1 The Struggle for Parliamentary Reform

The men who came into power as a result of the Tory revenge against Wellington and Peel had had much experience of opposition, but very little of office. They were headed by one who had grown old in the Whig cause. Charles Grey, who as a young man had supported the 'Society of the Friends of the People' and opposed all Pitt's repressive legislation, and who in middle age had fought against the Corn Law and the Six Acts, was now an elderly nobleman, but he remained true to many of the things for which his great leader Fox had stood. Into his hands in 1830 fell the task of constructing a Whig Ministry pledged to reform Parliament—and so to open a new epoch in British history.

The formation of a Whig Cabinet was made easier by an event which had occurred a few months before the downfall of Wellington. George IV, 'bewigged and gouty, ornate and enormous',[1] had passed away in July 1830. The 'First Gentleman in Europe', as he liked to be called, had been a little strange in the head in his later years—he frequently asserted, even in the presence of Wellington, that he had led a cavalry charge at Waterloo—and he had long since proved, by his opposition to all reforms, that his early association with Fox and the Whigs was inspired solely by a desire to annoy his Tory father, George III. In fact, a Whig Ministry under George IV would have been almost an impossibility, and Grey was therefore fortunate in having to deal with his brother and successor, the 'Sailor-King', William IV. This 'bursting, bubbling old gentleman, with quarter-deck gestures, round rolling eyes, and a head like a pineapple',[1] might be difficult to handle but, unlike George IV, he would act with other than purely selfish ends in view. As far as the Whigs were concerned he was likely to be a great improvement on the late King.

Though the Whigs were committed to parliamentary reform, they had no intention of thrusting power into the hands of the working classes, who were mostly too ignorant and illiterate to form an intelligent electorate. The Whig tradition was one of

Earl Grey

Death of George IV and accession of William IV, 1830

Whig intentions

[1] Lytton Strachey, *Queen Victoria*.

108

opposition to the power of Church and King in politics—a tradition which under Fox's leadership had grown into a general championship of the liberty of the individual against the Government. Led by Anglican landed aristocrats, the Whigs depended largely on the support of substantial traders, many of whom were Protestant Dissenters. Such a party was essentially a moderate one; though it might be prepared to remove some obvious abuses and to admit the more prosperous members of the middle class into a minor share of government, it would not for a moment dream, as the Radicals did, of turning Britain into a fully-fledged democracy.

The formation of a Whig administration was not an easy matter, since outstanding Whigs had become a rarity after so many years in opposition. Having filled several positions with his relatives, Grey then managed to find ability combined with moderation in some of the 'Canningite' Tories. Huskisson was on the point of accepting an office when he was unfortunately knocked down and killed by one of George Stephenson's engines at the opening of the new Liverpool–Manchester railway.[1] A more lasting recruit from the Tory ranks was Viscount Palmerston, who had spent years in office as Secretary-at-War, but had parted from his Tory colleagues on the question of parliamentary reform. Viscount Melbourne, a Whig who had accepted office under Canning, also occupied a leading position in the Ministry. With such men forming the new administration a measure of reform was certain—but only a moderate measure. *Grey's colleagues*

There were, however, apart from Grey, at least two members of the administration who regarded parliamentary reform with great enthusiasm. One of these was Lord John Russell,[2] who was largely responsible for drawing up the new Reform Bill and piloting it through the House of Commons. The other was Henry Brougham.[3] Brougham had ideas of introducing a stronger measure of reform than the rest of the Cabinet—who heartily disliked him—desired. Grey accordingly removed him from the Commons and pacified his reforming ardour by making him Lord Chancellor.

The Great Reform Bill was introduced into the Commons by Russell in March 1831. The formal first reading was punctuated by ironical cries from the members for rotten boroughs, all of which the measure proposed to abolish. The second reading was followed by a fierce debate, and amid tremendous excitement the *Introduction of the Great Reform Bill, March 1831*

<hr>

[1] See page 341.   [2] See page 104.   [3] See page 96.

Defeat in
Committee

Bill was carried by one vote. Then came the Committee stage (in which Bills are discussed not as a whole, but clause by clause, and in which amendments may be introduced). On two points during this stage the Government was defeated, so Grey resigned

General election

and demanded a general election. William IV agreed to dissolve Parliament, and on a wave of popular enthusiasm the Whigs came back with a strong majority (136). A slightly revised Bill

Defeat of
revised Bill in
Lords

was then passed through all its stages in the Commons, and in October 1831 was presented to the Upper House. Their lordships promptly threw it out.

Popular excitement now grew intense. The Lords' action challenged not only the direct interest of the middle classes but the fervent hopes of the lower classes; for though the Radicals were at first bitterly disappointed by the substantial property qualification proposed for a vote in the boroughs—the occupation of a house rated at £10 a year or over—they had come to regard the

Agitation in the
country

Bill as at least a first instalment of reform. Widespread demonstrations therefore occurred—two newspapers appeared with black edges, muffled bells were tolled as a sign of mourning, riots took place in the Midlands, and at Bristol a mob attacked the Tory M.P., sacked the Mansion House and burnt the Bishop's palace. Order was restored only by the time-honoured cavalry charge.

Embarrassed but strengthened by these demonstrations, the

Third version of
the Bill

Whigs in December introduced a third version of the Bill. After going through all its stages in the Commons again, this passed two readings in the Lords, for by now many peers had become

Refusal of
William IV
to create fifty
Whig peers.
Resignation of
Grey

convinced of the impossibility of resistance. In the Committee stage, however, the Lords tried to postpone consideration of some important clauses. Grey then asked William to create fifty new Whig peers to swamp the Tory majority. William refused to go beyond twenty, and the Government resigned.

Then followed a curious episode. Of all the opponents of the Reform Bill, none was more bitter than Wellington. The Duke had led the opposition to all the various versions of the Bill in the Lords, and had made the most forthright prophecies of red ruin if the measure should pass: 'You may rely upon it that neither Lord Grey, nor any nobleman of his order, nor any gentleman of his caste will govern the country six weeks after the Reform Parliament will meet, and that the race of English gentlemen will not last long afterwards.' Yet it was to Wellington—who was so unpopular at this stage that he had to fit iron shutters to the

The "System" that "Works so Well"!!. or The Boroughmongers GRINDING Machine.

(Cruikshank, 1831, from a print in the British Museum)

A cartoon which appeared during the height of the parliamentary reform agitation. The House of Commons, St Stephens, is represented as a mill supported on cannon. The slats on the mill wheel bear the names of rotten boroughs; and beneath the structure lies the discarded chaff—the corpses of the poor. From the mill, down a chute supported on bayonets, pours a stream of pensions, places, sinecures, etc. The boroughmongers, or owners of rotten boroughs, stuff their pockets with these, and are well content to leave matters as they are.

windows of his house in Piccadilly—that William IV turned in the hope that he could carry a Bill through the Lords less extensive than Grey's.

Attempt of Wellington to secury Tory support for a modified Bill

The Duke, as in the case of Catholic emancipation, was prepared for duty, however unpleasant. He tried to form a Tory administration to carry such a measure. The thing could not be done. Other Tory politicians had a less elastic view of party principles than the Duke, and refused to do what they regarded as the Whigs' dirty work for them. Moreover, at the prospect of being baulked of the Whig measure, the country burst into a blaze of agitation. Everywhere the demand was for 'the Bill, the whole Bill, and nothing but the Bill'. Led by Thomas Attwood, a banker and economist who had founded a prominent reformist society (the Birmingham Political Union), a movement spread to refuse the payment of taxes. Francis Place carried this idea a step further by organizing a mass run on the banks to withdraw deposits and so threaten the Government's financial stability. Placards were displayed all over London with the advice—'To stop the Duke, go for gold'. With revolution staring him in the face Wellington wisely beat a retreat, and within a week Grey was back in office on his own terms. Armed with a promise from William to create all the peers needed to force the measure through the Lords, he found the rest easy. Rather than see the peerage cheapened to no useful purpose, the Tory Lords and bishops followed Wellington's orders, abandoned their opposition, and kept away from Parliament during the passage of the Bill. The whole process had taken over a year of the bitterest struggle.

Renewed popular agitation

Return of Grey to office

The Bill becomes law, May 1832

Terms of the Reform Act

The Reform Act altered both franchise and representation. The old franchise had been uniform in the counties through the ancient forty-shilling freeholder qualification, but highly variable in the boroughs, ranging from votes for all householders to votes only for the Mayor and Corporation. In place of this the Act of 1832 set up two uniform franchises. For county elections the qualification was now holding freehold land of annual value 40s., copyhold land (an old form of lease) of annual value £10, or ordinary tenant or leasehold land of annual value £50. Thus the better-off tenant-farmers were added to the old voters for the county M.P.s. In the boroughs, however, where the new qualification was possession or occupation of a house of annual value £10, a few places like Preston and Westminster lost their extremely democratic franchise, though in most the middle classes were admitted to the franchise for the first time. How far the Parliament of 1832 was from contemplating democracy may be seen by the fate of an amendment suggesting the franchise for all householders in place of the £10 qualification. For this bold proposal exactly one vote was cast.

The redistribution of seats was perhaps even more important. Fifty-six rotten or pocket boroughs (defined as those of less than 2,000 population) lost both their members, and thirty rather less rotten boroughs lost one member. The seats thus gained were used either to increase the representation of the counties or else to provide members for the new industrial towns. Manchester, Birmingham, Leeds, Sheffield, Bradford, Swansea and some important districts of London were among the places which received separate representation for the first time. Scotland and Ireland, in parallel Bills, received similar treatment, though on a less complete scale.

The real import of these changes was much less than the Duke feared. An electorate of 435,000 before 1832 was increased to 652,000—not an overwhelming difference, for five out of six adult males still remained without a vote. In the boroughs the wealthier middle classes might now reign supreme, but the landed gentry were still almost as strong in the counties. Until the secret ballot replaced open voting on the hustings in 1872, the landlord could still control the votes of his tenants by bribery or intimidation, and could create dozens of votes by selling small forty-shilling freeholds to suitable supporters. The result was that for many years to come the composition of Parliament differed very little from that of the old days. More Radicals were returned (including Cobbett for Oldham), but in general the upper classes still held the reins with a firm hand; for even if membership of Parliament was now more possible for the middle classes (and there was still a high property qualification for M.P.s), entry into the charmed circle of Cabinet rank was quite another matter.

Significance of the Act

When all this is said, however, the Reform Act of 1832 still made a vital breach in the great wall of aristocratic privilege. It proved to be precisely what the Radicals hoped it would be, and what Grey hoped it would not be—a beginning. The day of working-class voters was not yet, and the dissatisfaction of the poorer middle and lower classes was soon expressed in the Chartist movement. But the Act gave power to those best fitted to exercise it at the time, and the wealthy commercial classes could now proceed with other reforms they regarded as essential. While not a democratic measure in itself, the Great Reform Bill thus opened the way immediately to social progress and eventually to modern democracy.

2 Grey: the First Burst of Social Reform

The reform of Parliament did not exhaust the activities of the Whigs. From 1832 to 1835 they pushed forward with a series of progressive measures more extensive than anything which had hitherto been attempted.

To some extent this was due not so much to the Whigs as to the Radicals, who urged the Whigs on to the very limit of their principles. In this work the few Radical M.P.s of course took a great share, but the dominant spirit was that of a man who had died the day before the Reform Bill became law—Jeremy Bentham (1748–1832). Bentham's influence was very strong in the reform of the penal code, the reform of legal procedure, and the reform of the Poor Law, but his great work lay less in any particular reform than in his attitude to all existing institutions. Discounting tradition, he had preached the new gospel of 'utility'. Not 'how old is it?' but 'what is the use of it?' was the searching test he applied to every institution. Did it lead to 'the greatest happiness of the greatest number'? Through this open-minded and unceasing criticism of all government activity and social custom, Bentham and his followers gave a great lead to public opinion. These Utilitarians, or 'Philosophical Radicals', as they were sometimes called, were not numerous, but their constant and informed agitation influenced the programmes of both the great political parties, and thus helped to place a variety of reforms on the statute book.

One of the first subjects to engage the Government's attention after parliamentary reform was the question of slavery in British colonies. British participation in the slave trade had been stopped in 1807, and Europe in general had followed this lead by condemning the slave trade at the Congress of Vienna, but much traffic still persisted. Moreover, conditions in the slave-ships had become still more disgraceful, for the greater the number of negroes packed into the vessel, the more worth while it was to risk defying the ban. Convinced that while slavery remained, slave trading would persist, Wilberforce and his friends, the

Influence of Bentham and the 'Philosophical Radicals' (Utilitarians)

Abolition of slavery in British Empire, 1833 (effective 1834)

'Evangelical' group of Churchmen,[1] assisted by some of the more Radical Whigs like Brougham, determined to strike at the whole institution of slavery. An Anti-Slavery Society was formed in 1822, and ultimately, in 1833, the dying Wilberforce was cheered by the news that Parliament had at last agreed to abolish the odious institution from the British Empire. By way of compensation £20,000,000 was allotted to the slave owners—roughly £37 a slave, the approximate market value. Unfortunately the sum was not fairly distributed, and the inevitable dislocation caused by the measure dealt the West Indies sugar trade a hard blow, as well as embittering the Boer farmers of the Cape against the British Government.[2]

Another great reform introduced in 1833 by Grey's Government was Lord Althorp's Factory Act—the first effective measure of its kind. Though two previous Acts had been passed (in 1802 to regulate the working conditions of pauper apprentices, and in 1819 to limit the hours worked by very young people), neither had been effective, simply for the want of any adequate means of enforcement. The 1833 Act took the important step of appointing paid factory inspectors, and as time went on there were more convictions against offending employers and better observance of the law. The provisions of the 1833 Act, applying to all textile factories except those manufacturing silk goods, were not in themselves very generous. Labour by children under nine was prohibited; children between nine and thirteen were to have at least two hours' schooling daily, with not more than nine hours' work in the factory (forty-eight hours a week); and young persons between thirteen and eighteen were to work not more than twelve hours daily (sixty-nine in the week). Harsh as these hours seem nowadays, they were nevertheless a considerable improvement on the average worked by children before 1833. Long hours for adults were left untouched, but at least in the system of factory inspectors there was now a means at hand for enforcing any future reform in this direction. *The Factory Act of 1833*

The year 1833 was also notable for the first government grant 'for the purposes of education'. Small as it was, it led to the growth of the whole State system of education.[3] *First government grant for education, 1833*

A measure of much greater immediate importance was the reform of the Poor Law. The old Elizabethan Poor Law, with its attempt to distinguish between the unable-to-work and the merely unwilling, had long since broken down. Under the *Need for reform of the Poor Law*

[1] See page 374.   [2] See page 410.   [3] See page 381.

pressure of the growing and increasingly mobile population, the upheaval caused by the Agrarian and Industrial Revolutions, and the distress arising from the wars with France and the post-war slump, the whole administration of relief had become scandalously inefficient. From 1795 onwards the 'Speenhamland system'[1] had been widely adopted all over the south of England. Farmers had lowered wages, large sections of the population had been reduced to accepting poor relief, and at the same time the local poor rates had reached monstrous proportions.

The 'last labourers' revolt'

This widespread and growing scandal thrust itself upon the Whigs' attention during the agricultural disturbances of 1830 and 1831, sometimes known as the 'last labourers' revolt'. With the return of peace in 1815 the artificial prosperity of England's wartime agriculture had collapsed, in spite of the Corn Laws, and many agricultural labourers had become unemployed. This had made the poor rates still higher—a burden which the hard-hit landowners and tenant-farmers greatly resented and counteracted by lowering wages. The justices of the peace also endeavoured to reduce the burden by scaling down the rates of relief. The consequence was spontaneous rioting by the agricultural poor all over the southern and eastern counties. Threshing-machines were destroyed, ricks of unpopular farmers or landowners were burnt, harsh overseers of the poor were ducked in village ponds; at the same time demands were framed for higher wages, lower rents, abolition of tithe and better scales of poor relief. Alarmed by all this—though no one (except a labourer) had been killed or seriously injured—Grey despatched a special commission of judges to the affected districts, where they carried out nothing less than a minor Bloody Assize. Nine men and boys were hanged (six for rick-burning), and many hundreds were transported or imprisoned. An unsuccessful attempt was also made to convict Cobbett of incitement.

From the tragic history of these riots the Whigs entirely failed to draw the obvious lesson, that eight or nine shillings a week was not enough to sustain life, and that the Government must therefore enforce a higher minimum wage. Their view was simply that the 'Speenhamland system', whereby labourers had come to expect poor relief as a normal adjunct to wages, was demoralizing the populace. To provide evidence for this conclusion, the Whigs appointed a commission charged with examining the whole question of the Poor Law.

Appointment of Poor Law Commission

[1] See page 85.

The report of the Poor Law Commission, issued in 1834, is The Commis-
one of the most important documents in the ninteenth-century   sioners' Report
history of Britain. Neglecting all the causes for distress in towns,
and approaching the matter with minds already made up, the
Commissioners placed the whole blame for bad conditions on the
Speenhamland system. Their main recommendation was thus
that able-bodied persons should no longer be supplied with 'outdoor relief', which should be reserved for the aged and the infirm.
For ordinary labourers the 'workhouse test' should be applied
rigorously—those who received aid from the rates must be prepared to enter a workhouse. To discourage the population from
regarding these institutions as desirable rest centres, workhouse
conditions were to be made more unattractive than 'the situation
of the independent labourer of the lowest class'. In justice to the
Commissioners, it must also be stated that they proposed to educate pauper children in separate workhouses, and to give the aged
and infirm either outdoor relief, or freedom to enjoy their indul-
gences in further separate establishments. Moreover, the work to
be done by the able-bodied was not to be 'repellent'—i.e. the
usual prison stone-breaking or oakum-picking.

If such a policy was to be carried out, it was clearly impossible
to leave each parish with its traditional independence in these
matters. The Commissioners therefore recommended the formation of a new poor law adminstration. Parishes were to be grouped
into 'Unions', each of which should maintain a workhouse system.
In each Union there would be paid poor law officials, supervised
by unpaid 'guardians of the poor', who were to be elected (from
the propertied classes) by local ratepayers. The policy applied
in the Unions by the guardians was to be laid down by a central
authority, to consist of three Commissioners appointed by the
Government.

Such were the broad lines of the report and recommendations The Poor Law
submitted to Parliament in 1834. The Poor Law Amendment   Amendment
Act of that year created the system of authorities demanded in the   Act, 1834
recommendations and left the new Commissioners to carry out
the policy which the enquiring Commission had suggested—and
in particular the abolition of the Speenhamland system. It was
not long before the Commissioners (the 'Three Pashas' or 'Ba-
shaws' of Somerset House, as they were soon nicknamed) were
the worst-hated men in England, and their new Union workhouses ('Bastilles') the worst-hated places. Especially detested
was the well-intentioned secretary of the Commission, Edwin

Chadwick—a Manchester man, a strong 'Benthamite' and a believer in efficiency to the point of ruthlessness.

Attempted abolition of 'outdoor relief'

Broadly speaking, Chadwick and the Commissioners (who often quarrelled) managed to abolish the Speenhamland system very speedily from the south, their policy being fairly peacefully accepted owing to a run of good harvests and the opportunities for employment afforded by the growth of the railways. The measure was hard upon the poor, who were deprived of a customary addition to their earnings, but in time wages rose—and poor rates certainly fell—and the whole process was not unlike a severe but necessary surgical operation. In the north, however, the policy of stopping outdoor relief to the able-bodied collapsed after dangerous riots. The reason for this was that the Speenhamland system had never really applied there, except perhaps in the case of underpaid hand-loom workers. The main use of out-relief had been not to supplement wages, but to provide a kind of unemployment pay when thousands of men were thrown out of work in temporary depressions in the textile trade. It was fantastic to think of presenting these victims of passing hard times with the choice of the workhouse or starvation. Notable figures like John Fielden of Todmorden, the famous factory owner and reformer, simply refused to apply the new system in their areas, and before universal hostility the Commissioners had to draw back. Outdoor relief thus continued in the north, though not in the Speenhamland sense of public allowances to men in work.

Failure to create different types of workhouse

In the other main point of their programme, that of making the Union workhouses more unattractive than the situation of the lowest labourer, the Commissioners succeeded only too well.[1] The Unions proved incapable of supporting separate workhouses for different types of poverty, and so young and old, respectable and depraved, sane and insane, were all too often herded together in the same establishment. Almost inhuman rules were usually enforced—for example, married couples were separated lest additional children should be born and further charges fall on the rates. Parents were often not allowed to see their children, visitors were forbidden except in the presence of the workhouse master, smoking was never allowed inside the walls, and all meals had to be consumed in silence. Unless an inmate chose to leave the workhouse entirely and risk starvation outside, he or she was rarely allowed out at all, except for visits to church—thereby

[1] Cf. Charles Dickens's description in the opening chapters of *Oliver Twist*.

(Cruikshank, from a print in the British Museum)

OLIVER ASKING FOR MORE

A famous scene from Dickens's *Oliver Twist* (published 1838). The faces
and figures of the young inmates are ample comment on the workhouse
conditions of the time.

making it difficult for the able-bodied, once in, ever to find out-side work again.

As for the work provided by the workhouse authorities, it soon degenerated into the usual stone-breaking and oakum-picking. Work on bone-crushing, however, was stopped when it became known that the inmates not only contracted disease from the occu-pation, but also on occasion fought like dogs for odd bits of putrid gristle still clinging to the bones. Nor is it difficult to understand such hunger, when the inmates' food is borne in mind—a kind of prison fare, in which bowls of skilly held a place of honour. Though many of these worst features were gradually abolished by pressure of public opinion, the horror of the work-house and the danger of applying for poor relief remained a dominant factor in the minds of the poor throughout the nine-teenth century.

Government activity against trade unionism: the 'Tolpuddle Martyrs', 1834

The unimaginative attitude of Grey's Government to the great problem of a livelihood for the lower classes was also seen in the rigid stand taken against the trade union movement. Disapprov-ing of the general spread of unionism which had followed the repeal of the Combination Acts, the Government was doubly alarmed by the growth of Robert Owen's 'Grand National Con-solidated Union'. This aimed at absorbing all the different craft or trade unions within one organization (thus placing within the hands of its leaders the weapon of a general strike) and then set-ting up a system of co-operative production. In its anxiety to cripple such a movement, which attracted much support from the working classes, the Government did not hesitate to strike at very small fry. Six men of Tolpuddle, in Dorset, were pro-secuted for indulging in secret oaths when they formed a local branch of the Friendly Society of Agricultural Labourers—a society which was affiliated to the 'Grand National'. Such oaths were in fact illegal, by an act passed at the time of the Nore Mutiny; but they were the usual practice of all unions at the time. The 'Tolpuddle Martyrs', as they came to be called in trade union circles, were therefore found guilty and sentenced to seven years' transportation—a savage sentence which Melbourne, the Home Secretary, refused to modify. Some two years later public opinion compelled their release. Such an incident explains why Grey's Government, valuable as so many of its measures were, was not exactly hailed among the poor as the last word in re-forming zeal.

3 Melbourne: the Pace Slackens. Chartism

In July 1834 the aged Grey gave up his office, to be succeeded by Melbourne, whose personality and talents made him as suitable for the position of Prime Minister as his views made him unsuitable. His sufferings in private life, for all his birth and fortune, had been considerable, since his wife had made herself ridiculous by her passion for Lord Byron, and his only son was an imbecile. Perhaps these events were responsible for his cynical outlook. Greville, the famous diarist, records how when Melbourne was invited to become Prime Minister 'he thought it a damned bore, and he was in many minds what he should do—be Minister or no'. It was in this spirit that Melbourne approached the task of governing a nation confronted with all the problems arising from the aftermath of the Napoleonic War, and from the Agrarian and Industrial Revolutions. Melbourne succeeds Grey, 1834

Melbourne took over Grey's Cabinet in the summer of 1834. Within a few months he quite unnecessarily offered William IV his resignation; and the latter, heartily tired of Whig reforms, was delighted to accept. In November 1834 Peel was accordingly entrusted by the King with the task of forming a Tory administration. Assisted by Wellington he assumed office, but lacking a majority in the Commons was defeated six times in as many weeks. In fact, the only important thing connected with this first ministry of Peel's was his election address to his constituents, the 'Tamworth Manifesto'. In this he accepted the principle both of the Reform Act and of 'redress for proved grievances'—in other words he showed that he had in mind a Toryism freed from the old oppressive views. From this document dated a new name for his party—the 'Conservatives'. Resignation of Melbourne Peel's first Ministry, 1834 The 'Tamworth Manifesto', 1835

By April 1835 Melbourne and the Whigs were back in office. The use to which Melbourne put this renewed spell of power was characteristic. One first-class reform, largely inspired by the Radicals, was passed, and then the Government sank into comparative lethargy. The reform in question was the Municipal Corporations Act of 1835, which was as badly needed for the boroughs as the Reform Act had been for Parliament. Melbourne's return to office, 1835

The local government of the great English towns was in an extremely varied and confused state. Two hundred and forty-six towns in England and Wales were incorporated—i.e. they were boroughs, having a charter of privileges, and a mayor and Defects of English municipal government corporation. But these boroughs included some of the smallest towns in the country—and even the non-existent Dunwich. On the other hand, many towns which were not boroughs, and thus still remained under the control of the local lord of the manor, were by 1834 among the greatest in the land, such as Manchester and Birmingham.

Apart from this fantastic disparity, there was a further great difference in the manner in which the boroughs themselves were governed. Some of them, such as Norwich and Nottingham, had large bodies of 'freemen' who acted as electors and thus ensured a fairly democratic municipal government. Most, however, had in the course of time become 'close' corporations; the aldermen were not elected by the inhabitants of the town, but were 'co-opted' to fill vacancies by those already on the corporation. This completely undemocratic system offended the Radicals, and became even more ridiculous when some sort of uniformity was introduced into national elections by the Reform Act of 1832. Moreover, nearly all the most valuable things that we associate with municipal government, such as street-lighting, sewage disposal and so on, were done—in so far as they were done at all—by a completely different set of authorities from either the corporation or the lord of the manor. These were the various Improvement Commissioners, either elected or nominated, who were authorized by Act of Parliament to manage some special kind of town improvement such as gas lighting, scavenging or street-paving—each activity being under a separate commission. English towns and boroughs before 1835 thus presented a remarkable picture of diversity of government, conflict of authority, corruption, and remoteness from popular control. In Scotland reform had already been introduced by the Burgh Act of 1833.

In 1833 a special Commission, on which Benthamite Radical feeling was well represented, was appointed by Grey to study the state of the municipalities. Its recommendations were accepted by Melbourne and embodied in the Municipal Corporations Reform Act. This abolished the 'close' corporations in the boroughs, and substituted instead a uniform body of borough councils, to be elected by all male ratepayers for a term of three years. The councillors themselves were to elect their mayor and aldermen—the latter constituting one-quarter of the council, and holding office for six years. Provision was made for non-corporate towns to become boroughs under certain conditions—Manchester, for example, sought incorporation in 1838 and Birmingham in 1839.

The Municipal
Corporations
Reform Act,
1835

Finally the new councils were permitted to take over the various Improvements Committees, if the latter agreed.

In spite of these great changes, progress in municipal services was not particularly rapid. Thirteen years after the Municipal Corporations Act was passed, a third of the English boroughs still had no provision whatever for draining or cleaning. Nevertheless, the groundwork of reform had been laid. Uniformity and order had been introduced, and the control of the middle classes over their towns had been established. What the middle classes made of these towns, of course, might not be very much—but at least they were now freed from the shackles of aristocratic privilege.

★   ★   ★   ★   ★

In their remaining five years of office the Whigs contented themselves with a very modest measure of reform. Indeed, one of their main preoccupations was to damp down a renewed blaze of reformist agitation among the lower classes. For the latter were deeply dissatisfied by the terms of the Reform Act of 1832, which left the mass of the people without any voice in public affairs; and the collapse of the Grand National Trades Union in 1834[1] had frustrated many hopes. A fresh series of slumps and the rigours of the New Poor Law added fuel to the flames, and by 1838 the Whigs found themselves up against an expression of discontent organized on a truly national scale. *Chartism*

The Chartist movement began in 1836 with the formation of the London Working Men's Association, a body of skilled working men with a reformist political programme. The secretary of this organization was William Lovett, its chief adviser the veteran Radical, Francis Place. These two men determined to draw up a programme of reform which would be acceptable to the broad masses of the country; and they were so successful in this object that very soon the societies affiliated to the L.W.M.A. reached a total of one hundred and fifty. The most important of these other groups were those centring upon Thomas Attwood, the Birmingham banker, and Feargus O'Connor, an Irish ex-M.P. who ran a violently radical paper in Leeds, *The Northern Star*. Lovett's programme was then drafted into a Bill of six points, called the *The London Working Men's Association, 1836*

---

[1] The union's ultimate aim of co-operative production had proved too far ahead of—or behind—the times. Owen, who wished to establish Socialism without affronting the capitalists, had also quarrelled with the other leaders over the desirability of strike action.

'People's Charter', and the whole Chartist movement was officially launched on the country at a big Birmingham meeting in
1838. The six points, which were common to most Radicals,
were: a vote for all adult males, the secret ballot, annual elections,
abolition of the property qualification for M.P.s, payment of
M.P.s, and equal electoral districts.

The next step was to persuade Parliament to accept these far-
reaching demands, and it was therefore decided to organize a
mass petition for the enactment of the Charter. A 'Convention'
was to be elected to meet in London and present the petition to
Parliament; if it were rejected the Convention was to organize
what the Chartists termed a 'National Holiday', or 'Sacred
Month', but what we should call a general strike.

The Convention duly met, in 1839, but found that only about
half a million people had signed the petition. So it decided on
further propaganda; torchlight meetings were held outside the
great towns, and the signatures rose to one and a quarter millions.
All this talk naturally brought to the head of the movement the
greatest talker—Feargus O'Connor, a showy idealist whose abilities lay exclusively in his tongue. Lovett was a far sounder character, but Lovett's influence was eclipsed during a spell in prison
which resulted from an incident in Birmingham—to which the
Convention had now moved. Defying a ban against speaking in
the Bull Ring, the Chartists provoked the Mayor into borrowing
a number of the new London police to deal with the situation.
A day of fighting and riots followed, in which the police had to
call for military assistance before they could gain the upper hand.
The Convention then issued a fierce denunciation of the authorities' conduct; and the authorities retaliated by arresting and imprisoning Lovett, who had courageously signed it.

At last, in July 1839, the petition was debated by Parliament,
Attwood proposing it and Lord John Russell leading the opposition on behalf of the Government. It was overwhelmingly rejected and the Chartist Convention duly called for the 'Sacred
Month'. The strike was bound to lead to clashes with police and
troops—were the Chartists really prepared to turn it into a full
revolution by arming, overthrowing the Government and setting
up a 'people's republic'? If not, the whole thing was nothing
more than a bluff which the Government could call by taking
vigorous measures against the strikers. On this crucial question
the Chartists never agreed—some like Lovett being quite opposed
to violence, some, like Frost, being prepared to go to any lengths,

some, like O'Connor, encouraging violence by their speeches while being completely unprepared to apply it in action. In the result, the plan of a 'Sacred Month' proved a fiasco, for the Convention found that support for the strike was by no means general even inside the Chartist ranks, and withdrew the order before it was due to come into effect. With all prestige lost from this contradictory policy, and with many of its leaders languishing in jail, the Convention then adjourned indefinitely, its objects all unaccomplished. Chartist disunity: adjournment of the Convention, 1839

To the story of frustration there was an epilogue three months later. A few extremists in Wales planned a general insurrection, to start with the capture of Newport and the release from jail of Henry Vincent, a Chartist leader. The attack was headed by John Frost, a draper who had been mayor of the town. His force of some 4,000 men, nearly all impoverished miners, was to meet two other contingents one night in November and advance on Newport during the hours of darkness. But bad weather sent the meeting arrangements astray, and Frost was left to attack unsupported after dawn had broken. The authorities, too, had wind of the scheme, and laid a trap, so that when the miners at last poured into the town they were met by volleys of fire from soldiers concealed behind the shutters of an hotel. These soon had their effect, and the crowd swept away, leaving several dead and dying. Frost was quickly arrested, and in company with others received sentence of death, afterwards commuted to transportation. Chartist leaders in other parts of the country were also rounded up, including O'Connor, who had apparently known very little of the plot, had tried to stop what he did know, and with unwonted tact had gone off to Ireland for a holiday. With their leaders imprisoned, their petition rejected, their whole movement disgraced in the eyes of sober citizens, the Chartists in 1840 seemed utterly broken. They had failed through their own confused counsels, the hostility of the middle classes and the vigour of the Government's actions. Nevertheless, the apparently dead body of Chartism still retained a kick or two of life, as later events were to show.[1] The Newport rising, 1839

Collapse of the movement

★   ★   ★   ★   ★

While Chartism occupied the centre of the political stage the Whig programme in Parliament was confined to comparatively minor measures. Among the most useful of these was the

[1] See pages 159–61.

Compulsory
registration of
births, mar-
riages and
deaths, 1836

introduction of compulsory registration for births, marriages and
deaths. This enabled accurate statistics to be kept, and thus provided the groundwork for later public health measures. Moreover, factory acts could be more strictly applied when a system
of birth certificates was introduced, for previously it had been
very easy for parents and employers to pass off children as older
than they actually were.

Ecclesiastical
reforms: the
Tithe Commuta-
tion Act

Between 1836 and 1840 the Whigs also passed some valuable
ecclesiastical legislation, notably the Tithe Commutation Act.
This made tithe an additional rent on the land, payable in money
to the parson or tithe-holder, and thus 'put an end to the quarrel
that had been renewed in the English village every year since the
Conquest and beyond, over the parson's tithe-pig and sheaves'.[1]
A further reform redistributed clerical incomes more fairly, and
placed the administration of Church lands and incomes under a
special body of Ecclesiastical Commissioners instead of leaving
individual bishops in unfettered control over them.

The penny
post, 1840

Finally, in 1840, the Whigs introduced a measure of prime
importance for the encouragement of trade, the penny postage.
The credit for this belonged entirely to Rowland Hill, a man of
original and inventive turn of mind. Hill showed that an enormous amount of time was lost by postmen having to wait at each
house for payment—for payment was made on delivery and at
different rates for different distances. He also insisted that existing charges—e.g. about 2s. from London to Dublin—were far
in excess of what could be afforded by the lower classes, and
that lower rates would bring a much greater use of postal facilities.
His proposals were that postage should be prepaid by means of a
stamp, and that there should be a uniform series of charges by
weight, beginning at a penny, irrespective of distance (within
the British Isles). In the next twenty-five years the number of
letters and packets carried annually by post increased nearly
tenfold, with enormous benefit to trade and social life.

Death of
William IV;
Accession of
Queen Victoria,
1837

By the time the Whig spell of office came to a close, a new
sovereign was on the throne. Victoria had succeeded her uncle in
1837. The new Queen, a girl of eighteen, was destined to rule the
Empire until the very end of the century. She more than made up
for her small physical and intellectual stature by her strong will-
power, her bursts of feminine realism, and her ardent devotion to
duty, while in 1837 the spectacle of a member of the British royal
family with a respectable private life was a pleasant novelty. Thus

[1] G. M. Trevelyan.

although in her reign she had phases of unpopularity, she ended by triumphantly rescuing the monarchy from the contempt into which George IV and his disreputable brothers had plunged it, and made the Crown the best-loved institution in the country.

The accession of Victoria in 1837 had involved a general election. Much to the relief of the Queen, who had been brought up in a strongly Whig environment, the Whigs were confirmed in power. It therefore fell to Melbourne to guide the new sovereign along lines acceptable to the British people. In this function he achieved his greatest success, rapidly establishing an affectionate relationship with the young Queen and training her in the model of a constitutional and not a despotic ruler. *Melbourne and Queen Victoria*

Much to the Queen's alarm she was soon threatened with the departure of the Whigs and their beloved leader, for in 1839 Melbourne, who had lost the support of the Radicals and the Irish, resigned. Victoria thus had to send for Peel, whom she intensely disliked—a 'cold, odd man', she thought him—and ask him to form a government from the Conservatives she so detested. *Resignation of the Whigs, 1839*

Peel was naturally anxious to make sure that his none too secure position should not be weakened by household intrigues in the palace. He therefore made it a condition of accepting office that the Queen should dismiss her leading Ladies-of-the-Bedchamber, who were all Whigs, and appoint Conservative ladies in their place. Thus arose the rather absurd 'Bedchamber Crisis'. Victoria, annoyed at having a choice of personal attendants dictated to her, refused to give way, although Melbourne had taken the correct course by advising her to yield. Touched by such loyalty to their cause, Melbourne and the Whigs then assured Victoria of their support, and agreed to take office again. In any case Peel was not anxious to lead another minority government, and soon had his revenge when the Whigs collapsed in 1841 and were defeated at a general election. *Peel and the 'Bedchamber Crisis'* *Resumption of office by the Whigs* *Whig defeat at general election, 1841*

The question of the Ladies was eventually decided against the royal view, but in any case it became less important with the Queen's marriage in 1840 to her cousin, Albert of Saxe-Coburg. This earnest young German, who was later accorded the title of Prince Consort, could never win his way to the heart of England, but that of Victoria was his without reservation. She soon came to respect his judgment as much as she idolized his person. It did not take Albert long to find out that there was a great deal to be said for Peel. The conversion of Victoria to the same view was not unduly delayed. *Prince Albert*

11. Peel and the Conservatives

1 Financial and Industrial Reform

By 1841 the reforming ardour of the Whigs had worn thin, and
their overthrow was no great blow to the cause of progress. Indeed, this was now well served by their opponents, for thanks to
Peel, reactionary Toryism was already fast developing into the
moderate Conservatism foreshadowed by the Tamworth Manifesto.[1]

Peel's problemsNotable as the period of Peel's Home Secretaryship had been,
it was to be dwarfed by his achievements as Prime Minister once
he had a majority behind him in Parliament. Yet the task which
confronted him in 1841 was no light one; for in addition to
troubles in North America, China, India, Scotland and Ireland,
he was faced with a critical situation at home. In spite of Britain's
growing industrial wealth, widespread distress persisted among
the lower classes, and though the Speenhamland system had been
abolished, one Englishman in ten was still a pauper. At the same
time the national revenue was falling off and the Whigs had
entirely failed to balance their budgets.

One of the causes of all this financial difficulty was the inefficient system of taxation resulting from the repeal of the income
tax in 1816. As a consequence of that concession, taxes on many
goods in common use had gradually been increased to make up
for lost revenue—in spite of the work of Huskisson—and in 1841
there were heavy customs duties on such everyday essentials as
corn, meat, sugar, tea, butter, soap and glass. Peel soon saw that
taxation of this kind, designed both to protect the home producer
from foreign competition and to bring in revenue, was producing
bad results. Not only was it placing necessary food beyond the
reach of the poorer classes, but it was actually failing to bring in a
good revenue, since duties were so heavy that some articles never
passed through the ports at all.

Having chosen Henry Goulburn, a sympathetic colleague, as
his Chancellor of the Exchequer, Peel brought his own keen
energies to bear on this thorny subject, and in 1842 produced

[1] See page 121.

possibly the most famous budget of the nineteenth century. This set up a new customs system based on a maximum duty of 5 per cent on raw materials, 12 per cent on semi-manufactured goods and 20 per cent on finished articles. Over three-quarters of the existing duties had to be substantially reduced to conform to these limits, and the budget was thus the largest single step towards free trade that had ever been taken. *The budget of 1842: reduction of duties*

Though Peel believed that in the long run tariff reductions would bring in a greater revenue through increased trade, he knew that at first a small sum—a quarter of a million pounds—might be lost to the Exchequer. This sum had to be made good, and money had also to be found to finance campaigns in India and China and to make up the deficit which had been a constant feature of Whig finance. Peel's solution was that of a brave man— he reintroduced income tax. Reimposed as a temporary measure for three years only,[1] it was to be collected at the rate of seven-pence in the pound on all incomes over £150 per annum. Duties which increased the general cost of living were thus replaced by a tax on those best able to afford it, and the whole national finances were set on a firmer and juster basis. *Reintroduction of income tax*

The transformation of the tariff system was carried still further by later budgets, especially that of 1845, which abolished duties on 430 articles. The virtual completion of free trade was to be the work of Peel's disciple, Gladstone (who as President of the Board of Trade under Peel already had some hand in these early measures), but in some respects free trade was already far advanced by 1845. All export duties had gone, together with nearly all duties on raw materials, and the vexed question of the Corn Laws was to be tackled in the following year. While Britain was industrially so far in advance of her competitors, free trade was certainly beneficial to her, and to Peel must go much of the credit for the great trade revival which marked the next twenty-five years. *Further steps towards free trade*

Peel also gave much attention to the problems of the British banking system. In the years following Waterloo many small banks had crashed—seventy in the one year 1825 for instance. The reason for this was at first thought to be that they were owned by private individuals or families, since the Bank of England alone was permitted to be a joint-stock concern. Even after other banks were allowed to operate on joint-stock lines, *Defects of the banking system*

[1] Thanks to increased social services and successive wars, the doomed infant is now well past the centenarian mark, and is still going strongly.

however, failures continued, and it became obvious that the main cause was the over-issue of currency by banks lacking sufficient reserves to tide them over difficult periods; for though the private banks were not allowed to issue notes of less than £5 denomination, they could—and did—issue without restriction notes of £5 and above. The temptation to banks to supply large quantities of currency beyond their real means was all the greater at a time when there were so many opportunities for the investment of large sums, as in the great railway growth of the 1840s; and even the Bank of England was not without fault in this respect.

Bank Charter Act, 1844

Peel's remedy for these matters was the Bank Charter Act of 1844. Its main aim was to limit note issue by banks. No new banks of issue could be created; the amounts issued by various banks were limited to their average issue in the twelve weeks before the passing of the Act; and all note issue by the Bank of England beyond £14,000,000 had to be backed by actual gold reserves. Possibly the Act restricted credit too much (a handicap later overcome by the growing use of cheques), for it had to be suspended three times in the next twenty-two years. But it certainly helped to establish that magic security of British finance which was so remarkable a feature of the rest of the nineteenth century, and it made 'safe as the Bank of England' a household phrase. The stability and honesty of British bankers were so well recognized the world over that the City became the chief market for raising capital and the safest place for keeping funds. A world-wide financial system was thus erected on the basis of Britain's world-wide trade.

* * * * *

The lowering of tariffs, the reform of taxation, the stabilization of the currency, the reduction of the National Debt—these were the remedies for distress naturally adopted by a man of Peel's outlook. If the commercial system of the country could be set firmly on its feet by low duties on raw materials, and if industrialists could work in the knowledge that the currency was stable, he was convinced that trade would inevitably expand and that the working classes would share in the general prosperity. For many men, however, particularly those of a rather younger generation, distress demanded more from the Government than merely clearing the ring for manufacturers to operate efficiently. The Government, they thought, must actively intervene to raise the standard of life where it was lowest by stopping the exploitation of women and children in factories and mines. The great leader of this school of thought during Peel's Ministry was Lord Ashley.[1]

The Christian conscience of Ashley, a fanatically sincere Evangelical Churchman, had been for many years disturbed by the horrors of factory life. It was his Bill in 1833 which had stirred the Whigs into passing the Factory Act of that year—an Act which in Ashley's opinion did not go nearly far enough. Together with John Fielden, the great and benevolent Todmorden manufacturer, he had long held a leading position in the 'Ten Hours' movement—the movement to secure a working day of ten hours for women and children in the factories. Such a measure would, of course, benefit men workers too, since the mills could not be worked economically by adult male labour alone; but men were supposed to be capable of looking after their own interests, and it was therefore good policy to stress only the claims of the women and children to protection. With this objective in view Ashley had managed to persuade the Whigs in 1840 to appoint a parliamentary committee to examine the working of the Factory Act of 1833. He had also secured the appointment of a special Commission to study the conditions of children employed in mines and other industries not covered by the Factory Acts. At this stage the Whigs had gone out of office, and the Conservatives, Ashley's own party, had come in.

Ashley and factory reform

Ashley himself did not hope for much from Peel, whom he regarded as too cold a man to be warmed by any generous enthusiasm for a great cause. 'Sat next to Peel last Saturday', he noted in 1841. 'What possesses that man? It was the neighbourhood of an iceberg, with a slight thaw on the surface.' Like Queen Victoria in 1839 with her 'such a cold, odd man', or O'Connell with his famous description of Peel's smile ('like the silver plate on a coffin'), Ashley had not penetrated the Prime Minister's reserve to the depths beneath. Nor did Peel, distrustful of Ashley's over-zealous Protestantism, at first offer the reformer anything better than a mere post in the Royal Household—'in which I could exhibit nothing good but my legs in white shorts', Ashley commented bitterly. Nevertheless, the enthusiasm of Ashley, coupled with Peel's willingness to listen to reason, produced two important measures of social reform during the Ministry.

The first of these sprang from the special Commission on child

[1] Ashley is better known under the title of the Earl of Shaftesbury, which he inherited in 1851.

labour in the mines which Ashley had secured in 1840. The Commissioners' report was written in unemotional language, but it presented a damning array of facts. County by county the tale was repeated—children five, six and seven years old were employed for twelve to sixteen hours a day at tasks like sitting in the dark opening trap-doors, standing ankle-deep in water working pumps, or dragging along trucks to which they were harnessed by a girdle and chain. Girls, too, shared in these labours, while women hauled carts, or carried huge baskets of coal on their heads up a series of ladders to the surface. Armed with such powerful ammunition, Ashley immediately introduced a Bill to abolish all female labour in the mines, together with that of pauper apprentices and boys under thirteen. His speech consisted of little more than a summary of the report, but it brought tears to the eyes of many M.P.s, and the bill had little difficulty in passing the Commons. In the Lords there was more of a struggle, for Lord Londonderry, Castlereagh's half-brother and a great coalowner, fought the proposals tooth and nail, and eventually managed to reduce the suggested age limit for boy labour by three years, and to knock out the clause about pauper apprentices.

In its final form the Act thus abolished all female labour in the mines, together with that of boys under ten.

Spurred on by his success over the Mines Act, Ashley renewed his efforts to achieve the Ten Hours limit for the factory workers. His opportunity came when the Government, following up the report of the parliamentary committee, introduced a Factory Bill going some way beyond the Act of 1833. For the first time it was proposed to regulate the hours of female labour, a twelve-hour day for women—a privilege already won in 1833 for 'young people' (aged thirteen to eighteen)—being suggested. As a concession to manufacturers, children were to be allowed into the mills at eight instead of nine years of age, but their working hours were to be reduced from nine to six-and-a-half a day. It was also proposed to bring silk mills into this system of regulation. This did not satisfy Ashley, who moved to reduce the suggested hours of women and 'young people' from twelve to ten. But his efforts were baulked by Peel, who believed that England would not survive foreign competition on a 'ten-hour day', and refused to accept any improvement on the Government's proposals.

2 Ireland and the Repeal of the Corn Laws

The problems which Peel had to solve in England were as nothing to those which confronted him in Ireland. Apart from all the long-standing religious and economic difficulties, he was confronted with O'Connell's agitation for the repeal of the Act of Union. In 1842 the Irish leader began a series of mass meetings to back his demand. His intention was to frighten Peel into surrender over the Union just as he had earlier frightened Wellington and Peel into surrender over Catholic emancipation; but, unlike the extremists of the newly-formed 'Young Ireland' movement, he was no believer in armed rebellion. Peel thus had little difficulty in dealing with him, for the Prime Minister was quite prepared to fight to maintain the Union, which to most Englishmen seemed a vital strategic necessity. Having made full preparations to counter resistance, Peel deliberately placed a ban on a mass meeting which O'Connell was to address at Clontarf. Tamely submitting—much to the annoyance of the 'Young Ireland' party —O'Connell soon found his influence at an end.

Peel and Ireland

O'Connell

Clontarf, 1843

With this firmness the Prime Minister strove to combine concessions to Irish religious opinion, such as increasing the Government grant to Maynooth College, an institution for training Catholic priests. But the religious difficulties in Ireland, almost insuperable as they seemed, were simple compared with the economic difficulties. Outside Northern Ireland there were no industries worth mentioning, and there was little coal or iron anywhere. The rapidly increasing population was thus compelled to rely entirely upon the land—but the land was nearly all owned by English or Anglo-Irish Protestants, who as often as not lived in England. The only way the Irish could get land was to rent it, and the demand for land was so strong that the original tenant would sublet a proportion of his holding to another, and he to a third, and so on. The result was an extraordinary number of smallholdings, usually leased at excessive rents to cover the profits of the many middlemen involved. Such a system naturally encouraged ignorant and unprogressive farming, for the peasants had neither education nor capital. There was little scientific crop rotation, hedging or ditching, and little incentive to progress, since any tenant outside Ulster who made improvements was liable to have his rent raised, or be evicted without compensation in favour of someone who would pay a higher rent. Nor could the

Peel's 'concessions' to Ireland

Irish economic problems

landlord himself make widespread improvements without first evicting large numbers of smallholders, pulling down the pitiful shacks which had sprung up, and generally making himself unpopular. Against such evictions the peasant's only defence was terrorism, which was mainly practised on the landlords' agents and cattle. And this in turn led to strong measures from the authorities, such as Coercion Acts suspending Habeas Corpus and trial by jury—all of which still further increased Irish ill-will. Such was the vicious circle which resulted from the Cromwellian land settlement and the eighteenth-century restrictions on Irish industry.

The standard of life which could be attained in conditions of this kind was possibly the lowest in Europe. Five-sixths of the population lived in single-room huts, often made of mud. Since land was so scarce, the peasant grew what would sustain him by the use of the least soil. To maintain a family of eight on bread would require 2 acres, but on potatoes it could be done with one. Potatoes were therefore the universal crop, and the staple diet. At least 4 millions out of the population of $8\frac{1}{2}$ millions could afford nothing better. It was a very precarious system; for if the potato crop should for any reason fail, Ireland would be up against starvation. In the summer of 1845 potato blight appeared in England; by the autumn it had spread to Ireland. The situation rapidly became critical. Peel had to act, or watch the Irish die by the thousand, the more so as the extremely wet summer had made a very bad corn harvest in England a certainty. His method of approaching the problem was to lead to his most famous political action, and to the end of his great spell of power.

Potato blight,
1845

*   *   *   *   *

The Conservatives and the Corn Laws

It so happened that the potato crisis in Ireland found Peel in an unsettled state of mind about the Corn Laws. At the beginning of his term of office he had reduced the sliding-scale duty on imported wheat, but beyond that he had refused to go. Though he had expressly reserved liberty of action for himself about the Corn Laws, his whole party was pledged to their retention. The great landlords were the backbone of the Conservative party, and the very kernel of their economic creed was protection for British agriculture against foreign competition. They might follow Peel along the paths of free trade in manufacture, but in agriculture never. If there was one thing they had taken for granted in 1841, it was that Peel, the guardian of their interests, would not give way to the growing popular clamour for repeal of the Corn Laws. And yet it was their own acknowledged leader who, to their surprise and fury, was soon to force Repeal down their throats. The reasons for this must be found in the great campaign fought by the Anti-Corn Law League, Peel's open-mindedness and sense of duty, the crisis of the Irish potato famine, and the inability of the Whigs to face the great issues involved.

The Anti-Corn Law League, a nation-wide organization, had been founded in 1839. Its leading spirit was Richard Cobden, a Sussex man of yeoman stock who had risen from travelling in textiles to owning one of the greatest calico-printing works in Manchester. As a collaborator he had John Bright of Rochdale, who was not only a wealthy factory-owner but also one of the finest orators of his time. These two men were strongly supported by nearly all the manufacturing class, and thus there was ample wealth available for financing agitation. Cobden's direction of the campaign was brilliant. Thanks to the recent reduction of the newspaper duty to one penny, two League newspapers were run. Pamphlets were distributed wholesale—it was no coincidence that Cobden had been one of the strongest supporters of the movement for a penny post. League 'orators' were sent to tour the country, and special attention was given to M.P.s and their electors. Every single elector in the country received a packet of anti-corn law literature, and League supporters were urged to buy 40s. worth of freehold land to qualify for a vote in the counties. In 1841 Cobden was elected M.P. for Stockport, and with Bright following him into the Commons two years later as the representative of Durham, the League forces were strongly arrayed for a frontal attack on the Prime Minister. *The Anti-Corn Law League*

The arguments which Cobden and Bright spread through the country and hurled at Peel across the floor of the House were cogent and convincing. The repeal of the corn duties would cheapen food. This would increase the purchasing power of the workers' wages and so result in greater prosperity all round, for the population would be able to afford either more food, or more manufactured goods, or both. Even the agriculturists would thus benefit, urged Cobden. Against this the agriculturists contended that to abolish duties on foreign corn would mean the end of British farming. They also asserted that the Leaguers really wanted cheaper food so that manufacturers could lower wages—a belief which O'Connor and many of the Chartists shared. *The League's arguments*

(Richard Doyle, 1845, reproduced by permission of the Proprietors of 'Punch')

PAPA COBDEN TAKING MASTER ROBERT A FREE
TRADE WALK

Papa Cobden: 'COME ALONG, MASTER ROBERT, DO STEP OUT.'
Master Robert: 'THAT'S ALL VERY WELL, BUT YOU KNOW I CANNOT GO AS FAST
AS YOU DO.'

The reluctant and apprehensive Peel is hustled along by the confident Cobden in
the direction of Corn Law Repeal.

Cobden's arguments, however, were not confined to the economic sphere. He also pointed out that protective duties of any sort were bad from the international aspect, since they led to ill-feeling between nations, and so increased the risk of war. This argument was strongly supported by Bright, a Quaker, who added that anything which artificially increased the price of food, God's bounty to man, and thereby kept it from the mouths of the poor, was not only an error, but a sin.

Before this battery of argument Peel, who had already moved so far towards free trade in many ways, was powerless. It was always a remarkable point about Peel that he was open to conviction by reason and fact, and by the spring of 1845 he had already realized that he could strive no longer against Cobden. After a particularly telling speech by the latter, the Prime Minister was seen to crumple up his notes for a reply, and heard to mutter to a colleague on the front bench, 'You must answer this, for I cannot.' Before very long he had decided that the Corn Laws must be repealed, but regarding his party as more or less pledged to Protection he hoped to wait until the next election a couple of years ahead, then announce his conversion, and come back to carry Repeal after an understanding to that effect with the electorate. *The conversion of Peel*

It was the wet summer of 1845 and the failure of the Irish potato crop which caused Peel to speed up this programme. By October it was clear that five-eighths of the crop would be ruined, and even sound potatoes were turned within a few weeks into 'masses of putrid slime'. One of the royal princes indeed maintained that rotten potatoes made perfectly good eating when mixed with grass, but the recipe was naturally not popular. Peel was in an agony of apprehension, particularly as to what might happen if the blight continued for another year—much to the amazement of some of his colleagues, who simply could not believe that the humble potato was so important. By the end of October he had come to the conclusion that the Corn Laws must be immediately suspended, but to this he could not get his Cabinet to agree. At the expression of the view, advanced both in the Cabinet and later on in the House, that his fears of famine were exaggerated, Peel grew really angry—'Are you to hesitate in averting famine which may come because it possibly may not come? Good God! are you to sit in Cabinet and consider and calculate how much diarrhoea and bloody flux and dysentery a people can bear before it becomes necessary for you to provide them with food? *Effect of the Irish potato famine* *Cabinet division*

Is it not better to err on the side of precaution . . .?' Wellington, though he later came round to support Peel and helped to put Repeal through the Lords, was at first one of the scoffers. 'Rotten potatoes have done it all!' he exclaimed; 'they have put Peel in his damned fright.'

The Whigs favour Repeal

While the Cabinet crisis was continuing, Lord John Russell, leader of the Whigs since the retirement of Melbourne, came out with a strong pronouncement in favour of Corn Law Repeal. Though Peel had now won over most of the Cabinet to his views, there were still several ministers opposed—the most notable was Lord Stanley[1]—and he therefore offered his resignation to the Queen. Russell then agreed to form a Whig Ministry to carry Repeal, although his own party were as divided about the matter as the Conservatives; but he could not get his leading supporters to agree about the offices they should occupy. Thoroughly disheartened, he abandoned his attempt, and (in the phrase of Disraeli) 'handed back the poisoned chalice' to Peel. Knowing that he was the only man in the country with sufficient authority to do so, Peel then agreed to form a government for the express purpose of repealing the Corn Laws. He thus laid himself open once more to the accusation of treachery to his party.

Resignation of Peel

Russell's failure to form ministry

Peel resumes office to carry Repeal

In January 1846, having left out Stanley from the Cabinet, Peel met Parliament with the proposal to lower the corn duty at once to a small sum and to abolish it entirely within three years. He encountered tremendous opposition. Though he had the backing of nearly all the outstanding men in his own party, he found the rank and file bitterly hostile; while the Whigs, who mostly supported him in Repeal, were not prepared to support him in anything else. All told, the Free Trade Conservatives could muster only a hundred votes, the Protectionist Conservatives well over two hundred. All that was lacking to these outraged landowners was a leader. To their surprise and delight an outstanding champion now emerged in the florid personality of Benjamin Disraeli.[2]

Disraeli

The son of a distinguished man of letters of Jewish race who had turned Christian, Disraeli had long nourished resentment against Peel. That austere figure had little use for one whose party politics followed strange lines of their own and whose dress was even stranger. The black velvet coat, the flame-coloured trousers broidered with gold, the scarlet, green, yellow or white waistcoat,

[1] Stanley succeeded to the title of Earl of Derby in 1851.
[2] Disraeli was created Earl of Beaconsfield in 1876.

the oiled ringlets, the flashing rings worn *over* white kid gloves
—all the paraphernalia with which he originally hoped to attract
attention—appealed not at all to Peel's sober English taste. Returned to Parliament at last in 1837, Disraeli had discovered
the drawbacks of extravagant dress and language—his maiden
speech had been greated with roars of laughter and he had been
forced to resume his seat. Thereafter he had toned down his
dress and his speeches, attached himself to Peel, and confidently
looked forward to a place in the Cabinet. Disappointed in this
hope, he had then pursued a curious conservative line of his own,
revolving in a small aristocratic circle which called itself 'Young   'Young England'
England'. This romantic Toryism, very feudal and very Anglican,
with its call for reform of working-class conditions by a benevolent aristocracy—aiming, in other words, at government by a
nobility which was really noble—had provided Disraeli with material for two novels (*Coningsby* and *Sybil*), some useful social
connections, and a parliamentary position from which to criticize
Peel. He had already twitted Peel with adopting only the measures
of his opponents—'The right honourable gentleman caught the
Whigs bathing, and walked away with their clothes. He has left
them in the full enjoyment of their liberal position, and he himself is a strict conservative of their garments.' Now, on Corn Law
Repeal, he had a magnificent opportunity. The infuriated Protectionists were overjoyed to find a leader who knew how to turn to
good account Peel's sacrifice of party principles, and they rejoiced
to see the Prime Minister writhe under the lash of Disraeli's
sarcasm.

To lend aristocratic backing to the onslaughts of the talented   Lord George
but ancestrally dubious Disraeli there also emerged Lord George   Bentinck
Bentinck, a racehorse owner who had sat for many years in Parliament without feeling the need to make speeches. Now, however,
all his sense of fair play was outraged by Peel's 'conversion', and
he devoted his shrewd if uncultured energies to punishing such
'cheating' as the proposed Corn Law Repeal. Bentinck's own
words were concise and to the point: 'I keep horses in three
counties, and they tell me I shall save £1,500 a year by free trade.
I don't care for that: what I cannot bear is being *sold*.' So he
disposed of his horses—and one of them afterwards went near to
breaking his late owner's heart by winning the Derby under
other colours—studied politics instead of Turf Guides, gave up
eating dinner in order to stay awake at debates, and wore himself
almost to death in a frantic effort to teach Peel a lesson. Their

conflict became so bitter that at one time Peel was restrained from challenging Bentinck to a duel only by a friend who threatened to inform the police.

Repeal of the Corn Laws, June 1846

So it came about that the passage of Corn Law Repeal was by no means easy. It was fought tooth and nail by Disraeli, Bentinck and the Conservative Protectionists for six months, till at last, in June 1846, it passed through the Lords by the influence of Wellington and the support of many Whigs. But meanwhile distress in Ireland had brought on a wave of crime and the Government had introduced a Coercion Bill to deal with it. The very same evening on which the Repeal Bill went through its third reading in the Lords, the Coercion Bill was defeated in the Commons by a

The Irish Coercion Bill— resignation of Peel

Coalition of Whigs, Radicals and Protectionists led by Bentinck and Disraeli. Two or three days later Peel resigned. His last speech included a deliberate tribute to his old enemy Cobden, and the expression of the hope that the name of Peel would be remembered affectionately by the toiling masses for whom he had sought cheaper food.

Peel's last years —1846–1850

For the remaining four years of his life, Peel occupied a position in Parliament almost above party. His life was cut short in 1850 as the result of a riding accident in Hyde Park.

The effects of Repeal

And what of the measure which had caused so much bother? How far were the predictions of the supporters and opponents of Repeal carried out? Strangely enough, this is still a debatable question. Nothing can be said, however, for the attitude of those Protectionists who argued that the famine in Ireland was purely imaginary. The famine was at any rate real enough to cause nearly a million deaths—mostly in 1847, the year after the blight ended. On the one hand, Repeal of the Corn Laws did not in itself greatly ease the famine, which also defied relief works like road-building, large-scale charitable subscriptions and the granting of outdoor poor relief. All the same, it did something, for it enabled more of the better-off peasants to afford wheat, and so release potatoes for the poor. It also kept down the price of the American maize which the Government imported and retailed cheaply— an unpopular but useful commodity rapidly nicknamed 'Peel's Brimstone'. Above all, Peel was psychologically right in his action, for at a time of famine any artificial restriction on the price of food was doubly resented, and might even have caused revolution.

Finally, on the broad question of general results—and it must be remembered that Peel regarded the Irish famine as only the 'last straw' which broke the back of the Corn Laws—Repeal did not quite justify the prophecies of either supporters or opponents. On the one hand British agriculture was not at once doomed by foreign competition—in fact, for the next thirty years it flourished as rarely before, enjoying a good though not excessive price for corn. This was because there was no great surplus of corn in Europe or elsewhere available at that time to flood the British market. Not till the opening of the great new sources of supply in the prairies of North America during the 1870s was British agriculture exposed to the full blast of competition—and then indeed some form of protection might have been beneficial. On the other hand, the claims of the Repealers were not fully justified —wheat did not drop sensationally in price, but was often quite as dear as before Repeal. The fact, however, that there was a general rise in prices of almost all commodities *except* corn during the next generation shows that the repeal of the Corn Laws, if it did not directly lower the price of food, at least stopped it from rising as it would otherwise have done. On the whole there can be little doubt that Repeal was a great social benefit, for it kept the price of bread at a reasonable level, and removed what many people felt to be a glaring injustice. Also, as Peel said, in many cases Protection simply led to slack and unintelligent farming.

But these were matters to be settled in the future. In 1846 the Conservative rank and file could not see beyond certain facts of the moment—that Peel had opposed Catholic emancipation, and then helped Wellington to carry it; had opposed Parliamentary Reform, and then accepted it; had opposed Corn Law Repeal—and then forced it through. It was too much. He had 'betrayed' his party, and therefore most of his party would have no more of him. But for the country his retirement and death were sad losses. Not for twenty years did a Prime Minister of comparable stature emerge.

12. Whig and Conservative Foreign Policy, 1830-1846

The Belgian revolt, 1830

The Paris rising of July 1830 not only brought the constitutionally minded Louis Philippe to the throne of France; it also touched off a revolution next door. Within a month the Belgians, weary of the unprofitable union with Holland which had been forced on them by the Vienna treaties, revolted against their Dutch ruler and declared their independence. Confronted with these events Wellington and his Foreign Secretary, Lord Aberdeen, very sensibly recognized Louis Philippe and secured his agreement to a policy of non-intervention in Belgium. A European Conference then met in London, an armistice was fixed up in Belgium, and the separation of that country from Holland was more or less agreed to by everyone except the Dutch.

At this stage Wellington fell from power and the Whigs came in. The Foreign Secretary selected by Grey was a newcomer to the Whig party—a Canningite Tory who had fallen out with the Duke over Catholic emancipation and parliamentary reform. For eighteen years he had occupied the minor position of Secretary-at-War in Tory Cabinets; henceforth Viscount Palmerston was never to be far from the centre of the stage.

Palmerston

The first task before Palmerston was to liquidate the Belgian affair. There was no agreement as yet on two vital questions—who was to rule the new state, and what were to be its boundaries? The danger of this was that at any moment the Belgians, if dissatisfied on these points, might appeal to the French, with whom they had linguistic and racial ties; and that the French, stepping in to help the Belgians, would remain to help themselves. This would leave a major naval power occupying the Belgian coast, and so violate a constant object of British foreign policy. It would also cause a European war, since none of the other great powers would stand idly by and watch fresh expansion on the part of France. Palmerston's problem was thus to secure Belgian independence from Holland, while avoiding war and keeping the new state free from French influence.

The process by which the Foreign Secretary achieved his ends was long and tortuous, but in the end it was completely successful. When the Belgians voted for a son of Louis Philippe as their new king, Palmerston took a strong line, and Louis Philippe, whose main anxiety was to establish his dynasty safely in France, cautiously declined the offer. Palmerston then managed to secure the selection of a more acceptable monarch, Leopold of Saxe-Coburg, who besides coming from a small state had the incidental advantage of being the favourite uncle of the future Queen Victoria. Then there was another crisis when the Dutch refused to recognize the new ruler and marched into Belgium. Their action was checked, with Palmerston's agreement, by the use of French troops. Once in Belgium, however, the French forces showed signs of staying there, so once again Palmerston acted energetically, and in concert with Prussia and Russia forced the French to retire. Various other complications followed, and not until 1839 was the whole incident wound up. In that year the Dutch finally recognized the loss of Belgium on condition that Luxemburg was retained by the Dutch crown. At the same time the European powers signed a treaty guaranteeing Belgian independence and integrity.[1] Thus, all told, Palmerston had scored a notable success—a European war avoided, and the infant Belgian kingdom preserved from the clutches of France.

King Leopold

Belgian independence guaranteed, 1839

There was plenty more to occupy Palmerston during these years, from helping to settle the ruler and boundaries of the new Greek kingdom to keeping Austria and France from clashing over revolts in Italy. He also gave valuable diplomatic support to the constitutional rule of the young Queens of Spain and Portugal, and helped to secure them against movements led by reactionary princes. The Polish attempt to throw off the Russian yoke in 1830 found him full of sympathy, but nothing more—Russia's behaviour might be objectionable, but there was no point in offending her needlessly, and there was no direct 'British interest' concerned. Besides, the British Navy would have found it very difficult to influence the fortunes of a campaign in Poland.

Minor problems —Greece, Italy, Spain, Portugal, Poland

All these were minor matters compared with the crisis in the Near East. Bitterly resenting the Sultan of Turkey's failure to pay the price of Egyptian help in the Greek War of Independence, Mehemet Ali in 1831 launched an expedition under his son Ibrahim Pasha against the Sultan's domain of Syria. Ibrahim swept through Palestine and Syria at such a pace that he soon

Egyptian invasion of Syria, 1831

[1] It was this treaty, in a renewed version, which the Germans violated when they invaded Belgium in 1914. See page 242.

threatened the heart of Turkey itself, while other Egyptian forces occupied most of Arabia. There was only one power which could intervene quickly enough to save the Sultan—and that was Turkey's great enemy, Russia. To Russia the Sultan therefore turned: 'a drowning man', the Turkish Foreign Minister remarked, 'will clutch at a serpent.' The serpent—for appropriately serpentine reasons—duly lent its aid, and the forces of Nicholas I barred Ibrahim's path to Constantinople. They did nothing, however, to disturb the Egyptian occupation of Syria and Arabia. The serpent then claimed—and received—his reward. By a secret clause of the Treaty of Unkiar-Skelessi, Turkey agreed to close the Bosphorus and the Dardanelles to foreign warships whenever Russia requested her to do so. The vital passage between the Black Sea and the Mediterranean thus came virtually under Russian control.

Russian intervention

Treaty of Unkiar-Skelessi, 1833

The secret articles soon came to Palmerston's ears—they were revealed by a patriotic Turk—but the British Foreign Secretary had to wait some time for an opportunity to wipe out Russia's advantage. His chance did not come until 1839, when on the death of the Sultan he persuaded the Powers that the Syrian question should be settled by their collective action.

Death of the Sultan—Palmerston calls a European Conference

The clash with France

Palmerston now faced the difficulty that France, as her chosen means of re-establishing her influence in the Eastern Mediterranean, was backing Mehemet Ali. Anxious at once to keep France out of this area and to destroy Russian influence at Constantinople, Palmerston aimed at bolstering up the Sultan's power and leaving Turkey indebted to Britain. He therefore went behind the back of France and fixed up an agreement with Russia, Prussia and Austria by which Mehemet Ali was to be turned out of Northern Syria. This at once brought threats of war from France —threats which alarmed Queen Victoria and shook the Cabinet, but which failed to make the slightest impression on the Foreign Secretary. Some Austro-British aid to a local revolt, and the presence of a British fleet in the Eastern Mediterranean, soon resulted in the expulsion of the Egyptians from Syria. And at the critical moment France climbed down, as Palmerston had always thought she would. The obstinate Mehemet Ali was then further punished by the loss of his other conquests.

Expulsion of Egyptians from Syria

Restoration of Mehemet's conquests to the Sultan

These considerable services to the Turkish cause were rewarded by a new Straits Convention. By this Turkey agreed to close the Bosphorus and the Dardanelles to the warships of all nations in

The Straits Convention, 1841

time of peace,[1] and so abolished the exclusive rights enjoyed by the Russians under the terms of Unkiar-Skelessi. Palmerston's triumph was thus complete. His bold diplomacy had set the Ottoman Empire on its feet again, and thereby reduced French and Russian chances of expanding at Turkey's expense. It had even resulted in a useful little acquisition for Britain, since the ruler of Aden had accepted a British 'protectorate' to save himself from Mehemet Ali. And all this had been accomplished without a war between the major powers, and with very little loss of British life. **Aden, 1839**

The Foreign Secretary's strong arm was soon felt even further afield. His anxiety to keep Russian expansion well short of India led to long-enduring complications in Afghanistan,[2] but before he left office in 1841 he had seen a quarrel with China well on its way to a thoroughly Palmerstonian settlement. **The Far East**

The events which brought on the 'Opium War' with China resulted on the one hand from the anxiety of the Chinese authorities to preserve their country from Western influence and commerce, and on the other from the determination of Western merchants—especially British merchants—to enjoy unrestricted trade with the East. This situation—which was repeated later in the century with Japan—was complicated by the desire of the Emperor Tao-Kwang to suppress the increasing importation of opium from India. This was not only demoralizing great numbers of Chinese, but was draining the country of much valuable silver, tea and silk in exchange. Matters finally came to a head in 1839, when the Chinese Government seized all British-owned opium in Canton and prohibited trade with Britain. **The 'Opium War' with China, 1840–1842**

Such an incident was exactly the kind of affair Palmerston rejoiced to handle, for British subjects were in need of protection and the opponent was no match for the Royal Navy. Brushing aside Gladstone's moral objections to forcing opium on the Chinese, he maintained that the ban against imported opium was merely a racket organized by the local Chinese opium manufacturers. He accordingly despatched a demand to Pekin for reparation and guarantees of future good behaviour, together with compensation for the stocks of confiscated British opium. The Chinese refused concessions, and a war then broke out in which Canton was bombarded and Chinese resistance broken.

It was left to Peel's Government to harvest the fruits of this

---

[1] Obviously he would open them to his allies in time of war.
[2] See page 397.

Treaty of
Nanking, 1842

activity in the Treaty of Nanking, by which all financial claims
were paid, including that for the confiscated opium, Hong Kong
was ceded to Great Britain, and five ports (including Shanghai
and Canton) were to be open for foreign trade under reasonable
tariffs. A year later the British were also granted 'extra-territorial
rights'—i.e. they were recognized as not subject to ordinary
Chinese law and law-courts. The 'Opium War' thus proved very
profitable. The fact that it entailed the bitter hostility of the
Chinese for many years to come did not specially worry Palmerston or most other Englishmen—China was not strong enough to
count in international affairs.

★ ★ ★ ★ ★

Peel's Second
Ministry: Lord
Aberdeen at the
Foreign Office

When Peel and the Conservatives took over from Melbourne
and the Whigs in 1841, Palmerston was succeeded at the Foreign
Office by Lord Aberdeen. The new Foreign Secretary, a quiet,
cultured Scot, had occupied the position once before under
Wellington.[1]

After the Chinese war had been wound up, there were the
troubles in Afghanistan and India[2] to deal with. The greatest
danger, however, was a crisis with the United States over the

The U.S.A.
boundary
dispute

Canadian boundary. To draw a frontier some 4,000 miles long
was obviously no easy matter, though a step of the greatest importance had been taken in 1817 when Castlereagh and the United

Early agree-
ments of 1817
and 1818

States agreed to abolish all fortifications and navies on the one
obvious boundary, the Great Lakes. The following year it had
been agreed that the boundary west from the Lake of the Woods
to the Rocky Mountains should follow the line of latitude 49
degrees. From the Rockies to the Pacific Coast, however, was left
'open ground', as it was so little occupied—though Pitt had
thought it worth saving from Spain during the Nootka Sound

Oregon

incident.[3] It was this huge area—known at the time as Oregon,
and bounded by the Rockies on the east, the Pacific on the west,
Russian Alaska on the north and California (then belonging to
Mexico) on the south—which now came under dispute. Obviously its strategic importance was very great, since complete
possession by the United States would shut British North America
off from the Pacific—and vice versa.

The Ashburton–
Webster
agreement

An older quarrel about the boundary between Maine and New
Brunswick was patched up successfully when Peel and Aberdeen
sent Lord Ashburton, a banker, on a special mission to reach

---

[1] See page 142.   [2] See page 397.   [3] See page 32.

agreement. The American negotiator, Webster, was also a banker, and between them the two financial experts arranged a compromise where all other efforts had failed. They also cleared up other matters of dispute, and left only the Oregon boundary as an outstanding question between the United States and Britain. This blazed up into dangerous proportions when Polk was elected President of the United States in 1844—for one of Polk's election slogans had been 'Fifty-four forty or fight'. The United States, in other words, were seriously claiming the whole of the Oregon area, for the line of latitude 54° 40' was the southern boundary of Russian Alaska. As against this Peel and Aberdeen urged the adoption of a boundary continuing the 49th parallel of latitude to the River Columbia, and thence following the river (i.e. south of 49°) to the sea. In negotiation Aberdeen eventually offered a boundary along 49° right up to the coast, except for a small deviation south to include Vancouver Island in British territory. Beyond this he would not yield, and Polk finally climbed down. Thus the last boundary question between Britain and the United States was safely disposed of, and Aberdeen could justly claim that the way was cleared for the growth of friendlier relations between the two countries.

President Polk: 'Fifty-four forty or fight'

The dispute settled: latitude 49°

The other great contribution to peace made by the Conservatives between 1841 and 1846 was the development of the Entente with France. The harmonious relations disturbed by Palmerston over the Syrian crisis were restored, and close friendship was established between the two ruling houses when Victoria and Albert, accompanied by Aberdeen, paid a visit to France in 1843 —the first by an English monarch since the time of Henry VIII. It was the good understanding between Aberdeen and the French minister Guizot which enabled a dispute over Tahiti to be settled without recourse to war.

The Entente with France

Tahiti

The methods of Aberdeen had very little in common with those of his predecessor. The downfall of Peel in 1846 was consequently greeted with dismay by ministries all over Europe, who knew that the return of the Whigs would mean the return of the dreaded Palmerston. Even the most pessimistic foreign government could hardly have guessed, however, that it would have to put up with Palmerston's activities almost uninterruptedly for another twenty years.

Return of Palmerston, 1846

13. Party Transition and Social Progress

1 The Ministries, 1846–1868

The party
groups

One of the few undeniable effects of the repeal of the Corn Laws was that it hopelessly divided the Conservative party. As a result Parliament for some years contained no less than five main groups. These were the Conservative Protectionists, led by Stanley, Bentinck and Disraeli; the Conservative Free Traders, led by Peel, Aberdeen and Gladstone; the Whigs, led by Russell and Palmerston; the Radicals, led by Cobden and Bright; and the Irish. Of these the Radicals usually supported the Whigs, but sometimes bitterly assailed them; the Irish supported whichever party—usually the Whigs—they thought would concede most to Irish demands; and the Peelites hovered uneasily between Conservatism and Whiggism. The shifting about of these groups explains why ministries in this period were not stable—why, in fact, there were no less than nine of them in just over twenty years.

Russell's first
Ministry (Whig),
1846–1852;
Derby's first
Ministry (Con-
servative), 1852;
Aberdeen's
Ministry (Whig-
Peelite Coali-
tion), 1852–1855

The Whigs began with a long spell of office under Russell. Then came the Conservatives under Derby, with Disraeli as Leader of the House of Commons and Chancellor of the Exchequer,[1] but they had no workable majority and fell within a few months. In the weakness of all parties a Coalition of the Whigs and Peelite Conservatives under Aberdeen was next tried, only to break up under the stress of the Crimean War. The Queen was then compelled to turn to the detested Palmerston, for whom the country was clamouring in the crisis. And Palmerston—though he was labelled by Disraeli 'an impostor, utterly exhausted, at the best only ginger-beer and not champagne, and now an old painted pantaloon, very deaf, very blind, and with false teeth which would fall out of his mouth if he did not hesitate and halt so in his talk'—was to dominate the political scene for the next ten years!

---

[1] He knew nothing of finance but accepted the position because, as Derby said, 'they give you the figures'.

Palmerston's first Ministry, which was almost entirely a Whig affair, ran from 1855 to 1858. It was followed by another brief Conservative interlude under Derby and Disraeli, but once more they lacked a majority, and by 1859 Palmerston was back in office. This time he had the support of the Peelites, and the Ministry lasted until 1865, when death at last removed the aged player from the stage.

After Palmerston's death Russell became Prime Minister for the second time. The Ministry saw the fusion of the Whigs, Peelites and Radicals into a more or less united party—the Liberals. When Russell retired from politics in 1867 the leadership of this amalgamation fell to Gladstone, whose work at the Exchequer had been outstandingly successful.

· Before Gladstone and the Liberals could come into their own, however, there was the third Derby Ministry. This was almost as powerless and pointless as the other administrations of that brilliant but largely ineffective aristocrat, who regarded politics as a boring duty and whose real interests were billiards, horse-racing and Homer. However, one measure of great importance was passed—the Second Reform Act of 1867.[1]

In 1868 Derby retired for reasons of health, and Disraeli achieved his ambition of becoming Prime Minister. But he was still virtually powerless, and the general election of that year gave his opponents, the Liberals, an excellent working majority of over a hundred seats. At last a strong unified party, under a strong leader, was about to take over. With the formation of Gladstone's first Government, a period begins in which the kaleidoscope settles down for a little, party issues are suddenly clear-cut, tremendous antagonists battle across the floor of the House, and the dates of ministries become much easier to remember.

Marginal notes: Palmerston's first Ministry (Whig),1855–1858. Derby's second Ministry (Conservative), 1858–1859. Palmerston's second Ministry (Whig-Peelite Coalition), 1859–1865. Russell's second Ministry (Liberal) 1865-1866. Derby's third Ministry (Conservative), 1866–1868. The Second Reform Act, 1867. Disraeli's first Ministry (Conservative), 1868. The Liberals in power.

2 Social and Industrial Reform

Compared with the years 1832–46 the period 1846–68 seems at first sight lacking in outstanding reforms. The governments of this latter period did not, for the most part, possess large enough majorities to carry great controversial measures, even had they wanted to; and in any case the high level of commercial prosperity made the demand for changes less keen. All the same, valuable

[1] See page 162.

steps were taken, mostly along paths already marked out. The three directions in which reform progressed most rapidly were the social and industrial, the financial, and the parliamentary.

When Russell came in with the Whigs in 1846, Fielden and Ashley renewed their struggle to achieve a ten-hour day in the mills. In 1847, with a great deal of Government support, Fielden managed to persuade Parliament to accept the proposal, and the great fight was at last over—or so it seemed.

Fielden's Factory
Act, 1847 (The
Ten Hours Act)

The echoes of Fielden's triumph were still ringing when ingenious employers, aided of course by still more ingenious lawyers, discovered a loophole in the new Ten Hours concession. The Act was not, of course, officially for the benefit of men operatives at all, but everyone knew that the men reckoned to benefit indirectly by the restriction of hours for women and young persons, since it did not pay to work a factory by male labour alone. When women's labour was restricted to ten hours many employers therefore began to adopt a kind of relay system, by which no more than ten hours' work was demanded in the day from any given woman or young person, but by which some of them were 'stood off' work for an hour or two in the morning, others for an hour or two in the afternoon, and so on. With some female and juvenile labour available throughout the fifteen hours a mill was normally open, the men could thus be kept working, with the exception of a break for lunch, for the whole of this time.

Evasion of the
intention of the
Ten Hours Act

The campaign for a strict ten hours was therefore resumed by Ashley. Unfortunately he lacked the support and guidance of Fielden, who had been defeated at the general election and died shortly afterwards. Doubting whether Parliament would agree to any fresh restriction, Ashley accepted a 'compromise' which was bitterly resented by the workers. In return for a clause that the labour of women and young persons might be taken only between 6 a.m. and 6 p.m. (2 p.m. on Saturdays) Ashley agreed on a ten-and-a-half-hour day instead of the ten-hour day. These terms were embodied in Grey's[1] Factory Act of 1850, much to the annoyance of operatives whose employers had never introduced the relay system, and whose labour was now increased by half an hour a day.

Ashley's
compromise

Grey's Factory
Act, 1850
(Ten-and-a-half
Hours)

Although Ashley's leadership of the shorter hours movement was now rejected by the textile workers, his services to the cause of factory reform had not yet ended. The early Acts had been confined to textile factories because they were the biggest and

[1] Sir George Grey was Home Secretary in Russell's Ministry.

most obvious factories of the time. It soon became plain, however, that conditions in many other trades were equally bad, or
worse, and Ashley now interested himself in extending the
benefit of the Factory Acts to workers in these industries.

Extension of
Factory Acts to
other industries

The first group of such trades was those in some way associated
with textile manufacture, and already by 1845, in Peel's Ministry,
Ashley had succeeded in extending the provisions of the 1844

(John Leech, 1849, reproduced by permission of the Proprietors of 'Punch')

PIN MONEY   NEEDLE MONEY

The gulf between rich and poor in Victorian Britain was very great. The leisured 'lady' has
pin (pocket) money to spend on jewels; the poor sempstress stitches from morn till night
in an attic, and still starves. The cartoon was inspired by the revelation that many London
sempstresses were receiving only 1½d. for making a shirt.

act to calico-printing. During Palmerston's second Ministry,
Ashley—or Shaftesbury, as he should now be called—enjoyed a
good deal of support from the Prime Minister, with whom he was
connected by marriage. This helped to secure protection—always
officially confined to women and children—for workers engaged
in bleaching, dyeing and lace-making. Palmerston also agreed to
set up a commission to enquire into general conditions of child
employment. This body revealed deplorable conditions in many

Calico-printing
(1845)

Bleaching and
dyeing (1860):
Lace manufac-
ture (1861)

The potteries
and the match
industry (1864)

General factory
protection

The Public
Health Act, 1848

Better treat-
ment of lunatics

Campaign
against employ-
ment of 'climb-
ing boys'

Evasion of the
1840 Act

industries—such as children of six working fifteen hours a day in pottery works, or women developing 'phossy jaw' from their work in match factories. The potteries and the match industry were included in the Factory Acts of 1864, while three years later Disraeli extended protection to those employed in any sort of workshop of a given size.[1]

Shaftesbury's benevolent activities were not confined to factory reform. Together with Chadwick and Dr Southwood Smith he succeeded in inducing Russell's Government, by the Public Health Act of 1848, to set up a Board of Health. The Board soon earned great unpopularity through its interference with local authorities, for neither Chadwick nor Shaftesbury, who were both members, was exactly tactful in his dealings, and opposition swept it away in 1854. But if it had not remedied appalling conditions, it had at least revealed them, and later approaches to the subject were better thought out and more successful.

Another great work of Shaftesbury's was the improved treatment of lunatics. As a Lunacy Commissioner for the greater part of his life, he was largely responsible for showing up the terrible conditions in both public and private asylums, and he constantly strove to abolish such inhumanities as chaining up, overcrowding, insanitary quarters, and unjustified certification. He waged a ceaseless war against neglect and cruelty in every form, and no one did more to enforce the vital principle of public inspection or control.

The 'climbing boys' employed by sweeps were another class to feel the benefit of Shaftesbury's wide pity. Here a well-known evil had persisted in spite of legislation from 1778 onwards designed to control it. The virtual selling of boys of six or seven to sweeps, the beatings to induce the young beginner to start his trade, the soakings in brine to harden bleeding knees and elbows, the deaths from suffocation or eventual consumption—all these horrors had been made public hundreds of times. An Act passed by Melbourne's Government (under pressure from Shaftesbury) had stated quite clearly that no one less than twenty-one years of age should climb a chimney, and that no boy less than sixteen should be apprenticed to a sweep. Yet this law, in spite of the great impression created by Dickens's *Oliver Twist* and later by Kingsley's *Water Babies*, was widely evaded. Housewives insisted that boys caused less dirt on the furniture than 'sweep-

---

[1] The ten-hour day was finally granted in 1874, during Disraeli's second Ministry. See page 190.

(Cruikshank, 1814, from a print in the British Museum)

WILLIAM NORRIS IN BETHLEM

In 1814 an official enquiry into conditions in Bethlem (Bethlehem or 'Bedlam') Hospital for the Insane revealed that one William Norris, an inmate who varied long rational periods with fits of violence, and who had fallen foul of his warder, had been kept in irons for over twelve years. An iron ring had been riveted round his neck, and this was attached by a short chain to a vertical iron bar on the wall, so that he could stand or sit, but not move away. Another iron band was riveted round his body and by means of projections to this his arms were pinioned to his sides. He could lie down only on his back. The investigators also discovered that many of the other patients were chained up, or naked, or kept in the dark; and that the House Surgeon, besides being frequently drunk, was himself insane.

ing machines', and property owners declined to rebuild their chimneys so that 'machines' could replace boy labour; so sweeps went on employing young boys—officially to carry the brushes, but actually to climb the chimneys. Magistrates were reluctant to convict, in spite of the evidence, for they were the very class whose large houses and rambling chimneys would have needed the most alteration.

Shaftesbury devoted years of labour and agitation to remedying this state of affairs. In 1864, in Palmerston's second Ministry, he secured a further measure by which sweeps were forbidden to employ boys under ten except on their own premises, or to allow boys under sixteen to be with them in a house where the chimney was being swept. But even this was ignored until a system of licensing was introduced in 1875. The police were specially charged to take notice of offences by sweeps, and any offence against the Acts of 1840 and 1864 was to debar the sweep from a licence to exercise his trade. After this the evil of climbing boys soon ceased. It had taken roughly a hundred years of agitation to achieve this simple reform.

Reform in factories, mines, lunatic asylums and chimney-sweeping, together with his lifelong interest in 'Ragged' schools —these were Shaftesbury's greatest achievements. Occasionally his moral fervour resulted in needless restrictions, as when he secured legislation against ritualism in the churches or campaigned successfully against the Sunday opening of the British Museum. These were the less amiable features of a great man, but it must be remembered that his evangelical churchmanship inspired his social reforms as well as his harsh religious creed, and that for Shaftesbury the one would have been impossible without the other.

Side by side with these efforts to improve conditions by legislation went a number of attempts at improvement by methods of self-help. In contrast to the mass of private industrial enterprises, there appeared, for instance, a new form of organization which aimed at securing the advantages of capitalism and large-scale operations while avoiding ownership by private persons. This experiment was co-operation, fathered in Britain by that great social reformer, Robert Owen.[1] His idea was that the whole of industry should come under the control of the workers, each factory being controlled and run by the men who worked in it. Early attempts to put into practice this idea of producers'

A further ineffective Act, 1864

Licences for sweeps, 1875

The co-operative movement

[1] See pages 120 and 123.

co-operation failed. Far different was the outcome of the scheme of consumers' co-operation launched in 1844 when twenty-eight flannel weavers set up a store in Toad (T'owd) Lane, Rochdale. Subscribing one pound each as capital, they decided to cut out the shopkeepers' profits by buying goods in bulk at wholesale prices, and distributing them without profit. As the scheme

The Rochdale pioneers, 1844

(Cruikshank, 1819, from a print in the British Museum)

PRETTY BOB   POOR BOB

The well-fed youngster becomes a sweep's 'climbing-boy', and suffers a tragic transformation.

developed, shops were set up where goods were sold at normal retail prices, the profits being shared among the customers as 'dividend' according to the amount of their purchases during the year. One result was to check adulteration, so widely practised then by ordinary shopkeepers, for the 'co-op.' had no reason to swindle its customers by adding water to their butter, sand to sugar, brickdust to pepper, or sulphuric acid to vinegar. The movement grew, especially in the north of England, until today the co-operative societies have many millions of members.

A similar effort in another field was the rise of the mutual benefit societies, often known as friendly societies. They were strongly devoted to the cause of temperance, and began to flourish from about 1840. In return for a modest weekly contribution, a working man could secure a relief payment when he was sick or otherwise unemployed, and a grant to cover funeral expenses at his death. The societies' business was administered largely by the members in their spare time, and so they provided wholesome practice in democratic control, while their names and ceremonies added cheer to working-class life—the Ancient Order of Foresters, the Royal and Ancient Order of Buffaloes, the Hearts of Oak. Some of the trade unions offered similar benefits, and private insurance companies,[1] working for profit, later entered the same field. Further means of thrift were also provided by savings banks —the Post Office Savings Bank was founded in 1861—and by the spread of life insurance.

3 Financial and Commercial Reform

If Shaftesbury was the dominant figure in social reform in the mid-nineteenth century, Gladstone soon became as unquestionably the leader in public finance. Like Peel, William Ewart Gladstone was the representative not of the old landed aristocracy but of the newer commercial and industrial forces. The son of a very wealthy Scottish corn merchant and shipowner who had settled in Liverpool and become a Tory M.P., he was educated at Eton and Oxford, and at the university achieved the same distinction as Peel—a 'double-first' in classics and mathematics. Entering Parliament in 1833 at the age of twenty-four, he had held minor office a year later under Peel, when his views were so far from liberalism that Macaulay described him as 'the last hope of the stern unbending Tories'.

In Peel's great Ministry of 1841–46, Gladstone had become President of the Board of Trade, where he gave powerful aid to Peel's policy of tariff reduction. After the death of Peel in 1850 he and Aberdeen stood out as the leaders of the Free Trade

[1] The Prudential started in 1848, and by 1900 14 million of its policies were current.

wing in their party. Their identity of view with the Whigs on this matter led to Aberdeen's Whig-Peelite Coalition of 1852, in which Gladstone served as Chancellor of the Exchequer.

Chancellor of the Exchequer, 1852–1855

In Gladstone's capable hands, finance was undoubtedly the most successful part of the otherwise ineffective Aberdeen Government. The Chancellor's views were comparatively simple —as little as possible must be spent, since government expenditure was nearly always devoted to undesirable purposes, such as armaments or warfare. To this end, and to enable manufacturers to produce cheaply and keep down the cost of living, taxation must be reduced to a minimum. Certainly no one has ever gone further than Gladstone towards this ideal. In his great budget of 1853 he abolished many duties on foodstuffs and semi-manufactured goods, besides halving nearly all duties on wholly manufactured goods. He also planned to reduce income tax until it should finally disappear in 1860. This taxpayer's dream was unfortunately shattered by the Crimean War, which sent income tax up from 7d. to 1s. 2d. in the pound.

Reduction of duties

Reduction of income tax

From 1855 to 1859 Gladstone was a somewhat isolated figure in politics, since he disliked Palmerston for his foreign policy almost as much as he detested Disraeli for his attacks on Peel. But in 1859 he threw in his lot with Palmerston, in whom he discovered a common enthusiasm for Italian liberation, and once more accepted the position of Chancellor of the Exchequer. Thenceforward he was associated with the Whigs and Radicals, until on the retirement of Russell in 1867 he stood forth as the leader of the new party formed by the fusion of Peelites, Whigs and Radicals—the Liberals.

Gladstone's isolation, 1855–1859

He joins Palmerston

Just as the Crimean War had ruined the brightest of Gladstone's earlier hopes, so his later work at the Exchequer was threatened when the activities of Napoleon III led to revived— but largely groundless—fears of France. Much to the fury of Cobden, Bright and the 'Manchester School' generally, Palmerston played on the public fears and demanded more battleships, together with fortifications for British dockyards. Panic waxed high, companies of volunteers were formed, and the Poet Laureate, Tennyson, with his sensitiveness to Victorian opinion, promptly obliged with an appropriate set of verses—*Riflemen, form.* All this was hateful to Gladstone, who thought the scare unjustified and likely to lead directly to war. In any case, Palmerston's proposals would involve increased public expenditure, and must be resisted. The nation was consequently presented with the

Chancellor of the Exchequer, 1859–1866

The French scare

Chancellor v.
Prime Minister
strange spectacle of the Chancellor of the Exchequer allying with
Cobden and Bright to outwit the Prime Minister.

The strategy of the attack on Palmerston was partly direct
(threats of resignation by Gladstone, who knew he was very
important to the Ministry) and partly indirect. The threats of
resignation—Palmerston said he set his chimney on fire with
them—came to little, for the Prime Minister declared that he
'would sooner lose Mr Gladstone than lose Plymouth'. The indirect approach took the form of an effort to allay tension by a
The Cobden
Treaty, 1860
commercial agreement between Britain and France. For this
purpose Gladstone sent Cobden to Paris, where he used his
unrivalled powers of persuasion on the Emperor and his
ministers. Cobden's object was to prevent war rather than to
score a success for British industry—'I would not step across the
street, just now, to increase our trade', he wrote to Gladstone.
'We have about as much prosperity as we can bear.' Ultimately
it was agreed that Britain and France should treat each other on
'most favoured nation' terms, while in return for a big reduction
of British duties on French wines and brandy, the French agreed
to lower their duties on British coal and a wide range of manufactured goods. The treaty certainly led to an expansion of trade,
for in the next ten years imports of French wine and exports of
British goods to France both doubled. Certainly too, it aided the
cause of peace and promoted friendlier feeling—though the panic
lasted until 1861 and Palmerston had his way about the fortifications and the ships.

Further
reduction of
duties
Besides concluding the commercial treaty with France, Gladstone swept away further duties, till there were only sixteen that
really mattered. Two of these were on tea and sugar, and both
were drastically scaled down. He also insisted—against the wishes
Repeal of
paper tax, 1861
of the Prime Minister—on repealing the paper tax, which he
termed 'a tax on knowledge', since it made books and newspapers
dear. Yet in spite of all this he managed to reduce income tax
Virtual
completion of
free trade
again until it stood at sixpence. In sum, by the time of Palmerston's death Britain was virtually a free-trade country, governed
with extraordinary economy at a cost of about £65,000,000 a
year.[1]

Financial
organization
These changes in national policy were accompanied by corresponding changes in the organization of commerce and industry.
In the early stages of the Industrial Revolution, the capital cost

[1] This may be contrasted with an expenditure of roughly £950,000,000
in 1938, or £6,000,000,000 in 1962.

of building a factory and equipping it with plant was met by a single individual out of his savings, or by a few individuals clubbing together as partners, or by borrowing from a bank. These homely methods, however, would not finance great undertakings like the railways that were built with such feverish energy and at such huge cost in the 1840s. So the joint-stock company, familiar already as a way of financing external trade, became a favourite device. Its drawback was that if it went bankrupt, the whole property of an investor might be seized in order to give satisfaction to the company's creditors. By Acts passed in 1856 and 1862 all companies were allowed the privilege of 'limited liability' if they followed certain reasonable rules. If a company should fail, the investor's liability would be limited to the sum he had invested, and so savings large and small could be invested with more safety.

Joint-stock companies

Limited liability

The new system attracted large amounts of capital, and created a class of people remote from the actual work of production who were interested in industry purely as owners. While the number of persons interested in each company thus tended to grow larger, the number of companies was growing smaller, and their scale of operation more extended. As the use of complicated machinery increased, so did the capital outlay, and there was little scope for the small firm.

Larger scale of undertakings

4 Chartism and Parliamentary Reform

The Chartist fiasco of 1839 had not killed the movement for further reform of parliament, though it had spoilt its chances of success. For some time to come only the broken and disorganized ranks of the Chartists took the subject seriously. In 1842 a second Chartist petition, containing 3,300,000 signatures, was presented to Parliament, and again rejected; and equally unavailing was the wave of strikes in the north known as the Plug Plot,[1] which had begun as a protest against wage cuts and expanded into an effort to enforce the Charter. Thereafter agitation died down for a few years, and many Chartists—though not Lovett or O'Connor—lent their energies to the far more efficiently run campaign against the Corn Laws. But in 1847, soon after Russell came into power,

The second Chartist petition and the 'Plug Plot', 1842

[1] The strikers marched from factory to factory knocking out boiler plugs. Peel's Government took a firm line: several hundred strikers were arrested, and seventy-nine were transported to Australia.

another slump occurred, and once more the working class turned to Chartism.

Revival of
Chartism,
1847-1848

A sign of the rising tide came with the election to Parliament of O'Connor. Then, in February 1848, came the news of the overthrow of Louis Philippe and the formation of the Second French Republic. When this was followed by the crash of governments all over Europe, with Italian and German princes, the King of Prussia, and even the Austrian Emperor compelled to accept popular demands, the excitement of the Chartists knew no bounds. They immediately set about organizing a third monster petition and electing another Convention. O'Connor even drew up a proposed constitution for a British Republic—with himself as President. The petition to Parliament was to be presented by a great procession on 10 April 1848, starting from Kennington Common.

The third
Chartist
petition, 1848

By now Russell's Government was seriously alarmed, fearing that the procession would be the signal for a general revolution. The Duke of Wellington, nearly eighty years old, was entrusted with the defence of London. Troops were called in, and thousands of special constables were enrolled from the middle and upper classes. The most interesting of these additions to the forces of law and order was the future Napoleon III, who was very appropriately given a beat on Piccadilly. The Government, which at first forbade both meeting and procession, ultimately sanctioned the meeting, while making special arrangements to hold the bridges over the Thames should the demonstrators try to approach Parliament. O'Connor thereupon made a speech to the assembled crowds at Kennington, and then proceeded to Westminster alone, bearing the petition, estimated by the Chartists to contain 6,000,000 signatures, in three cabs. In so inglorious a fashion did the vast demonstration end, while to complete the discomfiture the authorities at Westminster announced that the names supporting the petition were fewer than 2,000,000—and that, even so, many of them were forgeries. Some of the signatures were in the same handwriting, and others purported to be those of Peel, Wellington, Queen Victoria, and Mr Punch!

Chartist
disturbances

In spite of the ridicule which now submerged the movement, some of the extremists still stuck to their guns. One determined leader planned riots in the suburbs of London on Whit Monday, 1848, to occupy the police while a confederate led a great crowd from Bishop Bonner's Fields (now Victoria Park, Bethnal Green) to attack Whitehall. The police, however, discovered the plan and blocked the exits from the Fields; and as it poured with rain the dispirited crowd was only too glad to go home. A final plot by a few desperate men to seize London on 15 August was betrayed by the *agent provocateur* who had largely created it, and some more Chartists were transported.

Nothing had gone right for the Chartists from first to last in 1848, and the last blow came when O'Connor's Land Company —a scheme to settle town workers as smallholders in the country —was declared bankrupt. For some time now his brain had been plainly softening. In 1852 he was confined to an asylum, and three years later he died. The last large Chartist gathering was that which attended the funeral of the man who had done so much to wreck the cause he cared for.[1]

Death of O'Connor

After 1850 widespread trading prosperity and increased emigration helped to lessen that economic distress which was at the bottom of Chartism. The movement for parliamentary reform therefore continued on much milder and more respectable levels. Several rather half-hearted attempts to alter the franchise qualification were made by the various parliamentary leaders, but they failed for lack of any general agreement on the details. Palmerston in particular was lukewarm about the need for further reform, and it was not until after his death in 1865 that the Whigs, under Russell, again took up the subject seriously. At the same time Bright, the Radical, believing that many of the working class would use their votes, if they had them, to support a more 'moral' foreign policy than Palmerston's, organized a renewed campaign in the country.

Reform efforts in Parliament, 1848–1866

Bright's campaign

Russell's proposals in 1867 would have increased the existing electorate of 1,000,000 by only another 300,000, and they were defeated. With his resignation the Conservatives under Derby again came in, though they were once more in a minority. By now there were obvious signs of working-class agitation again— there was an attempt to hold a monster meeting in Hyde Park, and the railings were pushed down when the authorities shut the gates. Bright, too, was in full cry in Lancashire. The

Russell's proposals

---

[1] Though the work of the Chartists came to nothing at the time, five of their six points were later conceded—abolition of the property qualification for M.P.s (1858), the secret ballot (1872), equal electoral districts (by successive stages in 1867, 1884, 1918), payment of M.P.s (1911) and adult male suffrage (1918). Annual elections nobody wants. Some of the discredited Chartist leaders also profoundly influenced the future by helping the Communist Karl Marx to found the International Working Men's Association in 1864.

Conservatives therefore decided to take the bull by the horns. The leading spirit in this decision was certainly the Chancellor of the Exchequer, Disraeli, but the Cabinet differed so much on the details that an agreed plan was not arrived at until an hour before he was due to explain the proposals to the House. Eventually Disraeli proposed a Bill enfranchising £6 borough householders and £20 county leaseholders. As it proceeded through the House this was substantially amended. Partly through some of the more progressive Conservatives, partly through amendments by Gladstone and the Liberals, the Second Reform Act finally took the much more democratic form of granting the franchise in the boroughs to all householders and £10 lodgers, and in the counties to £12 leaseholders. Besides this there was a slight redistribution of seats, the boroughs of less than 10,000 population losing one of their members, and the resulting forty-five seats going to the counties and the big new towns.

The Second Reform Act practically doubled the existing electorate. Its most striking feature was the household franchise in the towns, which meant that many of the working class now enjoyed the vote for the first time. The possible consequences of this innovation caused some trepidation—Carlyle, for instance, wrote of 'Shooting Niagara', and Derby spoke of 'a leap in the dark'. The immediate political result of the measure was certainly not in accordance with the calculation of Derby and Disraeli. Both men claimed to have 'dished the Whigs', but if they hoped that the new electorate would vote Conservative to show its gratitude they were sadly mistaken. The next election saw Gladstone and the Liberals returned with the biggest majority for twenty-two years.

Disraeli's proposals

The Second Reform Act, 1867

Results of the Second Reform Act

14. The Supremacy of Palmerston: Foreign Policy, 1846-1868

1 Palmerston as Foreign Secretary, 1846–1851

The return of the Whigs in 1846 brought Palmerston back to the Foreign Office, and Europe held its breath.

There was not long to wait before a crisis developed with France. This arose from the French attempt to secure a hold on **The Spanish** Spain by arranging two marriages, one of which was between the **marriages** Spanish Queen's sister and a son of Louis Philippe. The possibility of Franco-Spanish union, though in fact it never came about, alarmed and infuriated Palmerston and British opinion generally to such a degree that the entente between Britain and France was broken. When Louis Philippe was faced with the Paris demonstrations of February 1848, Palmerston therefore did nothing to help the old king—except to afford him shelter in England as an exile.

The year 1848 gave Palmerston, in company with every other **The revolutions** European statesmen, a great deal to think about. Amid the general **of 1848–1849** toppling of thrones Palmerston kept one fixed idea in mind. It was his guiding principle not only in 1848, but in all other years, to see that no harm befell British interests. Beyond this he tended to approve the liberal side as opposed to the autocratic, and to show sympathy with nations struggling against foreign oppression. This sympathy, however, disappeared entirely if it conflicted with his view of Britain's well-being. With Palmerston it was always Britain first, liberalism a very poor second.

Following this simple principle, Palmerston recognized the new French republic—much to the indignation of Queen Victoria **Recognition of** —as soon as he was convinced that it did not intend to start **the Second** revolutionary wars all over Europe. He also helped the Italian **Republic** effort to drive out foreign and despotic rulers—without the knowledge of the Queen and his colleagues he allowed guns to go from Woolwich to the rebels in Sicily—since an Italy free from foreign **The Sicilian** control would cease to provide Austria and France with pretexts **revolt** for interference or expansion. In the same spirit, appreciating that

163

Spain

the Spanish liberals were more likely than the absolutists to keep their country free from dependence on France, Palmerston advised Spain in 1848 to mend her ways and employ a liberal ministry—an interference which resulted in the expulsion of the British Ambassador from Madrid. All this brought Palmerston into strong disfavour at Court and in the Cabinet, for he consulted no one in his high-handed actions, and frequently avoided submitting despatches to the Queen on the ground that they could not wait for her perusal.

The liberal side then, on the whole, came in for his diplomatic support—but not much more—in France, Spain, Portugal and Italy. With Germany he was not greatly concerned, never imagining that the national movement could come to anything. But in the Austrian Empire—outside Italy—the liberal and national revolutions got no support at all from Palmerston. The Hungarians, for example, repeatedly besought Palmerston's aid in their revolt against Austrian domination, but received not the slightest encouragement. This was not because he approved of Austrian absolutism—very much the reverse—but because he regarded the Austrian Empire in Central Europe as a useful bulwark against Russia. The Hungarians, therefore, were left to stand alone, though Palmerston did not mince his words in condemning Austrian brutality during the suppression of the revolt.

The Hungarian revolt

Palmerston had barely ridden the storms of 1848 and 1849 when he was faced with a squall of his own creation in the famous Don Pacifico incident. Pacifico was a Portuguese Jew who happened to have been born in Gibraltar, and could therefore claim British nationality. His house in Athens had been burned down in a riot, and he had submitted a grossly exaggerated claim for compensation to the Greek Government—a claim which included £26,000 for destroyed 'documents'. Palmerston, while not necessarily swallowing these figures, resolved to enforce Pacifico's claim, since the Greeks had shown themselves generally hostile to British influence. Typically Palmerstonian measures were therefore employed—the Piraeus was blockaded, and Greek shipping was seized to the value of the British claims.

The 'Don Pacifico' incident, 1850

The Greeks were not the only party to resent this high-handed action. France, a guarantor of Greek independence, had her offers of mediation flouted by Palmerston even when the British Cabinet had accepted them. The French Ambassador was withdrawn from London, and the House of Lords, inspired by Aberdeen, passed a vote of censure on Palmerston. Then it was the turn of the Commons. Peel, in his last speech, Gladstone, in his first oration on foreign affairs, Cobden and Bright, ever sensitive to 'reckless' diplomacy involving the possibility of war, all rose to the attack. But the imperturbable Foreign Secretary dominated the occasion with a tremendous speech. For over four and a half hours he held forth, reviewing his whole conduct of foreign affairs since 1830—and it was typical of Palmerston's mastery of his subject that two thousand volumes of Foreign Office papers were used to furnish the material for his defence. His concluding sentences were to become famous: 'As the Roman, in days of old, held himself free from indignity when he could say "Civis Romanus sum", so also a British subject, in whatever land he may be, shall feel confident that the watchful eye and the strong arm of England will protect him against injustice and wrong.' The doctrine was, after all, eminently pleasing to most Englishmen, even if Don Pacifico was a somewhat unworthy representative of the nation, and Palmerston came through the vote safely.

Don Pacifico's claims were scarcely disposed of before Palmerston was involved in another storm, this time not with Parliament but with his old antagonist the Queen. One autumn day in 1850, General Haynau, an Austrian who had behaved with extreme brutality in suppressing the Hungarian revolt, visited Barclay & Perkins's brewery in London. The draymen and brewery workers, mindful of his floggings of Italian and Hungarian women, greeted 'General Hyena' with a 'rough house'. He was rescued, but Palmerston made an awkward incident worse by remarking that the mob, which had merely succeeded in tearing Haynau's clothes and pulling his whiskers, should have 'tossed him in a blanket, rolled him in the kennel, and then sent him home in a cab'. The Austrians complained, not unnaturally, at such comment from the Foreign Secretary, while Queen Victoria was extremely angry at the insult offered to a distinguished guest. In his 'apology' Palmerston replied that the General would have done better to stay in Austria—and despatched this fresh piece of provocation without letting the Queen see it. It was this kind of thing that made Palmerston enormously popular with the people—and enormously unpopular at Court.

The visit of General Haynau, 1850

If Palmerston's activities in 1850 caused storms at Court and in the Cabinet, those of 1851 positively upset the boat. With difficulty restrained from the tactlessness of receiving Kossuth, the escaped Hungarian rebel leader, in his London residence, he proceeded to commit a blazing indiscretion. On 2 December 1851

Louis Napoleon Bonaparte, nephew of the great Napoleon and President of the new French Republic, carried out a *coup d'état*, imprisoning his opponents and extending his presidential power for a further ten years. This proved to be merely a step towards a revived Bonaparte Empire, which duly followed a year later when the President proclaimed himself the Emperor Napoleon III. Since he regarded Louis Napoleon as less dangerous to British interests than either the extreme Republicans or the Orleans family, Palmerston gave a warm welcome to the 1851 *coup*—entirely on his own initiative. He also commended Louis Napoleon's methods—in a despatch unsubmitted to the Queen. The Cabinet, however, was not prepared to take sides at all, while the sympathies of the Court were strongly Orleanist. This time the old man had really gone too far.

No one was more furious at Palmerston's action than the Queen. In taking decisions and sending off despatches without submitting them for the Crown's approval Palmerston was undoubtedly in the wrong. The Foreign Secretary's point of view was readily intelligible—the Queen was a novice in foreign affairs compared with himself, her husband was a priggish young foreigner with too German a viewpoint, and anyway it was an unnecessary bother; in 1848 alone, for instance, he had sent off 29,000 despatches. But the Court was determined to enforce its control, for Palmerston was a breezy and outspoken figure who might at any moment cause an international crisis by insulting some important crowned head or other. Already in 1850 he had promised to mend his ways, and here he was back at his old tricks. It was the last straw, and this time the royal pressure succeeded. Russell, who generally approved of Palmerston's policy if not always of his methods, was now in agreement with
the Queen, for the Foreign Secretary had flouted the Cabinet as well as the Crown. He was accordingly dismissed from his post.

Palmerston's revenge took precisely three weeks to accomplish. Within that time he had defeated the Government over Russell's Militia Bill and let in the Conservatives. Before many months
had passed he was back in office in Aberdeen's Whig-Peelite Coalition. But as no one would trust him at the Foreign Office and Gladstone had obvious claims to the Exchequer, he had to be content with the position of Home Secretary. At sixty-nine he thus entered a new sphere of duties, while the conduct of foreign affairs passed mainly to Aberdeen as Prime Minister and Russell as Foreign Secretary.

2 Aberdeen, Palmerston and the Crimean War

The Ministry of Aberdeen was perhaps the most distinguished group of statesmen ever to govern the country. This did not prevent it from drifting quite unnecessarily into the Crimean War.

For many years Russian ambitions at the expense of the Turkish Empire had been obvious, while more recently the Russian advance towards Afghanistan had seemed to threaten the British position in India. To these weighty considerations of foreign policy there was added the force of British (and French) popular opinion, which was strongly hostile to the whole institution of Tsardom. Nicholas I was trebly detested as the ruthless autocrat who had maintained serfdom, destroyed Polish liberties, and helped Austria to suppress the Hungarian revolt. It is against this background of distrust and dislike that the incidents leading up to the Crimean War must be seen. *British hostility to Russia*

The particular dispute which occasioned war in 1854 developed from a revival of ancient French claims to the guardianship of the Christian Holy Places of Palestine. The Sultan agreed to the French guardianship of the Nativity Church and the Holy Manger at Bethlehem, whereupon Russia, who also had treaty rights on behalf of the Orthodox Church, protested strongly, and advanced a new and far-reaching claim to the Protectorship of all Christians in the Ottoman Empire. These Christians certainly needed protection; but to allow the Tsar this right would have given Russia a pretext for constant interference in Turkish affairs. Though they were no match for the Russians the Turks nevertheless refused the demand, relying on the fact that Britain and France would be extremely unwilling to see Constantinople in Russian hands. *Events leading to the Crimean War*

The British Cabinet had thus no responsibility for the original crisis, but its reluctance to take a strong line helped to make matters worse. Although Aberdeen and his colleagues were from the first determined to defend Constantinople, they could not make up their minds to attempt to avert war by undertaking the defence of the Russo-Turkish frontier—i.e. the districts of Moldavia and Wallachia, now known as Rumania. Even when the Russians invaded Moldavia in July 1853 the Cabinet was still divided. Aberdeen himself was so sincerely desirous of peace that the Russians misjudged him: they went too far before they *Russian invasion of Moldavia, 1853* realized that there were actions which even Aberdeen would not tolerate.

Meantime an international conference in Vienna had been considering without success innumerable suggestions for compromise. At last, in October 1853, the Turks attacked the Russians in Moldavia, and in the following month the Russian fleet destroyed a Turkish flotilla at Sinope, on the Black Sea. This last action was regarded in Britain as an unwarranted massacre, and the demand for active intervention grew. Finally, after British and French fleets had been ordered into the Black Sea without making any impression on the Russians, Britain and France—not waiting for Austria, who was really much more vitally concerned—sent an ultimatum to Nicholas. This demanded the withdrawal of the Russian troops from Moldavia and Wallachia. When it was refused a state of war was declared.

In the summer of 1854, before the British and French had come to grips with the Russians at all, the Russian force retired from Moldavia and Wallachia. The reason for this was partly their failure to beat the Turks there, partly an ultimatum by Austria. The official objective of the allies had now been achieved, but the distrust of Russian intentions remained. Moreover, a war without any fighting seemed rather an anti-climax, so the British and French now agreed to deal a crushing blow at Russian naval strength by capturing and dismantling Sebastopol, the great naval base on the Black Sea. Palmerston, among others, was strongly in favour of this project, which it was supposed would be comfortably accomplished within six weeks.

The military history of the Crimean War is even more depressing than the diplomatic stupidity which led up to it. The allied troops, consisting of some 26,000 British, 30,000 French and 5,000 Turks, made a safe landing on the Crimean Peninsula north of Sebastopol. The first great obstacle to be overcome was a Russian army placed in the path of the allies along the steep banks of the River Alma. This was successfully dislodged by the British under their Commander-in-Chief, Lord Raglan, a veteran who had last seen active service forty years before. But the French refused to co-operate in following up this success, and the best chance of the war was lost. It then became necessary for the allies to skirt inland to more protected positions south and south-west of the fortress. Here they prepared for the grand assault which was to finish the war.

Meanwhile the Russians had not been idle. Under the inspira-

Sinope, 1853

The Anglo-French ultimatum

Russia's withdrawal from Moldavia and Wallachia

The Anglo-French objective: Sebastopol

The landing, 1854

tion of Todleben, a skilled military engineer, Sebastopol began to look a much more difficult nut to crack. Then in October the Rusian field-army organized a surprise attack on the British base at Balaclava. The ensuing battle was distinguished by two cavalry charges which have firmly established themselves in popular legend. First the heavy brigade, 900 strong, charged uphill against 3,000 Russian cavalry and prevented the enemy from sweeping down on the British positions. Then the light brigade, ordered by Raglan to charge the retreating Russians and recapture some guns they were bearing off, charged right up a valley over a mile long which was dominated at head and sides by Russian artillery. The magnificent troops, firmly led by Lord Cardigan, a keen though intensely unpopular commander, captured the guns, at a cost to themselves of 113 killed and 134 wounded out of 673. Unfortunately the order—which was badly worded—had been misinterpreted, and it was the wrong position they had charged and the wrong set of guns they had captured. The survivors therefore had to ride back again, exposed once more to extreme danger, though now aided by French attacks. The episode was fairly typical of the Crimean War. Tennyson, of course, supplied the appropriate poem.

Balaclava, 1854

Frustrated in October, the Russians tried again in the following month, this time attacking the forward British positions at Inkerman with greatly superior forces. The British Commander added needlessly to his difficulties by at first refusing French reinforcements, but in the end the attack was beaten off with heavy Russian losses.

Inkerman, 1854

By now an allied attack on Sebastopol was impossible till the following spring, when reinforcements and improved transport conditions would help matters. The allies therefore settled down to a Crimean winter. The full deficiencies of their military organization soon became apparent. A blizzard destroyed the tents and wrecked a large number of supply ships in harbour. The single mud-track from Balaclava to the heights outside Sebastopol became virtually impassable. There was no road-making or transport corps, and it was long before anyone thought of building a light railway. Food, forage, fuel, clothing, shelter, all were hopelessly, tragically inadequate. In such conditions, in the grip of winter, the toll of sickness mounted to enormous proportions—and the medical services were the most neglected and ill-equipped of all.

The Crimean winter, 1854–1855

There is no space to tell here the story of Florence Nightingale's

(Sir John Tenniel, 1854, reproduced by permission of the Proprietors of 'Punch')

HOW TO GET RID OF AN OLD WOMAN

Punch's suggestion for disposing of the ineffective Prime Minister, Lord Aberdeen. Pack him off to the Crimean War as one of Florence Nightingale's nurses!

heroic struggle against dirt, disease, inadequate supplies and official opposition; but as the one positive gain of the Crimean War must be reckoned the transformation in British military hospital services brought about by this remarkable woman. The work of Florence Nightingale in producing a smoothly functioning hospital organization from the chaos at Scutari was powerfully aided by W. H. Russell, the special correspondent of *The Times*, who showed up abuses and aroused public opinion in Britain.

Florence
Nightingale

The Times cor-
respondent—
W. H. Russell

The same journal was also responsible for revealing the military deficiencies in the Crimea itself—the censorship was less strict in those days, and presumably as inefficient as the other military departments—and the demand grew for an enquiry into the conduct of the war. When, in January 1855, Parliament demanded such an enquiry, Aberdeen felt bound to resign, and the country turned to the unquestioned man of vigour in the Cabinet. Thus Palmerston became Prime Minister 'to win the war'. He promptly agreed to the commission of enquiry, sent it out to the Crimea in March 1855, and accepted its severe strictures on the supply services and the Cabinet. Then he set about remedying the supply and transport deficiencies, stopped some of the ridiculous overlappings and subdivisions of authority, and soon infused new life into the whole conduct of hostilities.

Resignation of
Aberdeen, 1855

Palmerston
Prime Minister:
military reorgan-
ization

The change of administration and the overhaul of War Office practice was soon evident in the reinforcements of men and material which reached the Crimea in 1855. By the spring both a road and a light railway from Balaclava to the heights were open to traffic. By June the allies, now reinforced by 15,000 Piedmontese (sent by Cavour to win the gratitude of Britain and France, a seat at the peace conference, and some possible help towards Italian unification), were ready for another attack on Sebastopol. It failed, but better success greeted a renewed attempt in August, when the French captured the Malakoff redoubt, which dominated the whole fortress. The Russians then abandoned their positions during the night, leaving Sebastopol in allied hands.

The Piedmon-
tese

The capture of
Sebastopol,
August 1855

The object the allies had set themselves was now achieved, but it was a year before peace was concluded. Russia was by no means at the end of her tether, and Palmerston was anxious to deal her further blows. It was Napoleon III who caused an alteration in these views, for he threatened either to withdraw his troops (which were now four times as numerous as the British) or else to extend the war into a grand European affair

(*Leech, Feb. 1855, reproduced by permission of the Proprietors of 'Punch'*)

NOW FOR IT!

A SET-TO BETWEEN PAM, THE DOWNING STREET PET, AND THE RUSSIAN SPIDER

When Palmerston replaced Lord Aberdeen, Britain (Mr Punch and British Lion) confidently looked forward to the fight against Russia (Nicholas I) being conducted in a more vigorous spirit.

involving the liberation of Poles, Hungarians and Italians. This was far too large an object for Palmerston, who accordingly gave way. The final and decisive step was, however, taken neither by Britain nor France, but by Austria, who in January 1856 sent Russia an ultimatum. The Russians then gave in, and a peace congress met at Paris. *The second Austrian ultimatum, 1856*

The terms of the Treaty of Paris had some important results in the Balkans, including independence in all but name for Moldavia and Wallachia, which soon became united as Rumania. From the British point of view, the most important clause was that which forbade the maintenance of warships and naval arsenals on the Black Sea. This would have kept Russia permanently out of the Straits and the Mediterranean, and so secured an admirable dividend from the war. Unfortunately, however, Russia was in a position to break the treaty after the allied forces were withdrawn—which she duly did in 1870, when the French were busy fighting the Prussians.[1] As for the protection of the Christians in the Turkish Empire, the Turks merely promised to reform their ways. Of course they did nothing of the kind, and of course Russia was still left with pretexts for intervention. So far from producing a permanent settlement, the Crimean War thus merely gave Russia (and Britain) a nasty jolt, leaving the Eastern Question to rear its ugly head on many an occasion in the future. *The Treaty of Paris, 1856* *Neutralization of the Black Sea* *The Eastern Question remains*

3 Palmerston and Russell, 1856–1868

The Crimean War was barely over when a further military task confronted Britain in the form of the Indian Mutiny.[2] This was very effectively suppressed, and Palmerston had thus steered his country through two difficult situations. *The Indian Mutiny, 1857*

Fresh trouble then arose in the Far East. Palmerston was determined to improve on the concessions exacted from China in 1841–42. His opportunity occurred when Chinese authorities boarded the *Arrow*, a vessel which was able to fly the British flag as its Chinese owner lived at Hong Kong, though its licence to do so had actually expired. There is little doubt that the ship had been engaged in illegitimate traffic, including smuggling and piracy, but Palmerston took a strong line, and a British squadron shelled some forts near Canton to persuade the Chinese *The second Chinese War: the Arrow*

---

[1] See page 188.   [2] See pages 399–402.

to apologize. This led to much criticism of Palmerston in Parliament. The Opposition, organized by Cobden—who always detested the Prime Minister's methods—was supported by both Gladstone and Disraeli, and the voting went against Palmerston by the narrow majority of fourteen. But if Parliament was momentarily against Palmerston, the country was not, for nothing pleased the electorate better than putting foreigners in their place. A general election was held and Palmerston came back with a majority, while Cobden and Bright, who had also become unpopular for their opposition to the Crimean War, both lost their seats. Palmerston's further demands on China then led to

more fighting, in which the British were supported by the French, and eventually a joint expedition reached Pekin in 1860. Finally the Chinese agreed to open Tientsin and other ports, to admit foreign ambassadors to Pekin, and to allow the import of opium.

In the midst of the Chinese misadventure Palmerston's Government had most unexpectedly fallen. The Conspiracy-to-Murder Bill, designed to discourage the hatching of plots in Britain by foreign exiles—like that of Orsini to assassinate Napoleon III—by classifying such activity as a felony, was a piece of perfectly good sense. That did not prevent its being rejected by a Parliament apparently now more Palmerstonian than Palmerston himself. The same ill-assorted combination of forces which had reproved the Prime Minister for being too high-handed about China was now disgusted at his submissiveness to France. English laws were good enough without alteration to please foreign despots, they stoutly maintained—and the astonished Palmerston found himself 'out'.

The short Derby administration of 1858–59 witnessed decisive events in the struggle for Italian freedom, but the ambition of Victor Emmanuel and Cavour to unite Italy under the leadership of Sardinia–Piedmont[1] got no encouragement from the Conservatives. Fortunately for the Italians Palmerston was soon back in office.

The influence of Palmerston and his Foreign Secretary Russell was powerfully exerted in favour of Cavour's plans on a number of occasions. Napoleon III had struck a bargain with Cavour to drive the Austrians out of Lombardy and Venetia in return for the cession of Savoy and Nice to France; and under the stimulus

[1] Victor Emmanuel's realm was still officially called the Kingdom of Sardinia, but Piedmont had come to be the industrial and political centre of his domains.

of his victories in the north, the inhabitants of the Central Italian duchies of Modena and Tuscany had expelled their foreign rulers. Palmerston and Russell joined the French Emperor in supporting the demand for a plebiscite to settle the future of these duchies— a plebiscite which could only result in a vote for union with Sardinia. Napoleon III's subsequent acquisition of Savoy and

(*Tenniel, 1861, reproduced by permission of the Proprietors of 'Punch'*)

THE LATEST ARRIVAL

Italy becomes a united kingdom and joins the party of nations. She is welcomed by John Bull and his wife Britannia, ignored by the Pope, and regarded askance by the monarchs of Prussia, Russia and Austria. Napoleon III would like to be friendly, but is restrained by his spouse, the Royalist-Catholic party in France.

Nice—although he had backed out of the war before he had freed Venetia—only increased British support of Cavour, for the view spread in the British Cabinet that a united Italy would be a useful counterweight to French power. Indeed it was for that very reason, together with the need to conciliate Catholic opinion in France, that Napoleon's own enthusiasm for the Italians now diminished.

Then, a little later, when the guerrilla leader Garibaldi—openly disavowed but secretly supported by Cavour—had freed Sicily from the Spanish Bourbon ruler, and was about to invade the mainland of South Italy, Palmerston and Russell quashed Napoleon III's plan for holding him off by Anglo-French naval action. Freed from this danger, Garibaldi crossed in safety and soon liberated Naples. Finally, when Cavour launched the Sardinian-Piedmontese army into the Papal States, Britain alone of the major powers lent him diplomatic support. Russell's despatch to the British Ambassador at Turin became famous: 'Her Majesty's Government can see no sufficient grounds for the severe censure with which Austria, France, Prussia and Russia have visited the acts of the King of Sardinia. Her Majesty's Government turn their eyes rather to the gratifying prospect of a people building up the edifice of their liberties, and consolidating the work of their independence amid the sympathies and good wishes of Europe.' It was all very infuriating for Victoria and Albert with their fondness for Austria and the rights of sovereigns generally, but they could do nothing against 'those two dreadful old men', as the Queen described Palmerston and Russell. So Britain gave her blessing to the creation of a united Italy, and Italy in turn remained duly grateful—until 1940.

Italian unity was only one of the three great questions which were fought out abroad during Palmerston's second Ministry. Much of the time of the two 'dreadful old men' was occupied with developments in the United States. In 1861 the American Civil War had broken out, the Northern states resisting the attempt of the Southern states (who were alarmed by the anti-slavery campaign in the North) to secede from the Union and form an independent Confederacy. Officially Britain's attitude was from the first one of neutrality, but as the war went on incidents occurred and sympathies developed which threatened to involve her in the struggle.

The American Civil War is so often thought of nowadays as a struggle to suppress slavery that it is difficult at first to understand how any section of British opinion could sympathize with the slave-owning South. In fact, however, upper-class Englishmen had more in common with the aristocratic tobacco and cotton planters than with the 'Yankee' industrialists of the North. Moreover, the President, the Northerner Abraham Lincoln, was not actually committed to abolish slavery when the war broke out; and to many Englishmen it thus seemed right to support the

The American Civil War, 1861–1865

Divided British sympathies

side which was struggling to be free—the South. Such views, however, were not those of the British working-classes, whose relatives were Northern industrial workers rather than Southern planters, and who concentrated on the anti-slavery aspect of the Northern cause from the beginning. Faced with a fierce division of opinion in the country, Palmerston and Russell were strengthened in their natural desire to remain neutral—'for God's sake, let us, if possible, keep out of it', as Russell summed up the matter.

British policy— neutrality

'Keeping out of it', however, became quite a difficulty when the *Trent* incident occurred. The Southern states, anxious to put their case before Russell, decided to send two special envoys to Europe. The Southern envoys escaped the Northern blockade (the existence of which caused a 'cotton famine' and the most widespread misery in Lancashire) and then took berths in a British ship, the *Trent*, from Havana. While they were on the *Trent* it was stopped by a Northern warship, whose Captain (acting without orders) compelled the British ship to surrender the two envoys. This was a clear violation of British rights at sea, and Russell drafted a stiff despatch, demanding that the Northern states should apologize and release the envoys within seven days. War might possibly have resulted—though it was not very likely, since neither side was in the least anxious for it—but the Prince Consort, as almost his last action in life, secured a toning down of the draft. This produced the release of the envoys within the stipulated seven days—but not the apology. Russell, for his part, gave no encouragement to the envoys when they reached London, and the incident was safely over.

The *Trent* incident

The war dragged on, and Palmerston and Russell wisely maintained British neutrality. A piece of carelessness on the part of Russell, however, led to another dangerous incident. In spite of timely evidence of her intentions, he acted too late to stop a newly-built ship, subsequently known as the *Alabama*, sailing from Merseyside to join the South. The vessel then proceeded to sink a great amount of Northern shipping until she was sunk two years later. Russell refused to acknowledge any responsibility or to pay compensation—though he was careful to see that no further warships sailed—and the incident remained an extremely sore point with the Northern states until 1872, when Gladstone submitted the case to international arbitration.[1] Meanwhile the North moved on to victory, the South was compelled to remain

Alabama incident, 1862

[1] See page 188.

in the Union, and the war finished without the calamity of British intervention. It left, however, an unfortunate legacy of ill-feeling in the United States against Britain—in the North because British newspapers and upper classes had so obviously supported the South, in the South because that support had consisted of words instead of deeds.

The Schleswig-Holstein question

Before the American Civil War was over another cloud began to blacken the international horizon. The interminable question of Schleswig-Holstein loomed up in ever more threatening form. Schleswig and Holstein were two duchies, the former Danish in character, the latter German, which were both ruled by the King of Denmark. They were, however, not part of the Danish kingdom, but enjoyed a separate status, with their own laws and customs, acknowledging their ruler not as King of Denmark but as Duke of Schleswig-Holstein. As nationalist feeling grew in the nineteenth century, Denmark became anxious to absorb the Duchies entirely into the Danish kingdom, while the German elements of the Duchies' population naturally looked for support against this to the German Confederation, of which Holstein (but not Schleswig) was a member. The ensuing complications, aggravated by a dispute about the succession, had already resulted in a war in 1848, after which the Treaty of London (1852) had defined the status of the Duchies and confirmed the rule of the King of Denmark.

The Treaty of London, 1852

The situation, never quiet, again became acute in 1863, when a new King of Denmark inherited the Danish throne through the female line. The law of the Duchies, however, recognized succession only through the direct male line. To make sure of retaining at least the more Danish of the Duchies, the King therefore issued a new constitution incorporating Schleswig into Denmark. This was a clear violation of the 1852 treaty. Austria and Prussia, in the name of the rejected German claimant of 1848 and the German Confederation, then began to put pressure on the Danes to reverse their policy and give up the Duchies entirely. This was where the question began to concern the other powers, and notably Britain, one of the signatories of the Treaty of London.

The Danish violation of the treaty; Austria and Prussia intervene

Britain's concern —as guarantor of the Treaty of London

Broadly speaking, Britain was strongly for the Danes, overlooking their first violation of the treaty and concentrating only on the fact that two great powers were about to commit a great violation. A marriage, too, had just taken place between the Prince of Wales and Princess Alexandra of Denmark, and the populace had warmly greeted the arrival of the beautiful 'sea-king's daughter from over the sea' (as Tennyson put it in his customary rhyming commentary). Palmerston and Russell both openly supported the Danes, and Palmerston declared in the midst of the preliminary 'war of nerves' that 'it would not be Denmark alone with which they [i.e. Austria and Prussia] had to contend'. This encouraged the Danes to rely on British help and defy their opponents. *Palmerston's encouragement of Denmark*

If Palmerston and Russell were thinking of war with Austria and Prussia they should obviously have obtained the alliance of France. Britain had no army which could possibly stand up to Prussia's, and the fate of Schleswig and Holstein could not be decided on the sea. Unfortunately, the British Ministers did everything to make co-operation with France impossible, for they imagined that the main result of Napoleon's intervention in Germany would be an extension of French territory along the Rhine. Only at the very last moment did Russell make belated efforts to revive the Entente. By that time, however, Napoleon was not only offended with Britain, but had been 'squared' by Prussia. There was thus nothing left for Palmerston to do—since he was much too shrewd to invite military defeat—but to climb down and retire shamefacedly from the scene, leaving Austria and Prussia to crush the Danes and strip them of both Schleswig and Holstein. *Failure to co-operate with France* / *Prussia secures French connivance* / *Palmerston climbs down: defeat of the Danes*

In their conduct of the Schleswig-Holstein question Palmerston and Russell thus made every mistake save that of finally plunging into a war which they had no chance of winning. The truth was that they did not understand German affairs, and failed to perceive that the Prussia of Bismarck was the rising power of Europe. From the purely military aspect their fears of France were groundless, and their whole energies should have been bent on allying with France to stop Prussia at all costs. But it needed several more lessons to convince the British public of this— notably Prussia's subsequent refusal to hand Schleswig over to the German claimant, her war against Austria in 1866 to gain control of Holstein and the whole of North Germany, and finally her victory over France in the war of 1870–71. Palmerston's last venture in foreign policy was thus somewhat pathetic—the same old gay interference, but this time coming to grief at the hands of a far abler diplomatist than himself in Bismarck, who called his bluff and walked away with what he wanted. The incident suggests that Palmerston may have scored his earlier successes only because he had weaker opponents than Bismarck to deal with. *British failure to realize the danger from Prussia*

Britain's diplomatic defeat over Schleswig-Holstein did not, however, interfere with the Prime Minister's popularity sufficiently to lose him the next general election. In 1865 the wonderful old man—he was nearly 81—was returned for a further spell of power, but before he could enjoy it he caught a chill and died. The other veteran, Russell, was then left to carry on the Government, which soon fell on a proposal for parliamentary reform.

The death of
Palmerston

Russell Prime
Minister

The hold of Palmerston over British public opinion for so many years is difficult to understand, even allowing for his constant care of British interests, unless it is remembered how much the English love a 'character'. His outspokenness, his cheerfulness, his courage, his contempt for pretence and high-falutin nonsense all combined to endear him to the people. They liked a man who took so much responsibility on himself—whether it was in settling his country's attitude to foreign questions, putting the Queen and the Prince Consort in their place, or merely ordering up a special train when the railway officials declared that to do so would be highly dangerous. The annoyance of foreigners at his general attitude—and the pleasure of his fellow-countrymen—may be well understood when one comes across a reference in his correspondence to 'a set of Russians, ten of whom killed are not the equivalent to one Englishman'. The very physical vigour of the man was also gratifying to a nation of sportsmen, who gazed delightedly at the spectacle of a politician rowing and swimming before breakfast, owning successful racehorses, riding and shooting well into his eightieth year, and in his last months of life still able to eat 'preliminaries' at dinner to the extent of two helpings of turtle soup, a portion of cod with oyster sauce, a paté, two entrées, and a plate of mutton garnished with a slice of ham, all before tackling the main dish of pheasant.

The appeal of
Palmerston's
personality

So England mourned when at last the evergreen 'Pam' passed away. On the whole his career had been very successful, with British prestige kept at its highest level until his very last years. A magnificent Englishman, he was certainly no internationalist, and his outspoken criticisms of foreign powers and personalities left a dangerous legacy of dislike for Britain abroad. But the foreign elements which most detested Palmerston were nearly always autocratic and corrupt governments, and rarely the continental liberals, who looked to Palmerston's Britain as an oasis of freedom in a desert of tyranny.

Palmerston's
achievement:
respect for the
power and
liberty of Great
Britain

No very vital steps in foreign affairs were taken by Britain in the two or three years following the death of Palmerston. The air was certainly electric on the Continent as Bismarck and the Prussian army drove Austria out of German affairs in seven weeks of warfare, annexed the minor states of North Germany, handed over Venetia to Italy and exposed the weakness of Napoleon III and France. These were momentous events, but the Derby and Disraeli Conservative Governments could hardly take any decisive rôle in them. Since the British had an army many times smaller than the Prussians, the logical thing to do was to abstain from interference in Continental struggles, and certainly it was better to abstain than to adopt the later Palmerstonian policy, aptly described by Derby as 'meddle and muddle'. So the formation of modern Germany proceeded, and Britain looked on, uneasy but impotent.

The Seven Weeks' War, 1866

Derby's non-intervention

15. Gladstone and Disraeli

1 Gladstone's First Ministry, 1868–1874

When the Queen's invitation to form a ministry was brought to him in 1868 after the Liberal success at the polls, Gladstone was engaged in his favourite relaxation of felling trees. 'Very significant', murmured the statesman, when he read the message—and

Gladstone and the Irish problem

proceeded with the work of destruction. Then after a while he stopped, leaned upon his axe and announced: 'My mission is to pacify Ireland.' For the remaining years of his long life the settlement of the Irish question was Gladstone's foremost objective.

Ireland, 1846–1868

In the period following the suppression of O'Connell's agitation and the repeal of the Corn Laws, relations between Britain and Ireland had not improved. In 1848 there had been a wild

The 'Young Ireland' Rebellion, 1848

attempt at rebellion by the 'Young Ireland' movement led by Smith O'Brien, but a more serious matter was the constant trouble in the countryside. Though most of the Irish were not disposed to join in open rebellion, they were more than willing

Landlord v tenant

to participate vigorously in the conflicts between landlords and tenants. And opportunities there were in plenty; for in the years 1849–51 alone, no less than 36,755 families suffered eviction.

The refusal of successive governments to tackle Irish problems fairly and squarely led before very long to a fresh outburst of revolutionary activity. This time the inspiration came from the

The Fenian Society

Irish emigrants in the United States, where in 1858 the Fenian[1] Society was founded. The secret organization was extended to Ireland, funds were sent across the Atlantic, and preparations were made for an armed revolt in favour of an independent Irish republic. Learning of the danger, the Government in 1865 arrested James Stephens, the 'Head Centre' of the Fenians, but he escaped and reached America, where he soon tried to launch the Fenians into an attack on Canada. By this time Habeas Corpus had been suspended in Ireland, and feeling was running high on both sides.

[1] A name derived from the Fianna, an Irish militia of ancient times.

182

Worse was to follow, for in 1867 Fenian Irish began to make trouble in England. At Manchester a prison van containing two Fenians was attacked, the prisoners released, and a policeman shot. This led to three of the rescuers being hanged, which in turn only further excited the Irish, who referred to the victims of justice as the 'Manchester Martyrs'. Later in the same year an attempt to rescue two Fenians from Clerkenwell prison by blowing down a wall with explosive led to twelve innocent people being killed and over a hundred injured. Fenian outrages in England, 1867

In conditions such as these Gladstone had come to the conclusion that only the removal of grievances could prevent the whole Irish people from rising in rebellion. His first measures when he came into power in 1868 were accordingly aimed against what he regarded as the two main troubles—the religious grievance and the land grievance. Given a solution to these problems, Gladstone thought (at this stage in his career) that the political agitation against union with Britain would automatically disappear. Gladstone's remedies

Within two months of taking office Gladstone—fervent churchman though he was—steered through Parliament a bill to disestablish and disendow the Anglican Church in Ireland. The Irish had always objected to the Anglican Church possessing large estates and extracting tithe from a Catholic population, and they disliked seeing the general advantages of State recognition as the Church of Ireland go to a religious body which represented only a tiny fraction of their numbers. Gladstone's measure was accordingly most acceptable to them. Irish Disestablishment, 1869

Gladstone then turned to the land question, which was a much more complicated business.[1] His solution, the Irish Land Act of 1870, unfortunately did not go far enough to meet the real needs of the situation. By the terms of the Act compensation had to be paid by landlords evicting tenants who had made improvements, while for the actual eviction a 'scale of damages' was enforced in all cases except where the eviction was caused by non-payment of rent. But there was no provision to see that rents were kept at reasonable levels, and landlords might thus raise rents to levels that tenants could not afford and then evict them for non-payment of rent. Thus the Act failed to give the Irish what they really wanted—fair rents and fixed tenures, or better still, outright ownership of the land. Agrarian crime therefore continued unabated, the Government was compelled to pass a Coercion Act, The First Irish Land Act, 1870 The problem continues

[1] See page 133.

and the Irish of both religions began to join a new Home Rule movement—of which much more will be heard later.

★　　★　　★　　★　　★

Deeply concerned with Ireland as Gladstone was, that unhappy country was far from being the only interest of his Ministry. In domestic affairs he attempted a great programme of reforms, the like of which had not been seen since the Ministries of Grey and Peel.

Reforms at home

In 1870 a very important Education Act was passed—the work of W. E. Forster, vice-president of the Privy Council Committee for Education.[1] It laid the foundation of a national system of elementary education, but offended Nonconformists by giving grants to Church schools, and Churchmen by setting up 'Board Schools' in which religious teaching was undenominational.

Forster's Education Act, 1870

Another educational advance was the removal of the last religious tests at Oxford and Cambridge. Though by the 1850s Nonconformists had been admitted to study and take degrees at both universities, they were still not eligible for scholarships, fellowships or university offices. It was these restrictions which the University Tests Act now swept away. Henceforward Nonconformists were admitted to Oxford and Cambridge on the same terms as Anglicans.

The University Tests Act, 1871

In the same spirit of breaking down unfair privileges, the Government decided to recruit the Civil Service (except in the Foreign Office) by open competitive examination. The decision proved of the greatest value, for it enabled the higher ranks to be staffed by some of the best brains in the country.

Civil Service examinations

Another very valuable reform was the introduction of the secret ballot in place of the old open voting at the hustings. The main effect of this was to discourage the bribery that still persisted at elections. There was no point in buying someone's vote if there was no means of seeing how he cast it, and so the Ballot Act, coupled with Disraeli's extension of the franchise, made electoral corruption unprofitable. But there was also another result, peculiar to Ireland. A young Irish landowner, strongly anti-English for all his social position and his Ulster Presbyterian background, saw the possibilities of using the secret vote to elect Irish M.P.s favouring Home Rule. Previously many Irish voters had been too afraid of incurring the displeasure of the local

The Ballot Act, 1872

[1] Forerunner of the present Ministry of Education. For details of the Act, see pages 382–83.

landlord to vote against his wishes. Now they no longer needed to fear victimization, and their votes went to candidates who put Ireland first and foremost. When Parliament agreed to the Ballot Act it certainly did not visualize the weapon it was placing in the hands of Charles Stewart Parnell and the Irish Home Rule movement.

More controversial in its character was Gladstone's trade union legislation. The position of trade unions had for long been unsatisfactory. By the repeal of the Combination Laws[1] unions themselves had been legalized, but their privileges had been left very vague. Could they strike? Could they 'persuade' blacklegs to join them in striking? Could they hold corporate property and enforce their agreements by suing in the law courts? All these vital questions were very much matters of dispute, in which the views of judges were usually adverse to the unions. Gladstone determined to settle the points at issue, and in 1871 the Government passed two measures to this end. The first, the Trade Union Act, gave the unions certain legal rights, enabling them to hold property and to have the protection of the courts, for example, against dishonest treasurers who had embezzled union funds. *The Trade Union Act, 1871*

The gratitude of the unionists for the Trade Union Act was tempered by their indignation at the Criminal Law Amendment Act, which was coupled with it. This reaffirmed the most stringent sections of the 1825 Act, those concerning the prohibition of 'molestation' and 'obstruction'. The terms of the Act made it most difficult for the unions to enforce a strike by picketing, and left many of the natural activities of unions, such as a threat to strike, at the mercy of the law of conspiracy as interpreted by the courts. *The Criminal Law Amendment Act, 1871*

Among the most remarkable reforms of Gladstone's first Ministry were those carried out by Edward Cardwell at the War Office. To begin with, Cardwell abolished flogging as a military punishment in peace-time. This was not only a humanitarian reform; it also attracted to the ranks men of a better type, so that Cardwell was soon able to abolish 'bounty money' for recruits and discharge notorious gaol-birds. Next he introduced the Army Enlistment (Short Service) Act. This altered the existing twelve-year period of service to six years with the colours and six years in the reserve. A double benefit resulted—enlistment was encouraged and the military authorities were able to build up a more adequate reserve. *Cardwell's Army Reforms* *Abolition of (peace-time) flogging* *Short service*

[1] See pages 47 and 101.

Abolition of
purchase of
commissions

The opposition to these measures among the higher ranks of the military was as nothing compared with the storm that greeted Cardwell's proposal to abolish the purchase of commissions. The reform was duly enforced, but nothing did more to destroy Gladstone's popularity with the upper classes—and nothing did more to increase the efficiency of the British army.

Cardwell's reforms did not stop at this point. The equality of status between the Secretary for War (the political head of the War Office) and the Commander-in-Chief (the military head), which had been productive of much mischief in the past, was abolished by subordinating the latter to the former. At the same time the whole War Office was reorganized. It was also thanks to Cardwell that the infantry was rearmed with a new breech-loading rifle.

Reorganization
of War Office

Redisposition of
infantry

Finally, Cardwell was responsible for a complete redisposition of the British infantry. He first called back to England the scattered garrisons in the self-governing colonies, which he entrusted with their own defence. This saved money and provided an increased force at home. Then he reorganized the entire location of the infantry, dividing Great Britain and Ireland into sixty-nine districts and making each the centre of a regiment. These new county areas were each to contain two battalions of the old regulars (whose regiments had previously been known by numbers, and who had no special local associations) while the local militia and volunteers, which were already organized on a county basis, were now for the first time connected with the regulars. Under the new system the two regular battalions took it in turn to serve overseas, and this 'linked battalion' principle proved invaluable for training youngsters thoroughly at home before sending them to relieve the seasoned veterans abroad.

All told, Cardwell, besides improving the organization and efficiency of the army out of all recognition, added 25 battalions and 156 field guns to its strength and multiplied by ten the number of reserves available for foreign service. Perhaps the most surprising thing of all was that he was able to leave annual expenditure on the army lower than he found it—a fact which undoubtedly helps to explain Gladstone's strong support for his work. The instrument which Cardwell fashioned so efficiently and economically served well in the colonial campaigns of the next thirty years—especially in the hands of the one outstanding military figure who supported the reforms, Sir Garnet Wolseley.[1]

[1] R. C. K. Ensor, in his *England, 1870–1914*, maintains that there were

While Cardwell was wielding his new broom at the War Office, other ministers were not idle. In 1872 the Home Secretary, Bruce, secured the passage of a Licensing Act. This courageous measure was designed to control some of the evils in the sale of drink. Many public houses were closed down in areas which were too generously endowed with these establishments, hours of opening were limited, and regulations were made against the adulteration of drink—including the common practice of putting salt into beer to whet the thirst of the consumer. But the Act was bitterly opposed—a bishop in the Lords plumped for 'England free rather than England sober', and rioting took place in several towns. Whatever the social benefits, the Licensing Act thus cost the Liberals a great deal of popularity, and the whole liquor trade with its enormous wealth and influence promptly deserted to the Conservatives.

The Licensing Act, 1872

The reforms carried by Gladstone's first Ministry were its great glory, but its record in foreign affairs was by no means bad, and there was none of those unfortunate incidents which marred Gladstone's second spell of power.

Foreign affairs

The most important episode with which the Prime Minister and his Foreign Secretary, Lord Granville, had to deal was the Franco-Prussian War. They followed the only practicable policy —neutrality. Even had Gladstone wished to side with one party or the other he was powerless, for whereas the Germans could put over half a million men into the field the British could not have mustered a trained and equipped expeditionary force of more than ten thousand. But there really seemed no valid reason for intervention, for the British Cabinet was not to know that the much-vaunted French army would collapse so swiftly before the legions of Prussia, and that the war would end with a new German Empire as the dominating power of the Continent. In any case, British popular opinion was not in favour of helping the French, for they had done much to bring the war on themselves.

The Franco-Prussian War, 1870–1871

But if there was no reason for British intervention, it was at least important that neither side should violate Belgian neutrality.

Protection of Belgian neutrality

---

only two great defects in military organization that Cardwell was unable to remedy. These were the continuation of the Duke of Cambridge as Commander-in-Chief and the failure to construct a proper General Staff. The second was a consequence of the first, which was in turn inevitable in view of Victoria's determination to retain a royal personage at the head of the army.

Gladstone and Granville accordingly suggested to both combatants a reaffirmation of the Belgian neutrality treaty of 1839, and threatened to co-operate in the defence of Belgium against whichever side first crossed her frontiers. This move was entirely successful, for Bismarck, who was determined never to fight more than one great power at a time, agreed at once, and Napoleon III followed suit later. Thus Belgium was preserved from occupation by a major power—always a prominent British interest —and the Cabinet had scored a distinct success.

Russia and the Black Sea

But though there was no difficulty with either of the combatants during the war, there was trouble with a fellow-neutral. After the combatants were well engaged Russia suddenly announced that she no longer intended to be bound by the clauses of the Treaty of Paris which forbade her to maintain a navy on the Black Sea.[1] This raised the question of what Britain, France and Turkey, the late allies of the Crimean War, were going to do about it. France, desperately struggling against Prussia, was quite unable to take on other tasks, and the question therefore amounted to whether Britain was going to wage a new Crimean War virtually alone. Thanks to the wise direction of Gladstone and Granville the hot-heads were resisted, and no war came about. At a Conference in London Russia saved the face of her ex-enemies by consenting to a general article that treaty arrangements must stand unless altered by friendly agreement, and then had her claims to a Black Sea navy allowed.

The *Alabama* award

One of the most successful, but at the same time most unpopular, achievements of the Ministry was the *Alabama* arbitration. The ill-feeling between Britons and Americans engendered by the *Alabama* episode[2] in the Civil War still persisted, and Gladstone accordingly concluded an agreement with the U.S.A. to submit the question of compensation to an international tribunal. When this eventually met—it took several years of negotiation to create, for there was nothing of the kind in existence—it refused to entertain the American claim for 'indirect' damages (i.e. those arising from prolongation of the war), but decided against Britain on several claims of direct damage. The final judgment was that Britain should pay the U.S.A. roughly £3,250,000, or about one-third of their claim for direct damage. The British public, however, resented paying anything, and Gladstone's popularity suffered severely. All the same, one must admire his determination to settle the dispute pacifically; and

[1] See page 173.   [2] See page 177.

his use of an impartial tribunal was a landmark in the development of international relations.

By 1874 the life of the Parliament in which the Liberals held their majority was drawing to a close. After the loss of a few by-elections, Gladstone decided to submit to the verdict of a fresh general election. He promised, if he were returned to power, to abolish the income tax. Not even the magic of this appeal, however, could persuade the electorate to renew his lease of office.

Defeat of the Liberals, 1874

To the defeat of the Liberals many causes contributed. There was the feeling that they had come to the end of their reforming programme—an opinion aptly expressed by Disraeli when in 1873 he had referred to the statesmen on the Liberal front bench as 'a range of exhausted volcanoes'. Then, too, there was the fact that every Gladstonian reform had affronted some important section of the community. The upper classes were offended by army and civil service reform and the recognition of trade unions; the Church by Irish disestablishment and the opening of Oxford and Cambridge on equal terms to Nonconformists; the Nonconformists by the Education Act (although it had equally annoyed Churchmen); the labouring classes by the refusal to permit 'peaceful picketing'; and all the innumerable devotees of alcoholic refreshment by the Licensing Act. The *Alabama* award, too, had been extremely unpopular. On the whole it was not surprising, in spite of their notable record, that the Liberals lost office. Gladstone himself had no doubt that the Licensing Act was the main cause of his defeat—'we have been borne down', he wrote, 'in a torrent of gin and beer'. After that the Education Act was probably the main grievance. So the Conservatives came in with their first workable majority since the days of Peel, and at long last Disraeli was to enjoy not only office but power.

2 Disraeli's Second Ministry, 1874–1880

Seventy years of age, Disraeli was now really—as he himself put it—'at the top of the greasy pole'. Racked by asthma, kidney disease and periodic fits of gout, the aged Prime Minister had now to husband his resources carefully, and the Ministry proved less fruitful of great reforms than his earlier teaching might have led the country to expect. As he grew older, too, he became more and more absorbed in foreign and imperial affairs. All the same, a number of useful domestic measures were passed, the guiding

Disraeli and reform

Home Secretary
Cross

spirit being Disraeli's extremely capable Home Secretary, Richard Cross.

The Artisans'
Dwellings Act,
1875

One of the first reforms achieved was the Artisans' Dwellings Act, a measure which aimed at providing better houses for the poor. The Act introduced no form of compulsion, but gave local authorities permission to embark—if they so desired—on slum clearance schemes and the building of housing 'estates'. It was in part thanks to this measure that the Radical Mayor of Birmingham, Joseph Chamberlain, was able to effect such vast improvements in his native city.

The Public
Health Act, 1875

Cross was also responsible for a new Public Health Act. This codified regulations laid down by over a hundred different statutes, and became the basis of public health work for the next fifty years. It was an important step along the lines Disraeli desired his party to pursue, and for which he suggested the jesting watchword 'Sanitas sanitatum, omnia sanitas'—or, as the Liberals scornfully termed it, 'a policy of sewage'.

Legalization of
'peaceful'
picketing

Perhaps the most far-reaching reform of Disraeli's ministry was the Conspiracy and Protection of Property Act introduced by Cross in 1875. Repealing Gladstone's Criminal Law Amendment Act, the new law definitely stated the legality of peaceful picketing, and provided a new safeguard for the unions by declaring that a group of strikers might, without fear of a criminal conspiracy charge, commit any act which it was lawful for one person to commit. These two changes would have very considerably increased the power of the unions to organize strikes if the courts had not, in the next twenty-five years, reached new heights of ingenuity in interpreting the law in a sense hostile to trade unions. For the moment, however, the new working-class voters were pleased with Disraeli's efforts on their behalf.

Employers and
Workmen Act,
1875

Another valuable measure introduced by the Home Secretary was the Employers and Workmen Act. This abolished the unfair distinction by which a breach of contract on the part of an employer was merely a civil offence liable to the payment of damages, whereas a breach of contract on the part of a workman could be classed as a criminal offence and punished by fine and imprisonment. Henceforth a breach of contract was a civil offence, whether committed by employer or workman.

The Factory
Act, 1874
(Ten-Hour Day)

Another measure of direct benefit to the labouring classes was the Factory Act of 1874, which cut the 60 hours week laid down in the Act of 1850[1] to 56 hours. The 'Ten-Hour Day' was thus

[1] See page 150.

at last achieved, for working hours in the industries concerned became 10 hours on Mondays to Fridays and 6 hours on Saturdays.

Useful work was also accomplished in other aspects of social reform. Agricultural enclosure, for so long practically unchecked, was now at last limited by an act of 1876, which laid down that further enclosure was not to be permitted unless it would constitute a public benefit. Two years later, in the spirit of this measure, a large area of Epping Forest was preserved from the hands of enclosers and saved as an open-air resort for Londoners. Another valuable piece of legislation was the Rivers Pollution Act, which secured rivers from further pollution by sewage, and compelled manufacturers to render harmless the discharges from their factories. All these measures, like the Sale of Food and Drugs Act (which prohibited harmful substances in food), were for the benefit of the nation's health, and so carried further the policy of which the Public Health Act was the foundation.

Other Public Health Reforms

At the same time another step was taken towards free and compulsory primary education by the Education Act of 1876.[1] At the other end of the educational system, Oxford and Cambridge were reformed by means of an investigating commission and an Act of Parliament which together made the extensive revenues of the Colleges more available for purposes of learning.

Education Act, 1876

Reform at Oxford and Cambridge

Perhaps the best-known reform of Disraeli's second Ministry, however, is one which was inspired by the eccentric and warmhearted Samuel Plimsoll, a former coal merchant who had entered Parliament. Plimsoll had written a book exposing the dastardly practice of overloading ships so that the owners could either cash in on a very profitable voyage, or else, if the ship went down, benefit from the heavy insurance thoughtfully taken out beforehand. Harassed by his agitation, the Government consented to introduce a Merchant Shipping Bill officially designed to stop such practices. The heart of the Cabinet, however, was not in the measure, for it was subjected, behind the scenes, to pressure from wealthy and influential shipowners. Moreover, a Commission appointed to study the subject had reported that Plimsoll's favourite remedy, a load-line clearly displayed on each ship, was impracticable.

The Safety of Merchant Shipping

Samuel Plimsoll

Finding itself pressed for time at the end of the session, the Government therefore announced its intention of dropping the Bill. At this, Plimsoll created a violent scene, shouted that he

[1] See page 383.

would unmask the 'villains' and 'ship-knackers' who sent the seamen to their doom, shook his fist at Disraeli, defied the Speaker, who was trying to restrain him, and took himself off in a temper. This focused public attention on the matter, and Disraeli wisely beat a retreat by putting through the Government proposals as a temporary measure. They were made more permanent by the Merchant Shipping Act of the following year. But the measure left much to be desired, for though a load-line was introduced, and the Board of Trade was empowered to stop an overloaded ship leaving port, the line was to be drawn where the shipowner thought fit! The principle of the line, however, had been obtained, and after some years of quarrels and disputes a further Merchant Shipping Act in 1890 authorized the Board of Trade to see that a scientifically devised line was drawn and respected.

The political atmosphere during the opening years of the Ministry, while the Government was largely concerned with social reform, was far less bitter than it afterwards became. This was partly due to the fact that Gladstone retired from the leadership of the Liberal party soon after Disraeli's accession to office. He was succeeded by Lord Hartington, who was a member of the Cavendish family, and afterwards became the eighth Duke of Devonshire. Hartington had very little of Gladstone's fire, and it distinctly suited Disraeli to have so much less formidable an opponent. The Prime Minister's pleasure in the change appears in a letter to one of his elderly female friends, describing Hartington's first appearance as Liberal Leader—'Harty-Tarty did very well: exactly as I expected he would; sensible, dullish and gentlemanlike'—while to the same sympathetic ear he retailed 'the new joke about the Whigs . . . you know Lord Derby, *père*, said the Whigs were *dished*; they say now they are Caven*dished*'. It was not long, however, before the old party bitterness returned; and it reached new heights when Gladstone emerged from his semi-retirement to lead an ardent campaign against the Government's foreign policy.

The Merchant Shipping Act, 1876

The 'Plimsoll line'

Gladstone's 'retirement'

Lord Hartington

The re-emergence of Gladstone

*   *   *   *   *

Disraeli was nothing if not an upholder of British power and prestige, and it was not long before he seized a remarkable opportunity of strengthening Britain's imperial position. This occurred when a large block of Suez Canal shares came on the market. The Canal, which had been opened in 1869, was the

The Suez Canal Shares, 1875

work of a Frenchman, de Lesseps; he had been largely financed by French capital, for Palmerston had opposed the whole project and Gladstone had doubted its engineering and financial soundness. By far the largest block of shares not in French hands belonged to the spendthrift Khedive Ismail of Egypt—and in 1875 Ismail had either to find £4,000,000 within a fortnight or declare the public bankruptcy of his Government. The Khedive therefore entered secret negotiations for the sale or mortgage of his shares—about seven-sixteenths of the total issued—to a group of French capitalists. When news of this was brought to the Foreign Office by a journalist, Disraeli determined to act swiftly, for he saw how much the security of the Indian Empire might depend on control of the new route, and how important it was that the French should not acquire a virtual monopoly of the shares. Winning the Cabinet round to his view, he borrowed the necessary money on behalf of the Government from his friends the Rothschilds (Parliament was not sitting, and speed and secrecy were essential), and within ten days had brought off the deal.

This rapid and successful transaction—which ensured reasonable rates for British shipping using the Canal, and gave Britain a prominent interest not only in the Canal but in Egypt—was quickly regularized by Parliament. Critics were not lacking, but on the whole the episode was regarded as a great triumph for Disraeli. And the Prime Minister, of course, took care to present the matter to the Queen in a light well calculated to secure her approval:

> It is just settled; you have it, Madam, . . . Four millions sterling! and almost immediately. There was only one firm that could do it—Rothschilds. They behaved admirably; advanced the money at a low rate, and the entire interest of the Khedive is now yours, Madam.

The following year Disraeli took a further action which, though of considerably less importance, was also intended to strengthen the Empire. In 1874 he had suggested that the Queen, to mark the direct relationship to the Crown in which India had stood since 1858,[1] should assume the title of Empress of India. The Queen was delighted with the suggestion, and soon compelled the Prime Minister to act up to it. But the proposal had a very bad reception from critics in Parliament—including Gladstone

The Royal Titles Bill, 1876

[1] See page 402.

(*Tenniel, 1875, reproduced by permission of the Proprietors of 'Punch'*)

MOSÉ IN EGITTO!

Disraeli, anxious to secure control over the short route to India, acquires the Khedive's shares in the Suez Canal. 'Moses in Egypt' is an opera by Rossini; the Prime Minister's Jewish ancestry makes it a specially appropriate title to this cartoon.

—and in the country generally, and it was only with great difficulty that Disraeli forced it through. Whatever the ultimate advantages of the new title in securing the loyalty of Indians to the Crown, there is no doubt that its most immediate effect was to secure the loyalty of the Queen to her Prime Minister. For the whole incident, with the niggling criticisms it brought forth from the Liberals, set the Queen violently against Gladstone and his party. An antipathy was thus formed, or confirmed, which was to colour politics for many years, and to make Gladstone's task much more difficult when he again assumed office.

But by far the most important incident in foreign affairs during Disraeli's second Ministry was the fresh crisis with Russia. In 1875 and 1876 the subject nations of South-Eastern Europe rose against their Turkish masters. The latter reacted with their customary vigour, particularly in the Bulgarian provinces, and indulged in ghastly atrocities and massacres; and this gave Russia the excuse to attack Turkey in the name of the Balkan Christians. Once more the Eastern Question demanded an answer. *The Eastern crisis / Revolts against Turkish rule / Russo-Turkish War, 1877*

In order to clear the decks for war with Turkey, the Russians first promised Austria-Hungary that they would not object if she annexed Bosnia and Herzegovina, which adjoined her territory. They then secured Britain's temporary neutrality by a promise, among other things, not to occupy Constantinople or close the Straits. Disraeli did not wish to connive at Russia's schemes, but he was in a difficult position because the Turks had refused all suggested reforms and because there was a rising tide of anti-Turkish opinion in this country. This was all the stronger because, misled by the British Ambassador at Constantinople, Disraeli had at first minimized the severity and extent of the Turkish cruelties, declaring them to be 'to a large extent inventions'. It had in fact been left to a Liberal paper, the *Daily News*, to bring the truth (though with some journalistic exaggerations) before the public; and to Gladstone, emerging from his semi-retirement, to lead the anti-Turkish campaign in the country. *Disraeli's attitude / Gladstone's attitude*

The opening barrage of Gladstone's campaign was an eloquent pamphlet, *The Bulgarian Horrors and the Question of the East.* 'Let the Turks', thundered Gladstone, 'now carry away their abuses in the only possible manner, namely by carrying off themselves. Their Zaptiehs and their Mudins, their Bimbashis and their Yuzhashis, their Kaimakams and their Pashas, one and all, bag and baggage, shall I hope clear out from the province they *Gladstone's pamphlet, The Bulgarian Horrors* have desolated and profaned.' The pamphlet had enormous influence; and a general political campaign on these lines by the Liberals made it impossible for Beaconsfield (as he now was) to support Turkey immediately on the outbreak of her war with Russia.

The Liberal agitation naturally did nothing to improve the relations of the two great British statesmen. Beaconsfield was bitterly resentful of Gladstone's attitude, for he considered it destroyed national unity in a time of crisis, and was liable to give direct encouragement to Russia; while Gladstone regarded Beaconsfield's apparent indifference to the sufferings of the Bulgarian Christians as simply immoral. Writing to his Foreign Secretary, Lord Derby, soon after the publication of Gladstone's pamphlet, Beaconsfield referred to it as 'of all the Bulgarian horrors, perhaps the greatest'; and a little later Lord Derby was treated to a description of 'that unprincipled maniac Gladstone—extraordinary mixture of envy, vindictiveness, hypocrisy and superstition: and with one commanding characteristic—whether Prime Minister, or Leader of Opposition, whether preaching, praying, speechifying, or scribbling—never a gentleman!' Gladstone for his part spoke less about personal characteristics, but he felt equally deeply.

The course of the Russo-Turkish War of 1877 caused a distinct change in British opinion. With the protracted and heroic defence of Plevna by the Turks, British opinion began to turn in their favour. Ultimately in December Plevna was compelled to surrender through starvation, and in January 1878 the Russians occupied Adrianople, where they were within easy reach of Constantinople. For Beaconsfield the critical moment had come, and none too soon for the martial ardour of Queen Victoria, who was threatening to abdicate if her Cabinet continued to countenance the Russian advance. 'She feels she cannot', the Queen wrote to the Prime Minister, 'remain the Sovereign of a country that is letting itself down to kiss the feet of the great barbarians. . . . She is utterly ashamed of the Cabinet. . . . Oh, if the Queen were a man, she would like to go and give those Russians, whose word one cannot believe, such a beating!'

Thus supported by the Queen, Beaconsfield now asked for a grant of £6,000,000 from Parliament for military purposes. Then came the news of an armistice between the two belligerents, but there were so many rumours of an intended Russian occupation of Constantinople that the British Mediterranean Fleet was

Plevna

Adrianople

Beaconsfield
takes action—
the Anglo-
Russian crisis

(*Tenniel, 1878, reproduced by permission of the Proprietors of 'Punch'*)

A BAD EXAMPLE

Dr. Punch: 'WHAT'S ALL THIS: YOU THE HEAD BOYS OF THE SCHOOL THROWING MUD! YOU OUGHT TO BE ASHAMED OF YOURSELVES!'

Gladstone and Disraeli, the two senior boys at St Stephen's Academy—i.e. the two party leaders in the House of Commons—caught in a bout of mud-slinging (in this case, mutual recriminations over the Eastern crisis). Headmaster Punch takes both to task.

ordered through the Dardanelles to the Turkish capital. The Russians answered this by moving forward to the very outskirts of Constantinople. War now seemed imminent, and the rising temper of anti-Russian feeling in Britain was reflected in the famous music-hall song—

> We don't want to fight, but by Jingo[1] if we do
> We've got the men, we've got the ships, we've got the money too.
> We've fought the Bear before, and while Britons shall be true,
> The Russians shall not have Constantinople.

The Treaty of San Stefano, 1878

The tension then slackened somewhat, but in March 1878 it again approached breaking-point when the terms of peace between Russians and Turks became known. The Treaty of San Stefano, among other provisions, assigned to Russia the eastern part of Armenia and created a very large state of Bulgaria, stretch-

'Big Bulgaria'

ing from the Black Sea to the Aegean. This 'Big Bulgaria', which was inhabited by many races other than Bulgarians, was to be administered and garrisoned for an initial period by the Russians. Such an extension of Russian power was welcome neither to Britain nor to Austria-Hungary, and both countries demanded that the terms should be submitted to a European Congress for revision. To show Russia that he meant business, Beaconsfield then called out the Reserve, and ordered several thousand Indian troops up to Malta. This bold action was taken against the advice of Derby, who was replaced as Foreign Secretary by Lord Salis-

The demand for revision by a Congress

bury, a much firmer and more skilful negotiator. Faced with this evidence of Britain's determination, and the additional fact that Germany, under Salisbury's persuasion, also declared for a Congress, Russia now agreed to submit the treaty to revision by the other great powers.

The Congress of Berlin, which lasted for a month in the summer of 1878, was Beaconsfield's greatest triumph. Beacons-

Beaconsfield's preliminary agreements—

field and Salisbury went to Berlin armed with three preliminary (and secret) agreements which they had been careful to make. The first was with Russia, who was by now convinced that Britain would fight unless the San Stefano terms were modified.

—with Russia ('Big Bulgaria' trisected)

By this agreement Russia consented to a drastic reduction of the 'Big Bulgaria'. The southern and western parts, including much of Macedonia, were to be handed back unconditionally to the Turks; the northern part, north of the Balkan range, was to be an independent principality, to be known as Bulgaria, and to be

[1] Thus was the word 'Jingoistic' added to the English language.

THE DECLINE OF THE OTTOMAN EMPIRE IN EUROPE 1783-1913

HUNGARY

R. Save
R. Danube
Belgrade

R. Dniester
BESSARABIA
(To Russia 1812)
R. Pruth
R. Bug
LITTLE TARTARY (To Russia) 1791
Ochakof

TRANSYLVANIA   MOLDAVIA

RUMANIA

WALLACHIA (1861)
Bucharest

BOSNIA
1878 (Austrian Occ.)   1908 (To Austria)
DALMATIA
HERZEGOVINA
1833
1817
SERVIA
1878

R. Danube
Plevna
1878
Sofia
EASTERN RUMELIA 1885
BULGARIA
1913

MONTENEGRO
1913
1913

BLACK SEA

To Rumania (1878)

Adrianople
TURKEY
1913
Constantinople
Bosphorus
Scutari
Sea of Marmora

ALBANIA
1913

MACEDONIA
1913

GREECE

Salonika
Gallipoli
Dardanelles

ANATOLIA

ADRIATIC SEA

ITALY

Corfu
EPIRUS   THESSALY 1878

1831

IONIAN SEA

Ionian Islands

Athens

MOREA   CYCLADES

AEGEAN SEA

MEDITERRANEAN SEA

Rhodes

Crete

K. C. Jordan

Legend

━━━━━ **Boundary of Turkish Empire 1783**

•••••••••• **Boundaries of Balkan States**
    at times between 1783 and 1913

•-•-•-•-• **Boundaries of Balkan States 1913**

⌗⌗⌗⌗⌗ **Boundary of Turkey in Europe 1913**

initially under Russian organization; while a smaller province, south of the Balkan range, was to be officially part of the Turkish Empire, but to possess a Christian governor and a considerable degree of self-rule. Russian influence would thus be excluded from the Mediterranean area, and a constant object of British foreign policy secured.

—with Turkey ('The Cyprus Convention')

Britain's second preliminary agreement was with Turkey. Since Russia refused to surrender her Armenian conquests, Beaconsfield determined to acquire a convenient base for dealing with any further Russian moves in the Middle East. To this end he persuaded Turkey, in return for a guarantee of her remaining Asiatic dominions against Russian attack, to surrender Cyprus —'the key to Asia', as he termed it—into British keeping. At the same time Turkey promised once more to reform her administration, and particularly the treatment of her Christian subjects.

—and with Austria-Hungary (Bosnia and Herzegovina)

Britain's third preliminary agreement was with Austria-Hungary. It promised that Britain would not object to an Austrian occupation of Bosnia and Herzegovina. This was to ensure Austrian support in the event of a conflict with Russia at the Congress.

The Congress of Berlin, 1878

Armed with these three agreements, Beaconsfield was able, in spite of his failing health, to dominate the Congress. On the whole, matters went smoothly, save on the details of the province south of the Balkan range. Beaconsfield wished the Turks to have the right of military occupation, since this would give them a good northern frontier against Russian influence—the Balkan mountains. Russia of course desired to forbid the entry of Turkish soldiers into the province. Beaconsfield also wanted the province to be called Eastern Rumelia, so that its name would imply no connection with the new Bulgaria, while Russia desired it to be called South Bulgaria. On both points Beaconsfield took a very firm line. He let it be known that it would be a question of war against Russia if she did not give way; backed up his ultimatum by ordering a special train to be ready to take the British delegation from Berlin; and triumphantly got his way on both matters. He also secured a few concessions from Russia in Armenia— before releasing the news about Cyprus.

The Treaty of Berlin, 1878

A new treaty embodying these terms—the Treaty of Berlin— was then drawn up to replace the Treaty of San Stefano. Among other important clauses, Serbia and Montenegro were slightly enlarged (though not to the extent contemplated by San Stefano) and declared entirely independent of Turkey; and Austria-

Hungary was allowed to occupy and administer Bosnia and Herzegovina.

The most divergent views may be taken about Beaconsfield's achievement at Berlin. On the one hand he had avoided war, checked Russian expansion and added Cyprus to the British possessions. On the other hand he had restored thousands of Serbs and Greeks (in Macedonia) to Turkish rule. The artificial division between Bulgaria and Eastern Rumelia on which he set so much store was undone within seven years, when the two territories proclaimed themselves united. The promises of good behaviour from the Turks were of little value, and before many years had elapsed the massacres of Armenian Christians were to exceed anything that the Bulgarians had suffered. Cyprus proved to be of little use, for within five years the British were firmly established in Egypt, a much more important centre.

There was thus little permanence about most of Beaconsfield's work in this connection, but in one respect at least it profoundly influenced the future. By the destruction of the 'Big Bulgaria' Russian influence in South-Eastern Europe was sharply limited; and by the Austrian occupation of Bosnia and Herzegovina (which Beaconsfield would have been in any case powerless to prevent), that of Austria-Hungary was decidedly increased. The effect was thus to place Russian and Austrian influence in South-Eastern Europe on a far greater equality than before, and the struggle for predominance between the two powers in this area became one of the great causes of the First World War.[1]

When Beaconsfield returned from Berlin, however, it was only apparent that he had avoided war, smacked Russia soundly in the face, and added territory to the British Empire. The aged statesman was therefore able to claim that he brought 'peace with honour'. The Liberals, however, were not inclined to agree about the 'honour'. They strongly disapproved of the return of the Greeks and Serbs of Macedonia to Turkish rule, and bitterly attacked the Cyprus Convention—not only because of the acquisition of the island, but because of the pledge to defend Turkey-in-Asia against future aggression. It was, thundered Gladstone, 'an insane covenant'—a criticism which inspired Beaconsfield's famous description of his opponent as 'a sophistical rhetorician, inebriated with the exuberance of his own verbosity, and gifted with an egotistical imagination that can at all times command an

[1] Moreover, the spark which started the conflagration came from Sarajevo, the capital of Bosnia.

interminable and inconsistent series of arguments to malign an opponent and glorify himself'. But, in general, the country approved Beaconsfield's work in no uncertain tones, and the Queen reflected popular sentiment when she invested the returning statesman with the Garter.

If Beaconsfield scored a notable popular success over the Eastern Question, he was soon to be in hot water over other problems in Afghanistan[1] and South Africa.[2] In each case a 'forward' policy carried out by Beaconsfield's nominees led to war and temporary disaster. A Zulu War, an Afghan War and a narrow shave with Russia all within two years was a little too much for the British public, unaccustomed to so rapid a pace in the conduct of foreign affairs. The Liberals did not fail to press home the moral, and Gladstone's verbal onslaughts during his campaign to win the Conservative seat of Midlothian were greeted with immense enthusiasm.

The tide was thus turning against the Conservatives. Besides the growing belief that Beaconsfield's foreign policy was following dangerous and even unrighteous courses, there were also the effects of the great agricultural depression. At the close of the 1870s foreign corn first began to flood the British markets; for with the new improvements in transport the products of the virgin soil of Canada, the 'Middle West', the Argentine and Australia could now be sold in the United Kingdom at a very cheap price. A disastrous succession of British harvests between 1875 and 1880, with a climax in 1879, the 'Black Year', only made matters worse. Many farmers were driven out of business, thousands of acres of corn land went back to grass, rents fell, and it was inevitable that the Government would be saddled with the responsibility for some of the disaster, however little it was in fact to blame. Indeed, the only thing Beaconsfield could have done would have been to impose, as in the old days, heavy duties against foreign corn. But he knew that duties on food, although he had defended them a generation earlier, would now lose so many votes for his party as to mean political suicide. In his own words, Protection was 'not only dead but damned'.

So it came about that at the elections of 1880 the Conservatives were decisively defeated. Beaconsfield thereupon resigned, and the Liberals returned to power, much to the chagrin of the Queen. Within a year the veteran Conservative leader was dead.

It is difficult not to be impressed by the genius of Benjamin

Afghanistan and South Africa

Gladstone's 'Midlothian Campaign'

The agricultural depression

Defeat of the Conservatives, 1880

[1] See page 403.   [2] See page 412.

(*Tenniel, 1878, reproduced by permission of the Proprietors of 'Punch'*)

A BLAZE OF TRIUMPH

The skilful Disraeli, walking the tightrope of the Congress of Berlin, manages to support Turkey and at the same time secure Peace—and Cyprus.

Disraeli's
achievement

Disraeli, Earl of Beaconsfield. Enthralled by the glamour of crowns and coronets, and an actor and *poseur* to his finger-tips, he nevertheless made a contribution of very great value to British political life. Whatever view is taken of his foreign policy, he was certainly conscious of the imperial destiny of his country, and, as Salisbury said, 'above all things he wished to see England united, and powerful, and great'. But posterity should perhaps be even more grateful for his constant stress on the duties rather than the privileges of the governing classes, and for his effort to guide his party along the path of social reform. In this object his success was, in the long run, considerable; and to all progressive Conservatives the work of Disraeli has remained, and will remain, a source of inspiration.

16. The End of an Era

1 Gladstone's Second Ministry, 1880–1885

With the end of Beaconsfield's period of power in 1880, the Liberal and Conservative parties had each enjoyed one good innings, and had scored freely by means of their favourite but differing strokes. From this time on the game of politics was to grow more serious, and the flow of the nation's life to be more often troubled. During the last years of the nineteenth century there began to appear the deep conflicts which doomed the stable structure of Victorian England. In Ireland nationalism threw down its challenge to English mastery; at home labour difficulties bore witness to a state of social conflict; abroad there appeared new threats to Britain's peace and security. The death of the Queen in 1901 after her long reign of sixty-four years indeed signalized, as some felt at the time, the end of an era.

The story of Gladstone's second Ministry is one of promise unfulfilled. The Liberals seemed to have everything in their favour, including a substantial majority in the Commons, a strong party organization, a veteran but immensely energetic leader, and a Cabinet of outstanding ability. Yet their lot was to be five years of difficulty and humiliation. *The Liberals in 1880*

Some causes of weakness were apparent at the outset. The Ministry had to face not only the opposition of the regular Conservative party, which was staid enough after the passing of Disraeli, but the stinging darts of a small group of 'Tory democrats' led by Lord Randolph Churchill, and well named 'the Fourth Party'. For there was no doubt that the Irish Nationalists, over sixty strong, were the third. Skilled in the tactics of obstruction, the Irish members were determined that if Parliament would not grant Home Rule to Ireland, it should carry no measures at all. They forced the Commons to adopt unwelcome rules limiting the scope of debate, and they provoked continual rows which seemed sheer sacrilege to all who venerated the traditions of Parliament, and particularly to Gladstone. *The Conservatives and 'the Fourth Party'* *The Irish Nationalists*

Worse than these trials were the divisions within the Liberal party itself. Many of the M.P.s for boroughs were Radicals who *Liberal divisions and difficulties*

205

owed their election to working-class voters; a few of them were of working-class origin themselves. On the other hand there was still a strong Whig element, best represented by Lord Harting-ton.[1] There was little in common between aristocrats of this order and Joseph Chamberlain, the successful screw-manu-facturer, who backed the demand for 'three acres and a cow'

(Tenniel, 1883, reproduced by permission of the Proprietors of 'Punch')

ATHWART THE COURSE

R–nd–lph Ch–rch–ll (an aggravating boy) 'IN THE WAY AGAIN! 'OORAY!!'

The cross-party sniping and shock tactics of Lord Randolph Churchill and his friends of the 'Fourth Party', together with the similar efforts of the Irish M.P.s, threatened to wreck not only Gladstone's Ministry but the whole system of parliamentary government.

for every land worker, and denounced the rich, 'who toil not, neither do they spin'. Gladstone himself tended to be a Radical in public and a Whig in the Cabinet; and this behaviour, com-bined with his personal aloofness—his followers' most intimate mode of reference to him in his absence was 'Mr G.'—resulted in neither section of his party fully trusting him.

[1] See page 192.

The situation in Ireland when Gladstone took office was Ireland again rapidly worsening. What small benefits the Irish peasantry had obtained from the Land Act of 1870 had been engulfed in the depression which struck the British Isles five years later, when bad weather and poor harvests at home combined with an influx of cheap American corn to ruin British agriculture. The only remedy was a change in farming methods, which in Ireland meant evicting small tenants and letting the land in large units to men who could put capital into their farming and make it pay. In 1880, 10,000 persons were accordingly evicted—five times as many as in 1877. In the same year, 1880, 2,500 outrages were recorded, for despair drove the peasants to violence. Previously they had made little response to the Fenian movement, or to the later Irish Republican Brotherhood. But now there was com- The Irish Land bustible material in plenty, and to make full use of it Michael League Davitt, a Fenian who had served a seven years' sentence for treason, organized the Irish Land League.

Meanwhile in Parliament an annual resolution urging Home Rule had produced nothing but derision from the English members, and a well-intentioned bill of Gladstone's to compensate unfairly evicted tenants was thrown out by the House of Lords. Then the Irish campaign began in deadly earnest, waged in Ireland against the landlord by rent strikes and terror, in Parliament against the Government by every resource of debate and obstruction.

The director of this double onslaught was Charles Stewart C. S. Parnell, Parnell. It is notable that the most powerful leader of the Irish 1846–1891 Catholic peasantry should have been a landowner, a Protestant, and not of true Irish stock. Parnell's power lay in his dominant personality. Hatred of England, even more than love of Ireland, was his consuming passion. In contrast to the volatile Daniel O'Connell, who alone can be compared with him in influence over his countrymen, Parnell was humourless, friendless, ungenerous; distant and reserved in manner, he spoke well only through practice. Yet by sheer intensity of purpose and force of character he became the unquestioned leader both of the Irish party in Parliament and of the Land League—in fact 'the uncrowned King of Ireland'.

The Land League's campaign was organized on the lines of a The League's strike. The League decided what was a reasonable rent for each campaign holding, and if a landowner refused to accept this, all the tenants on his estate withheld their rents. If they were then evicted the

League organized a boycott[1] of the offending parties—landlord, agent and new tenants. Methods often went beyond persuasion. 'Moonlighters' went out nightly to maim cattle and burn ricks, conveying sinister hints by digging graves before people's door-steps—graves which were not always left unprovided with an occupant.

Gladstone's remedies— Coercion Bill, 1881—

To deal with these tactics, the Government brought in a Coercion Bill suspending the Habeas Corpus Act, so that suspected persons could be imprisoned without trial. This roused the Irish M.P.s to their greatest efforts of obstruction, but though they kept the House sitting for forty-one hours, they could not prevent the passage of the Bill. It was rapidly followed by a more constructive measure—Gladstone's Second Irish Land Act, which gave Irish tenants the 'three F's' they had long asked for —Fixity of tenure, Fair rents (to be assessed by special courts) and Free sale. Together they ensured that a tenant could not be evicted while he paid his rent, that the rent could not be made excessive, and that the tenant could sell his lease, without his landlord's permission, to anyone who would give him a fair price for it. This last provision meant that the tenant could recover the cost of any improvements he had made.[2]

—Second Irish Land Act, 1881

Parnell's rejoinder

Parnell did not view the Land Act as a matter for gratitude. On the contrary, he calculated that if so large a concession had been won by pressure and violence, it would certainly pay to continue the pressure—if not the violence. Parnell's aim, in fact, was not to solve the agrarian problem in Ireland, but to keep it alive as a proof that Ireland could not be governed by Englishmen. So the Land League, after giving the new courts a brief trial, boycotted them, and evictions and outrages went on as before. To meet this defiance, the Government used its powers under the Coercion Act to arrest Parnell and other leaders of the League, lodging them in Kilmainham Gaol, Dublin. Nevertheless, Parnell's campaign was not without effect, for Gladstone now questioned whether any solution put forward by a British government could ever win acceptance from the Irish people. The Liberal leader's conversion to Home Rule had begun.

Meanwhile another approach was tried, for the Government did not wish to be forced back on mere repression. Contact was made with Parnell, and a 'gentleman's agreement' was reached,

[1] The name of an early victim, Captain Boycott, became a new word in the language.
[2] See page 133.

(Tenniel, 1881, reproduced by permission of the Proprietors of 'Punch')

THE RIVALS

The fair Hibernia (Ireland) is wooed on the one hand by Parnell's **Land League** with daggers and dynamite, and on the other by Gladstone with the **Second Land Act**. At this stage Mr G.'s prospects seem rosy.

The Kilmainham 'Treaty' known as the Kilmainham 'Treaty'. A Bill would be introduced to clear off the arrears of rent into which half the tenant-farmers had fallen, while Parnell, who was to be released, would call off the campaign of outrage—which was indeed no part of his policy. To carry out the Government's intentions, a new Viceroy and Chief Secretary for Ireland were appointed. But they had no sooner arrived in Dublin than the Chief Secretary, Lord Frederick Cavendish, and the permanent Under-Secretary, Phoenix Park murders, 1882 Burke, were murdered by a gang of assassins in Phoenix Park.[1] Thus were the best hopes of peace ruined by extremists—a secret group calling themselves 'The Invincibles', who were not discovered till later. But many people attributed the vile deed to Parnell's own influence, and in any case it so blackened the reputation of Irishmen in general that the policy of conciliation was handicapped. The Kilmainham 'Treaty' was only half carried out, for the Arrears Act that was passed did little for the peasants, and there was a new Crimes Act to legalize trial of serious offences without a jury. Yet outrages continued, with an increase in the number of murders. Before the year was out, however, the Invincibles were brought to trial.[2] The remaining years of Gladstone's Ministry saw some improvements in conditions through the working of the Land Act and Arrears Act, but no abatement of the Irish demand for Home Rule, and no attempt by the Government to advance towards it.

Ministry's poor record in South Africa and Egypt Imperial affairs also went badly. Delay in granting self-government to the Boers led to the disaster of Majuba Hill,[3] and the subsequent recognition of the independence of the Transvaal seemed like a spineless surrender. Gladstone showed a different temper in ordering the occupation of Egypt, but this enterprise brought in its train the tragic loss of Gordon.[4] The Government incurred the deepest odium by its failure to rescue him, and escaped a motion of censure by only fourteen votes. It regained some credit, however, by its handling of an Afghan border incident with Russia.

The Third Reform Act, 1884 In contrast with Gladstone's earlier period of office, the years 1880–85, fraught with trouble abroad, witnessed only one important domestic reform—the Third Parliamentary Reform Act.

---

[1] Burke, a permanent official, was the intended victim; his normal escort of detectives had fallen too far behind, and Cavendish, who was unknown to his assailants, perished in trying to save his companion.

[2] One of them turned 'Queen's evidence' and was pardoned. An avenger murdered him on board the ship in which he was being smuggled to South Africa.   [3] See page 412.   [4] See page 421.

Since the previous Reform Act of 1867, all town householders had enjoyed the vote, but in the country it was limited to the ancient 40s. freeholders and the tenants of a £12 leasehold, so that the landlord influence was still very strong. The main feature of the new Bill—for which Chamberlain, with his strong views on the unearned privileges of the landed aristocracy, was largely responsible—was to equate the county with the borough franchise. Its effect, together with that of a companion Act for the redistribution of seats, was to give the vote in the counties to all householders, adding about 2 million voters to the existing 3 million, and to re-map the constituencies on a more drastic plan than either of the earlier Reform Acts. Towns with fewer than 15,000 inhabitants lost their separate representation; towns with fewer than 50,000 were to have one member only—an approach to the ideal of equal single-member constituencies. The two chief consequences of the Act were unintended. One was to increase the power of the Irish Nationalist Party, which now swept the board in Catholic Ireland. The other was to weaken the Whig element in the Liberal party, for Whigs had got in usually by pairing with the more popular Radical candidates in two-member boroughs, many of which were now abolished.

In 1885, as a result of further Irish complications, Gladstone's Government fell. The Cabinet was more hopelessly divided than ever over a project of Chamberlain's for local self-government in Ireland; and Parnell and his followers, nibbling at bait held out to them by the Opposition, joined their votes with the Conservatives to defeat the Ministry on the Budget. Gladstone thereupon resigned, and the Conservative leader, Lord Salisbury, took office.

Parnell allies with Conservatives: defeat of Liberal Ministry 1885

2 Parnell, Gladstone and Salisbury

Salisbury had no majority, and could only carry on the business of government until an election could be held. The seven months of this 'caretaker' administration saw much manœuvring. Chamberlain bid for a Liberal—or Radical—victory in the forthcoming election with a striking programme of social reform. Parnell too held good cards, for he could sway not only the Irish constituencies but also the large Irish vote in cities like Liverpool and Glasgow. After some bargaining with the Conservatives, Parnell received the impression that they might, if returned to

Salisbury's 'Caretaker' Ministry, 1885–1886

The election of 1885

power, give Ireland Home Rule, and he consequently used his influence with the Irish voters in England on the Conservative behalf. Thanks largely to Chamberlain's programme, however, the election resulted in a Liberal majority of eighty-six over the Conservatives. But Parnell's Nationalists, triumphant in Ireland, reached the same figure, so that it was now in his power either to keep the Liberals out of office or to put them in.

The Liberals and Home Rule

Even after the election Gladstone would have preferred to solve the Irish question by agreement between the parties, but it became known—against his wishes—that at heart he favoured Home Rule. The Conservatives then dropped it, and the Irish vote in the House of Commons was promptly used to help the Liberals, so that Salisbury's Ministry was defeated as soon as the new House met. Gladstone thereupon became Prime Minister for the third time. He was now dependent on Irish votes and virtually pledged to give Ireland Home Rule, though by no means all his colleagues favoured such a departure.

Gladstone's third Ministry, 1886

The first Home Rule Bill, 1886

The first Home Rule Bill was introduced in 1886. It proposed to set up in Dublin an Irish parliament to control all the affairs of government except certain reserved subjects, of which the most important were defence, foreign affairs and external trade. A tremendous debate took place in the Commons, in which Gladstone was opposed by two of the finest orators of his own party, Hartington, leader of the Whigs, and Chamberlain, leader of the Radicals. Chamberlain believed in local self-government for Ireland but was a determined opponent of Home Rule. Largely through his influence ninety-three Liberals voted with the Conservatives, and the Bill was rejected by thirty votes. Once again, as in 1829 and 1846, a powerful ministry was brought down and a great party split asunder by an Irish problem. This time it was the Liberals who suffered, and for the next twenty years, with one short interval, they languished in opposition. Home Rule would certainly have been a wise policy; but England was not yet prepared to concede it.

★   ★   ★   ★   ★

Salisbury's second Ministry, 1886–1892

Lord Salisbury now entered on a period as Prime Minister which was to occupy thirteen and a half of the next seventeen years. He accepted the Premiership without enthusiasm, his main interest being foreign affairs. At home he was sceptical of all projects of reform, adopting them only when he could not help it.

The Conservative remedy for the troubles in Ireland was 'twenty years of resolute government'. This they began to apply first in the shape of a new Crimes Act under which all offences against law and order in Ireland would be tried without a jury, and secondly by a modest measure to assist tenants to buy their farms. The country relapsed into smouldering rebellion. The latest device of the Land League was the Plan of Campaign, by which the tenants on each estate decided what was a fair rent, and if their landlord would not accept it, paid it into the campaign fund instead. There were many evictions, and the law was rigorously enforced by the new Secretary for Ireland, Salisbury's nephew A. J. Balfour, whom the Irish soon dubbed 'Bloody Balfour'.

The policy of coercion was not popular in England, and opinion swung in favour of Home Rule. Parnell reached the height of his prestige when a series of letters published in *The Times*, implicating him in the Phoenix Park murders, were proved to be forgeries. Everything seemed to point to a victory for Liberalism and Home Rule at the next election. Then came the tragic fall of the Irish leader. He was cited as co-respondent in a divorce suit brought by Captain O'Shea, a worthless Irish ex-officer and M.P., against his wife. Parnell's connection with Katherine O'Shea had lasted for some years, and was tolerated by O'Shea until a regular income he was drawing from his wife's family dried up. But the revelation was a severe shock to Parnell's Catholic following, and to the Nonconformists who were such an important element in the Liberal party, and all Parnell's will-power and generalship counted now for nothing. Gladstone's advice that he should resign his leadership of the Irish Nationalist Party in the interests of his cause was stubbornly rejected; and when most of his followers deserted him he still clung tenaciously to his position, wore himself out in a desperate battle to maintain it, and ten months later died a broken man at the age of forty-six. Meanwhile Balfour endeavoured to combine firm government with a policy of 'killing Home Rule by kindness'.

It was not only the death of Parnell that lowered the excitement of the parliamentary scene; until the end of the century the important developments were taking place elsewhere. The Government's record of legislation was a fairly busy but very ordinary one, in which little trace could be found of the Radical enthusiasms which Lord Randolph Churchill had imported into the Conservative party as Chamberlain had formerly into the

Local
Government
Act, 1888

Liberal party. The most important reform was the Act which set
up County Councils—elected bodies which took over the
administrative duties performed since Tudor days by nominated
Justices of the Peace. The landowner was thus deprived of a
large sphere of influence in local affairs—though the J.P.s retained their duties as magistrates—and the country people were
given the same control over local government as borough
residents had enjoyed since the Act of 1835.[1] The London area,
except the City, was erected into a new County, while other towns
with populations over 50,000 enjoyed as County Boroughs the
same powers as the counties. The new councils replaced a vast
muddle of administrative bodies, estimated to number 27,000,
all of them entitled to levy rates for one purpose or another. To
the original duties of county councils many new charges were
later added, among them education, health and public assistance.

Salisbury's
foreign policy

In international relations the period was one of stress, in which
the 'massive wisdom and calm temper' of Salisbury, who was
Foreign Secretary as well as Prime Minister, were a great asset
to his country. It fell to him to achieve the agreements by which
Africa was partitioned without violence,[2] and to maintain British
interests on a European stage dominated by Bismarck. His
greatest single difficulty arose from the British occupation of
Egypt, which he was no more able than Gladstone to bring to a
close. Bismarck did everything possible to foment trouble there
between the British and French—not that much stimulus was
needed, for friction was constantly occurring at all points of contact, and Salisbury pronounced France to be 'an insupportable
neighbour'.

Salisbury, like Pitt, Palmerston and Disraeli before him, entertained a profound suspicion of Russian intentions in the Near
East. Some years earlier he had seconded Disraeli at the Congress
of Berlin in destroying the 'Big Bulgaria' planned by Russia, and
in restoring Turkey once more to a position of some strength.[3]
But he now came to the conclusion that in supporting Turkey
as a bulwark against Russian penetration Britain had 'backed the
wrong horse'. The correct course would rather be to encourage
the Balkan nationalities to a genuine independence. So when the

Bulgaria, 1885

Bulgars defied the arrangements of the Congress and united the
two parts of their country to form a single state, he prevented
any action being taken against them to enforce the Berlin Treaty
—greatly to the annoyance of Russia, which had found the new

[1] See page 122.   [2] See page 425.   [3] See pages 198–200.

Bulgaria unexpectedly obstinate and now wanted to keep it as weak as possible.

The term 'splendid isolation',[1] sometimes used to describe Lord Salisbury's foreign policy, is misleading. He tried to limit engagements with other states because he thought the risks greater than the advantages, and because he considered that long-term alliances could not honourably be undertaken in a democracy, where changes of popular opinion were always liable to upset them. He did not, however, avoid commitments altogether. Though he discouraged German ideas of a defensive alliance, he gave some support to Germany's friends in the Triple Alliance —Austria and Italy. In the two 'Mediterranean Agreements' concluded in 1887, Britain promised to support Italy's interests in the Mediterranean against France, and joined Italy and Austria in an undertaking to prevent any disturbance of the Balkans— presumably by Russia. Relations between Britain and Germany were further improved immediately after Bismarck's retirement by the Convention of 1890 dealing with East Africa and Heligoland.[2]

'Splendid Isolation'

In sum, Salisbury carefully preserved his country's interests at a time of great difficulty when Britain, despite a comfortable supremacy over all her rivals on the sea, could have taken no immediately effective part in a Continental war.

*   *   *   *   *

In the election of 1892 the Conservatives won more seats than the Liberals, who therefore depended on their alliance with the Irish party for a majority of forty in the Commons and their ability to form a Ministry. It was in any case Gladstone's intention to introduce a second Home Rule Bill, and he took office as Prime Minister for the fourth time with this single aim. In the keenly contested debates which occupied eighty-two sittings of the House of Commons, Gladstone, at the age of eighty-three, proved to have lost none of his grasp of intricate detail or his oratorical magic. But the Bill which he drove successfully through the Commons with such persistence was given short shrift by the large Conservative majority in the House of Lords. Their justification for rejecting the Bill was that a majority of British voters, excluding the Irish, had declared against it. The reply to this argument would have been to dissolve Parliament

Gladstone's fourth Ministry, 1892–1894

The second Home Rule Bill, 1893

[1] First used in the Canadian House of Commons in 1896.
[2] See page 425.

and hold a fresh election, which Gladstone, untiring in the fight, wished to do. But he was overborne by his colleagues, and early in the following year resigned.

Whatever views are taken of Gladstone's political principles, few would deny him the title of Grand Old Man. Grand in physique and energy he certainly was, as the long tale of trees felled at Hawarden may witness, or the thirty-mile walks in all weathers when he was past sixty. As an orator and master of the parliamentary stage he has never been surpassed, and few statesmen, in the harassing turmoil of politics, have so persistently kept sight of moral ends. A deep religious conviction was the mainspring of his whole political creed, for he lived, like Milton, 'as ever in his Great Taskmaster's eye'.

Gladstone had long seemed to be the only man who could lead the Liberals, and they had difficulty in replacing him. His successor, Lord Rosebery, was neither his choice, nor the party's, but the Queen's—a notable example of the exercise of personal power by the Sovereign. Rosebery, endowed as he was with every talent and gift of fortune, failed to make a great political career through lack of constancy and purpose, and was ill-fitted to hold together a party divided over Radicalism and Imperialism. He was not on speaking terms with Sir William Harcourt, who led the Liberals in the Commons, while the party's Nonconformist followers were upset by the success of Rosebery's stables in twice producing a Derby winner—once while he was Prime Minister. The chief occupation of the Rosebery Ministry was the melancholy one of putting measures through the House of Commons only to have them rejected by the House of Lords. The drastically Radical 'Newcastle Programme', adopted by the Liberals in 1891, thus came to nothing. The one measure of importance to escape the massacre was Harcourt's introduction of progressive death duties in the Budget of 1894. These heavier duties were execrated as sheer confiscation, but they proved so easy a means of increasing revenue that every subsequent Chancellor of the Exchequer has been profoundly grateful for their introduction and many have increased the rate of incidence.[1]

[1] One commented on their comparatively low yield in a certain year: 'People have not been dying up to expectations.'

3 New Trends: Socialism and Imperialism

While there was no great parliamentary issue to rival Irish affairs in the interests of the British public, new forces were revealed by startling developments in the late 'eighties. From the time of the collapse of Chartism there had been no sign of revolutionary activity in England. The socialist ideas of Robert Owen seemed forgotten, and for thirty years the main working-class organizations had been friendly societies, co-operative societies, and trade unions of a limited scope. These trade unions were recruited from the more skilled and better-paid workers, had a high subscription of about a shilling a week, and provided generous benefits when members were sick or otherwise unemployed. The chief aim of each union was to safeguard the interests of workers in a particular craft against the competition of the untrained and unskilled mass. The members of these unions were less inclined to Socialism than were many of the middle-class Radicals, and those few of their leaders who entered Parliament did so as Liberals.

In spite of the complacence of these working-class spokesmen, the 'eighties witnessed a sharp and sometimes violent movement in favour of Socialism. The most obvious cause was the trade depression which began in 1873 and reasserted itself after 1883. Wages went down, and there were large numbers of unemployed, most of them with the still harsh Poor Law as their only resource. The poor were less inclined to be passive under their misfortunes than in the past, for elementary education had taught many to read, and a few to think. *Growth of Socialism*

These changes declared themselves in an outbreak of strikes and demonstrations—there were 500 strikes in 1888—and in the rise of Socialist organizations. The most important strike was that of the London dockers, who subsisted entirely by casual labour paid at shocking rates. When they paraded daily through the City to their meeting-place in Trafalgar Square, carrying fish-heads to show what they had to live on, many Londoners began to learn what life was like for the poor The strikers, though disciplined and moderate, were on the verge of defeat when suddenly subscriptions began to pour in to their aid from all over Britain, from Australia and from Europe. They were thus enabled to hold out for their terms—sixpence an hour ('the *The dockers' strike, 1889* dockers' tanner'), and a minimum of four hours' work at a time —until the employers had to give in. The strike did much to arouse public opinion on labour questions, and speeded the formation of trade unions for the great body of unskilled workers who had so far lacked protection. These new unions differed from the old in two respects: they were usually organized on an industrial instead of a craft basis (i.e. they aimed at the enrolment of all the workers in an industry, whatever their type of work), and they took far more interest in political and economic questions—flirting with Socialism, if not always embracing it.

The new trade unions

By 1900 the trade unions had enrolled two million members, and by constant pressure and frequent strikes had gained for the working class a larger share of the national income, even in a period of severe foreign competition and general trade depression (1873–95). But their battle was not fought without bitter defeats. When the mineowners called for a 10 per cent reduction in wages in 1893 there was a lock-out which lasted fifteen weeks; and when the engineers, who still had the biggest and richest union, attempted in 1897 to maintain their restrictive rules (limiting the number of apprentices, for example) and to secure an eight-hour day, they were defeated after a thirty weeks strike—the worst setback the trade union movement had suffered for many years. Still worse was to come. The House of Lords, in its capacity of court of appeal, decided in favour of the employers a case brought by the Taff Vale Railway Company against a railwaymen's trade union that had called a strike: the union had to pay £23,000 damages to recoup the company for the loss suffered through the stoppage. It had previously been assumed that trade unions, as voluntary bodies without full legal personality, were immune from such actions. The new decision meant that any strike would cause the financial ruin of a union, since its funds would have to bear the losses of the employers as well as furnishing strike pay for its members.

Taff Vale case, 1901

Only Parliament could reverse this decision and restore to the unions the full use of the strike weapon. But useful as this weapon was, it seemed that more might be done to improve the condition of the wage-earners by legislation in Parliament than by strikes. The working class had received little help of this kind from the Conservatives, and expected no more from the Liberal Party, whose middle-class followers often paid the wages. Moreover, the Liberals had so far failed to introduce payment of M.P.s or to give much encouragement to working-class candidates for Parliament. So at last trade union leaders were prepared to strive for separate representation of Labour in Parliament, instead of being satisfied with the few working-class Radicals who had sat and voted in the Commons as Liberals.

In this new endeavour the trade unions were to have a variety of allies, not always like-minded with them nor indeed agreed among themselves. The conditions of the late nineteenth century worked on the consciences of many people to produce a passion for the investigation and reform of social evils. Thus arose diverse groups and opinions. The doctrines of the German Jew, Karl Marx, were taken up by H. M. Hyndman, a very untypical old Etonian, and his colleagues of the Social Democratic Federation. They proclaimed the class war and the inevitable success of revolutionary action to overthrow capitalism. This was doctrine too strong for even the more militant trade unionists, and the S.D.F. drifted into isolation and impotence. Less extreme, though still strongly socialist, was the Independent Labour Party, formed from local groups of a decidedly working-class character. The most prominent figure in the I.L.P. was Keir Hardie, the Scottish miners' leader; elected to Parliament in 1892, Hardie *Socialist Groups —Marxists*

I.L.P.

had arrived at the House wearing instead of a 'topper' a cloth hat—horrifying augury of things to come!

Very different from either the S.D.F. or the I.L.P. was the Fabian Society.[1] Its members were middle-class intellectuals much less interested in co-operating with other socialist bodies than in permeating the Liberal and Conservative parties with their ideas of reform, their aim being, as Beatrice Webb said, 'to make thinking persons socialistic'. She and her husband, Sidney Webb, by tireless research into the history and problems of industry, local government and the Poor Law amassed the facts which were intended to convince influential people of the need for socialist measures, and to show how these could be grafted on to Britain's parliamentary democracy. Thus the moderate tendencies of the older trade unionism were reinforced by a new and influential propaganda. It used the platform as well as the Press, one of the most effective Fabian speakers being the red-bearded, brilliant and forceful Irish playwright, George Bernard Shaw. *Fabians*

Finally there were many champions of social reform who were content to campaign as an advanced Radical wing of the Liberal

[1] The name was taken from the Roman general Fabius, who wore down Hannibal's Carthaginians by a strategy which avoided pitched battles.

(*Partridge, 1909, reproduced by permission of the Proprietors of 'Punch'*)

FORCED FELLOWSHIP

Suspicious-looking Party: 'ANY OBJECTION TO MY COMPANY, GUV'NOR? I'M AGOIN' YOUR WAY'—(*aside*) 'AND FURTHER.'

How the Labour party was regarded by the great majority of citizens during its early days. The Labour ruffian accompanies the harmless old Liberal gentleman —i.e. votes with him in Parliament against the Conservatives. But the brute's intention is only to knock his companion over the head with the cudgel of Socialism and make off with his property.

party or to co-operate closely with it. Foremost among these was John Burns, a Londoner who had worked as an engineer and taught himself a great deal about economics and politics. Striking in appearance, with black hair and beard, he became a most effective open-air speaker. He was prominent in the dock strike of 1889, particularly in organizing relief. As the only working-class member of the first London County Council he learnt how to apply socialist ideas to the practical affairs of local government. Elected to Parliament for Battersea in 1892, he took a Radical rather than a socialist line in national affairs; later, as President of the Local Government Board in Asquith's ministry, he was the first artisan to become a Cabinet Minister. *John Burns*

To combine these diverse groups and policies was no easy matter, but Keir Hardie won over the trade unions to the idea of a new parliamentary party, and they with the main socialist groups set up in 1900 the Labour Representation Committee, with J. Ramsay MacDonald, a self-educated Scot from a poor family, as its secretary. The trade unions paid one penny per member per annum to finance candidates who would form 'a distinct Labour group in Parliament'.[1] *Birth of the Labour party, 1900*

Their chances improved by a secret compact with the Liberals, fifty candidates stood for election in 1906 and twenty-nine were elected. There were twenty-four more M.P.s elected to represent working-class interests who in time merged with the L.R.C. members and swelled the ranks of the Parliamentary Labour Party, whose first leader was Keir Hardie. A new force had appeared in the political arena so long dominated by the two ancient parties.

* * * * *

After the election of 1895 the Liberal party was out of favour and its ideas in confusion. The trend of public opinion was for some years with the Conservatives, whose main driving force was to be found not so much in their leader, Lord Salisbury, as in their new and popular recruit, Joseph Chamberlain. *Liberals in eclipse*

Chamberlain's recipe for the success of the Conservative party was Imperialism with a dash of Radicalism. In his early days he had been a most successful mayor of Birmingham, initiating a policy of slum clearance, housing estates, adequate sanitation, public baths, parks, libraries and art galleries. While in the Liberal party he had taken a leading part in promoting the *Chamberlain's programme*

[1] Not until 1918 did the new party definitely adopt the socialist creed.

Education Act of 1870 and the Reform Act of 1884, and—despite the monocle in his eye and the orchid in his buttonhole—had posed as the champion of popular interests against the aristocracy. When, however, he got among the Conservatives, who had no enthusiasm for bold reforms, the dash of Radicalism was diluted to vanishing-point, and only Imperialism remained.

The new Imperialism

In order to teach his countrymen to 'think imperially' Chamberlain chose the comparatively humble post of Colonial Secretary in the new Conservative Ministry. His aim was to build up the Empire into a great economic unit that would enable Britain to keep abreast of rivals like Germany and the United States. New colonies would provide raw materials and markets for industrial products; and the sacred obligation to advance the welfare of the natives—'The White Man's Burden'—could be agreeably combined with empire-building and profit-making. As for the self-governing dominions, it was Chamberlain's hope that they would enter into a federation with the Mother-Country, thus forming a great political as well as economic unit. Imperial propaganda of this kind was greatly assisted by the celebrations of Queen Victoria's Jubilee and Diamond Jubilee in 1887 and 1897, when colonial contingents from all over the world paraded before London's fascinated gaze. Indeed, the British public became more than a little unbalanced in its enthusiasm, and was ready to applaud the Government's ventures wherever they might lead —to the brink of hostilities with France at Fashoda in 1898,[1] and into war with the Boer Republics in 1899.[2]

Venezuela incident, 1896

These crises were preceded, however, by one which was not at all of Britain's making. President Cleveland of the United States intervened in a dispute between Britain and Venezuela over the boundary of British Guiana to declare that the boundary would be drawn by an American commission and the result enforced by the U.S. Government. The President was moved to this utterly unreasonable behaviour allegedly by respect for the Monroe Doctrine,[3] but in fact by a desire to win the approaching Presidential election on the popularity gained by 'twisting the lion's tail'. The matter was reasonably settled by quiet diplomacy behind the scenes; it was agreed to send it to arbitration, whereupon all the main British claims were successful. But the affair had given Britain a sharp reminder of the dangers of her position. In a war with the U.S.A. she would have had no support from any European Power. During the Boer War, which came soon

[1] See page 422.   [2] See pages 414-15.   [3] See page 77.

(Linley Sambourne, 1903, reproduced by permission of the Proprietors of 'Punch')

HISTORY REVERSES ITSELF

PAPA JOSEPH TAKING MASTER ARTHUR A PROTECTION WALK.

Papa Joseph: 'COME ALONG, MASTER ARTHUR, DO STEP OUT.'
Master Arthur: 'THAT'S ALL VERY WELL, BUT YOU KNOW I CANNOT GO AS FAST AS YOU DO.'

See inset and page 136. Just as Cobden had once led the reluctant Peel in the direction of the Repeal of the Corn Laws, so Joseph Chamberlain now urges the reluctant Arthur Balfour in the direction of Protection.

afterwards, foreign opinion was almost uniformly hostile to Britain; isolation seemed not so much splendid as perilous.

Unfortunately Imperialism left this government little time to attend to anything else. After all the promises made at the election the only social reform was a Workmen's Compensation Act, by which an employee could obtain compensation for injury at work without having to prove negligence on the part of his employer. In Ireland there was one useful administrative reform —the Irish Local Government Act of 1898, which gave Ireland County Councils like those set up in England ten years earlier.

Workmen's
Compensation
Act, 1897

In 1902, after winning an election at the end of the Boer War, Salisbury retired. He had been four times Foreign Secretary, and Prime Minister for over thirteen years, even longer than Gladstone. Skilful and effective in foreign affairs, he had been inclined to let the growing problems at home look after themselves. He showed more interest in his scientific experiments at Hatfield House than in bold projects of reform, in which he had no faith. The County Councils had been set up and free elementary education had been provided[1] not because the Prime Minister had a plan, but because something had had to be done. He rather deplored, in private, what he called 'Joe's war' in South Africa,[2] but did little to prevent it. The difficulties of the times called for more positive ideas. Not even Salisbury's highly intellectual nephew, A. J. Balfour, who succeeded him, was able to provide them. Distracted, like so many leaders before him, by Ireland, and then by the tariff reform scheme of Chamberlain—who had ideas in plenty—Balfour was unluckily destined to lead his party into the worst defeat it had ever met.

Salisbury retires

Balfour's
Ministry,
1902–1905

In Ireland the Conservatives continued their attempt to 'kill Home Rule by kindness', and a Land Purchase Act introduced by Wyndham was by far the most thorough attempt ever made to solve the land problem. To enable all tenant-farmers to purchase their farms, the Government was prepared to lend £5,000,000 a year up to a total of £180,000,000. The purchasers, by an annual redemption payment ($3\frac{1}{4}$ per cent) which was less than a normal rent, would become the owners of their farms after sixty-eight years.[3] In six years a quarter of a million tenants took up the scheme. With so great a proportion of farmers on the way to owning their land, and the rest paying 'fair rents' which

Ireland—
Wyndham's
Land Purchase
Act, 1903

Success of
Conservative
policy

[1] See page 383.   [2] The Boer War; see page 415.
[3] The payments were made with great regularity until de Valera's Government intercepted them in 1932. See page 277.

were on the average 20 per cent lower than before Gladstone's Act of 1881, the Conservatives could indeed claim to have solved the Irish land problem.

As well as pacifying Ireland, the new Prime Minister was anxious to improve the country's efficiency in industry and trade, and this was the motive of the other important measure his Ministry produced—the Education Act of 1902,[1] which set up a system of secondary schools. Important as this measure was in its promise of greater national efficiency, it failed to satisfy Joseph Chamberlain, who now brought forward his master-plan for securing Britain's supremacy over her rivals—a plan so drastic that his Cabinet colleagues would not swallow it.

Education Act, 1902

Chamberlain's aim was to unite all parts of the Empire in a customs union, which by fostering an exchange of products among its members would create new ties of commerce and new common interests. But to admit colonial goods into Britain on more favourable terms than foreign goods meant imposing import duties on the latter; in other words, Britain must abandon the free trade on which her great commercial prosperity had been built. Chamberlain accordingly set to work to change opinion in the country. He resigned from the Ministry, founded the Tariff Reform League, and opened his campaign in Birmingham in 1903. 'You want an Empire', he urged; 'do you think it better to cultivate the trade with your own people or to let that go in order that you may keep the trade of those who are your competitors and rivals?' He conjured up the vision of a great trading unit embracing 300 million people, and called upon the Free Traders to recognize in this the realization of their ideals.

Empire trade

Tariff Reform, 1903

Tariff reform was the pivot of Chamberlain's whole programme for the Conservative party, for the proposed import duties would finance social reforms at home and development in the colonies, as well as meeting the increased cost of the Navy. The scheme would appeal to Conservatives because it would avoid higher taxes on land and on big incomes. But Chamberlain had no success. The great industries—iron and steel, coal and cotton—were flourishing without protective duties, which would increase the cost of living for their million workpeople and lead to demands for higher wages. Trade with foreigners was worth twice as much as trade with the Empire, so it seemed bad business to decrease the former for the sake of increasing the latter. Chamberlain's campaign not only failed to

Chamberlain's failure

[1] See page 387.

win over the country from free trade but proved disastrous to his party. Doubt and division were sown in the ranks, and a few free trade members, Winston Churchill among them, even left the party and joined the Liberals. To these the new programme was a godsend. Doubly divided over social reform and Imperialism, they could nevertheless rally round the ancient banner of Free Trade. When Balfour resigned in December 1905 the Liberal leader, Sir Henry Campbell-Bannerman, accepted office and promptly appealed to the verdict of a general election. In this the Liberals fought as a united party, their main argument being represented by a poster showing a big loaf, to be enjoyed through Liberalism and Free Trade, and a little loaf—the penalty of Conservatism and Tariff Reform.

'Chinese slavery'

Another Liberal poster which seemed, surprisingly, to decide many votes portrayed a Chinese coolie. The Government had approved a scheme to solve a shortage of labour in the Transvaal gold mines by importing into South Africa large numbers of indentured Chinese labourers. They were confined in squalid conditions in barrack-like compounds, and though they were paid wages they were being treated rather as a usable commodity than as human beings. The Liberals with some reason raised the cry of 'Chinese slavery', and successfully aroused the anger of many of the British public. The Conservative ministry seemed to do nothing right. Even Balfour's Education Act, an excellent measure in itself, lost the votes of indignant Nonconformists.

The election of 1906

Yet no one expected the 'Liberal landslide' of 1906, the most complete reverse in the history of party warfare to that time. The new House of Commons contained 377 Liberals, 53 men of the Labour and kindred groups, 83 Irish Nationalists, and only 157 Unionists—the official name of the Conservative party after the Liberal Unionists were merged in it in 1901. There were three main reasons for the Conservative disaster, apart from the general ineffectiveness of Balfour's Ministry. The country was disappointed over social reform, many people were sickened of Imperialism by the Boer War, and Chamberlain had split his party over the protection issue. Instead of inspiring the country to follow him in an imperial crusade, he had only sown the suspicion that he wished to tax the poor for the benefit of the rich. It was a sad end to a career in which boldness, energy and exceptional ability had produced little positive achievement outside the municipal affairs of Birmingham.

17. Liberal Rule in the New Century

1 The Great Liberal Reforms

The years between the Liberal victory of 1906 and the outbreak of war in 1914 were filled with great reforming activity. But they were marred by bitter and violent political controversies and by an ever-increasing tension in international affairs.

The premiership of Sir Henry Campbell-Bannerman has been described as 'common-sense enthroned'. Shortly before his death in 1908 he was succeeded by H. H. Asquith, who included in a brilliant ministerial team Lloyd George, Sir Edward Grey, R. B. Haldane, John Morley and Winston Churchill. The Radical wing of the Liberal party was well represented in the Ministry, and counted the Prime Minister himself among its members. Everything pointed to such a spate of progressive legislation as the country had not yet seen.

Liberal Prime Ministers: Campbell-Bannerman, 1905-1908; Asquith, 1908-1916

The main obstacle to the fulfilment of Liberal desires was the House of Lords, which had so effectively blocked the path of the previous Liberal Ministry (1892–95). The Conservative majority in the Upper House promptly threw out two Government Bills, but discreetly passed a Bill which reversed the Taff Vale decision (so safeguarding union funds from claims for damages arising from strikes)[1] and at long last freed the trade unions from their anxieties over the law of conspiracy and the use of pickets to enforce a strike. Nor did the Lords obstruct the provision of free meals for necessitous schoolchildren (1906) or the introduction of Old Age Pensions on a modest scale in the budget of 1908— 5s. a week at seventy when other sources of income were not more than 8s. a week. Among other useful measures a Trade Boards Act was passed in 1909 to set up wage-fixing machinery for some of the industries where 'sweating' was worst; it was later extended to cover a very large number of the least organized workers. In the same year the first labour exchanges were set up to assist in placing men in suitable employment.[2]

Trade Disputes Act, 1906

Old Age Pensions, 1908

Trade Boards Act, 1909

---

[1] See page 218.
[2] The task of organizing them fell to a Civil Servant named W. H. (later Lord) Beveridge.

In spite of the general success of their reforms thus far, and of their liberal and statesmanlike policy in South Africa,[1] the Government were convinced that the measures they had most at heart, and for which they had an unmistakable verdict from the voters, could not be carried through unless the powers of the Upper House were curtailed. In 1909 this question was put to the test in the most uncompromising manner. The Chancellor of the Exchequer was David Lloyd George, who as a fatherless Welsh lad had been brought up by an uncle—a bootmaker and local preacher—and had later made his way into the law and into Parliament. He now introduced a Budget full of novel and far-reaching experiments which were bound to be resented by the Conservative peers. Either they must swallow the Budget in contradiction of every principle they believed in, or they must reject it, a step without precedent in modern history. Lloyd George had already fairly stated the real issue: 'whether the country was to be governed by the King and the Peers or by the King and the People.'

The need for a large sum for the Navy to maintain a lead over Germany, the expense of Old Age Pensions, the reduction of tax on small incomes by allowances for children, and grants of money for various new ventures such as the Road Board, meant that the Chancellor of the Exchequer had to produce nearly £16,000,000 by new taxation. Lloyd George proposed to find this money by various means, including an increased rate of death duty on estates over £5,000, a new super-tax (payable in addition to income tax) on incomes over £3,000, and a revolutionary tax on unearned increase in land values, to be paid whenever land changed hands. This last proposal, which involved valuing all the land and buildings in the country, aroused more violent opposition than all the rest. The Conservative advocates of Tariff Reform saw that one of their main arguments would disappear if revenue could be raised by these new methods instead of by import duties, and of course the party rose as one man to defend the landowning interest.

The Welsh David had supplied himself with a suitable stock of pebbles, and slung them with force and zest. Though the Conservatives in both Houses fought the Budget bitterly, Lloyd George in his public speeches concentrated on the Lords, using every device of rhetoric to bring them into hatred and ridicule as a selfish and obstinate caste. 'Should 500 men' (the peers),

[1] See page 417.

he demanded, 'ordinary men, chosen accidentally from among the unemployed, override the judgement—the deliberate judgement—of millions of people who are engaged in the industry which makes the wealth of the country?' and 'Who made 10,000 people owners of the soil, and the rest of us trespassers in the land of our birth?'

(*Sir Bernard Partridge, 1914, reproduced by permission of the Proprietors of 'Punch'*)

CRESCENDO
or THE TUNE THE OLD COW'S LIKELY TO DIE OF
The Cow: 'STOP, STOP! THIS ISN'T MILKING, IT'S MURDER'

Lloyd George, Chancellor of the Exchequer in Asquith's Ministry, doubles the new super-tax and raises the standard rate of income tax to 1s. 3d. in the pound to pay for social reforms and increased armaments. (Since then the same cow has been murdered many times, with increasing brutality, but curiously enough still survives.)

The Lords almost deserved Lloyd George's strictures. Their House was supposed to act as a revising chamber, yet in fact its members tended to lie dormant during periods of Conservative rule and only came to life when the Liberals were in office. This tendency they now carried to impossible extremes. By a huge majority, in a House unusually well attended, they rejected the Budget.

The Lords reject the Budget

'We have got them at last!' exclaimed Lloyd George. The

Commons having passed a resolution declaring the action of the Lords unconstitutional, Parliament was dissolved, and an election was held (January 1910). Other issues besides the future of the Upper House arose, and the result was by no means a triumph for the Liberals. They had only a narrow majority over the Conservatives, and so depended—not for the first time in their history— on the Irish Nationalists. The Lords yielded to the extent of passing the Budget they had formerly rejected. This of course did not save them. Asquith introduced a Bill which would come near to destroying the powers of the peers. It provided that the House of Lords should lose all power to amend or reject a Money Bill; that any Bill passed by the House of Commons in three successive sessions, though three times rejected by the Lords, should nevertheless become law; and that the maximum duration of a Parliament should be shortened from seven to five years. (The last provision was to ensure that the veto of the Lords could still operate when the House of Commons was over three years old and therefore out of touch with the electorate.) This Bill the peers of course determined to reject.

A round-table conference of party leaders was then called, but failed to find a way out of the crisis. At this stage the new King, George V, gave an undertaking to the Prime Minister that if the proposals for altering the powers of the Lords were put before the people at another election and approved, he would create all the new peers—a list of some 250 names was prepared—needed to outnumber the opposition. A second election had a similar result to the first, the Bill was brought in again, and after a struggle, but without the creation of Liberal peers, it was accepted by the Lords. The Liberals had achieved one of the few deliberate and drastic changes ever made in the Constitution.

After the long interruption of the constitutional crisis, the Liberals resumed their activity in reform. First came the payment of salaries[1] to M.P.s, a democratic step which had been included in the People's Charter of 1838, and in the Liberal party programme since 1880.

Next, and most important of the social reforms of this Ministry, was the National Insurance Act. This was due mainly to the initiative of Lloyd George, but was copied fairly closely from the German scheme of some twenty years earlier. The first part of the Act dealt with sickness, and covered most of the wage-earning population. Sickness benefit comprised free treatment and medi-

First election of 1910

The struggle for the Parliament Act

King George V, 1910-1936

Second election of 1910; the Parliament Act, 1911

Payment of M.P.s, 1911

National Insurance Act. 1911

—sickness

[1] £400 a year, since raised to £3,250.

cines from a general practitioner and a weekly payment during absence from work, but neither was extended to the families of insured persons. Hospital care was not included in the scheme, but the hospitals, maintained by charity, gave free treatment in any case to those unable to pay for it. The scheme was to be administered not by the government but by 'approved societies', several thousand in number. Most of the work was in fact in the hands of the great insurance companies and the well-established friendly societies.[1] The second part of the Act provided unemployment benefit for workers in building, engineering and shipbuilding. Both kinds of insurance were compulsory and were financed by contributions (in the form of stamps stuck on a card) of 4d. a week from workers and 3d. from employers, to which was added a grant reckoned at 2d. a week from the State. The Conservative party, having failed to prevent the passage of the measure through the Commons and being now unable to block it in the Lords, did their best to stir up opposition to it in the country, representing it as an attack on the wages of the poor. Lloyd George retorted that they were getting '9d. for 4d.' The doctors, too, protested, but found, when they got over their initial dislike, that it brought them a profitable increase in patients.

If the Insurance Act cost much money, a little was saved by the government's prison reforms. An Act of 1907 introduced the probation system, a valuable means of dealing with offenders and an alternative to prison. The Criminal Justice Administration Act of 1914 required the courts to allow reasonable time for the payment of fines before committal to prison for non-payment. Another measure was the introduction of Borstal prisons for young offenders.

The Government also came again to the rescue of the trade unions, which had suffered another setback from the House of Lords in its legal capacity. The Osborne judgment of 1910 had made it illegal for a trade union to use its funds in supporting candidates for Parliament, a practice which had been more general since the foundation of the Labour party, and was indeed objectionable to trade union members who happened to be Conservatives. The Liberals had already remedied this in part by providing salaries for M.P.s; they now passed an act to legalize expenditure for political purposes, provided that this was approved by a special ballot of the members and that any member could 'contract out', i.e. decline to contribute for this purpose.

[1] See page 156.

Disestablish-
ment of the
Welsh Church,
1914
A characteristic Liberal measure to disestablish the Anglican Church in Wales was delayed by the House of Lords as long as possible, and became law only in 1914. The Church of England opposed it strongly, fearing that it would be followed by disestablishment in England, but Wales was in fact a special case, because of the devotion of most of her people to their Nonconformist chapels.

In the years following 1906 the Liberals had achieved valuable reforming legislation, and had tackled some of the outstanding problems of the time. Yet there were other questions which so divided public opinion or so strained the Liberal creed that no solution was found for them on parliamentary lines.

The suffragettes
One such issue was women's suffrage. Since 1867 the claim of women to the vote had been put forward, usually by and on behalf of educated women. In 1903 a new movement was begun when Mrs Emmeline Pankhurst with her daughter Christabel founded the Women's Social and Political Union. Their object was to obtain the remedy of the vote for their less fortunate sisters who suffered exploitation in industry and other social injustices. Scorning the older methods of quiet propaganda, their followers heckled and interrupted at political meetings, forced themselves on the attention of M.P.s at the Houses of Parliament, and organized huge meetings and processions. The Liberals were divided on the issue, and the Cabinet refused to upset its programme by bringing in a Women's Suffrage Bill. But the militant 'suffragettes' only intensified their campaign, and were arrested in large numbers. Many were sentenced to imprisonment, and some began hunger-strikes to bring about their release. They were very successful in this until the Government had a measure passed, popularly known as the 'Cat and Mouse Act', by which a hunger-striker could be released, and later sent back to prison without further formalities.

Results of their
campaign
From 1911 the militant suffragettes resorted to general lawlessness, burning down buildings, firing the contents of pillar-boxes, placing bombs (one was found under the Coronation Chair in Westminster Abbey), slashing pictures in the National Gallery, and chaining themselves to the railings of Buckingham Palace. Many people felt that these women were proving not their fitness but their unfitness for political responsibility. On the other hand, the suffragettes suffered much for their beliefs, and their sacrifices—one woman threw herself beneath the King's racehorse in the Derby of 1913 and was fatally injured—did not fail to

win some sympathy for the principle of equality of political rights between the sexes.

Impatience and a tendency to violence also declared themselves in industrial disputes. Wages, which had risen generally in the previous period, remained stationary from 1900 to 1914, though the cost of living continued to increase. The many workers still outside the unions were often very badly paid, and a large proportion of the working class suffered from shocking housing, inadequate social services and fluctuating employment —conditions which, together with the new freedom to strike secured by the recent Trade Disputes Act, bred the most acute industrial strife Britain had yet known. In 1911 a railway strike paralysed a large part of the country, and in the following year 850,000 miners were idle for several weeks, with resulting unemployment in other industries. These strikes and a number of lesser ones led to violent incidents, several of which involved the use of troops by the Government. Another feature of the period was the 'sympathetic strike', when men of one union came out to help another. Such strikes were really aimed not at the employers but at the Government, which ended the coal strike, for example, by introducing a minimum wage act. The resort to violence which failed the suffragettes brought some success to the trade unions; the scene of its chief triumph, however, was the country where violence was no stranger—Ireland. *Strikes, 1911–1912*

2 Ireland, 1906–1914

Greater prosperity, assisted by the Conservative reforms, had blunted the edge of political agitation in Ireland. In 1910, however, when the Liberals once more needed Irish votes to maintain them in office and help them defeat the House of Lords, Home Rule again became a possibility. The Parliament Act once passed, John Redmond, leader of the Irish Nationalists, claimed the price of his support, and Asquith accordingly moved the third Home Rule Bill in April 1912. *Third Home Rule Bill, 1912–1914*

It was the problem of Ulster, already a difficulty in the days of Gladstone and Parnell, that wrecked the third attempt to give Ireland self-government. Protestant Ulster had a traditional hatred of southern Irish Catholicism, and a suspicion of the designs of the agricultural south upon her industrial wealth. These feelings were stiffened at the end of the nineteenth *Ulster* by Ulster's greater prosperity and self-confidence, by the contagion of nationalism spreading from the south, and by the stimulus deliberately applied by English Unionists. The latter, defeated over the 1909 Budget and the Parliament Act, were determined not to let the Liberals have their way over Home Rule, and hoped that the separation of Ulster from the rest of Ireland would make Home Rule unworkable. Everything was therefore done to encourage Ulster's resistance, which from 1910 onwards was led by Sir Edward Carson, a Dublin Protestant lawyer and M.P. His policy was not only to oppose the Home Rule Bill in Parliament, but to prepare a stand against it in Ulster by making ready a 'provisional government', enrolling volunteers, and importing arms from Germany. In this policy 'General' Carson received the open support and encouragement of the English Unionists, especially 'Galloper' Smith (F. E. Smith, later Lord Birkenhead).

Sir Edward
Carson

However genuine their principles, the Opposition party could no doubt be criticized for encouraging Ulster in rebellion.[1] At the same time Asquith's lack of decision and firmness were deplorable. He could not drop Home Rule, or coerce Ulster into accepting it; and when he tried to amend the Home Rule proposals so that Ulster was left out, Redmond would not agree. Redmond himself was no firebrand, but he was under pressure from the rapidly growing Sinn Fein[2] movement founded by the journalist Arthur Griffith, which was winning over Catholic Ireland from Home Rule to a policy of complete independence. Asquith, however, should have forced his decisions on Redmond, and above all he should have prevented the formation of private armies in Ireland. The Ulster Volunteers were soon matched by the Irish Volunteers (Nationalists), the only difference being that the Ulstermen had been allowed to import arms, and the Nationalists were prevented, until they defied the Government's ban. The passing of the Home Rule Act, after the two years' delay enforced by the House of Lords, seemed likely to be the signal for the outbreak of a terrible civil war.

When the Government took precautions against this danger, they found that the officers of the British Army were strongly Unionist and pro-Ulster in their sympathies. Instructions to excuse from service officers actually resident in Ulster were so

---

[1] In 1886, over the first Home Rule Bill, Lord Randolph Churchill had written: 'Ulster will fight; and Ulster will be right.'
[2] Sinn Fein = We Ourselves.

mishandled as to bring forth a declaration from the officers of the 3rd Cavalry Brigade at the Curragh, the Army's headquarters in Dublin, that most of them would 'prefer to accept dismissal if ordered north'. In face of this warning, the heads of the War Office gave written assurance to the officers concerned that they would not be required to enforce the Home Rule Act against Ulster.

A dissolution at this time would probably have resulted in a severe Unionist defeat and have given Asquith the authority he so badly lacked, but the extremely serious international crisis made it out of the question. A last effort was made to get an agreed solution by postponing the inclusion of Ulster under the projected Irish government, but a special conference of all the parties concerned broke down on the day of the Austrian ultimatum to Serbia (24 July 1914). The operation of the Home Rule Act was then suspended for the duration of the war, and Englishmen forgot about Ireland until the Sinn Fein rebellion of Easter 1916 jogged their memories.

The Curragh incident, 1914

Home Rule becomes law but is suspended

18. The European Crisis and the First World War

1 The End of British Isolation, 1902–1914

The foreign policies of Palmerston, Disraeli and Salisbury rested comfortably on firm foundations—British wealth and British naval supremacy. At the close of the nineteenth century, however, these foundations were being undermined; for the Germany of the young and headstrong Kaiser William II, not content with Bismarck's achievement of dominating the Continent, was now set on building up a big navy, acquiring a great overseas empire, and becoming the strongest power in the world.

The ambitions of Germany

This situation was fraught with peril not only for Britain, but for every other country which stood in Germany's way. Among other effects it induced France and Russia in 1893 to sink their considerable differences and join together in a Dual Alliance. From this date onwards these two powers therefore stood opposed to the rival combination formed in 1882—the Triple Alliance of Germany, Austria-Hungary and Italy.

Dual Alliance v Triple Alliance

The mounting danger from Germany was not immediately realized in Britain, since there was plenty of material for dispute with the members of the opposite camp. Relations with France were poisoned by French resentment at the British occupation of Egypt, while Russian designs on the Balkans, China and India had invariably encountered Britain's opposition. For a time, indeed, Britain positively favoured the Triple Alliance. From 1895, however, the divergence of interests between Britain and Germany became increasingly plain, not only in Europe but also in Africa and the Far East. The clearest danger signal was the German Navy Law of 1898, which was designed to raise the Kaiser's fleet from the fifth place among the world's navies to equality with the first. At every point Britain seemed to collide with Germany, while the trade rivalry between the two powers was growing ever more acute.

Anglo-German friction begins, 1895

During the Boer War Germany's jealousy—the Kaiser had

earlier congratulated Kruger on the failure of the Jameson Raid[1] —and Britain's lack of friends became more obvious than ever. In fact, her dangerous and exposed position caused the whole policy of isolation to be called in question, and even before peace was made with the Boers the first move in an opposite direction was taken. Under the inspiration of Lord Lansdowne, Foreign Secretary in the closing years of Salisbury's Ministry, Britain made an alliance—the first since the Crimean War—with Japan, each promising to be neutral if the other were at war with one power, and to give armed help if the other were at war with more than one power. This was to prevent the intrusion of other states into China, and particularly to repel the Russian advance into Manchuria and Korea. These objects were secured by the astonishing victory of Japan over Russia in 1905, when Russia was deprived of possible allies by the new Anglo-Japanese treaty Japan's success had world-wide consequences, for it helped to bring on revolution in China and later in Russia, to stir up nationalism among the people of Asia, and to set Japan herself on the ambitious road that led to Manchuria in 1931, Pearl Harbour in 1941, and Hiroshima in 1945.

Anglo-Japanese Alliance, 1902

Russo-Japanese War, 1904–1905

Having taken one step away from isolation, Britain found it easier to take the next. Balfour's Cabinet felt the need of a friend in Europe, and it was decided that Lansdowne should make a thorough effort to clear up difficulties with France. A state visit to Paris by King Edward VII helped to create the right atmosphere, and the Entente Cordiale came into being in 1904. The formal agreement dealt only with colonial and trade questions. In particular Britain was to have a free hand in Egypt, and France in Morocco, instead of each hampering the other as they had done before. The two states promised, therefore, only to stop quarrelling; they did not promise to co-operate. How far they would do so would depend on other factors in the international situation.

Anglo-French Entente, 1904

The Anglo-French accord was soon tested. When France set out to secure control of Morocco in 1905, Germany tried to prevent her. By German insistence a conference of the powers was called at Algeciras, in Spain; but there France received strong support from Britain, and so was able to proceed with little hindrance. By this time the Entente was taking on a practical shape, for the British and French military staffs had already begun a regular exchange of information.

Morocco, 1905–1906

The Entente was the work of a Conservative government; it

---

[1] See page 414.

(*Partridge, 1905, reproduced by permission of the Proprietors of 'Punch'*)

THE MATCH MAKER MALGRÉ ELLE

Mlle La France (*aside*): 'IF SHE'S GOING TO GLARE AT US LIKE THAT, IT LOOKS AS IF WE MIGHT HAVE TO BE REGULARLY ENGAGED.'

The bullying attitude of Germany towards France over Morocco drives France and Britain still closer together. Some circles in France raise the question whether the Entente should be made into a formal alliance.

was not upset when the Liberals came into power in 1906. Faced with the continued threat from Germany, Sir Edward Grey, Foreign Secretary in Campbell-Bannerman's Ministry, decided that since Britain had made friends with France, it was logical to make friends with France's ally, Russia. A long history of mutual suspicion and hostility was forgotten—or overlooked—in the need of the hour, and in 1907 an Anglo-Russian agreement was signed. It referred only to Afghanistan and Tibet, which the Russians promised to leave alone, and to Persia, where 'spheres of influence' for each power were mapped out. But, like the Anglo-French Entente, the treaty with Russia meant more than it said And when it was concluded the Triple Entente—Britain, France and Russia—confronted the Triple Alliance. Thus far had German ambitions driven Britain along the road from isolation. Anglo-Russian agreement, 1907

The Triple Entente had hardly been formed when Russia received a severe rebuff. In 1908 Austria-Hungary annexed two nominally Turkish provinces which she had administered since 1878—Bosnia and Herzegovina.[1] This extension of Austrian power endangered the age-long Russian ambition of an advance to Constantinople, and the prestige of Russia in the Balkans could hardly survive another such reverse. Bosnian crisis 1908

The Triple Alliance next probed the strength of France. When the French sent troops into Morocco 'to suppress disorder', the Germans despatched a gunboat to Agadir as a warning that they considered their interests to be threatened—an action which might easily have led to war. But they in their turn received a warning from Britain in a speech by Lloyd George and withdrew—though not without compensation—from Agadir. Round two had gone to the Entente. Agadir incident, 1911

While the new British friendships were being formed and tested under German pressure, the country's capacity for self-defence was being reviewed. From 1904 Sir John Fisher, First Sea Lord, an officer equally possessed of pugnacity and vision, energetically reformed the organization and armament of the Navy. He was well supported by his political chief, Lord Cawdor, First Lord of the Admiralty. In 1906 was launched a ship which outclassed all existing battleships and caused the navies of all the powers to be rebuilt—the 'Dreadnought', of 17,900 tons, armed with ten 12-inch guns, and capable of 21 knots. In Fisher's opinion, this ensured seven years of peace, since the Germans would have to spend that time enlarging the Kiel Canal to make full use of Reorganization of the Navy The 'Dreadnought'

[1] See page 201.

comparable vessels. With a good start, Britain could easily have retained her supremacy by building each year the four ships of the 'Dreadnought' class that Fisher proposed; but the Campbell-Bannerman Government abandoned this programme as too provocative and too expensive, and Germany was able to re-enter the naval building race. However, the prospect of her outbuilding Britain in Dreadnought-class battleships and battlecruisers forced the Liberals in 1909 to change their minds. In that year Asquith proposed to start four of these vessels immediately, and four more if need were shown; but a popular outcry, with the slogan 'we want eight and we won't wait', induced him to sanction eight at once. Altogether eighteen of these vessels were laid down from 1909 to 1911.

Another of Fisher's changes had far-reaching consequences. His reorganization of the battle-fleets had involved taking most of the British battleships out of the Mediterranean to concentrate them nearer Germany. In pursuance of this policy it was agreed with the French in 1912 that they should take responsibility for the Mediterranean, while British ships should guard the North Sea, the Channel and the Atlantic—an arrangement which made it difficult, if not impossible, for Britain to stand aside when a German attack on France took place.

Naval arrangement with France, 1912

Though Britain concentrated her main resources on the Navy, the Army was not neglected. R. B. (later Lord) Haldane, the Liberal Secretary of State for War, like Cardwell increased the Army's efficiency while reducing its cost. Provision was made for the rapid mobilization of twenty divisions, seven of which formed an Expeditionary Force, complete with artillery, transport, and medical services, and backed by adequate reserves. As second-line troops, quickly available for service overseas, the Territorial Force was formed out of the old yeomanry and volunteers. The Officers' Training Corps was set up in public and secondary schools to produce the officers required by an enlarged army in wartime. It was due to the careful planning of Haldane that a small but highly efficient force was transferred to France without a hitch within a fortnight of the outbreak of war in 1914.

Haldane's Army Reforms, 1906-1909

In Western Europe the powers were locked in a conflict arising largely from the new competition in industry, trade, and overseas expansion. In Eastern Europe the crisis was due by contrast to a long historic process reaching its climax—the decay and dissolution of the Turkish and Austrian Empires. In seizing Bosnia and Herzegovina in 1908, Austria-Hungary started an undisguised

Collapse of Turkish Empire in Europe

scramble for what remained of the Turkish Empire in Europe, and set up a ferment of national passion in the Balkans which spread into the rotting fabric of the Habsburg Empire itself. After banding together against the Turks and vanquishing them in the Balkan War of 1912 the Balkan peoples were flushed with triumph; the Serbs in particular, victorious in a further war (against their ex-ally Bulgaria) in 1913, were now ardently longing to free their Bosnian compatriots from Austrian rule. They knew that Russia could not afford to fail the Slav cause a second time. Germany and Austria, on the other hand, felt the balance tipping against them, and were tempted to strike before their chances became worse. *Balkan Wars, 1912 and 1913* *Preventive war?*

On 28 June 1914 the Austrian General Staff and Foreign Minister were given—or created—the excuse they wanted. The Archduke Francis Ferdinand, heir to the aged Emperor Francis Joseph, was sent with his wife on an official visit to Sarajevo in the newly annexed province of Bosnia—a hot-bed of Serbian agitation. As the Archduke and his wife drove through the streets a young Bosnian Serb hurled a bomb at their car; they escaped injury, only for another young Bosnian later in the day to shoot them dead. The murder was the work of a few fanatics; but the Austrians, having first secured a promise of support from Germany, found it convenient to assume the complicity of the Serbian Government, and confronted Serbia with demands which would have gravely intruded upon her independence. Eight of the ten points were accepted by the Serbs, and the remainder they offered to submit to international arbitration; but this was not good enough for the Austrians, who thereupon declared war. At this Russia, determined to maintain her prestige and position in the Balkans by protecting the Serbs, mobilized her forces. Germany then followed suit and demanded that Russia halt her mobilization. When she refused, a German declaration of war against Russia followed. Next the Germans turned on France, who, true to the terms of her alliance with Russia, was also mobilizing, and demanded guarantees of French neutrality. Failing to secure these, Germany then declared war on France. But the easiest road to Paris lay through Belgium. On 3 August the main German forces in the west entered that country and, on being refused a free passage, opened fire on the forts of Liège. *Sarajevo, 28 June 1914* *Austria declares war on Serbia* *Russia mobilizes* *Germany declares war on Russia and France* *Belgian neutrality violated*

What would Britain do? Until 3 August (which was Bank Holiday Monday) no one knew, for though France and Russia were her friends and associates, she had no military alliance with them. Sir Edward Grey had done everything possible to save peace, except pledging support to France. He did however give on 2 August an assurance that if the German Fleet attacked the French Channel ports the British Navy would intervene, and he demanded an undertaking from Germany to respect the neutrality of Belgium. When Parliament met on 3 August it was almost certain that Belgium would be invaded, and that knowledge resolved all doubts; for if Britain's obligation to France was uncertain, her obligation to defend Belgium, undertaken in the treaty of 1839,[1] was clear and precise. So the final refusal of Germany to give the required undertaking was answered on 4 August by the British declaration of war, supported by an almost unanimous nation.[2]

Britain declares war, 4 August 1914

'Militarism run stark mad' was an American description of Europe in May 1914. Issues were being decided by the advice of soldiers rather than diplomats, and in the absence of any kind of international authority or even any machinery of conference it was almost impossible to prevent the conflict. In the words of Lloyd George, the governments of Europe 'stumbled and staggered' into war—a war that was to cost over ten million lives.

2 The First World War, 1914–1918

The Schlieffen plan

The German plan for victory in a war on two fronts had been long prepared—by a former Chief of Staff, Count Schlieffen. Since the cumbrous Russian war machine would be slow to gather momentum, the East was to be left almost unguarded and everything was to be staked on a quick decision against France. This was to be achieved by placing relatively light forces on the left of the line, and by packing the whole weight of the offensive into the right, which would sweep irresistibly through Belgium and North-Eastern France, engulf Paris, swing round upon the rear of the French right on the frontiers of Alsace and Lorraine, and finish off the war in the West within six weeks. After this the Russians could be dealt with at leisure; while Britain, deprived of an ally in Western Europe, would have to make peace.

The scheme came within an ace of success. At first the French

---

[1] See page 143.
[2] Two members of the Cabinet, however—Lord Morley and John Burns —had resigned after the promise on August 2nd to protect the French Channel ports.

(Partridge, 1914, reproduced by permission of the Proprietors of 'Punch')

UNCONQUERABLE

The Kaiser: 'SO YOU SEE—YOU'VE LOST EVERYTHING.'
The King of the Belgians: 'NOT MY SOUL.'

The gallant refusal of the Belgians to tolerate a German march across their country was greatly admired in Britain. It united nearly all sections of British opinion in support of war against Germany.

took the offensive in Lorraine and lost thousands of men in heroic but entirely futile bayonet charges against machine-gun posts. Meanwhile the Germans demolished the Liège forts and massed their armies for the attack. In record time they swept through Belgium; and the small British Expeditionary Force under Sir John French, which had rapidly crossed to France, no sooner pushed forward to Mons than it was forced to retreat. But at this point the Germans made a series of mistakes. They diverted two army corps to the east, where the Russians had gallantly invaded East Prussia to relieve the strain on France; they kept their right wing too short to pass Paris on both sides; and when they attempted to pass on the east they left their right flank insufficiently guarded. So, while the main Allied armies turned about in their retreat, a reserve French army in Paris struck out at the passing flank; forward German units which had crossed the Marne were ordered back to give support; the British, who had been retreating south with the French, advanced into the gap created in the front; and soon the whole German force was retiring north from the Marne to the Aisne. The first—and greatest—crisis was over.

After the Marne the French and British armies made several attempts to get round the German right flank, until both Allied and German forces had extended their lines to the Belgian coast and were held in deadlock. The campaign then solidified into a vast siege operation, with the opposing forces facing each other in lines of trenches from the Swiss frontier to the North Sea. From the end of 1914 until the great offensives of 1918 these lines never varied by more than some twenty miles to east or west, and the small strip of Flanders where many of the attacks took place became a hell in which hundreds of thousands were slaughtered in trying to gain a few acres of pock-marked mud or one of the rare dominating ridges. Defence prevailed over attack; and the machine-gun, the dominating weapon until the last year, took a fearful toll. To counter this power of the defence, attacking forces relied chiefly on terrific artillery barrages. These were intended to flatten the enemy's barbed wire, obliterate his trenches, silence his guns, and allow the infantry to go 'over the top'. But since the opposing trenches were not usually greatly affected, their occupants brought their machine-guns into play as soon as the barrage lifted, and mowed down the advancing troops by the thousand.

Attempts to loosen the military deadlock with new weapons had

Germans invade France

Russians invade East Prussia

Battle of the Marne, September 1914

Deadlock on the Western Front

New weapons—

for a long time comparatively little effect. The Germans' use of poison gas in 1915 gave them a temporary success, but protective measures robbed it of its worst terrors, and retaliation soon redressed the balance of advantage. Tanks were the most striking invention of the war, though their initial surprise value was wasted, for they were first used in small numbers in the later stages of the Somme battle (1916), instead of being reserved for a mass attack. Properly used in force, however, they finally proved decisive in 1918. Great developments were also seen in military aviation: the aeroplane, at first simply a means of reconnaissance, was soon engaged in air fighting, in harassing ground forces, and in bombing bases and communications. Large-scale bombing of enemy resources, however, was only in preparation when the war came to an end. Competition in the production of aeroplanes of improved types was intense; but the Royal Air Force had established a general superiority over the enemy before the end of hostilities.[1]

Gas

Tanks

Aeroplanes

Immediately on the outbreak of war Lord Kitchener was asked to take over the War Office. He was one of the very few who guessed at an early date how long the war would last, and he set himself with determination and thoroughness to organize a great military force.[2] By the end of 1914 a million men—all volunteers—had been enrolled in 'Kitchener's Armies'.

'Kitchener's Armies'

The stalemate on the Western Front caused both sides to try in 1915 to achieve results in the Eastern theatre, though few believed events here could be finally decisive. The scope of the war had been extended to the whole Middle East in October 1914, when Turkey, influenced chiefly by her perennial clash of interests with Russia, had thrown in her lot with Germany. Early in 1915 certain members of the British Cabinet, notably Lloyd George and Winston Churchill, were urging the great advantages to be won by a successful stroke in south-eastern Europe. It was decided to try to force the passage of the Dardanelles Straits and seize Constantinople. This would have brought results of the utmost value to the Allies—the exchange of supplies between Russia and the West, the rescue of Serbia, the entry of the other Balkan

Turkey supports Germany, October 1914

---

[1] In August 1914 the combined resources of Royal Flying Corps and Royal Naval Air Service totalled 260 aircraft and 7 airships; in November 1918 the Royal Air Force, formed in April 1918 by combining these two services, had more than 22,000 aircraft on charge (of which over 3,000 were in the first line), as well as 103 airships.

[2] An effective poster showed the figure of Kitchener with pointing finger and the legend 'Your Country needs YOU'.

states on the Allies' side, and the removal of the Turkish threat to the Suez Canal; and it might well have shortened the war by two years. An attempt in February and March to force the passage of the Dardanelles by warships alone having failed, troops were landed on the Gallipoli peninsula dominating the entrance to the Straits. The first forces numbered 75,000, including a large contingent from Australia and New Zealand—the 'Anzacs'. They were within reach of success at an early stage, but never wrested from the Turks the ridge which forms the backbone of the peninsula. In face of an unyielding resistance the campaign had to be given up, the whole force being evacuated in December with such extraordinary skill that not a casualty was suffered. This was the exception to a series of blunders which had frustrated a brilliantly conceived strategic plan.

Gallipoli campaign, 1915

In the vast spaces of Eastern Europe the war remained mobile, instead of settling into the static pattern of the West. In the first weeks of hostilities Hindenburg repelled the hastily prepared Russian attacks on East Prussia, almost destroying the invading Russian armies at the battle of Tannenberg, and during the summer of 1915 the Russians were driven from Poland in a rapid campaign. Thus relieved of Russian pressure, Austria was better able to defend herself against her new enemy, Italy, who had declared war in May[1]; and she could also, with German help, make a fresh onslaught on Serbia. The gallant Serbs had twice defeated the Austrians and had won back Belgrade, their capital, but now succumbed to the double blow of the Austro-German attack and a stab in the back from Bulgaria, who in October joined what appeared to be the winning side. At about the same time an Anglo-French force was landed at Salonika, in Greece, but it was too late to help the Serbs, and too small to influence the situation in the Balkans after it had taken so unfavourable a turn. The year 1915 was thus on the whole a bad one for the Allies, but they were holding their own on the all-important Western Front, while the British armies were growing and the naval blockade of Germany was beginning to tighten.

Russian reverses, 1915

Italy joins Allies, May 1915

Defeat of Serbia, 1915

On the home front it was long before the British people realized what endurance and effort would be required of them, and the transformation of a civilian people into a nation in arms was

The home front

[1] Italy, though a member of the Triple Alliance, had refused to support Germany and Austria in 1914 on the ground that they had committed aggression and that she had no obligation to fight against Britain. She was induced to join the Allied side in 1915 by promises of Austrian and Turkish territory.

carried out with much difficulty and strain. People soon ceased to move coloured pins on maps of the Western Front, and their only excitement came when bad news was released. The Government failed to give a firm lead. General conscription of adult males, including married men, was imposed only after long delay, in May 1916, and systematic rationing—of meat, bacon, fats and sugar—was not enforced till 1918. Meanwhile, expenditure rose above £5,000,000 a day and income tax to 5s. in the pound, and a great savings effort was encouraged by the introduction of War Savings Certificates. Daylight Saving was introduced in 1916, partly as a war measure to save fuel. The labour problem was solved by women taking up scores of occupations they had never engaged in before, both as auxiliaries in the armed forces and as workers in factories, in the transport services and on the land. For the first time for many generations war began to come home to the ordinary British civilian, in the form of raids by Zeppelin airships and by aeroplanes; and though the attacks were only occasional, and extremely light compared with those of the Second World War, there was great alarm and a considerable loss of production.

The British Government's most acute problem was the supply of munitions. The demand for guns and shells exceeded all previous estimates, and the public believed, despite the complacency of the War Office, that British lives were being thrown away for lack of artillery ammunition. The problem was effectively tackled only when Lloyd George was given the new post of Minister of Munitions in Asquith's remodelled Ministry, a coalition consisting of twelve Liberals, eight Conservatives, and one representative of Labour. Lloyd George threw himself into his task with dæmonic energy, overcoming the manufacturers, who resented interference, the trade unions, who mistrusted a sudden influx of new workers as a threat to their standards, and even the War Office, which tried to withhold information. *Shortage of munitions, 1915* *Asquith's Coalition Ministry, May 1915*

The munitions crisis was only one example of the failure of ministers and soldiers to get on with one another. The generals spoke of the politicians as 'our worst enemies after the Germans'; the politicians found the generals too limited in their outlook and short-sighted in their planning. Kitchener as Secretary for War shared the Army's views, and his disagreements with other ministers became widely known. In 1916 he was lost with a cruiser that was taking him to Russia, and his death was felt as a national disaster, for by his strength of character, organizing ability and *Politicians and soldiers* personal prestige he had done more than any other man to make the British a nation in arms.

Germany attempts to gain a decision

Both sides expected 1916 to be a year of decision. The Germans had come to regard Britain, as Napoleon had done, as the 'arch-enemy', but their plan for 1916 was to destroy France, Britain's 'best sword' on the continent of Europe. The Germans decided to attack the historic French fortress of Verdun, hoping to attract to its defence the best troops of France, and so 'bleed her to death'.

Verdun, 1916

The French forces at Verdun, commanded by Pétain, suffered terrible losses, heavier than those of the attackers, but not heavy enough to be decisive. Meanwhile, Russia staged an offensive in Galicia of which no one had thought her capable, taking prisoner 250,000 Austrians, and helped not only once again to divert German forces from the Western Front, but also to bring Rumania into the war on the side of the Allies.

Russian offensive, 1916

Battles of the Somme, 1916

The British Army, profiting from the respite afforded by the German concentration on Verdun, went into action in 1916 with greatly increased numbers and equipment. The sector chosen was astride the River Somme, and on 1 July the attack began. The enemy was well prepared, despite the drain of Verdun on his reserves, while the British commanders had thought out no way of overcoming the defensive power of carefully sited machine-guns except the usual artillery bombardment, which in this battle was not sufficiently intensive. The infantry were sent against the unsubdued defences at a terrible cost; there were nearly 60,000 casualties during the first day—the heaviest day's loss of the whole war, and the heaviest day's loss in the whole history of the British Army. Disappointed in his hopes of a break-through, Sir

Sir Douglas Haig

Douglas Haig, who had earlier succeeded Sir John French in command, nevertheless persevered in a battle of attrition through an autumn of wretched weather. By mid-November the result was that six or seven miles of ground of no great tactical value had been gained at a total cost of half a million casualties.[1] The British Army had, however, engaged half the German forces of the Western Front, and thereby relieved the French of an intolerable strain.

Battle of Jutland, May 1916

The one great sea battle of the war was also fought in 1916, off Jutland. In 1914 a small German force, after some successes in the South Atlantic, had been destroyed at the battle of the

[1] The total of British casualties in these five months on this one front was thus almost half that of the British and Commonwealth forces on all fronts during the whole of the Second World War (1¼ million).

Falkland Islands. Otherwise, German warships had scarcely ventured beyond the Baltic except for a few tip-and-run raids to bombard British east coast towns. The British Grand Fleet, commanded by Admiral Sir John Jellicoe, was constantly at sea, if only because there was no properly defended harbour on the whole east coast where it could anchor. At last, however, the German Fleet came out on a large-scale venture. The battle that followed was indecisive; both commanders were cautious, and the two fleets never properly closed for action. After nightfall the Germans, aided by chance, were able to escape and reach their base, having inflicted losses more serious than those they had suffered. This drawn encounter was a disappointment to British hopes, but Jellicoe's caution was to some extent justified by the fact that, in Churchill's words, he was 'the only man on either side who could lose the war in an afternoon'. The Germans also had the best of reasons for keeping their fleet in being, if only in harbour, for so long as they could do so the British Fleet must be kept together, with its great protective screen of destroyers, which were urgently needed for dealing with the submarine menace.

For the submarine campaign had come to be one of Germany's chief hopes of victory. Not only had Britain's own supplies of food and raw materials to be fetched from the four corners of the earth; British ships had also to supply the war needs of the Allies and to convey millions of fighting men and their equipment to the theatres of war. That the resources of the world were thus available to the Allies, while the Central Powers had to live on the limited resources of one part of Europe, was the advantage which would decide the result of a long war. This advantage the Germans determined to wipe out by sinking ships in such numbers as to strangle the British war effort. Since a submarine increased its own risk by any delay, and since it was vitally important to Germany to sink neutral vessels trading with the Allies, the U-boats were ordered to sink ships on sight, armed or unarmed, enemy or neutral. In response to American protests, this policy was moderated for a time, but in February 1917 it was resumed. In the April of that year 423 Allied and neutral ships were sunk, totalling 840,000 tons. Losses at such a rate would soon starve Britain into surrender.

Yet the decision of the German Government to resume unlimited submarine warfare was a mistake, for it brought into the war the one nation whose resources and manpower could turn

Submarine (U-boat) menace

'Unrestricted' warfare: losses in 1917

U.S.A. joins Allies, April 1917

the scale. The Germans knew their action would have this consequence, but they counted on winning the war before the intervention of the United States could take effect—and they very nearly did. The Americans, though generally sympathetic to the Allied cause, had at first regarded the war as no concern of theirs, except that they had deemed it their duty as well as their interest

THE YPRES SALIENT BY NIGHT

A picture by one of the official artists of the First World War. Trenches, 'tin hats' barbed wire, shells, shell-holes, tree-stumps, Very lights—all were unforgettable elements in the abomination of desolation that was the Western Front.

to maintain the rights of neutrals. In so doing they had raised continual objections to the operations of the British blockade, and at one time a declaration of war against Britain had seemed by no means impossible. Fortunately the U-boat campaign turned American protests, and ultimately American action, against Germany.

The U-boat campaign in 1917 presented as grave a threat as

the German land advance in 1914. But shipping losses were eventually reduced by the somewhat tardy adoption of the convoy system (which was more or less forced on the Admiralty by Lloyd George), by the help of the American Navy, and by the development of new devices such as the hydrophone and the depth-charge, so that when American troops were ready they were brought across the Atlantic in almost complete safety.

Defeat of the U-boats

In addition to the crisis on the war fronts, Britain had been hampered by difficulties elsewhere. Once more, as when she had fought Philip II, Louis XIV and Napoleon, her troubles were Ireland's opportunity. The Third Home Rule Bill, which had become law in September 1914, had not been put into effect, because of the Government's need to concentrate on the war. From the moment hostilities in Europe began the Irish Nationalist party, who were in favour of helping Britain, lost ground to the Sinn Fein movement, which aimed at complete independence, and looked upon the war as a chance to win it. At Easter 1916 about 2,000 Sinn Feiners raised a rebellion in Dublin, armed partly with German guns. They seized several public buildings, including the Post Office, and held out for five days. Irish opinion, which for the most part regarded them as madmen, turned sharply in their favour when fifteen of their leaders were subsequently executed by the British Government.

The Sinn Fein Rebellion, Easter, 1916

There were also troubles within the Cabinet itself. Asquith's direction of affairs had long been causing dissatisfaction, and he was now forced to resign, after some intrigues in which Lloyd George played a prominent part. Lloyd George had shown himself the most active member of the Coalition Government, and was the obvious person to take Asquith's place, which he did with the support of most of his Liberal and Conservative colleagues. Under his direction a small War Cabinet was formed; in theory free from departmental cares, it could devote itself to rapid decisions on major issues. Its members, in addition to the Prime Minister, were Balfour, Curzon and Milner (Conservatives), and Henderson (Labour). Later there was the innovation of including Dominions Prime Ministers who were visiting Britain, particularly Smuts of South Africa.

Resignation of Asquith, December 1916

Lloyd George succeeds him

The War Cabinet

The gain to the Allied cause of America's support was more than balanced at first by the loss of Russia. The Tsarist régime had always suffered from corruption and incompetence, and Russia's achievements in the war had been due to her tremendous reserves of manpower and the courage of her soldiers, who in

The Russian Revolution, March 1917

places during 1915 had only one rifle between three men. In March 1917 the Government at last met its merited fate, and fell to a revolution in the capital. The spirit of revolt soon spread to the Army, which began to melt away; and in November the new Liberal and Socialist government of Kerensky was swept aside by a great social upheaval which only the Marxist Bolsheviks, led by Lenin and Trotsky, knew how to ride. Paralysed for the time being, Russia had to submit to ruinous terms of peace dictated by the Germans at Brest-Litovsk, and she dragged down Rumania with her.

The Bolsheviks in power, November 1917

Meanwhile, on the Western Front the spring of 1917 had witnessed a deep German withdrawal between Arras and Soissons. It proved to be a voluntary move designed to shorten their line, leaving a belt of scorched earth in front to hamper the Allies; for the enemy fell back upon the most formidable defensive works yet constructed—the Hindenburg Line. This withdrawal upset the French plans for a renewed offensive, which the new French Commander-in-Chief, Nivelle, nevertheless insisted on carrying out. Another costly failure resulted.

Allied reverses. 1917

The morale of the French troops was seriously affected by this further slaughter, and for a time the French armies were weakened by mutinies. So, to take the weight off their ally, the British mounted a further offensive. It turned out to be yet another ghastly blood-bath. Even worse than the battles of the Somme in its misdirection and futility, it petered out in the mud of Passchendaele. Elsewhere, events brought the Allies little comfort, for the Italians were routed at Caporetto by the Austrians and Germans, and had to be stiffened by troops withdrawn from the Western Front. The only brightness in the picture shone from the Middle East, where the British after their earlier reverses conquered Mesopotamia, while Allenby, advancing from Egypt, was in Jerusalem by Christmas. A notable part in Allenby's campaign was played by the scholar-soldier T. E. Lawrence, who led the tribes of the Arabian Desert against their Turkish masters.

Third battle of Ypres (Passchendaele)

Caporetto

Victories in Mesopotamia and Palestine, 1917

To the Germans the early months of 1918 held out the last hope of victory. Their long-sustained effort was draining their resources in minerals, chemicals, rubber, food and men; the crumbling power of Austria-Hungary had to be supported; and their Turkish ally was faring badly. Their U-boat campaign and other aggressions had brought in against them not only the U.S.A. but a host of lesser states all over the world, so that the total of

1918: Germany's difficulties

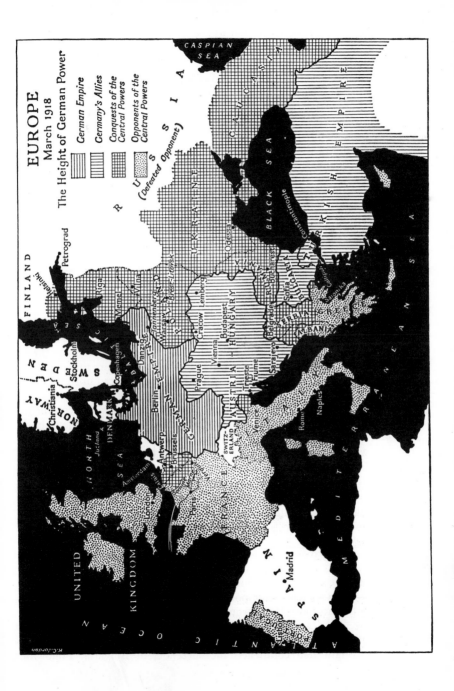

EUROPE
March 1918
The Height of German Power

German Empire

Germany's Allies

Conquests of the
Central Powers

Opponents of the
Central Powers

U S S R
(Defeated Opponent)

R.G.Jordan

states finally arrayed against the Central Powers was no less than twenty-seven. But Russia was knocked out, and 400,000 men, switched to the Western Front before American reinforcements could arrive, might there achieve the break-through, the decisive stroke which neither side had yet been strong enough to produce.

Germany's final bid

So a new blow was aimed by Ludendorff, Hindenburg's Chief of Staff and the brain behind his campaigns, at the point where the French and British sectors joined. Its objectives were Arras and the Channel ports.

It was fortunate that the Allies had improved upon their early leaders. Lloyd George with his fiery energy and uncanny gift of vision was a born war premier. Clemenceau in France checked the spread of defeatism and rallied the nation to a final effort.

Single command on the Western Front

And at last the Allied armies on the Western Front were put under a single command, though not until the German offensive threatened them with defeat. The new generalissimo was Foch, a Frenchman of penetrating intellect and indomitable spirit.

German offensive, March 1918

When the Germans launched their attack on a forty-three-mile front on 21 March a whole British army on the Somme—the Fifth Army—was swept away. Two great bulges were pushed into the British front, but neither Amiens nor Arras fell. A later thrust against the French brought the Germans once more to the Marne, but nowhere did they break through. Foch waited until the Germans were exhausted by their efforts and the Allied armies had recovered, and then began a series of counter-strokes, commencing with the inviting flanks of the bulge. The main blow, how-

Allied counter-offensive, August 1918

ever, came from Haig, who attacked before Amiens on 8 August, which Ludendorff called 'the Black Day of the German Army'. From this time the Germans were given no respite. Haig's untiring optimism now came into play with good effect, for he convinced Foch that victory was possible before the end of 1918. By July 300,000 Americans were in France, and, untried soldiers though they were, they proved invaluable. The weight of effort, however, fell mostly upon the British, who not only held the main German mass on the northern part of the front, but drove

Hindenburg Line breached

it back, and in late September, by a splendid feat of arms, breached the Hindenburg Line.

The Germans were not convinced of the inevitability of defeat until bad news came from an almost forgotten theatre of war— the Balkans. The Allied force had broken out from Salonika after three years of inactivity, and in a brilliant campaign of a fortnight had compelled the surrender of Bulgaria. Following upon the defeats in France and reports of trouble on the home front, this news convinced Ludendorff that Germany must give in. On his advice President Wilson was asked for terms of peace on 3 October. The decision could have been postponed, for the German armies in the West, though defeated, were not broken. But there could be only one end. The Turkish Army in Palestine was destroyed, the Austrians were routed on the Italian front and their subject peoples were on the brink of revolt, while Germany herself was being strangled by the relentless pressure of the blockade. The smouldering hopelessness of the German people broke out in revolution, started by a naval mutiny at Kiel, and the Kaiser fled to Holland. At 11 a.m. on 11 November 1918 an armistice came into effect; the thunder of the guns died away, and the world sighed in relief that the 'war to end war' was at last over.

Surrender of Bulgaria, September 1918

Germany sues for peace

Revolution in Germany

Armistice, 11 November 1918

So many factors contributed to the defeat of Germany that no one of them can be regarded as in itself decisive. Among the most important were undoubtedly the prolonged and heroic endurance of France, the prodigious reserves of Russian manpower, the arrival of huge American armies to turn the scale when both sides were virtually exhausted, and the simple fact that Germany took on far too much. It may be doubted, however, whether any nation made a greater contribution to victory than the British. The great military forces so quickly built up from almost nothing and sustained for so long in the field, in spite of casualties which amounted to nearly a million dead; the vast quantities of money and goods furnished to the Allies; above all, perhaps, the retention of supremacy at sea, with the consequent ability to maintain overseas trade, supply overseas forces and impose a pitiless blockade on the enemy—all these played a vital part in the overthrow of Germany.

19. Between the Wars

1 The Peace Treaties and the Resettlement of Europe

The Paris Peace
Conference,
1919 The Conference which met in Paris to draw up the peace settlement consisted of representatives of 27 Allied states, but all the important decisions were made by 'the Big Four'—the leaders of the British, French, American and Italian delegations. None of these was an ideal peacemaker. Lloyd George, though he was a brilliant negotiator, came fresh from an election which had brought forth such slogans as 'Squeeze Germany till the pips squeak!' and so was not entirely free to consider European problems on their merits. Clemenceau, 'the Tiger', was old and disillusioned, and interested only in security for France. Woodrow Wilson was by contrast a man of ideals, intent on making a just peace and laying the foundations of a new world order, but he lacked experience of European politics and politicians. The main concern of Orlando was merely to secure a rich reward for Italy.

Principles of the
peacemakers In the hands of these four men lay the destinies of war-torn Europe. The victors agreed in condemning as the villains of the tragedy the great autocratic and militarist empires of Germany and Austria-Hungary. Since both the throne of the Kaiser and the Empire of the Habsburgs had collapsed in 1918, the first part of the peacemakers' task was done for them. Europe, however, had to be rebuilt. Wilson, with much support from British opinion, had supplied the principle on which this should be done. Germany had sued for peace on the basis of 'Fourteen Points' enunciated by Wilson in January 1918; and, with modifications, the Allies had agreed that the Peace should be built upon these 'Self-determina-
tion' points. Running through them all was the principle of self-determination—the right of all peoples to choose the state to which they should belong. This was to be the foundation-stone of the treaties. Liberty and nationalism, the twin watchwords of the nineteenth century, were proclaimed anew so that free young nations might arise from the ruins of the destroyed tyrannies.

Two looming shadows darkened this hopeful prospect. One

was Communist revolution, which in Russia was maintaining itself against Tsarist and Allied forces, and was threatening to spread to the rest of Europe. The other danger, ally of the first, arose from the widespread ruin and chaos, hunger and disease that war had left in its wake. The policy of the victorious Allies towards Russian Communism was first to attempt its overthrow by armed force, and when this failed, to protect Western Europe from its contagion. This they were able to do by recognizing the new states which, escaping from Russian dominion, had sprung up along the whole of Russia's western frontier, and which the Allies hoped would form a barrier against the spread of Communist infection. The second danger—economic ruin—was beyond the power of a peace conference to remove, and no permanent body was evolved to cope with it.

The peacemakers turned first to the problem of Germany. In the west, France of course recovered Alsace and Lorraine, and when the time came for the treaty to be signed, the ceremony was held in the same Hall of Mirrors in the Palace of Versailles where Bismarck had humiliated France in 1871. The French demand for a frontier on the Rhine was not, however, accorded; baulked by Wilson and Lloyd George, Clemenceau had to be satisfied instead with the demilitarization of the Rhineland and a guarantee from Britain and the U.S.A. of France's security—which the U.S.A. subsequently failed to confirm. Nor did France obtain possession of the Saar basin, with its rich coal mines, for though taken from Germany it was placed under international control for fifteen years, after which a plebiscite was to determine the eventual ownership. *Treaty of Versailles 1919* *Germany's reduced frontiers*

A far greater blow to Germany was the loss she suffered in the east. West Prussia and Posen, which were inhabited by Poles, became part of a reconstituted Polish state, thereby forming a 'corridor' for Polish access to the Baltic, and leaving East Prussia separated from the rest of Germany. Danzig, the great port at the mouth of the Vistula, being mainly German in population, was placed under international control.

Besides thus losing four million subjects in Europe, together with great resources in iron and coal, Germany had to surrender her colonies overseas, her warships and aircraft, and most of her mercantile fleet. Her army was limited to 100,000 men, and conscription was abolished. In addition, she was ordered to pay sufficient in cash and kind to cover all the loss she had caused during the war to civilian life and property. The amount, later *Other penalties* fixed at £6,600,000,000, would have taken a long time to pay off, and nothing like the full sum of these 'reparations' was ever extracted.

Break-up of Austria-Hungary

Germany's main allies suffered worse than herself. The Habsburg dominions had fallen apart in 1918, and the peacemakers had little to do except to recognize accomplished facts. A tiny Austria, a much reduced but independent Hungary, and three states created or enlarged out of the former Austro-Hungarian territories—Czechoslovakia, Rumania and Yugoslavia—emerged from the upheaval in Central Europe and the Treaty of Trianon. The Turks likewise lost almost all their subject populations, including their Arab dominions. From this wreckage of the Habsburg and Ottoman empires Italy picked up far less than she expected, and she remained disappointed and resentful.

Treaty of Trianon

End of the Ottoman Empire

The new nations

The post-war treaties brought freedom to many people, for the total of subject 'minorities' was reduced from 45 million before the war to 19 million. But it was a precarious freedom, for no one asked whether the small new sovereign states were strong enough to defend themselves and rich enough to provide a decent livelihood for their peoples, or whether they would co-operate with one another to achieve these ends.

The League of Nations

Wilson knew that the peace treaties fell far short of the standards he had set up, but relied upon the great new creation of the League of Nations to right any injustices and generally make the world a better place. The setting up of an 'association of nations' was one of the Fourteen Points, and British and American thinkers had prepared plans for co-operation between all nations of the world. Upon their work was built the Covenant of the League, which by Wilson's insistence was made the first part of all the peace treaties. Among the objects of the League were disarmament, the prevention of war, the improvement of social welfare, better labour conditions, and care of backward peoples. Most important were the arrangements for maintaining peace. Each state that signed the Covenant undertook to help any fellow-member that was attacked, and to act against a member that resorted to force in defiance of the Covenant.

Mandates

Among the duties of the League was the supervision of the 'mandate' system. The former German colonies in Africa and the Pacific, which had all been captured during the course of the war, were not annexed outright, but were placed under the care of Allied states, including the British Dominions and France, but not Italy. Britain herself became responsible for Tanganyika

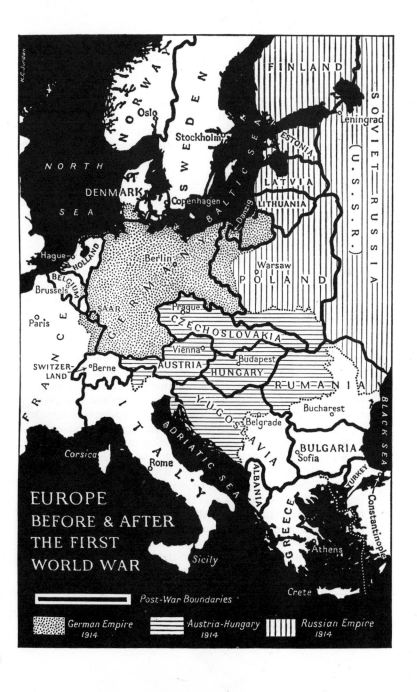

K.C. Jordan

EUROPE
BEFORE & AFTER
THE FIRST
WORLD WAR

Post-War Boundaries

German Empire
1914

Austria-Hungary
1914

Russian Empire
1914

(formerly German East Africa) and parts of German West Africa, and temporarily took charge of Iraq and of Palestine, where a Jewish National Home was to be established. The mandatory powers undertook to place the welfare of the native inhabitants of these territories before their own interests, and to ensure that the resources and trade of the areas should be open equally to all nations. The League was responsible for seeing that the powers proved faithful to their trust.

★   ★   ★   ★   ★

U.S.A. rejects Wilson's work

The new order in Europe was beset with difficulties from the start. Wilson had neglected public opinion in America, with the result that Congress rejected the pledge to France, the whole of the peace arrangements and membership of the League of Nations. With Germany and Russia also outside the League, Britain and France were left to give effect to its guarantees. Unfortun-

Reparations difficulties

ately they had very different ideas as to how the League should work; they also quarrelled throughout a series of eighteen conferences (1920–22) over the amount Germany could be made to pay in reparations, and the division of the payments between themselves. Finally, when Germany made some minor defaults on promised payments, the French Prime Minister Poincaré, without consulting the British Government, sent French troops to occupy

French occupation of the Ruhr, 1923

the Ruhr valley, so as to secure the products of Germany's greatest industrial area The step was ill-advised but perhaps excusable. The French had lost both the guarantees they had asked for—a frontier on the Rhine and an Anglo-American pledge of assistance. Now Germany was evading the penalties of defeat. The French got little out of the Ruhr, which they left in 1924.

'Inflation' in Germany

Meanwhile the German currency, already suffering from inflation, completely collapsed. The mark became utterly worthless, the savings of Germany's middle class disappeared, and until a new currency could be introduced, based on foreign loans, the country was in economic chaos.

There were others who resorted to force with less excuse than Poincaré. The Allies' settlement of the Near East was overturned

Mustapha Kemal

by Mustapha Kemal, a determined and ruthless officer who became the dictator of Turkey. In the space of two years he overthrew the Sultan, drove out the Greeks from Asia Minor and threatened to re-occupy the demilitarized Straits zone. War with Britain and France was averted by a narrow margin, and a new settlement was negotiated with the Turks at Lausanne, by which Greece had to give up the territories she had gained in 1919.

Treaty of Lausanne, 1923

In Italy the distress of the post-war period and the incompetence and corruption of the politicians in office opened the way for Mussolini. Under the threat of a 'March on Rome' by his bands of Fascists,[1] he took over the Government and soon suppressed every form of opposition. He gave an early taste of his methods in foreign affairs when, to coerce the Greek Government into settling a minor dispute on Italy's terms, the Italian Fleet bombarded Corfu, killing many civilians—a piece of scoundrelism which went unchecked by the League of Nations and Italy's former allies.

Italian Fascism, 1922

In the atmosphere produced by these events it was not likely that the general disarmament promised in the League Covenant would proceed very far. Even Germany began secretly to re-arm without much difficulty, and the rest clung to their weapons for lack of any other guarantee of their security. Great reductions were of course made in the forces existing at the end of the war. Britain cut down her army and air force to very small proportions, and France went back to a two-year period of conscript service. But of a general beating of swords into ploughshares there was little sign.

Failure to disarm

There were, however, two hopeful moves which brightened the international outlook. By the Washington Naval Treaty, Britain, U.S.A., Japan, France and Italy, having first agreed on consultation and co-operation in all problems of the Pacific, fixed a ratio for the number of large battleships each should have—Britain 5, U.S.A. 5, Japan 3, France $1\frac{3}{4}$, Italy $1\frac{3}{4}$. This ratio gave Britain a comfortable superiority in Europe, while in the Pacific agreement was easy because the naval bases were, in the conditions then prevailing, out of striking distance of each other. Secondly, in 1925, Austen Chamberlain, the British Foreign Secretary, Briand of France, and Stresemann of Germany made the Locarno Treaty, by which Germany affirmed her acceptance of her new frontiers in the west, while Britain and Italy undertook that if ever those frontiers were violated by either France or Germany they would go to the help of the state that was attacked. Following this, Germany was admitted to the League of Nations,

Washington Naval Treaty, 1922

Locarno Treaty, 1925

[1] Fascism, from the *fasces* (rods and axe) carried before a Roman consul as a symbol of authority—a form of dictatorship involving the destruction of parliamentary government and the pursuit of national greatness before all else.

Germany joins
the League, 1926
and four years later the last Allied troops were withdrawn from
the Rhineland. At last there seemed to be some promise of
European harmony.

2 Britain after the First World War

Post-war
conditions
At home as well as abroad, the years which followed the war were
a time of confusion, disappointment and unrest. The war itself,
diverting the nation's efforts for four years into tasks of destruction, had caused immense economic dislocation. Among the signs
of this was a steep increase in prices, so that the pound sterling
of 1914 was worth only 8s. 3d. in 1918; the National Debt (up
from £650 million to £7,000 million) and taxation increased even
more steeply, income tax having risen from ninepence to six
shillings in the pound, never to fall substantially again. The
powers of the Government and the numbers of civil servants had
grown far beyond all previous limits, yet the Government lacked
the knowledge and experience for dealing with the transition
from war to peace, to say nothing of the trade crisis which lay
just ahead. These circumstances, jointly considered, were likely
to arouse in the minds of even the more fortunate members of the
public an unusual degree of discontent and impatience with their
rulers.

At first, however, there was rejoicing that the war was at last
over, and optimism prevailed. The Coalition Ministry had found
Fourth Parlia-
mentary Reform
Act, 1918
time before the war ended to introduce the fourth Parliamentary
Reform Bill, which gave the vote to all men over twenty-one and
to women over thirty[1]—an obvious measure of justice to citizens
who had contributed so much to the war effort. The first election
on the new register (with eight million new voters, of whom six
million were women) followed immediately on the ending of
hostilities. The supporters of Lloyd George's Coalition Ministry
fought the election as a united group, being furnished each with
The 'coupon'
election, 1918
a letter—scornfully described by Asquith as a 'coupon'—signed
by Lloyd George and Balfour and vouching for his loyalty to the
Coalition that had won the war. The Coalition triumphantly
won the election.

The Prime Minister now turned some of his superabundant
energy to the tasks of reconstruction. With his usual gift for the
arresting phrase, Lloyd George spoke of creating 'a land fit for

[1] But only women who were ratepayers or the wives of ratepayers.

heroes to live in'. The vision was soon to fade as the country struggled in a morass of economic difficulties and stumbled into industrial strife. While the post-war optimism lasted, however, the Government brought in two measures of social reform which were of considerable importance. By the terms of the Housing Act of 1919 the state for the first time came to the help of local authorities by providing housing subsidies; this measure brought little result for the time being because economy cuts soon followed. The Unemployment Insurance Act of 1920 was a great advance on the scheme of 1911,[1] which was limited to building, engineering and shipbuilding. Now all employees earning up to £250 a year, except farm workers and domestic servants, were covered. Twelve weeks' contributions ensured up to fifteen weeks' benefit, at the rate of 15s. for men, 12s. for women. Though these rates were low and there was no provision for families, it was recognized for the first time that the unemployed should generally be protected by the state. Protection was likely soon to be demanded whether or not it was paid for by contributions, on the principle that the state had a duty to care for the unfortunate— a principle only scantily recognized by the harsh Poor Law of the nineteenth century, which had been much more concerned to deter applications for relief than to comfort the needy. The new scheme was soon to be submerged, however, by unemployment on a scale never before experienced.

Housing Act, 1919

Unemployment Insurance Act, 1920

For a short time after the armistice British industry indeed enjoyed a 'boom'. Everywhere there was a big demand for goods such as textiles which had become scarce during the war. But when more normal conditions of trade returned, the factors which had retarded British expansion before the war reasserted themselves—backwardness in methods, low productivity and depressed agriculture.[2] Foreign rivals less affected by the war had forged ahead; markets lost to Britain were difficult to recapture. Moreover the Government chose this very moment to decrease the proportion of paper currency to gold reserve. This, by increasing the real value of money, caused a general fall in prices; declining profits declined still further, and with the shrinkage of trade appeared the black spectre of mass unemployment, involving, of course, a fall in wage rates. By the end of 1921 there were nearly two million unemployed. The 'slump' was on.

The post-war 'boom', 1919–1921

The slump

In these circumstances industrial struggles became rife, especially in the coal industry. The miners objected to the

Coal troubles, 1921

[1] See page 231.   [2] See pages 363–4.

Government, which had directed the industry during the war, handing back the mines to private control, and demanded shorter hours, higher wages and nationalization of the mines. The Government introduced by law a seven-hour day and a wage-increase dependent on output, but made no attempt to change the ownership of the mines. When the coalowners resumed full control, the miners rejected a proposed decrease in wages, and a lock-out took place which lasted several months. The miners were relying on the support of the railwaymen's and transport workers' unions, their partners in 'the triple alliance', to stage what would virtually have been a general strike to begin on Saturday, 16 April. But when the miners rejected a last-minute request by the Government to continue discussions, the other unions withdrew their support and the strike was cancelled. The day was called 'Black Friday' in the trade union movement. The miners after much suffering had to admit defeat. The stoppage was reckoned to have caused the country a loss of £250 million.

Rebellion in Ireland

At the same time affairs in Ireland reached a final crisis. The Sinn Fein movement[1] had continued to grow, and in the election of 1918 it swept away the moderate Nationalists. Refusing to take their seats at Westminster, the Sinn Feiners set up a parliament of their own in Ireland, and waged a guerrilla rebellion better armed, more boldly led and more formidable than any in the long story of Irish resistance. The Government reinforced the Royal Irish Constabulary with recently demobilized soldiers, who wore the R.I.C. black cap with their khaki. These 'Black and Tans' took at least one Irish life for one English, without the formalities of arrest and trial. The bitter and sanguinary struggle only made the Irish more determined on freedom, and their persistence was rewarded. Lloyd George met the Sinn Fein leaders, and made with them a 'treaty' which took effect in 1922.

The 'treaty' of 1922

Ireland was to have a status similar to that of a Dominion, remaining in allegiance to the Crown. Ulster was to be allowed to separate herself from the rest of the country, and promptly did so, choosing to continue as a part of the United Kingdom, though with a parliament for local affairs. But within a few months two of the Irish leaders who had negotiated the treaty—Arthur Griffith and the military chief Michael Collins—were dead, the latter murdered by extreme Sinn Feiners for whom any agreement with the English was treason. In fact a civil war now broke out in Ireland between the new Sinn Fein Government and the

[1] See page 251.

extremists, or Republicans, and it was some time before the latter were suppressed.

The concessions made to Sinn Fein, together with troubles in the Near East[1] and at home, helped to bring about the collapse of Lloyd George's coalition. The end came in 1922 when the Conservative rank and file, finding the Liberal leader more of a liability than an asset, withdrew their support and compelled their leaders to break up the Coalition. Some Liberals remained faithful to Lloyd George; others, who had never forgiven his treatment of Asquith, opposed him. Thus the party which, inheriting and improving upon the principles of the Whigs, had fought for so many great causes in the nineteenth and twentieth centuries, suffered a split from which it never recovered. *Fall of Lloyd George, 1922*

This proved, too, to be the end of Lloyd George's effective career, after more than fifteen years continuously in office. He lived for twenty-three years more, and again led the Liberals in the House, but he gave few signs of his former greatness. First prominent through his outspoken condemnation of the Boer War, he had risen quickly to high office, framed the 1909 Budget and defeated the Lords' attempt to destroy it, and done much to lay the foundations of the Welfare State. An inspiring leader of the nation in war, he had shown a fortitude in disaster which won the lasting admiration of Churchill, who was later to steer the nation through still greater perils. At the Peace Conference of 1919 he had displayed an almost uncanny skill in diplomacy; and it was Lloyd George who at long last found a solution to the Irish problem. A hater of landlords and a genuine champion of the depressed classes, he finally entered the House of Lords as an earl in 1945; a Prime Minister of infectious energy, he distrusted his subordinates and schemed to undermine official persons; a politician of genius, he was too liable to persuade himself that what he wanted was both possible and right. But though he may have lacked moral scruples, he had charm, courage, vigour, and an enormous zest for life, and his outstanding services alike in peace and war ensure him a place among great British statesmen.

Asquith's career also had now virtually come to an end. A distinguished Oxford classicist and then a successful barrister, a Cabinet Minister after only four years in Parliament, Home Secretary at the age of forty, Prime Minister for eight consecutive years—it had been a triumphant career for a middle-class boy who, like Lloyd George, had lost his father at an early age. *End of Asquith's career*

[1] See page 260.

His complete mastery of any subject on which he spoke and a quite extraordinary command of language marked his prowess in the House of Commons. As Prime Minister he displayed more the qualities of a judge than those of a leader, but his powers of work were remarkable. Even in the first years of the war he had got through his day's tasks in five hours, read a book every evening and found time for social pursuits—habits which no doubt helped to impair his reputation as a war leader. His main achievements had been the victory over the House of Lords and the social security measures of 1908–11, when under his leadership Liberalism had marched proudly to meet the new century—whose forces after all were to prove too much for it.

Bonar Law Prime Minister

The next Prime Minister was Bonar Law, who had earlier been the Conservative chief in Lloyd George's ministries, but who had retired from office on account of ill-health. It was his willingness to return to the arena as leader of his party and of an all-Conservative Government that had made possible the break-up of the Coalition. Though deprived of the support of most of the leading Conservatives, who had wished to continue the Coalition, he secured a workable majority in the election that now followed. When he was forced by his illness to resign early in 1923, he was replaced by Stanley Baldwin, whose Cabinet career had been comparatively short, but whose distrust of Lloyd George had been decisive in the latter's overthrow.

Election of 1922

Baldwin Prime Minister

Faced with mass unemployment at home and disturbed conditions abroad, Baldwin decided that protection was the only remedy. Two steps away from free trade had been taken already, when in 1915 and 1921 import duties were imposed on certain manufactured articles. Baldwin now wanted a complete protective system, but when he appealed to the country for approval, his policy was rejected. This time the Conservatives found themselves with only 258 seats, while Labour had 192 and the Liberals 157.

Policy of protection

Election of 1923

With Liberal support the Labour party could now take office. Asquith was more in agreement with Labour than with the Conservatives, especially on the need to preserve free trade, and decided, in spite of many appeals to keep the Socialists out, to put them in. He could eject them from office at any time, and was to do so after only nine months. MacDonald chose a Cabinet of moderates, and even filled a few places with persons from outside the Labour party. In some ways, however, a new epoch seemed to have begun. A Labour Minister wrote of their first

The Labour Government, 1924; MacDonald Prime Minister

interview with the King: 'As we stood waiting for His Majesty, amid the gold and crimson of the Palace, I could not help marvelling at the strange turn of Fortune's wheel which had brought MacDonald the starveling clerk, Thomas the engine-driver, Henderson the foundry labourer and Clynes the mill-hand to this pinnacle.'

There was time only for MacDonald to prove his ability in foreign affairs, while his colleagues produced a new Housing Act and some relaxation of restrictions on unemployment benefit and educational expenditure, before the first experiment in Labour government came to an end.

The election of 1924, the third in three years, was famous for the 'Red Letter'. The newspapers published a document released by the Foreign Office and alleged to have been sent by Zinoviev, the Russian Chairman of the Communist International, to tell British Communists how to promote revolution in Britain. This happened at a time when the Labour Government had been trying to arrange a loan to Russia and a trade treaty. The implication that the Labour party could not be trusted to take care of British interests helped to lose them 42 seats, though by running more candidates they actually polled more votes than in 1923. It was in fact the Liberals who suffered worse, losing 116 seats and retaining only 42. The country now appeared to find that the Labour and Conservative parties presented the real political alternatives; the latter, with 415 seats and a clear majority of 200, could expect five secure years in office. *The 'Red Letter' election*

The Prime Minister was again Baldwin, who was becoming associated in the public mind with a pipe, suggesting plain English honesty and a placid disposition—a reputation which did insufficient credit to his shrewdness. Head of a great iron firm, he represented the manufacturing and business interests which were so prominent in the Conservative party during the period between the wars—though he was certainly exceptional in that he anonymously gave £120,000—a fifth of his fortune—to help reduce the National Debt. His Cabinet was strengthened by prominent Conservatives of the former Coalition ministries such as Austen Chamberlain, Foreign Secretary, and the Earl of Birkenhead, Secretary for India, while Winston Churchill, who had not been a Conservative since 1903, came in as Chancellor of the Exchequer. To help the country's trade the new government planned to cut down its expenditure, which proved impracticable, to restore the pound sterling to its full value in terms of *Baldwin's second Ministry. 1924–1929*

Remedies for trade depression

gold, which raised the price of exports and so proved a mistake, and to use tariffs and subsidies, which came to stay. They also

Local Government Act, 1929

tried to help industry by the de-rating clauses of the Local Government Act (1929), whereby farms were exempted from rates altogether and factories from all but a quarter, the loss to the local authorities being made up by the Government. The relief was helpful to industries in difficulties, but where profits were being made already it was a gift from the taxpayer to the manufacturer. The same Act was a landmark in the long history of the Poor Law. The Guardians of the Poor, who had functioned since the reign of the first Elizabeth, were abolished, and their work taken over by the County Councils, which set up Public Assistance Committees to administer relief and to manage the hospitals for the old and infirm. Not until the buildings which had long housed these unfortunates were replaced by modern ones would the miseries of the old system entirely disappear, but the stigma of the workhouse, for so long dreaded by the poor, was now largely removed. The main author of this Act was Neville Chamberlain, son of Joseph, as Minister of Health, and it owed much to the support of Winston Churchill at the Exchequer.

Pensions Act, 1925

The Conservatives were busy with other measures of which all parties could approve. A new Pensions Act extended the National Health Insurance scheme so that contributors could draw Old Age Pensions at sixty-five. Under the Electricity Act a Central

Electricity Act, 1926

Board was set up to control the generation of electric power and make it available everywhere by means of a national 'grid', which

B.B.C., 1927

was completed in 1933. Broadcasting, which otherwise would have been developed by competing private companies, was also

Fifth Parliamentary Reform Act, 1928

brought under government control. Finally, this staid Conservative Parliament gave the franchise to women on the same terms as men, so that all persons over twenty-one shared in political rights, and the work begun in 1832 was made complete.

More coal troubles

A renewed crisis in the coal industry might have been foreseen and should have been forestalled. The foreign demand for British coal fell off sharply, especially with the recovery of the Ruhr, so that prices, profits and wages declined. The mineowners asked for still further reductions in wages to enable them to meet foreign competition, but the miners were determined to have 'not a minute on the day, not a penny off the pay'. Baldwin provided a government subsidy to keep the industry on its feet while an enquiry was held by a Royal Commission, but neither side entirely accepted its proposals, and the Government began to support the owners' contention that at least as a temporary measure the working day should be increased once more to eight hours. The embittered miners turned to the General Council of the Trade Union Congress for aid, and the Council undertook to declare a general strike to force the Government to give way to the miners' demands. The strike began on 3 May 1926, workers being called out in sections, transport men first. The unions offered to let food and health services continue—illogically, since the whole point of a general strike was to hold the country to ransom, and the more ruthless the stoppage the surer its success would be. Moscow observers of the British scene, hopeful of a social revolution, were presumably perplexed and disgusted to learn that some of the strikers were beguiling their idle days with friendly games of football with the police!

The General Strike, 1926

A week passed and nothing happened to bring the issue nearer a decision. The Government had plans ready, and complete paralysis was avoided. Business people somehow contrived to get to work, and volunteer strike-breakers enjoyed the novel experience of driving trains, buses and lorries. Newspapers virtually ceased publication, but the Government was able to provide regular news through the B.B.C. and *The British Gazette*, an official government news-sheet edited by Winston Churchill. The country's major industries were of course brought to a standstill, but to gain victory the strikers would have had to endure not one but many weeks without wages or strike pay. They would also have had to be prepared for violence; as it was, ugly incidents occurred and there were several baton charges by the police. But there was little spirit for a fight to the bitter end. The union leaders had wished merely to help the miners, not seeing that success would mean the surrender of power by the country's lawful government—in fact a revolution. It was this that made the Government unyielding, the public in general hostile to the strikers, and the union leaders themselves irresolute. In fact they were ready to seize on any excuse for calling off the strike, and did so on 12 May without demanding or obtaining any concession from the Government. Some strikers did not get their jobs back; there were 3,000 prosecutions for seditious speeches or violence; the miners were left to struggle on alone. The British working-class movement, with little thought of what it was doing, had picked up a deadly weapon of revolution, fingered the trigger —and laid it down.

The coal stoppage went on for seven months before the miners gave in. They had to accept lower wages and longer hours, their unions were penniless, more markets had been lost, and one miner in six remained permanently out of work. Even then nothing was done towards the necessary reorganization of the industry. But the Government promptly took steps to weaken the unions and prevent another general strike. The Trade Disputes Act of 1927 prohibited general or sympathetic strikes; any strike which had an object beyond the furtherance of a trade dispute in one industry, or which was designed to coerce the Government, was rendered illegal. Trade union funds could not be used to support political activity, i.e. the Labour Party, unless the member stated his wish to contribute for this purpose.[1] The whole trade union movement suffered from its failure in this contest, and a membership figure of 8,300,000 in 1920 was reduced in the next ten years to less than half by the combined effects of trade slump and strike fiasco.

Trade Disputes Act, 1927

3 The Economic Crisis

In spite of the fiasco of the general strike, it was the Labour party that proved victorious when an election fell due in 1929. Ramsay MacDonald therefore took office for the second time, though dependent as before on Liberal support. It was his Government's misfortune to meet the worst economic crisis the world had ever known.

The second Labour Government, 1929–1931

The breakdown of trade and finance that occurred in 1931 may be traced in part to the First World War and the subsequent confusion over reparations and debts. In 1923, for example, Baldwin as Chancellor of the Exchequer had undertaken that the British Government should pay the U.S.A. £920,000,000 over a period of sixty-two years. The Allies exacted as much as they could from Germany so that they might repay their debts on the other side of the Atlantic, but such reparations as Germany paid in cash were made possible only by her borrowing from America and Britain. The full payment of reparations and debts would have required a vast one-way flow of trade. But as the creditor countries could not have their workers sitting idle while their debtors supplied their needs, most of them, and especially the U.S.A., imposed high duties on imported goods, so that debts

World economic crisis, 1931

[1] This was called 'contracting in'; the Act thus reversed the provisions of the Trade Union Act of 1913 (see page 231).

simply could not be paid. Europe just managed to keep going while America continued to lend, but when in 1929 America was shaken by a financial slump and stopped lending abroad the whole unstable edifice collapsed. Gluts of unsaleable goods accumulated, and everywhere people were thrown out of work. In three years world trade shrank by two-thirds.

Britain, far more dependent than most countries upon external **Effect on Britain**

THE MORNING AFTER.

(David Low, October 1929, reproduced by permission of the 'Evening Standard')

An American financier wakes up after the boom-time of the 1920s. After a final frenzy of speculation on Wall Street, he finds that shares have crashed and the world economic crisis has begun.

trade, was one of the worst sufferers. Her means of earning by shipping and exports were cut down, and the resulting decline in profits and employment reduced the demand for goods at home. By the end of 1931 there were 2,900,000 people unemployed—a fifth of all insured workers. Expenditure on unemployment benefit was rapidly mounting, while the yield of taxes was falling. The crisis grew more acute when British financiers lost heavily through bank failures in Austria and Germany. Foreigners began in alarm to withdraw their money from London, thus obliging the Bank of England to borrow again from the U.S.A. and from France. These creditors would lend no more unless the British Government balanced its budget.

To this end, a special economy committee recommended many cuts in expenditure. These included reduced pay for teachers and the armed forces, and a reduction of unemployment

(*By permission of Mrs Strube and Beaverbrook Newspapers Ltd.*)

'J'accuse'

By agreeing to form a 'National' Government, Ramsay MacDonald was widely regarded within his own party as a traitor to the Labour movement. Here Strube of the *Daily Express* depicts MacDonald and J. H. Thomas as aristocrats charged before a Revolutionary Tribunal—the General Council of the Trade Union Congress backed by the rank and file of the Labour Party (Morrison third from left behind balustrade, Lansbury on stairs). Strube's famous 'Little Man'—the ordinary harmless and bewildered citizen—peeps from behind the curtain (Sept. 1931).

benefit by ten per cent.[1] One argument for this was that it would facilitate a general reduction of wages, and thus the lowering of costs and improvement of trade. To solve the country's problems by imposing sacrifices on the poorest was so objectionable to ten of the twenty-one members of the Labour Cabinet that they refused to agree to it, and the Cabinet broke up. In this crisis MacDonald, urged by King George V, accepted the task

[1] Benefit for a man with wife and three children would then be 29s. 3d. a week—subject to a household means test.

of forming a new ministry with the co-operation of the Con- MacDonald's
servative leaders and some Liberals. Supported by only three 'National
Labour colleagues, foremost of whom was his Chancellor of the Government'
Exchequer, the hard-grained and puritanical Philip Snowden, 1931–1935
MacDonald completed a small Cabinet with four Conservative
and two Liberal ministers. This was described as a National
Government, and certainly the solution of a coalition in time of
crisis appealed to the greater part of the nation. To the majority
of the Labour Party, on the other hand, MacDonald appeared to
have betrayed the working class, to champion whose cause the
party had been created.

In the long and bitter controversy that ensued it was contended
that the economies were too small to warrant breaking up a ministry, that there was no need to balance the budget, and that it was
a mistake to try to keep the gold standard—that, on the contrary, devaluation of the pound was the correct remedy for the
country's difficulties. Until it happened, however, everyone
thought that 'to go off gold' would have the most disastrous consequences. MacDonald had acted on the best financial advice,
and thought it his duty as head of the Government to secure the
agreement of the Cabinet to the measures declared necessary to
obtain foreign loans and save the pound. Later theories were to
favour managed currencies and budgeting for a deficit; but the
past experience of other countries showed that unsound finance
was the way to catastrophe. MacDonald could of course have
resigned and left an unpleasant duty to the Conservative and
Liberal leaders; but this would have been to confess his own
complete failure as a prime minister.

The economies so painfully decided on were not fully enforced.
When the 12,000 men of the fleet in harbour at Invergordon The Invergordon
learned (from the newspapers) of the cuts in their pay, which fell mutiny
heaviest on the lower ranks, they staged a quiet and orderly
mutiny—or at least refused to take their ships out of harbour for
exercises. They were successful; the cuts were modified; even
the teachers, who did not strike, lost only ten instead of fifteen
per cent. Moderate and good-tempered as the episode was, however, the spectacle of a government surrender to a sailors' revolt
plunged the money market into a state of real alarm, and the
flow of foreign funds out of London became a flood. The loan
negotiated by the National Government was rapidly exhausted,
and there was no prospect of another. The Government therefore
had to take the very step its formation had been meant to avert—

Britain went off gold. If the same thing had been done a month earlier by the Labour Government it would of course have been regarded by financial authorities at home and abroad as a catastrophe. As it was, no dreadful consequences followed. The pound lost nearly one-third of its value, but the change proved for the moment beneficial, for British goods thus became cheaper for the foreigner to buy, and export trade improved.

MacDonald had expected that after a brief 'interlude' of all-party government Labour would return to power and himself to the leadership of the party. Instead he had to face the unrelenting opposition of his former followers. This was in part the cause
of his decision to consult the electorate later in the year. The election was a triumph for the National Government, and a disaster for the Labour Party. The Government won $14\frac{1}{2}$ million votes, its opponents less than half that number; in the Commons, however, such was the exaggeration of the electoral system, 554 M.P.s were pledged to support the Government, and Labour was reduced to 51; nearly all its leaders were swept away, except those who were in alliance with their former opponents. The party elected George Lansbury as leader. When he resigned in 1935 because his pacifist principles would not allow him to accept the party's policy on armaments, he was succeeded by Clement Attlee, a respected but minor figure who thus took a notable step towards his later eminence as Prime Minister.

The National Government's policy for trade recovery was protection. Since this was entirely a Conservative policy it was a bitter pill for MacDonald and Snowden to swallow; still more so for Sir Herbert Samuel, the leading Liberal representative in the Cabinet. Snowden and Samuel were with difficulty dissuaded from resigning early in 1932, and did so before the end of the year, leaving the ministry more obviously Conservative in complexion than before. Neville Chamberlain, as Chancellor of the Exchequer, then appropriately put into effect the policy of protection urged by his father thirty years earlier. A duty of 10 per cent was levied on almost all imports, with an exception for Empire products; and a Tariff Commission was set up to fix higher rates of duty for particular articles, according to the need of home industries for protection. Imperial preference was to
be an essential part of the scheme, so in 1932 an Imperial Conference met at Ottawa, the capital of Canada, to arrange a great system of exchange among the countries of the Empire. The results were disappointing, for the simple reason that the

Dominions would not admit British goods free of duty to the damage of their own products. Nor would Britain give the desired advantage to Dominion foodstuffs by taxing those from foreign countries—for a dear food policy would be too unpopular at home. The Empire did not therefore become a great free-trade unit; instead of lowering duties on each other's products, Britain and the Dominions raised those on foreign goods.

However, Britain suffered less and emerged more quickly than many countries from the world-wide depression. By 1936 output per worker was 20 per cent above the 1929 figure; in the same period prices went down while wages remained stable; cuts in unemployment benefit were restored in 1934, in salaries in 1935; the total of unemployed was reduced, though never below two millions till 1936; there was a favourable balance of external payments. The Government was able to adopt a cheap money policy, that is, to borrow at lower rates of interest and to enable others to do the same. It is unlikely, however, that the improvement was entirely due to the Government's financial policy, which had been operated to only a modest degree, whether through economies, tariffs, or balanced budgets.[1]

Economic recovery

Having put through Parliament Bills to nationalize civil air lines and London's transport,[2] the ministry in its last year became absorbed, somewhat to the exclusion of other problems, in the Government of India Bill, which was hotly opposed by Churchill and some other Conservatives.[3]

In the summer of 1935 Ramsay MacDonald surrendered the leading position in the Government to Baldwin, his last task being the drafting of a *Statement Relating to Defence* which explained the need for increased expenditure on armaments. In 1937 he resigned from the ministry, and later in the year he died. From his election as Secretary of the Labour Representation Committee in 1900 he had been the chief architect of the growing fortunes of the Labour Party. An 'intellectual' in a party normally suspicious of the type, he had nevertheless established himself as its leader by his brains, hard work, fine presence, and skill as a parliamentarian. He had secured the control of the political side of the movement over the trade unions, and his own control over the party in Parliament. After his virulent opposition to the First World War had virtually excluded him from politics, he had recovered his position, and thereafter followed a moderate line,

Second 'National' Government; Baldwin Prime Minister, 1935-1937 MacDonald retires

---

[1] For other causes see page 366.
[2] See page 366.   [3] See pages 406-7.

firmly resisting extremist policies or any association with Communism. In his last years his vanity and aloofness weakened his hold on his followers, while as an apostle of social betterment and international peace he was frustrated by economic depression and growing militarism. It was mainly due to him, however, that Labour had become one of the two main parties in the state.

Election of 1935

Slow start on rearmament

The election which followed on MacDonald's resignation from the premiership produced a smaller but still comfortable majority for the National Government. Secure though he was in Parliament, it was Baldwin's way 'to wait for events to push him', and in the vital matter of rearmament lack of leadership brought serious results. The Government were well aware of the speed and menace of Germany's war preparations, but they did not show the sense of urgency which inspired the repeated warnings of Winston Churchill, not himself a member of the ministry, nor did they speak plainly to the people of the dangers which lay ahead. The country thought it could have security on the cheap by supporting the League of Nations, and its leaders, of all parties, failed to teach the unpalatable truth—that Britain's safety, and her influence in world affairs, required a sacrifice of wealth and economic liberty.

The abdication crisis, 1936

In 1936 occurred the death of King George V. He and his consort, Queen Mary, had done much, particularly during the First World War, to maintain the respect and increase the affection in which the monarchy was held, as the rejoicings at their Silver Jubilee had recently shown. The stability of the monarchy—and the qualities of Baldwin—now served to tide it over a crisis of an unusual kind. It was the Prime Minister's painful duty to make clear to the new King Edward VIII that he must choose between his throne and his affection for the lady he wished to marry—a lady who, having had two husbands already, the second of whom she had conveniently just divorced, would not in the general opinion of the nation and of the Dominions Governments be a suitable queen. Edward VIII accepted the position, signed a dec-

King George VI, 1936–52

laration of abdication which was given legal effect by the British and Dominions Parliaments, and left the country. He was succeeded by his eldest brother, who became King George VI.

Baldwin retires

After the coronation of the new king in 1937 Baldwin resigned his office and retired from politics. Someone once described him as 'the plain man raised to the nth'. He had a strong sense of fairness and a genuine belief in the importance of conciliation and moderation, and this did much to reduce the bitterness of politics at the time of Labour's first challenge. His faith in common sense and his readiness to appeal to moderate opinion in all parties gave him a strong hold over the House of Commons and the country. Sparing of activity though he was, he several times showed himself good in a crisis, not least in the way he restrained his more militant colleagues in the Cabinet during the General Strike. He may indeed be compared with MacDonald, so different in many other ways, in his command of parliamentary skills, his long-sustained control of his party, his dislike of extremism— and the decline in authority and reputation of his last years in political life. Baldwin, however, in his transparent and unaffected sincerity, and in his deep love of his country, expressed from time to time in speeches and writings which combined simplicity with keen perception, captured the affection of Parliament and the nation to a far greater extent. As a statesman, his greatest defect was a basic lack of interest in foreign affairs, which resulted in his failure to grasp with sufficient speed the full implications of Adolf Hitler.

The new Prime Minister was Neville Chamberlain, whose efforts were to be almost entirely absorbed in the management of foreign affairs, in which he took a most active part. One of his first tasks, however, was to bring to an end a troublesome dispute with Ireland, where the extreme Republicans under de Valera had come into power in 1932. De Valera had been sentenced to death for his share in the Easter rising of 1916, but reprieved because he was of American birth. He had later headed the opposition to the 'treaty' with England in 1922. Determined to sever all remaining ties with the British Crown, he and his new government now agitated ceaselessly against the partition of Ireland— the separation of the prosperous six northern counties and their union with the British Crown. To bring pressure on the British Government, Southern Ireland (now named Eire) cut off the annual payments by which the British Government's loans to assist land purchase[1] were being repaid. This action led to a tariff war—to the harm of both countries. A settlement was reached in 1938, which however left the issue of partition untouched. The land loans were wiped out by a final payment of £10,000,000, the trade war called off, and the three harbours in Southern Ireland which the British Navy had so far continued to use were, with remarkable lack of foresight, handed over to the

Chamberlain Prime Minister, 1937–1940

Agreement with Eire, 1938

---

[1] See page 224.

M.B.—K

Eire Government. Their loss and the neutrality of Eire were a severe handicap to Britain in the Second World War.[1]

4 The Gathering Storm

It had been hoped that with the defeat of the autocratic states in 1918 the world, in Wilson's phrase, would be 'safe for democracy'. Even by 1925 this was beginning to be doubtful. Mussolini had set up his Fascist dictatorship in Italy, there was a Communist dictatorship in Russia, and in both Spain and Greece impatient generals had forced themselves into power. In Germany the former Austrian house-painter and ex-corporal Adolf Hitler was building up his National-Socialist (Nazi) storm troops, and winning votes by ceaseless propaganda against the alleged causes of Germany's troubles—the Versailles Treaty, the Communists and the Jews. By 1933 Hitler's party was strong enough to take over the Government, and he himself became Chancellor and Führer (Leader) of Germany—a position in which he rapidly silenced his opponents by the use of concentration camps, torture and all the other loathsome methods of Nazi dictatorship.

Meanwhile, the League of Nations, the main hope of world peace, was weakened by a series of calamities which began with the seizure of Manchuria from China by Japan in 1931. The League condemned Japan, but in view of the difficulties involved did nothing to restrain her, and Japan merely left the League (1933). This disaster was rapidly followed by that of the World Disarmament Conference, which met after years of preparation in 1932. It was soon floundering in argument over rival schemes, and was finally wrecked by the withdrawal of Germany in 1933 when her demand for immediate equality of armed strength with other nations was refused. This was the first of the steps by which Hitler gave notice to the world of his intention to assert his country's claims in complete disregard of every other consideration.

Events elsewhere gave Hitler much encouragement. Mussolini proceeded to satisfy the Fascist thirst for empire and glory by a totally unprovoked attack on Abyssinia, almost the last remaining independent country in Africa. The League could not have been faced with a clearer case of aggression, but in the hour of need it

Rise of dictatorships

The Nazis

Hitler, Führer of Germany, 1933

Failure of Disarmament Conference, 1933

Italy's attack on Abyssinia 1935–1936

[1] In 1949 Eire placed her status as a republic beyond all doubt and severed the last link with the Commonwealth.

failed. Italy was declared at fault, but the sanctions invoked against her stopped short of the point where they would have been effective, for neither foreign supplies of oil nor the use of the Suez Canal were denied to her. When, however, Sir Samuel Hoare, the British Foreign Secretary, agreed with his French counterpart Laval on a proposal to let Italy have part of Abyssinia, he was forced to resign by a public outcry, and Anthony Eden took his place. This did not stop Italy finishing off the Abyssinians and establishing an 'Empire' in East Africa.

Hitler, emboldened by Italy's successful defiance of the League, and profiting by the concentration of British forces in the Mediterranean, now sent his troops into the Rhineland and announced that he would no longer recognize the clauses of the Versailles Treaty which demilitarized this region of Germany. His action went unchallenged, the British view being on the whole that the Germans could reasonably do what they liked in their own country. German troops in the Rhineland, 1936

Germany and Italy then became associated in an understanding which they chose to describe as a European 'Axis'. The fruits of their fellowship were soon seen. Spain, where the monarchy had given place to a republic in 1931, was now engulfed in a fierce civil war, in which military leaders and sympathizers with Fascism, supported by the Church, raised the standard of revolt against the Government and its following of anti-clericals, Liberals, Socialists, Communists, Anarchists, and other left-wing parties. The British attitude was to treat the matter as an internal quarrel, and to isolate it by means of a 'non-intervention' committee of which all the interested Powers, including Germany and Italy, were members. But these two states shamelessly poured weapons and men into Spain to help the rebels, while the Spanish Government in turn received some help from Soviet Russia. The Opposition in Parliament clamoured for action against Hitler and Mussolini, but Chamberlain, impressed with the menace of Germany, was determined to seek an understanding with Italy on the basis of respect for each other's interests; in pursuance of this policy he allowed—indeed partly provoked—Eden to resign. As Eden had advocated opposition to Italian aggression in Abyssinia and Spain, this was bound to appear a success for the dictators. The 'Axis' The Spanish Civil War, 1936–1939

In 1938 Hitler began to force the pace. Early in the year Austria was occupied by German forces and incorporated in the 'Third Reich', or new German Empire. Czechoslovakia, now three parts German occupation of Austria, March 1938 encircled, was plainly to be the next victim, and as the summer passed Hitler inspired a ferocious propaganda campaign against the alleged sufferings of the three million Sudeten Germans within the country. The tension mounted, and at his chosen moment Hitler presented a series of impossible demands to the Czechs. To avert this threatened attack and the general war which suddenly appeared inevitable—for France had an alliance with Czechoslovakia—Chamberlain flew to Germany to intercede with Hitler.

The outcome of the Czechoslovak crisis was the Munich settlement, by which the Czechs had to surrender their Sudeten borderlands, with their carefully prepared defences, into German hands. The main bastion barring Germany's march to the east and southeast had fallen. Many said Czechoslovakia had been betrayed, but Chamberlain returned from Munich claiming that he had secured 'peace in our time'. This unfortunate boast obscured the only possible justification of the Munich policy, which had lowered British prestige the world over—that Britain had to gain time, to postpone, if only for a year, a war for which she was unprepared.

A year's respite and no more was won. Fortunately that year was put to good use in at least one direction. The expansion and

re-equipment of the Royal Air Force, begun in 1934, was now beginning to show results. In September 1938 there were in Fighter Command thirty squadrons; of these only seven were armed with modern aircraft—the all-metal monoplanes which were to become famous as the Hurricane and the Spitfire. A year later, the strength of Fighter Command had risen to thirty-nine squadrons; and nineteen of these were of up-to-date types. Moreover, the new (and then very secret) device of radar, which in September 1938 gave 'cover' along the coast only from Suffolk to Kent, in September 1939 reached from Dundee to the Isle of Wight. Britain had thus achieved by the postponement of war a reasonable chance of withstanding the formidable German Air Force, the very threat of which had already forced other countries into submission.[1]

Meanwhile, in March 1939, Hitler had marched the Germans into the truly Czech parts of Czechoslovakia, contemptuously breaking his undertaking at Munich. The policy of appeasement

---

[1] Defence against air attack by night was far less advanced at this time. Fortunately the science of attack by night had not been greatly studied or developed by the German Air Force.

had clearly failed, and Hitler's appetite was shown to be insatiable. The British Government reacted quickly. Before the month was out, decisions were taken to double the Territorial Army, to introduce conscription, to concert all possible military measures with the French, and to extend guarantees of help to the most likely objects of Hitler's further attentions, Poland, Rumania and

British guarantee to Poland

"EUROPE CAN LOOK FORWARD TO A CHRISTMAS OF PEACE".*(HITLER)*

(*Low, October 1938, reproduced by permission of the 'Evening Standard'*)

...t and after Munich, Hitler's prophecies of peace hoodwinked many British politicians. ...ut Winston Churchill and others, including the cartoonist Low, were well able to ...enetrate the German Führer's genial disguise. Austria had already disappeared into ...anta' Hitler's bag, Czechoslovakia was half-way in, and Poland and the other nations ...f East and South-East Europe were all likely to follow before long.

Greece. If Germany persisted in her programme of loot, the next step would mean war.

Hitler, however, was too well used to dealing in threats to be perturbed by those of others. He continued to nourish his designs on his next victim, Poland—for the recovery of Danzig, the elimination of the 'Corridor', and the acquisition of a great 'living-space' for Germans in the east. British and French guarantees or

Germany and Poland

protests, as at Munich, might easily come to nothing; even if they were enforced, he felt strong enough to deal with the West once the East was settled. And in no way could Britain and France bring effective help to Poland before she succumbed to the German 'Blitzkreig'—only Russia could do that. The Western Powers therefore approached Russia, though with little confidence in her policy or her strength, her army being at that time weakened by the extensive purges of the higher ranks carried out by Stalin, who in 1924, after a brief struggle with Trotsky, had succeeded Lenin in supreme power in Russia. A Russian alliance alone could have saved peace, but Russia chose to play the German game in what she conceived to be her own interests. With her distrust of the Western Powers deepened by Munich, she was well content to see Germany embroiled with Britain and France, while she herself gained time to prepare for the coming storm.

Russo-German Pact, August 1939

In August 1939 the announcement of a Russo-German pact told the world that Hitler was free to attack Poland. On 1 September the German armies marched.

When Hitler's Germany went to war there was only the choice of submitting to the evils of Nazism or giving fight. Never had Britain faced a plainer danger. A ruthless dictator had proclaimed his scheme of world domination, and was felling his victims one by one. His conquest of Europe would be surely followed by the destruction of the British Empire and the extinction of British independence.

Britain at war, 3 September 1939

The result for the world would have been such a blight upon the human spirit as it had not known since the Dark Ages. No less an evil could have justified the choice of war.

20. The Second World War

When Britain and France in September 1939 took up once more the challenge of Germany, it was in a mood of profound sadness. The struggle of 1914-18 had made the horrors of armed conflict so manifest, so much a part of general experience, that there could be none of the old blare of trumpets and beating of drums, none of the 'pride, pomp and circumstance of glorious war'. The task that lay ahead would be arduous and bloody; but neither in her own interests nor in those of civilization could Britain stand idly by and watch the naked evil of Hitlerism spread unchecked across Europe.

If the mood of the two Western democracies was sober and realistic, there was nevertheless no lack of confidence. Clearly their intervention could not save Poland from being overrun; but at least it could restore Poland to the map of Europe after the war. And though Britain's cities would certainly suffer from the attentions of the all too formidable German Air Force, she could count a number of assets of immense value—notably the Commonwealth, great industrial strength, a strong Navy, an extremely efficient Air Force, the large French Army and the benevolent neutrality of the United States. So France and Britain had little doubt that they could keep the German armies at bay in the west, reduce the enemy's power to resist by a merciless blockade, and in the fullness of time build up big enough forces to smash through the Siegfried Line. *Anglo-French strategy*

For a few months, in that period which American journalists christened the 'phoney war', all seemed to be going fairly well. True, Poland was knocked out with unexpected speed; and the Russians advanced into the eastern half of the country while the Germans were overrunning the west—a little piece of 'compensation' arranged in the Russo-German pact of the previous August. But a common frontier between Russia and Germany could surely not endure for long untroubled, and so the situation, even in Eastern Europe, was not without hope. Meanwhile in the west the armies made no move, and the air forces did little beyond reconnaissance, pamphlet-dropping and attacks on warships. So the small British Expeditionary Force established itself in France; *The opening moves* *Poland, September 1939* the Allied navies cleared the seas of German commerce; the Russians set upon the Finns, but met with a valiant resistance; and in Britain life went on very much as usual. For the average British citizen only a few inconveniences like the black-out, the closing of theatres, the evacuation of large numbers of children from the big towns to the less populated areas, and the extraordinary number of news bulletins broadcast by the B.B.C., marked the transition from peace to war.

Norway and
Denmark,
April 1940

This pleasant state of things could not last long, and the first shock to Anglo-French complacency came in April 1940. Anxious to safeguard his supplies of Norwegian and Swedish iron-ore, Hitler invaded Norway, at the same time occupying Denmark as a stepping-stone. British opinion confidently expected the Navy at once to sever German communications, and at the same time to land a large force for the succour of the Norwegians. Unfortunately it failed to realize that British surface warships could not operate off Southern Norway for fear of the German Air Force; nor was it aware that, with a big German offensive daily expected in the west, the Allies could not spare more than two or three divisions for fighting in Norway. So in a few weeks the Germans were able to overrun the country, thereby not only safeguarding their iron-ore supplies, but also gaining valuable bases for the conduct of their air and U-boat offensive.

Coalition in
Britain under
Churchill

All this caused so great a volume of criticism against Chamberlain's Government that the Prime Minister was compelled to resign, and the new ministry—a coalition of all parties—took office under Winston Churchill. Its formation coincided with the next, and far greater, shock. On 10 May 1940 Hitler launched his long-expected offensive in the west, striking at France through Holland, Belgium and Luxemburg. These lesser powers, clinging to their neutrality with great obstinacy, had refused to co-ordinate

France and the
Low Countries,
May–June 1940

plans with Britain or France against German aggression; but inoffensiveness was no protection against Hitler. Now the logic of events made them, like Norway, combatants in a common cause. So, while the right wing of the French armies sat secure in the Maginot Line, the left wing (which included the B.E.F.) at once advanced into Holland and Belgium, to meet the Germans as far forward as possible. But the enemy, with a decisive superiority in tanks and aircraft, swept everything before him. Holland was overrun in five days, Belgium in not much more than a fortnight. The French positions on the Meuse were overwhelmed, and the German panzers tore across France to the Channel, splitting the

Allied armies in twain. Cut off in the north, the B.E.F. and the French 1st Army found themselves with only one hope of escape —an evacuation from the port of Dunkirk and the neighbouring beaches. It seemed impossible that they could be plucked in time from the path of the all-conquering enemy; but by a supreme endeavour on the part of the Navy, the merchant seamen, the amateur yachtsmen, the Royal Air Force and the troops themselves, over 300,000 British and French soldiers were safely evacuated. These nine days of ceaseless effort, carried out under the nose of the German armies, and under ceaseless bombardment from the German Air Force, brought about what Winston Churchill aptly called 'a miracle of deliverance'. *The Dunkirk evacuation, 26 May–4 June 1940*

But, as the Prime Minister also pointed out, 'wars are not won by evacuations'. The British forces had been saved—but they had lost all their equipment. And the remaining French armies, and the few British troops still with them, were quite unable to stop the Germans sweeping over the length and breadth of France. Stunned and bewildered, the unhappy French now felt the spite of a new foe, for Mussolini hastened to bring the Italians in on the winning side. Faced with such unparalleled disasters, most Frenchmen saw no alternative but to give in; there was little support for the opinions of General de Gaulle, who was all for continuing the struggle from French North Africa. So, on June 25, less than seven weeks from the opening of the German attack, France came to terms with her enemies. In consideration for retiring rapidly from the struggle, she was allowed an 'unoccupied zone' in the centre and south of France, with a capital at Vichy; the northern half of the country and the Atlantic coastline came under the occupation of the Germans. *Italy joins Germany, June 1940* *The fall of France, June 1940*

Britain, supported by her Dominions and Colonies, was now left to face the combined might of Germany and Italy. Indeed, there was even some danger of war with France, for the Royal Navy had to bombard the French Fleet (in the North African port of Oran), to make sure that it did not come under German control. At this melancholy stage in Britain's fortunes Hitler certainly expected her to give in; but he had miscalculated the temper of the race, and he was forced to prepare plans for an invasion. This was a task for which the German Navy had naturally little relish, and Hitler's naval commanders made it clear that they could not get the German Army across the Channel unless the superiority of the British Fleet had been neutralized by the German Air Force. But before the German Air Force could do this, it had *British action against the French Fleet, July 1940* first to overcome the Royal Air Force—or in other words to gain air supremacy over the Channel and Southern England.

The Battle of Britain, August–October 1940

So the Battle of Britain began. In a sense everyone helped, for from Dunkirk onwards a tremendous national effort sent up the production of arms and aircraft, while citizens enrolled in the newly formed Local Defence Volunteers—later renamed the Home Guard—to keep watch for and repel the invaders. But the fighting was all done by a few hundred young men in the Royal Air Force. It was done by the reconnaissance crews, who brought back priceless information of the enemy's preparations; by the bomber crews, who attacked the airfields and the shipping concentrations across the Channel; and above all by the fighter pilots, who, heavily outnumbered as they were, inflicted unacceptable losses on the German Air Force and defied all its efforts to gain air superiority over Southern England. So, lacking the first prerequisite for transporting his troops across the Channel, Hitler was forced first to postpone, then to call off the invasion. As at the Marne in 1914, the great flood of German success had been halted, and flung back; the cause of civilization was saved. And once more it was the Prime Minister who crystallized everyone's feelings in a phrase: 'Never in the field of human conflict was so much owed by so many to so few.'

The Battle of Britain raged throughout August and September 1940. Even when it was clear that his invasion plan had collapsed, Hitler still kept up the pressure. But as his hopes of a successful landing faded, his tactics changed. Finding it too expensive to drop any appreciable load of bombs on precise objectives by day, but simple and cheap enough to hit urban areas by night, he

The night 'Blitz' against Britain—September 1940–May 1941

turned to a night air offensive. Night attacks had already been delivered as a supplement to the daylight attacks of the Battle of Britain; now they were greatly intensified. The targets were Britain's big cities and ports, with the triple object of cowing her population into submission, reducing her industrial output and restricting her imports. The last purpose was also furthered by an

The U-boat war

intensified U-boat campaign, for which the newly-acquired German bases on the French Atlantic coast came in extremely handy.

The night 'Blitz', as it was popularly called, was highly vexatious. From September 1940 to May 1941 there were few nights on which London was not raided; and many of the provincial cities—notably Liverpool, Coventry, Hull, Plymouth, Bristol, Birmingham and Manchester—also suffered severely, if not so frequently. But it was quite unsuccessful, either in seriously restricting trade and production or in shaking the morale of the British people. Fortunately, in May 1941 it died away—not as a result of Britain's defensive measures (though the night-fighters, thanks to airborne radar equipment, were becoming increasingly proficient), but because the German Air Force was required

THE ARMY TOES THE LINE

(*Low, October 1940, reproduced by permission of the 'Evening Standard'*)

Nazi Germany's allies and friends in the early part of the war were not all equally ready to play Hitler's game. Italy (Mussolini), Spain (Franco) and Japan (Konoye) seemed firm in the Fascist ranks; but Vichy France (Pétain) was a broken reed, and Soviet Russia (Stalin) obviously had ideas of its own.

elsewhere. For Hitler, seeing a golden chance to settle matters to his lasting satisfaction in the east while there was no land fighting in the west, was about to double-cross his temporary collaborator, Stalin.

The attack on Russia was the greatest of Hitler's many mis- takes. Even more surely than in the case of Napoleon, the decision proved fatal to its author. Time and again Hitler was to come

The German attack on Russia, June 1941

within an ace of success as the German armies swept forward in their summer offensives; but always the Russians somehow held, and struck back in the winter, which they knew so well how to turn to their advantage. New depths of barbarity were plumbed in the fighting, and millions perished on either side. Against an implacable and tireless foe whose territory offered seemingly endless room to retreat and manœuvre, the German armies wore out their heart and soul.

The war in Africa

While Hitler was finding the British homeland too tough a nut to crack, Mussolini was having much the same experience with Britain's overseas possessions. With the entry of Italy into the war in June 1940, fighting had spread to Africa and the Mediterranean. At first the Italians held the initiative; the British were compelled to evacuate British Somaliland, and to give a little ground on the Egypt-Libya frontier. But Italian dreams of occupying Egypt soon came to nothing, and their large invading army was first held up, then thrown back to Benghazi and beyond, by the ridiculously small British forces under General Wavell.

Wavell's offensive, December 1940

Defeated and disgraced, the Italians in Africa now had to accept German help, and early in 1941 Rommel's Africa Corps began to arrive on the scene. But Libya was not the only embarrassment for the Italians; for Mussolini, trying to score a cheap success against the Greeks, had also bitten off more than he could chew in South-Eastern Europe. So here, too, he had to be rescued by his fellow-dictator; and to forestall the German attack, British troops were hastily withdrawn from Egypt and Libya and rushed across to Greece. It was an understandable but a disastrous decision. The small Anglo-Greek forces, even with the Yugoslavs also deciding at the last moment to resist Hitler, were quite unable to hold the German onslaught; while the weakened British army in Libya was simultaneously driven back to Egypt.

German aid to the Italians

German conquest of Greece and Yugoslavia, April 1941

British retreat to Egypt

With the Balkans—save Turkey—in their hands, the Germans next jumped to Crete, which they captured by an extremely costly airborne invasion. This exposed shipping in the Eastern Mediterranean to heavy air attacks, and at the same time threatened the whole British position in the Middle East. But a pro-Axis revolt in Iraq went off before the Germans were ready to take advantage of it, and the occupation of Syria by British and Free French forces stopped the Vichy French authorities in that country conniving at the German schemes. The 'back door' to

German conquest of Crete, May 1941

Iraq and Syria, May-July 1941

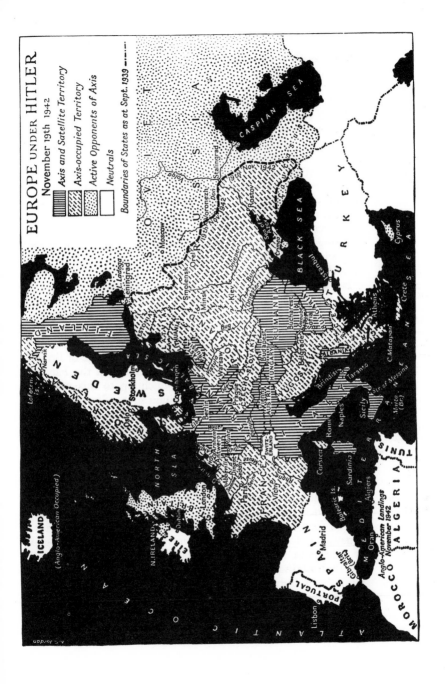

EUROPE UNDER HITLER
November 19th 1942

Axis and Satellite Territory
Axis-occupied Territory
Active Opponents of Axis
Neutrals
Boundaries of States as at Sept. 1939 -------

Egypt was thus made secure, as well as the front door to vital British oil supplies in Iraq and Persia.

Second British advance into Libya, November 1941

With Egypt and the Middle East removed from immediate danger, with Italian East Africa by now entirely in British hands, and with the main German armies fully occupied in Russia, the British forces in Egypt could renew their efforts to capture Libya. An offensive launched in November 1941 again carried them to Benghazi, but once more hopes were cheated by the same combination of factors as before—difficulties of supply, and a fresh crisis elsewhere—and some of the newly-gained ground had to be given up. A feature of the fighting during this series of exchanges

Malta

was the tremendous hammering given to Malta by the German Air Force, operating from Sicily. Nevertheless Britain's 'unsinkable aircraft carrier', from which bombers (and submarines) operated with deadly effect against the Axis supply routes to Africa, defied all efforts to subdue her.

Japan attacks Britain and U.S.A., December 1941

It was while the British Eighth Army was advancing on Benghazi for the second time, and while Hitler's legions were enjoying their first experience of a Russian winter, that an act as decisive as the invasion of Russia occurred on the other side of the world. Japan, who in 1937 had joined the 'Axis' and begun an undeclared war on China, decided to take advantage of Britain's preoccupation elsewhere to acquire an empire in the Far East. Knowing that the United States, which up to this point had acted on the formula of 'all aid to Britain short of war', would not stand idly by and witness further Japanese expansion, she struck out not only at Malaya and Burma, but at the American Pacific Fleet in its Hawaiian base of Pearl Harbour. Germany and Italy instantly lent their support to their new ally by declaring war on the United States, and at a stroke the war had become world-wide.

Pearl Harbour, December 1941

The damage inflicted on the American Fleet at Pearl Harbour, and the total inadequacy of the British forces which could be spared for the Far East, gave Japan for the moment a series of

Loss of Malaya, February 1942

runaway victories. Malaya was overrun, the vaunted stronghold of Singapore falling with an appalling loss in prisoners; the Dutch East Indies succumbed no less quickly; and the uneven

Loss of Burma, May 1942

struggle in Burma could have only one result. Within a few months Japan had stripped Britain of her Far Eastern possessions, and advanced to the very gates of India.

The Japanese held

But if the onslaught of Japan made Britain's task doubly difficult for the moment, it also in the long run ensured victory, for it brought in as a full ally the United States—incomparably the greatest industrial power in the world. After a period of difficulty, the Japanese were held off India and Australia, control of Far Eastern waters was gradually asserted by the American Navy, and before the close of 1943 the initiative was within the Allies' grasp. It was rightly decided, however, to concentrate the main Allied effort against Germany and Italy before turning in strength to the Far East, and for some time Japan was thus able to hold on to most of her conquests.

The first task was to clear up the war in Africa. A new British offensive in Libya was prepared for the summer of 1942, but Rommel struck first. The British lines were penetrated, and in a flash the situation was transformed, with the Eighth Army in full retreat towards Egypt and the Italo-German forces in hot pursuit. Not until only sixty miles lay between him and Alexandria was Rommel halted; and there, at El Alamein, the Eighth Army first checked the enemy onrush, then, after reinforcement and reorganization throughout the autumn, turned once more to the offensive. The final battle at El Alamein, in October 1942, was the beginning of the end in Africa. Thenceforth Rommel was on the run; and the British forces soon harried him out of Egypt, right across Libya, and into Tunisia. Meanwhile the epic defence of Stalingrad was proving the turning point of the war in Russia. *The setback in Africa, June 1942*

El Alamein: the turn of the tide

Stalingrad

As soon as General Montgomery was assured of success at El Alamein, the first of the great combined Anglo-American expeditions was launched. In November 1942 forces under General Eisenhower landed in Morocco and Algeria. Except at Casablanca there was very little resistance from the local French authorities, and the force was able to move quickly east into Tunisia. The strategical purpose was of course to bottle up Rommel's line of retreat and to regain control of the Mediterranean. The Germans reacted very strongly, moving into the hitherto unoccupied zone of France and despatching powerful forces by air to forestall the Allies at Tunis and Bizerta. And since Rommel succeeded in withdrawing part of his forces from Libya to link up with the newly-arrived reinforcements in Tunisia, the end was somewhat delayed. Nevertheless, it was reasonably certain, and by May 1943 the whole African campaign was over. The final scene came when 300,000 Germans and Italians, driven into the extreme north-east corner of Tunisia, had no alternative but to surrender; for the Anglo-American naval and air forces had strangled their sea communications, and there was no possibility of a German 'Dunkirk' *Anglo-American landing in French North Africa, November 1942*

The conquest of Tunisia: the end in Africa, May 1943

The Allies now concentrated their energies on Europe. The programme at this stage was threefold—to win the long and grim struggle against the U-boats, to wage a redoubled bombing offensive against Germany and to knock out Italy. Of these tasks the last was the simplest. Once the North African shores were cleared of the enemy, Malta could be built up as an offensive base and everything prepared for the invasion of the Italian homeland. In July and August 1943 the second of the great Anglo-American ventures under Eisenhower captured Sicily; and by September it was time to invade the mainland. Before the landing was made Mussolini, disgraced by incessant defeat, had been overthrown, and the new Italian Government had secretly adhered to the Allies. But the Germans were in most of the key-positions throughout the country, and after a quick advance as far as Naples the Allied progress settled down into a long slogging-match up the peninsula.

Anglo-American conquest of Sicily, July–August 1943

The fall of Mussolini

The invasion of Italy

The Battle of the Atlantic

Meantime the U-boat menace was being mastered. The decisive factor was the increasing use of very-long-range aircraft operating from both sides of the Atlantic, equipped with searchlights and radar detection devices, and employing depth-charges. By the end of 1943 the Battle of the Atlantic was virtually won; and though the U-boats were to offer a fresh danger before the end of the war, when they began to be equipped with a device for recharging their batteries without surfacing, the new threat was too late to be effective.

The air offensive against Germany

At the same time the bombing offensive against Germany was mounting in intensity. On the whole the Americans, operating by day, attacked precise targets like factories; the Royal Air Force, operating by night, concentrated on large industrial areas. As the Allied air forces grew in size, and their radar and other navigational aids improved, the weight of bombs falling on Germany, and on vital objectives in the occupied territories, increased sharply. The Ruhr, the North German ports, Berlin—all these were scenes of ruin and devastation before 1943 was out.

While this vital work of weakening German industrial and economic capacity continued, the Allies were preparing for their greatest venture—the liberation of North-West Europe. General Eisenhower and most of his victorious team of commanders were recalled from Africa and Italy and placed in charge of the new operation; the most meticulous preparations were made, including the construction of two artificial harbours to be towed across the Channel; and in March 1944 the pre-invasion air programme began. It was directed mainly against the enemy's communications, transport facilities, radar stations and coastal batteries.

When the British, Canadian and American armies came to touch down on the Normandy beaches on 6 June 1944, they found that the work of the Allied air forces had been well done, and that the German powers of resistance and reinforcement were decisively weakened. A tough struggle followed to build up the Allied forces in the lodgements they had gained; then, towards the end of August, came the break-out by the American forces on the right, and soon the Germans were reeling back to the Seine. Almost without pause the pursuit went on, while a further Allied force landed in the South of France to strike up the Rhône valley. At lightning speed France and Belgium were liberated, bringing relief not only to the local populations, but also to the inhabitants of London, who for some months had been bombarded from bases on the other side of the Channel by Hitler's 'secret weapons' (the V1, or flying-bomb, and the V2, or long-range rocket). But the attempt to jump the barrier of the Rhine came to grief with a disastrous airborne landing at Arnhem, and the Allied armies had to settle down to develop adequate port facilities and communications before completing the liberation of Holland and striking into the heart of Germany.

In the midst of these preparations, in December 1944, the Germans struck a final desperate blow—an offensive through the Ardennes aimed at Antwerp. After some initial progress in foggy weather it was soon held, and the effort proved fatal to a prolonged German resistance. Meanwhile, the Allied air forces were not only reducing German cities to rubble, but were strangling the enemy's communications and destroying the synthetic oil plants on which his aircraft and mechanical transport depended. The only vital thing which they failed to destroy was the German will to resist—though the strength of this doubtless owed much to the difficulties of opposition under Hitler.[1]

With the spring the Allied armies soon crossed the Rhine, captured the Ruhr, and struck deep into Germany. At the same time the Russians, who had been advancing steadily since the heroic defence of Stalingrad at the end of 1942, were bursting across the German borders in the east. Still Hitler, caring nothing for the ruin of his country, fought on. At last, with the Russians in the suburbs of Berlin, and the German armies in the west split

Marginal notes:
'D' Day, 6 June 1944

The liberation of France and Belgium, 1944

Hitler's 'secret weapons'

The last German effort: the Ardennes, December 1944

The effect of Allied air power

The crossing of the Rhine, March 1945

[1] A plot to assassinate him, involving many Germans, including officers of high rank, failed in July 1944.

into fragments by the Anglo-American advance, even Hitler acknowledged the inevitable, and committed suicide. With Hitler
gone the German generals and admirals hastened to arrange Germany's unconditional surrender, and on 7 May 1945 a general
armistice was signed at Rheims.

The German domination of Europe, while it lasted, had been
as horrible as the Nazi creed had promised. From the outset war
was waged indiscriminately, with deliberate attacks on civilians,
the cities of unoffending peoples like the Dutch and the Belgians
being devastated without warning. The advancing German armies
terrorized even populations which might have been won over,
like the Ukrainians of western Russia. Torture and massacre
were employed to repress resistance in occupied countries. Hundreds of thousands of men were taken off to provide slave labour
in Germany. Worst of all, in pursuance of the absurd Nazi racial
doctrines, 'non-Aryans', which meant mainly Jews but also gyp-
sies, were transported to the number of six million to extermination centres where they were done to death, men, women and
children alike, in gas chambers, and their bodies consumed in
vast incinerators. In Germany itself mental defectives were put
to death or sterilized, and victims in concentration camps were
subjected to appalling medical experiments. The most cruel of
earlier oppressors of mankind—barbarians like Attila and
Genghiz Kahn—had been outdone by the leaders of a European
nation priding itself on its greatness and civilization.

Germany defeated, the Allies could now concentrate on the
destruction of Japan. An offensive was already making good progress in Burma, and this was brought to a successful conclusion.
Preparations were made to recapture Malaya and the Dutch East
Indies, and to invade Japan itself; but neither proved necessary.
From bases in China, and on islands captured within striking distance of Japan, the American air forces were already destroying
the Japanese homeland. On 6 August, they employed for the first
time a new and infinitely terrible weapon when they dropped an
atomic bomb on Hiroshima. Two days later Russia declared war
on Japan; and on 9 August the Americans dropped a second
atomic bomb—on Nagasaki. Warned of the ghastly fate that would
be theirs if they continued to resist, the Japanese instantly
surrendered, and on 14 August 1945 the Second World War was
brought to a triumphant if disquieting conclusion.

Although it was somewhat overshadowed by the work of the
Americans in the final phases, and although the resistance of the

The German
surrender,
May 1945

Europe under
Germany

The reconquest
of Burma

The 'atom-
bombs' on Japan,
August 6 and 9,
1945

The Japanese
surrender

Russians was the key factor in wearing out the German Army, the contribution of the British Commonwealth towards winning the war was very great. The British Navy, Army and Air Force were all weapons of the highest value; the natural, industrial and financial resources of Britain, the Dominions and the

The British effort

(Low, May 1945, reproduced by permission of the 'Evening Standard')

The shades of Pitt and Lloyd George, Prime Ministers during two great national struggles of the past, help Winston Churchill up to the pedestal reserved for the greatest war leader.

Colonies were used to the full, regardless of the future; British science made an outstanding contribution, particularly in the field of radar and the atomic bomb; and the toughness of the British people, in conjunction with the skill and valour of the Royal Air Force, first sent Hitler's plans awry. After the first disasters the British effort was consistently directed with skill and vision. This time the British troops were plunged into no interminable bloodbaths, no Sommes or Passchendaeles. For this the credit was due very largely to the combined wisdom of the Prime Minister and the Chiefs of Staff of the three Services.

Churchill's
contribution

Indeed, no individual contribution towards winning the war was greater than that of Winston Churchill. Though at times, and particularly in the early days, he made mistakes, there was never any question that in Churchill Britain had a leader of unique vigour, power and understanding. Among other things, he steadfastly cultivated the friendliest relations with the United States and its great President, Franklin Roosevelt, so that generous help was coming from America long before she entered the war; he at once, in spite of his strong anti-Communist views, welcomed Russia fully into the fold when the German attack made her, in spite of herself, our ally; and throughout he rallied and sustained the nation not only by his supreme eloquence but also by his superb moral and physical courage. Nor was this moral influence exercised only over his own peoples; to the forces of resistance and freedom everywhere—in occupied Europe no less than in the United States—the spirit of Churchill was the spirit of unconquered Britain. It was an inspiration—and a guarantee.

★   ★   ★   ★   ★

Life in wartime
Britain

The effect of the war on life at home was severe beyond comparison with any previous struggle. The sight of the men returning from Dunkirk in 1940, and soon afterwards the battles in the skies over southern England, left little to the civilian imagination —except the experience of enemy occupation. Soon there fell on Britain a rain of high-explosive and incendiary bombs from the night sky in raids that went on for many months. When this form of attack had been mastered there followed in 1944 the assault of the flying bombs and rocket bombs, of which more than a thousand fell, mainly in the London area. 60,000 civilians were killed by enemy action, and as many again were seriously injured. Life when things were more normal was subject to the depression of five years' black-out and to the harassment of rationing and shortages which stopped only just short of hardship; the clothes ration was a half of the pre-war rate of consumption; diet, for lack of imported foods, was monotonous though adequate. The evacuation of schoolchildren from the cities broke up families; billeting in the country mixed them with results that were not always happy.

The war effort

Despite these difficulties the country's effort was immense. With four-and-a-half million men drawn off into the armed forces the nation nevertheless produced 70 per cent of the enormous quantity of munitions they required; 10 per cent came from the rest of the Commonwealth and the remaining fifth from the U.S.A., mainly in the form of 'Lend-Lease', President Roosevelt's ingenious name for supply without any strict form of payment. The production of food was increased by 70 per cent, its import reduced by half. Twenty-two million men and women—all up to the age of forty-five—were registered for military service

(From Lancaster: 'Assorted Sizes', by permission of John Murray Ltd.)
'Thaird floor: No crockery, no hardware, no toys, and precious little baby linen.'
A useful British asset is the ability to find humour in difficult circumstances. Osbert Lancaster here draws a little fun from war-time shortages—and the eternal British female (1944).

or work in industry; three million men served in the Home Guard or in civil defence after their day's work was done. Financial sacrifices matched the rest; to cover expenditure six times greater than in 1938 the Government raised the standard rate of income tax to 10s. in the pound, and altogether took one-seventh of personal incomes in direct taxes. Though the expected invasion of Britain's shores never came, the nation spent six years in battle order.

21. Britain since 1945: Home Affairs

Labour victory, 1945 The general election which was held after the defeat of Germany in 1945 marked the end of a parliament which had lasted for ten years and of the wartime Coalition which had lasted for five. The Labour and Liberal ministers were unwilling to continue with the Coalition, and the election was fought on party lines. The Conservatives reckoned on the tremendous reputation of Winston Churchill, their leader, to bring them success. But the voters returned the Labour Party to power with the largest majority in the party struggles of modern times—393 to 189 for the Conservatives—larger even than that of the Liberal victory of 1906. The verdict seemed an act of ingratitude to the great war leader, but the voters were thinking less of the struggle just ending than of social benefits to come. In so far as they thought of the past it was the bad days of the 1920s and 1930s, mainly under Conservative rule, that they remembered.

The end of the war, 1945 So Clement Attlee found himself, somewhat to his surprise, Prime Minister, and at once took over Churchill's place at the Potsdam Conference of the Allies which was dealing with the future of Germany. The first duty of the new Government, however, was to finish off the war with Japan. This was easy; the main decisions had already been taken, and the Americans did most of the work. The Government was soon busy, therefore, with plans for a new Britain, which had been prepared in outline for some time.

The Labour ministry, 1945 The Cabinet contained a number of recognized stalwarts of the Labour movement, and several who had held office in the wartime Coalition; Attlee himself had been Deputy Prime Minister. Among his chief colleagues now were Herbert Morrison, son of a London policeman, with a long experience of politics, partly as leader of the Labour majority on the London County Council; Ernest Bevin, of the Transport and General Workers Union, who took charge of the Foreign Office; Hugh Dalton, an Old Etonian, as Chancellor of the Exchequer; Sir Stafford Cripps at the Board of Trade; and Aneurin Bevan, a Welshman of great forcefulness

298

and eloquence, as Minister of Health. Attlee was quiet in manner and unimpressive as a speaker, but he ran the Government efficiently and managed his somewhat difficult team with skill. It was not perhaps the fault of this ministry if the simultaneous tasks of recovery from the war, social reconstruction, and trying to establish a new international order were too much for it.

At home the Government was determined on several measures of nationalization, but approached them without undue haste. Their first concern was to repeal the hated Trade Disputes Act of 1927,[1] and so to restore the full power of the trade unions. Next the Bank of England was taken into public ownership. Among the great industries coal was given pride of place; an act to nationalize the mines was passed in 1946. Cable and Wireless Limited, with its great network of overseas communications, was also taken over by the state. By 1948 the transport services of the country, both by rail and road, were with few exceptions put in charge of the British Transport Commission, a government agency, and the electricity and gas industries were treated similarly. There was remarkably little opposition to these measures; the case for their nationalization had been clearly made, often by independent committees of enquiry set up by Conservative governments. Very different was the case of the iron and steel industry, which was next on the Government's list. This was not a public utility but a manufacturing industry. It made profits; the relations of management and labour were good; large sums had recently been invested in it. But because it held a key place in the national economy the Government meant to have control of it. There was not time, however, to pass a Bill through both Houses of Parliament before a general election fell due—that is if the Lords used to the full the power of delay which had been left them by the Parliament Act of 1911.[2] The Government therefore introduced in 1947 a new Parliament Act to reduce from two years to one the Lords' power of delay, and in this way were able to pass the Bill for the nationalization of the iron and steel industry before the end of the Parliament elected in 1945, in which they had so overwhelming a majority. But in the country the attack on the iron and steel firms aroused powerful opposition, and the Conservative Party, which had been almost in despair after the defeat of 1945, recovered its voice and its confidence.

Outside Parliament much was happening to weaken the credit of the Labour government and to bring grist to the Conservative

Marginal notes:
Repeal of the Trade Disputes Act

Nationalization of the Bank of England, coal, overseas communications, transport, electricity, gas, 1946–1948

Parliament Act, 1949

Nationalization of iron and steel, 1950

Economic and financial troubles

[1] See page 270.   [2] See page 230.

mill. Since the end of the war in Europe economic recovery had been slow, handicapped as it was by general shortages of materials and manpower. In the year 1947 the effects of six years of destruction came to be fully felt; it was a time of economic crisis and almost unrelieved gloom. While during the war Britain had depended largely on Lend-Lease supplies from the U.S.A., these were abruptly cut off as soon as hostilities ceased. Instead the Government negotiated a loan from the U.S.A. and Canada—in dollars—of £1,300 million. Not only was this used up in half the time that had been calculated; it was a condition of the loan that after one year British currency should be fully convertible— i.e. that pounds could be changed at the will of their owners into any other currency. This would usually be dollars, of which

Dollar shortage all countries were in dire need to buy American goods. The result by 1947 was a drain of dollars and gold out of Britain, which, if unchecked, would soon have left the country unable to pay its way, for a great increase of necessary imports had not been matched by a corresponding rise in exports.[1] Drastic cuts were imposed: imports of food were reduced, petrol could be used only

Cripps and austerity for approved purposes, and all foreign travel, except for business, was forbidden. And, in addition, the convertibility of the pound was suspended. In September 1947 Sir Stafford Cripps became Chancellor of the Exchequer and was given general control of economic affairs. His name became almost a byword for the austerity which was his own by personal character and now became the nation's lot by hard necessity.

The fuel crisis, 1947 The crisis was made much worse by the most severe winter that England had known since 1881. Frost and snow pushed up the demand for fuel but paralysed transport. The generating stations could not nearly meet requirements, and continual power cuts hindered production, so that in March 2,300,000 people were out of work. Everything finally depended on coal, yet output was 50 million tons below the pre-war figure. The industry when taken over by the state was ill-equipped and inefficient. There had not been time to reorganize it or to win the goodwill of the miners, who in fact transferred their traditional suspicion of the owners to their new masters, the National Coal Board, and frequently expressed it by unofficial strikes. The fuel crisis helped to cause the disastrous dollar shortage of the summer, and probably delayed the country's recovery by a whole year, though there was some improvement by the end of 1947.

[1] See page 368.

An impoverished Britain was indeed asked to shoulder a staggering burden. Commitments abroad required armed forces of nearly a million men and the spending overseas of £200 million a year. The Government were trying at the same time to boost exports and to carry out great measures of social reform. The Labour ministers would not be deterred from raising the school-leaving age by a year in 1947, depriving industry of a year's supply of recruits at a critical time, nor from launching the National Health Service in 1948. These were advances of the kind the Government's supporters expected, and indeed considered to be their due after the effort and suffering of six years of war. *Burdens abroad and at home*

The National Insurance Act and the National Health Service Act were the outcome of plans which had been prepared under the Coalition Government, the former being shaped by Sir William Beveridge, formerly a civil servant and an expert on social questions. The Beveridge Plan was a great scheme of social insurance to be provided, in the case of employed persons, by contributions from employees, employers and the state. But self-employed persons such as farmers and shopkeepers, and non-employed persons such as dukes, were also to contribute, so that everyone in the country was covered. Benefits were payable in case of unemployment or illness, and were to cover dependants as well as the insured person. Industrial accidents were also provided for, and grants were made for maternity, to widows, and to meet funeral expenses. Retirement pensions were made available to all, for men at sixty-five, for women at sixty. A weekly allowance was to be paid to parents for each child after the first. Finally, a complete medical service was set up, controlled by regional boards under the Ministry of Health. This enabled patients to have the attention not merely of a general practitioner as before, but free treatment in a hospital or sanatorium, with spectacles, dentures, and surgical appliances if necessary. All these were free at first; part payment for spectacles, dentures, prescriptions, and dental treatment was introduced later. In the first year eight and a half million people received dental treatment and five and a quarter million pairs of spectacles were provided; the total cost was £400 million—3½ per cent of the national product. There was no money, however, to build the projected health centres and new hospitals. The National Health Service was recognized by its advocates and enemies alike as the deepest invasion so far of the private sector. The doctors at first *National Insurance scheme, 1948* *National Health Service, 1948* objected bitterly to a scheme which would half convert them into salaried civil servants, but the campaign of the British Medical Association finally collapsed in face of Aneurin Bevan's determination, and most doctors came into the scheme. It is unlikely that Parliament had ever before passed measures that meant so much to ordinary people as this comprehensive insurance against the commonest incidents and disasters of family life, protecting the citizen 'from the cradle to the grave'—whether he wished to be protected or not.

The Government's plans for social security were generally approved. There was growing opposition, on the other hand, to the programme of nationalization, which seemed to have done nothing to improve production in the mines or efficiency in the power and transport services. The easement which had appeared in the trade position late in 1947 was maintained in 1948, but by the middle of 1949 dollars and gold were again fast running out, and

Devaluation of sterling, 1949

Cripps decreed devaluation of the pound in September,[1] with some resulting benefit. An increase in the allowance of newsprint, which had cut down the daily papers to a meagre four pages, and a limited restoration of private motoring made life in post-war Britain a little less grim.

The election of 1950

The Labour Government, which had maintained the remarkable record of never losing a by-election, was nevertheless to suffer heavy losses when a general election fell due in 1950. The party's enthusiasm for nationalization—its traditional remedy for economic injustice—had wilted; only the sugar-refining, cement and chemical industries were now on its list of proposals. The Conservatives, on their side, did not urge general denationalization, but merely demanded more efficient and more local control of the state-owned industries. They concentrated their electioneering attack on the generally miserable condition of the country under Labour rule. The voters returned only 315 Labour members to the House, and 298 Conservatives. But the Labour majority over all possible opponents was merely six, a margin impossibly small by all previous parliamentary experience. Yet Attlee carried on for eighteen months, to the intense weariness of M.P.s who had to be in constant attendance in the House for fear of losing a division—or of missing a chance to win one. The Labour ministry was in a very different position from that of 1945, which had embarked full of hope on what it called, with some reason, 'the peaceful revolution'

[1] See page 369.

The Conservatives, on the other hand, who had been thoroughly demoralized after their defeat in 1945, were now in good fighting trim. Lord Woolton, the wartime Minister of Food, reformed the organization of the party, while R. A. Butler and a team of young colleagues worked out a policy more attractive to

Conservative revival

(*By permission of the Executors of Sir David Low's Estate and Beaverbrook Newspapers Ltd.*)

'All I ask is that you get it properly balanced.'

Gaitskell as Labour's Chancellor of the Exchequer, riding the British camel, had a difficult task to adjust the competing financial claims of the welfare services and of defence (supported by Service ministers E. Shinwell and J. Strachey). Both of these loads threatened to break the camel's back (Feb. 1951).

the voters. The Labour Government was weakened at this time by the deaths of Ernest Bevin and Stafford Cripps, and by the resignation, in protest against large increases in military expenditure and new charges for National Health services, of Aneurin Bevan and Harold Wilson. Fearing that the tide was beginning to flow against his party, Attlee decided on an election in October 1951.

The election of 1951—Labour's defeat

Labour had given Britain a system of social security which few countries in the world could match; there was full employment with higher wages and for most employees holidays with pay. A great new programme of military preparation, to cost £3,400 million in three years, had been launched as a result of the Korean War.[1] India had been set free.[2] But the voters in 1951 were mindful of the miseries and restrictions of the previous six years, when everything was in short supply and the black market flourished, when homeless 'squatters' seized Army huts and empty houses, when money seemed to be constantly losing its value. Some people, too, were coming to the conclusion that Labour was retaining many forms of restriction from a love of controls for controls' sake. The election of 1951 gave the Conservatives a majority of seventeen and Churchill returned to power.

Churchill's last ministry, 1951-1955

His Government inherited trouble. On examining the finances Churchill said the position was worse than he had expected; the payments deficit was bigger than just before devaluation in 1949. Exports had not increased enough to pay for dearer imports; there was a shortage of labour and of raw materials. Imports were immediately cut by £350 million, and R. A. Butler in his first budget reduced the school building programme, giving priority to the Conservatives' promise to build 300,000 houses in the year. The armaments programme drafted by the Labour ministry was to be spread over five years instead of three. These

Economic difficulties persist

economies alone could not of course solve the persistent difficulties which were to harass a succession of Conservative ministries.[3] Reserves of gold and foreign currencies were never large enough to tide over comfortably a period of reduced exports of goods or increased export of money; wages rose faster than production, and so caused inflation. When home consumption and therefore prices rose too quickly the Government applied the brake by increasing taxation and restricting credit. When production fell off and exports declined it used the accelerator, reducing taxes

'Stop-go'

and the bank rate. This 'stop-go' technique was obviously a somewhat vexatious way of regulating the national economy, but no one seemed able to suggest anything better. At the same time, however, real wages advanced fairly steadily, and it was a period of increased prosperity for the greater part of the nation.

Denationalization of iron and steel and road haulage

True to its election promises, Churchill's ministry returned to private ownership the iron and steel industry and most road

[1] See page 315.   [2] See pages 407-8.   [3] See page 370.

haulage business. Another concession to the principle of private enterprise was the decision that the B.B.C.'s monopoly of broadcasting should no longer apply to television; commercial companies, financed by advertisement and only lightly controlled by the Independent Television Authority, were to be set up. All these measures were duly criticized in Parliament by the Labour Party, but its effectiveness in opposition was reduced by division in its own ranks; Aneurin Bevan continued to find support for his objections to a level of expenditure on armaments which the majority of the party accepted as necessary.

Commercial television, 1954

On the death of King George VI in 1952 his elder daughter Elizabeth succeeded to the throne. She had married Prince Philip, who was connected with the Greek royal family but had been brought up in Britain and served in the Royal Navy. The coronation of the new Queen, witnessed by millions for the first time on television screens, was attended by a good deal of wishful talk about a new Elizabethan age which might match the first—a reaction no doubt against the prevalent materialism, and an antidote to the uncomfortable realization of Britain's reduced rôle in world affairs. Not that signs of national spirit and achievement were entirely lacking. The day of the Queen's coronation brought the stirring news of the first conquest of Mount Everest, scaled by a British expedition led by Sir John Hunt; the summit was reached by Sir Edmund Hillary, a New Zealander, and the Sherpa, Tensing. In 1954 Roger Bannister was the first man to run a mile in less than four minutes. In 1958 a British party led by Dr Vivian Fuchs made the first crossing of the Antarctic continent—2,200 miles in ninety days.

Elizabeth II, 1952

In 1955 Sir Winston Churchill, the oldest Prime Minister since Gladstone, resigned the premiership and was succeeded by Sir Anthony Eden, who had again held the post of Foreign Secretary. Sir Winston was to serve another nine years in the House of Commons, which he had entered in 1900, but this was the end of his active career.

It had been a career unmatched in variety and achievement. It had embraced military service on the N.W. Frontier of India, in the Sudan and in France; the drafting and administration of pioneer measures of social security; strenuous political campaigns in a variety of causes; a consistently remarkable rôle in the House of Commons. Out of office, for he was never an orthodox Conservative—for twenty years in fact he was a Liberal—he had in the 1930s struggled, perhaps perversely, against the Government

Winston Churchill, b. 1874, M.P. 1900–1965

of India Bill, but with utter justification to warn the country of the danger from Germany. His leisure had produced notable historical works and memoirs and numerous paintings. Never an easy man to work with, for he could insist unreasonably on his own ideas, he so inspired others that working with him was the greatest experience of their lives. His generosity and strong sense of humour made him as much loved as his honesty and mastery of his task made him respected. His vitality and courage— courage such that he positively enjoyed a struggle against adversity—shone most brightly in time of war, and most of all in what he called the nation's finest hour, as it was certainly his own, in 1940.

Eden's ministry, 1955–1957

Eden's first decision was to recommend a dissolution of Parliament which proved well-timed, for the ensuing election increased the Conservative majority in the Commons to seventy. This was the first time for nearly a century that a party in power had increased its votes at an election, but the balance in the country was still fairly even, Conservatives winning just under 50 per cent of the votes and Labour 46 per cent. Apart from the usual economic worries, which resulted in a restrictive autumn budget to correct a too optimistic one just before the election, Eden's ministry was to be concerned mainly with foreign affairs,[1] including the Suez fiasco, and was unfortunately cut short by his own breakdown in health. He had to resign office in January 1957, to be succeeded by Harold Macmillan.

Macmillan's ministry, 1957–1963

The new ministry was soon engaged in an overhaul of the country's defence policy.[2] The heavy expense of the armed forces, still 690,000 strong, the revolutionary developments in weapons of aggression, the striking evidence of Russia's progress in technology—she tested her first hydrogen bomb in 1953, launched the first earth satellite in 1957 and the first manned spacecraft in 1961—all demanded a reshaping of Britain's defences. Though these could not be altogether independent of the much more powerful forces of the U.S., whose Air Force used bases in Britain, it had been resolved before Churchill's retirement that Britain should develop her own hydrogen weapon.

It was now decided to rely mainly on nuclear weapons and rocket missiles in the event of a major war—or by possession of them to prevent one. This would make possible the reduction of

[1] See page 317.
[2] A Ministry of Defence was set up during the Second World War. By 1964 the three Service ministries were completely subordinated to it.

the armed forces to 375,000 men and the ending in 1960 of compulsory military service, which had been maintained since the end of the war. The army was to have a reserve in Britain which would be made mobile by a fleet of transport aircraft, and the world-wide network of bases and garrisons would be largely dismantled—a process harmonious with the granting of independence to former colonies. The development of the manned bomber would be stopped. The Navy would be reorganized and the number of ships reduced. The new programme did not proceed without its troubles, though the first hydrogen bomb test at Christmas Island in the Pacific was successful. 'Blue Streak', intended as the chief rocket weapon, was found unsatisfactory and given up in favour of the American 'Skybolt', launched from aircraft. This was in its turn abandoned by the Americans, who offered Britain instead the 'Polaris' weapon, which could be fired from a submerged submarine. Britain having launched her first nuclear-powered submarine in 1960, the offer was accepted.[1]

Britain's hydrogen bomb, 1957

Events within the Labour Party ensured that a change of government would not lead to the abandonment of nuclear weapons. In 1955 Attlee, who had presided over the post-war social revolution with 'deceptive mildness', accepted an earldom and handed over the party leadership to Hugh Gaitskell, who, though one of the 'intellectuals', now gained a firm grip on the rank and file of the party. Though in 1960 the annual conference voted in favour of unilateral nuclear disarmament by Britain in spite of its leader's urgings to the contrary, Gaitskell held to his policy and defeated an attack on his leadership in the Parliamentary Labour Party.[2] Later the party conference was persuaded to change its mind, and Labour opinion came to favour the merging of Britain's nuclear power in a general allied force, on the ground that Britain could neither independently produce nor effectively use her own 'deterrent' weapon. It was only outside Parliament and the party that the determined opponents of the possession of nuclear arms prosecuted their campaign. Their annual Easter marches to the nuclear weapons research station at Aldermaston and their 'sit-down' demonstrations in Trafalgar Square provided the main political spectacles of the time, but failed to attract widespread support.

[1] Doubts of a different kind arose from three spy trials in Britain which revealed the sale of secrets to the Russians and weaknesses in the security services.

[2] His premature death in 1963 was a great loss to the party. He was succeeded as leader by Harold Wilson.

Macmillan's Government indicated its readiness for some degree of change by three minor measures. It sponsored a Homicide Act which limited the death penalty to five specific categories of murder, substituting life imprisonment for the rest. It instituted life peerages for distinguished men and women, so that the House of Lords for the first time included a feminine element. And it set up a Restrictive Practices Court to enquire into cases of alleged monopoly or restriction harmful to the public interest. This ministry also restored an element of competition in a sphere from which it had been almost excluded since the war—the renting of houses. Of eleven million dwellings under control half were now released, as tenants moved, to be let at their market value. Many tenants had to pay higher rents—or quit—but more houses came on the market; and large numbers of older dwellings, going to rack and ruin because landlords could not afford repairs, were given a new lease of life.

A more controversial measure was an Act to restrict, for the first time, immigration from Commonwealth countries. Attracted by plentiful employment and a higher standard of living, large numbers of immigrants came to Britain in the 1950s, mainly from the West Indies, but also from India and Pakistan. Taking in general the worst-paid jobs, and congregating in the poorer areas of great cities, where their pattern of life was different from that of their white neighbours, they created something of a social problem and aroused some degree of racial hostility. The Act of 1962, reluctantly introduced by the Government and strongly criticised by the Labour Party, made it possible to refuse admission to immigrants unless they had in advance found recognized employment. This considerably reduced their number— at the expense of the right of free movement which had been one of the advantages of Commonwealth membership.

Whatever the ups and downs of the economy—and in 1958 the Chancellor of the Exchequer, Peter Thorneycroft, having committed himself to stern measures to improve it, had resigned rather than accept the more liberal expenditure that his colleagues favoured—employment remained generally high and wage-earners were enjoying a much improved standard of living. So Macmillan was able to point out, in a speech delivered in 1957, that most people had 'never had it so good'. This view on the whole received the approval of the voters, who proceeded in the election of 1959 to give the Conservatives a further increased majority of a hundred seats in the House of Commons. This House

Margin notes:

Homicide Act, 1957

Life peerages, 1958

Restrictive Practices Court, 1956

Rent Act, 1957

Commonwealth Immigrants Act, 1962

The election of 1959

was destined to run its full five-year term, so that the Conservatives enjoyed thirteen consecutive years in office. 'Enjoyed', however, is not perhaps the right word for the last two years of this period, which produced first an unsavoury scandal involving the Secretary of State for War, and then a sharp rebuff from France to the Government's efforts to join the Common Market.[1] Finally, when Macmillan had to resign through illness, there was a not entirely dignified search for a new Prime Minister, conducted as it was partly in a glare of publicity at the Conservative Party Conference, and partly—as was more usual—behind closed doors. The search ended when the Foreign Secretary, the Earl of Home, renounced his peerage, as a recent change in the law allowed, accepted the call to the Premiership, and re-entered the House of Commons as Sir Alec Douglas-Home.

Douglas-Home Prime Minister. 1963

When, in October 1964, he recommended a dissolution, the election that followed was contested without much excitement but with an extremely close result. Labour gained a majority of only five over its opponents in the House of Commons. Harold Wilson took office as Prime Minister with a majority as slender as Attlee's in 1950, and inherited a financial crisis as formidable as that which had confronted Churchill in 1951.

Election of 1964: Labour's narrow win

Wilson Prime Minister

[1] See page 320.

22. Britain since 1945: Foreign Affairs

Europe after the war Not even in the aftermath of the First World War did Europe present a scene of distress and confusion to compare with her condition in 1945. The ravages of war had been more fierce than ever before; cities had been reduced to rubble and vast industrial regions left incapable of production. Whole populations were in the grip of famine. Hundreds of thousands of war prisoners and deported workers awaited repatriation; millions of refugees moved across the face of the Continent. The tiny handful of neutral states could do little to help; the belligerent nations were themselves exhausted. Fortunately, from the United States, its productive power actually increased by the war, came handsome financial support for the United Nations Relief and Rehabilitation Administration, which, moving in behind the armies, provided most effective first-aid in the form of transport, food and materials for friend and former foe, Communist and non-Communist states alike.

The division of Germany The best hope of recovery would have been found in the wholehearted co-operation of the major wartime Allies, but it soon appeared that this was not to be. The point of their closest contact, and their most pressing problem, was Germany. Britain, the United States, France and Russia, meeting at Yalta in the Crimea early in 1945, had agreed to split Germany into four occupation zones, and Berlin, the capital, was similarly divided into four sectors. The intention was that the occupying powers should concert and apply a common policy. This from the beginning they failed to do, a failure which was the more serious because the Russians held the mainly agricultural East while the Western powers controlled nearly all the industrial areas. The bargain between them required that machinery from the western zones should be handed over as reparations to the Russians in compensation for the devastation by the Germans of their industrial centres, and this was done, but there was no corresponding obligation on the Russians to send food to the western zones. The merging for economic purposes of the British and American

310

K.C. Jordan

NORWAY

Oslo

NORTH

SEA

DENMARK

SWEDEN

Stockholm

Copenhagen

BALTIC SEA

FINLAND

Leningrad

ESTONIA

LATVIA

LITHUANIA

SOVIET RUSSIA (U.S.S.R.)

Hague

HOLLAND

BELGIUM

Brussels

Bonn

WESTERN GERMANY FEDERAL REP.

Berlin

GERMANY

EAST. DEM. REP.

Warsaw

POLAND

Paris

FRANCE

Prague

CZECHOSLOVAKIA

SWITZER-LAND

Berne

AUSTRIA

Vienna

Budapest

HUNGARY

RUMANIA

Trieste

Fiume

YUGOSLAVIA

Belgrade

Bucharest

BLACK SEA

ITALY

ADRIATIC SEA

BULGARIA

Sofia

Corsica

Rome

ALBANIA

Sardinia

GREECE

TURKEY

EUROPE
IN 1950

Sicily

Athens

Constantinople

Dodecanese Is.

Crete

············· Boundaries of 1938 afterwards changed

▭▭▭ 1950 Boundaries

//////// Territorial gains by Russia

≡≡≡ Territorial gains by Poland

zones into one brought some relief, but the Western powers had for some time to pour food into their zones if they were not to watch the Germans starve.

Meanwhile the Allied powers lost no time in setting up the United Nations, with its headquarters in New York, as an organization to replace the League of Nations, which was quietly buried. Its main bodies were, similarly, an Assembly in which all member states took part, and a Security Council in which the five great powers—Britain, U.S.A., U.S.S.R., France and China —had permanent places while others were elected to it in turn by the Assembly. The great powers were invested with a power of veto which could prevent any action being taken by the Council —a power insisted on by Russia and used by her with great frequency to frustrate the policies of the non-Communist majority of states. For some years, too, Communist and non-Communist states voted against the election of those new members favoured by their opponents, until at length it was agreed to elect all the candidates impartially.

Though the problem of a German settlement was not even approached, a series of conferences in 1946–47 produced peace treaties which the other defeated nations were required to accept. In these difficult negotiations Britain was represented by Ernest Bevin, who showed the robust qualities developed by his trade union experience, Russia by Molotov, America by Byrnes and France by Bidault. Italy paid the price of Mussolini's ambition by the loss of Fiume to Yugoslavia and of the Dodecanese Islands to Greece, while the whole of her African empire was given up. Russia advanced her western frontier almost everywhere, at the expense of Rumania in the south and of Finland in the north, while she had swallowed the three Baltic states of Esthonia, Latvia and Lithuania and absorbed a very large slice of Poland, seized by agreement with Hitler in 1939. Poland was compensated by acquiring a considerable part of eastern Germany, including most of East Prussia, up to the river boundary of the Oder–Neisse line. Heavy indemnities were demanded from all the defeated states, but in view of their distressed condition were soon waived by the Western powers. Austria was separated from Germany, but had to support armies of occupation until a peace treaty was signed in 1954.

The division of Europe into two antagonistic parts soon became painfully apparent. In the West, elections produced governments of various hues, but in none of them was a Communist party represented for long, in spite of the former prominence of Communists in wartime resistance movements. In the East, on the other hand, the presence of the Red Army was used in every country to secure the domination of the government by the Communist element. parliamentary
democracies in
the West

The exercise of Russian influence in Eastern Europe was sanctioned by the agreement reached between the Allies at the Yalta Conference of 1945, but Western opinion was shocked to see one-party rule established by the ruthless suppression of rival groups in Poland, Hungary, Rumania, Bulgaria and Albania. In Yugoslavia Marshal Tito followed a similar course, though relying on the liberation forces under his own command instead of on the Russians. The only exceptions were Finland and Czechoslovakia. The Russian government decided that Finland could safely be allowed a régime of its own choosing. But Czechoslovakia, which had enjoyed genuine parliamentary rule between the wars, was the victim of a determined *coup* in 1948, when the Communists secured control of the police and the organs of propaganda, fomented wide-spread strikes, and brought down the government. Thus Russia had in three years established a chain of so-called 'people's democracies' to extend her influence far into Europe, a situation only spoiled for her by Tito's preference for taking the line he thought best in Yugoslavia's rather than Russia's interests. 'people's
democracies'
in the East

Meanwhile consolidation went forward in Western Europe on different lines. Alarmed by the possibility of a complete economic breakdown in Europe, the United States came forward with the most magnificent offer of help that history records. That it was not inspired merely by fear of a spread of Communism is shown by the fact that the offer was made to all countries needing help in their recovery. Many Communist states were at first tempted to accept, but were compelled by Russia to reject the American offer because the Russian government expected to see a general collapse of the capitalist economies, but meanwhile feared an extension of American influence. Eighteen countries, including Britain, joined in the American scheme, which required them to plan their production and estimate their need of dollars for some years ahead, to stabilize their currencies, and to increase their trade with each other by lowering tariff barriers and setting up an Organization for European Economic Co-operation. In the first year of the operation of the Plan, named after General Marshall, the American Secretary of State, a total of £1,325 million was paid out in dollars by the U.S., which asked only slight The Marshall
Plan, 1947 trade concessions in return. American aid became the basis of the economy of most of the free countries of Europe, and particularly of that of Western Germany.

'The cold war' Within three years of their victory over Germany, the mutual suspicions of Russia and the Western powers had generated a state of tension commonly referred to as 'the cold war'. At every point their policies clashed; only in the trials of German war criminals at Nuremberg did they effectively co-operate. In wider German affairs they were constantly at odds, and in 1948 their antagonism almost reached flash-point. Britain, the United States

Recovery of Western Germany and France wanted to set Western Germany on its feet. In 1948 a new currency was established and at the same time controls were removed. The change worked like a miracle, and the Western zones were soon launched on a remarkable recovery. This was to be followed by the setting up of a German government for the western part of the country. The Russians feared the increase of prestige which this success would bring to the Western powers, and the contrast with their own poverty-stricken zone of East Germany, from which they continued to take reparations on a large scale. As a counter-measure they decided to drive the Western

The Berlin blockade, 1948–1949 powers out of Berlin; they barred all routes into the city in June 1948, intending to starve out both the Allied forces in the city and its two million inhabitants. The reply of the Western powers was not to shoot their way through, which would have been to

The air-lift start a general war, but to organize an air-lift on a huge scale and at enormous expense. 100,000 tons of goods were ferried in the first month; later the rate rose to 8,000 tons a day. In this remarkable operation, which quite defeated Russia's calculations, the R.A.F. took a large part. The Russians refused to negotiate unless the whole German problem was discussed, and vetoed consideration of the crisis by the United Nations. But in May 1949 they abandoned the blockade, and Berlin was saved to remain an outpost of the West in Communist East Germany—and a gateway through which nearly two million Germans passed from East to West until in 1962 the building of a wall across the city shut them in. The first phase of the cold war thus ended in defeat for Russia.

The danger from Russia had drawn together Britain, France, Belgium, Holland and Luxemburg into an alliance, unprecedented in peace-time, with a permanent military organization. In 1949 it was vastly extended by the incorporation of the United States and Canada, with Italy, Iceland, Norway, Denmark and

Portugal, to form the North Atlantic Treaty Organization. No- N.A.T.O., 1949 thing less than the short-sighted and provocative policy of Russia could have produced such a formidable union of powers or have persuaded the U.S.A. to become so closely involved in the affairs of Europe. It was now the policy of the U.S.A. to contain the Communist power by undertaking, in the words of President Truman, 'to support free peoples who are resisting attempted The Truman Doctrine, 1947 subjugation by armed minorities or by outside pressure'—a far cry from the negative principle of the Monroe Doctrine[1] which had been the basis of American policy until 1941.

The determination of the Western powers was next put to the test in the Far East. As soon as Japan was defeated in 1945 there was bitter strife in China between the Nationalists, the old revolutionary party, and the Communists, led by Mao Tse-tung. By 1949 the Communists had prevailed, and Chiang Kai-shek, the Nationalist leader, could only hold the island of Formosa— and that with American protection. The scene of trouble in 1950 was Korea. Released in 1945 from Japanese rule, it was, like Germany, divided for purposes of occupation, Russian troops holding the North and American the South. By the time these were withdrawn the North was under the control of a thoroughly Communist government, whose forces in 1950 crossed the line and invaded the South, assisted by Russian tanks and aircraft. War in Korea, 1950–1951 On South Korea's appeal to the United Nations Security Council, from which Russia had temporarily withdrawn in protest against the exclusion from the U.N. of Communist China, the aggression United Nations condemns aggression of North Korea was condemned, and U.S. naval and air forces were soon in action. Britain too supplied a strong naval force and was one of nine member states to send army or air force units.

On the part of the U.S. the intervention was heavy; within a few months the North Korean forces had been thrown back with the loss of 140,000 prisoners, and the U.N. forces were not far from the country's northern frontier with Manchuria. This possible threat to her territory led to Communist China's inter- China intervenes vention on a massive scale. The U.N. forces now faced a new army of 200,000 men, and though these were ill-supported by ships, aircraft, armour or heavy artillery they were formidable in guerrilla warfare behind the U.N. lines as well as in mass attacks on the front. It was a bitter and exhausting struggle, costing over 75,000 lives to the South Korean and U.N. forces, Americans suffering particularly heavily. Yet the conflict was one which

[1] See page 77.

the powers were anxious to limit. Russia sent no troops to Korea; the U.S. neither bombed nor blockaded China, nor used atomic bombs, of which she alone then had a supply. Fighting was halted in 1951, and two years later an agreement was at last reached whereby the former boundary between North and South, the 38th parallel, was restored.

The Palestine problem

Meanwhile a more limited but extremely difficult problem, that of Palestine, had found Britain and the United States in disagreement, and had defied a peaceful solution. Hitler had determined on the extermination of all the Jews in Europe, and in the countries occupied by the Nazis this dreadful aim was nearly achieved by the cold-blooded and systematically organized murder of six million people. Most of those who survived wanted at the end of the war to seek refuge in Palestine, designated a Jewish National Home at the end of the First World War and administered by Britain under a League of Nations mandate.[1] The plight of the Jews now aroused the strongest sympathy in the United States, whose government favoured unrestricted immigration into Palestine. The British government, however, doubted whether the country could support a large new influx, at any rate without harm to the interests of the Arab population. Moreover Bevin, the Foreign Secretary, was anxious not to upset the Arab states, who were sworn enemies of the Jewish National Home from the start, because he feared the effect on Britain's strategic position in the Middle East, particularly on her access to the vast oil reserves of that region. He therefore wished to maintain the limit of 75,000 immigrants fixed by the British government in 1939. An Anglo-American commission now recommended that 100,000 Jews should be admitted as soon as possible, but the Palestinian Arabs would agree to no increase at all in the number of Jews or of the area of land under their control. The Jews, on the other hand, would accept no restriction of immigration, and aimed at nothing less than national independence. They began to organize illegal immigration on a large scale, and British attempts to stop it provoked world-wide indignation. Extremist Jewish organizations unleashed a terrorist campaign against the British, while armed Arab bands infiltrated into the country to harass the Jews.

End of the mandate, 1948

Faced with deadlock, Attlee's government determined to give up the mandate and hand over the problem to the U.N., which decided on a partition of Palestine (the whole country was only the

[1] See page 260.

same size as Wales) and the establishment of two independent states, Arab and Jewish. The Arabs would not accept partition, and Britain refused to enforce it, withdrawing her troops in 1948. The Jews promptly declared the independence of the state of Israel, and were attacked by the armed forces of all the neighbouring Arab countries. The war soon went in favour of the Jews, however, and when the fighting stopped they had gained a larger area than the U.N. proposals would have given them—though the cease-fire line cut Jerusalem itself in two. The chief sufferers were the 650,000 Arab refugees, some of whom had left Palestine before the war began in expectation of a speedy return, others fleeing for their lives when hostilities opened. The unabated hostility of the Arab states towards Israel prevented any settlement in the Middle East, and was soon to produce a first-class international crisis.

Meanwhile another trouble-centre developed in the Far East. Before Malaya could recover from the effects of the Japanese invasion Communist rebels drawn from the Chinese population terrorized large areas of the country, finding refuge in the jungle when pursued by the British forces. Malaya being an indispensable source of tin and rubber, the paralysing of the country would have been a major success for the Communists in the 'cold war'. It was only when General Templer was appointed High Commissioner in 1952 that the insurrection began to weaken, and it was finally overcome not long before Malaya became independent within the Commonwealth in 1957. *Communist insurrection in Malaya*

It was Eden's government that had to face the next crisis in the Middle East, still seething after recent events in Palestine. It had been agreed with the Egyptian government in 1954 that British troops—never out of Egypt since 1882[1]—should leave the Canal Zone in 1956, though a British base maintained by civilians was to remain. As soon as the troops had left, Colonel Nasser, who had prompted a successful revolution against King Farouk and had become the dictator of Egypt in 1954, declared the Suez Canal to be the property of the Egyptian government. This was in retaliation, he said, for the refusal of Britain and the U.S. to finance the building of a great new dam at Aswan on the Nile. Eden considered the seizure of the Canal an outrageous proceeding, and one most dangerous to British interests. He saw Nasser as a new Hitler, and his ambitions as likely to embrace the whole Middle East. Meanwhile the Israelis had been getting new *Suez crisis, 1956* *Nasser seizes the Canal*

[1] See pages 419–21.

supplies of arms from France and were only waiting for an opportunity to use them against Egypt. Eden had been reluctant to
join in any plot with the Israelis; and he respected the views of
President Eisenhower, who was urging restraint in dealing with
Egypt. But Nasser's seizure of the Canal removed Eden's doubts;
it meant, he said, 'Nasser's thumb on Britain's windpipe.' He
was ready (though the British forces for some weeks were not)

**Israel invades
Egypt**

to join France in immediate action. It was the Israelis, however,
who first attacked Egypt, and they appeared to do so in confident
expectation of British as well as French support. This they received in a curious form, for as they advanced into the Sinai
peninsula Britain and France presented both combatants, Israel
and Egypt, with an ultimatum: there must be a cease-fire
within twelve hours and an occupation of the Canal Zone by
British and French forces. The alleged purpose was to keep the
combatants apart, though in fact the Egyptian forces would be
caught between the advancing Israeli army to the east of them
and the Anglo-French forces on the Canal to the west.

**British and
French landing**

On Egypt's rejection of the ultimatum British bombers attacked targets in Egypt, and five days later British and French
forces landed, quickly capturing Port Said and Port Fuad at the
northern end of the Canal at some cost in casualties to both sides.
In another forty-eight hours they would have seized the whole
Canal. But a powerful outcry was raised throughout the world.
There came a rebuke from the United Nations, threats of rocket
warfare from Russia, strong remonstrances from the United
States, and a sudden run on the pound, of which the last two
were the most effective.

The resolution of the British and French governments accordingly weakened, and the day after the landing, both British and
French forces ended hostilities. Rarely had a British government
encountered such a storm of hostile opinion. In the United

**—condemned
by U.N.**

Nations Assembly a resolution of condemnation was passed by
64 votes to 5; in the Council Britain had earlier used the veto
for the first time to block a motion calling for a cease-fire. Of
the Commonwealth countries, Australia withheld her support,
and India openly condemned the whole enterprise.

It was not only the Commonwealth that showed signs of strain.
There were bitter recriminations in Parliament, and opinion in
the country was divided as it had not been since the days of
Ulster and Home Rule. Accusations of collusion between Britain,
France and Israel were naturally made, but were strenuously

denied. Some thought the Government had been wrong only to stop short of recovering the stolen property—the Suez Canal. Others charged it with flouting the U.N., jeopardizing relations with America, risking a third world war, and giving a shocking example to the world of resort to violence. Whatever view was taken, the attempt had turned out an appalling failure, and it lost the two Western powers international goodwill at a particularly unfortunate moment, for the attack on Egypt coincided with the Russian intervention, likewise condemned by the majority of the U.N., to suppress an anti-Communist revolt on a national scale in Hungary. In the end, the British and French troops were withdrawn, and an international force was sent by the U.N. to police the border between Egypt and Israel, a measure largely due to Canadian leadership. Egypt emerged from the affair in possession of the Canal, Nasser's prestige and influence in the Arab world were greatly enhanced, and Britain's strategic interests as well as her reputation had suffered serious harm.

Failure of intervention

Under the strain of these events, and weakened by previous illness, Eden's health broke down, and he retired from office. On succeeding him, Macmillan found that his most immediate concern was to repair the damaged relationship with the United States. This task he pursued with very fair success in two meetings with President Eisenhower during 1957. His Government continued, however, to be harassed by difficulties in the Commonwealth.

Following Palestine and Malaya, it was Cyprus, intended after the loss of Suez to be an important British base, that made political trouble for the Government and gave uncongenial employment to the Army. In 1954 a revolt began, pursued by the usual guerrilla and terrorist methods, with the object of throwing off British rule and achieving a union ('Enosis') with Greece. Not only was this aim obnoxious to the large Turkish minority in the island, but the Government held continued British control to be indispensable, and rejected the idea of independence, then or later. After four and a half years of obstinate struggle, however, independence was conceded, to take effect in 1960, and Archbishop Makarios, the picturesque leader of the Greek Cypriots, returned from forced exile as head of the new government and in due course made his appearance among the Commonwealth Prime Ministers gathered in London. The constitution of Cyprus was guaranteed by Greece and Turkey, Britain's right to maintain bases in the island was accepted, and an uneasy peace descended upon it—to be broken again in 1963.

Revolt in Cyprus

While Britain's anxieties persisted, little reduced by successive grants of independence to Commonwealth countries,[1] the general outlook improved a little.

Death of Stalin, 1953: Khrushchev

The death of Joseph Stalin in 1953 was gradually found to have resulted in some moderation of Soviet policy towards the outside world. His successors, notably N. S. Khrushchev, were less narrowly fanatical, and seemed as well aware as the Western leaders of the suicidal character of nuclear war. Moreover, the increasing prosperity of the Soviet Union tempered the revolutionary ardour of the earlier days of struggle and hardship. More was now heard of 'peaceful co-existence' with capitalist powers.

'Peaceful co-existence'

However, in view of the Marxist belief in the inevitable downfall of capitalism, which was to be assisted by all means short of war, there was little difference between Russia's 'peaceful co-existence' and the West's 'cold war'. Moreover, the problem of a divided Germany, as a 'summit' meeting at Geneva showed in 1955, made any real understanding between the great powers extremely difficult. So there was nothing more than a slight relaxation of tension, and Britain continued to rely on her 'special relationship' with the United States and on a series of alliances in which the U.S. was the dominant partner—NATO[2] (in which Greece and Turkey had been included) for Europe, CENTO (the Central Treaty Organization) for the Middle East, and SEATO for South-East Asia, which had become one of the most critical areas for the containment of Communist power.

The Cuba crisis, 1962

In the most acute crisis of the East-West rivalry Britain was little more than a spectator. This occurred in 1962 when President Castro's pro-Communist government of Cuba allowed the Russians to begin installing nuclear missiles in the island—an action which would have rendered useless the warning system of the U.S. and so put that country in mortal peril. With great courage and decision President Kennedy ordered a blockade of Cuba and demanded the withdrawal of the missiles. Russia complied with the demand, and war, which had been imminent, was narrowly averted. The improvement of relations between Russia and the U.S. that followed was perhaps a sign that neither power would be likely to venture so near the brink again.

Britain's concern at this time was mainly with a choice of great difficulty between her ties with the Commonwealth and those with Europe. Political bonds with the Commonwealth were loosening as its independent members grew in number and

[1] See page 440.　　[2] See page 315.

variety,[1] and the proportion of British trade carried on within the Commonwealth was declining. Across the Channel, on the other hand, there was now a group of six powers with which Britain had much in common. If she joined them she would belong to an economic union greater in population, greater perhaps in potential, than the United States of America. If economic union should produce some form of political union, as it well might, the barrier thus erected against the advance of Communism could be insuperable. In 1961 Macmillan's government decided, though public opinion was sharply divided, to apply for membership of the European Economic Community, or Common Market.[2] Every effort was made in the negotiations that followed to safeguard the interests of Commonwealth countries, and even to advance them by providing for them access to the Common Market. However, negotiations broke down when success seemed near. General de Gaulle, as a single-minded champion of French interest, disliked the prospect of an increasing British political influence in Europe—disliked especially, perhaps, Britain's 'special relationship' with the United States. His veto put an end to the negotiations, at any rate for a considerable time, and Britain was forced to remain content with her other economic connections— the European Free Trade Association[3] and the Commonwealth.

Britain applies to join the E.E.C.

—and is rejected

The apparently interminable negotiations on disarmament at last in 1963 produced some result. Britain, the U.S. and Russia agreed to cease testing nuclear weapons in the atmosphere. The fall-out from test explosions was producing an amount of radioactive material that could have become dangerous. The ban did not extend to subterranean explosions, these being more difficult to detect, and no agreement was reached on measures of inspection. Nor did France, having just carried out her first test of a nuclear weapon and being anxious to develop it, take part in the agreement. It showed, however, some advance in mutual confidence, and offered hope of further and more positive measures of disarmament.

Nuclear test ban agreement, 1963

[1] See pages 440–1 for the progress of the colonies to independence.
[2] See page 371.   [3] See page 371.

23. Scientific Progress

1 Science in the late Eighteenth and early Nineteenth Centuries

The most important feature of the nineteenth century, whether reckoned by its effect on politics, on religion or on the life of the people, was the development of science.

The seventeenth century

Modern scientific thinking based on observation had begun in the seventeenth century, when Galileo set a new standard of curiosity about the universe, the Irishman Robert Boyle founded chemistry as an exact science, and William Harvey made the brilliant discovery of the circulation of the blood. In the same period many of the essential instruments of science were invented or improved—the telescope, microscope, micrometer, thermometer and barometer. To crown this early development came Isaac Newton (1642–1727), the supreme scientific genius, who gave mankind the idea of a universe regulated in every particular by unchanging laws.

The task of the nineteenth century

By 1800 sound scientific principles had thus been established in many fields, but some ancient and mistaken ideas still survived, such as the Greek notion of earth, water, air and fire as the basic elements, and the belief that living creatures could arise from lifeless matter. Before these conceptions could be dispelled, science had to master the systematic use of measurement to determine such matters as specific gravities and boiling points. Joseph

Black, 1728–1799

Black of Edinburgh, and Lavoisier, until the French Revolutionary Tribunal sent him to the guillotine, had pointed to the need of testing all theories by the use of the balance, and much work of this kind was done as the new century wore on. Britons played a big part in the discoveries of this period, but science was an international concern—as witness Sir Humphry Davy, who, at a time when Britain and France were locked in combat, was received by French scientists in Paris with every mark of honour.

Dalton's atomic theory, 1808

It was an Englishman, John Dalton, who was responsible for the oustanding scientific achievement of the early nineteenth century—the formulation of the atomic theory. The idea that all matter consists of minutely small particles was centuries old, but Dalton, starting from the fact that the same two elements will combine in different ways to form two different compounds, showed that this combination always takes place in a simple ratio, the weight of the compound being produced by the addition of one part of one element to one, two, three or more parts of the other. From this he deduced that an element consists of atoms all identical in size, weight and behaviour, which can be linked up with the atoms of other elements in varying proportions. There was thus a mathematical order in chemistry which could be expressed in equations, and possible combinations of elements could be forecast and the weights of the compounds foretold.[1]

While Dalton was expounding the atomic structure of matter, Sir Humphry Davy had begun to explore the relation of electrical to chemical phenomena, splitting up compounds by electrolysis—the process of passing through them an electric current. During a life crowded with activity which brought him widespread fame and attention Davy discovered the new elements chlorine and iodine, experimented with nitrous oxide (later used as an anaesthetic), and after a study of firedamp (marsh gas) invented the miner's safety-lamp. *Davy, 1778–1829*

Davy's chosen assistant and pupil, Michael Faraday, said to be 'Davy's greatest discovery', outshone even his master by his brilliant achievements in physics. Faraday discovered two simple laws governing all the processes of electrolysis, and then turned his attention to the properties of electric currents themselves. This brought him to the discovery of electromagnetic induction, or the fact that an electric current passing through a circuit can induce a current in another circuit insulated from it. Upon this fact are based almost all forms of electrical machinery, including the electric telegraph and the dynamo.[2] *Faraday, 1791–1867* *Electromagnetic induction, 1820*

Other important discoveries of the early nineteenth century concerned the conception of energy, particularly the nature of light and heat. Newton had explained light as consisting of the movement of minute corpuscles through space, a notion that fitted in with his general explanation of the universe as material bodies moving in space and controlled by a mutual attraction—

[1] Twenty elements were recognized by Dalton; later researches have carried the list to 102, of which ten are artificial.
[2] Electric telegraphy was being used in England by 1840, but no useful electric motor was devised till 1870

the force of gravity. Former ideas of heat had likewise pictured it as a fluid substance passing into the heated object. But in the 1840s appeared the idea that energy was a general phenomenon independent of particular substances, and that different forms of energy were convertible into one another. The question was settled by James Prescott Joule when he proved heat to be a

(*Rowlandson, from a print in the British Museum*)

CHEMICAL LECTURES

Lectures on the new Chemistry were a fashionable diversion at the end of the eighteenth century.

Joule—Law of Conservation of Energy, 1843

form of energy. He measured the amount of heat liberated by the expenditure of mechanical work, and from this went on to propound the law of the conservation of energy, which means that energy cannot be lost or gained, but only changed into another form. This has been described as the most valuable scientific discovery of the nineteenth century, because it provided a new method of investigation not only into a great number of the problems of physics but also into biological problems concerning the working of living bodies.

2 The Doctrine of Evolution

Of the vast number of scientific ideas produced in the nineteenth century it was the doctrine of evolution, as propounded by Charles Darwin in *The Origin of Species*, that most affected general thought. The idea of evolution itself was not new. It had been popular with philosophers for some time, and the scientists themselves had begun to accept it, particularly Erasmus Darwin, grandfather of Charles, and the Frenchman Lamarck, who suggested how evolution had come about. Lamarck's theory was that changes were caused in organs of the body by a creature's habits, which were due in turn to its environment—thus the neck of the giraffe might have become long through many generations of stretching to reach foliage. The theory was false, and Charles Darwin put forward another explanation of the mode of evolution, which he supported by an immense amount of evidence. The new theory burst upon the public like a thunderclap.

Two events helped to lead Darwin towards his thesis. The first was his five years' voyage in South American waters as official naturalist in the Government discovery ship *Beagle*. The second, after his return, was his reading Malthus's *Essay on Population*, which provided him with the main clue for his explanation of evolution. The first factor in evolution was the existence of variations among members of a species; these variations might be slight but were innumerable. They were well recognized, for example, among breeders of animals, who selected the varieties of which they approved to breed the next generation. What had not so far been explained was how the existence of these variations could lead in the natural state to evolution, i.e. to a gradual change in the character of a whole species, and in time to the emergence of a new species. How did Nature select individuals for breeding? This was where Malthus's book, with its emphasis on the unceasing struggle of human beings to survive under the onslaughts of starvation and disease, gave Darwin his clue. He decided that changes in species come about because certain individuals who differ from the rest are better able by means of these differences to adapt themselves to their environment; they thus survive when the rest perish. Those giraffes which happened

Darwin's The Origin of Species, 1859

The problem of selection

'Natural Selection'

to be slightly taller and longer-necked than the rest would be able to find food when the others could not, and would thus survive and propagate offspring, which would also be of the longer-necked variety. In the course of time all giraffes would have long necks, which would distinguish the whole species from other species of animals.

How the variations occurred in the first place Darwin never claimed to know. Later work, based on the discoveries of the German Abbé Mendel, has shown that those variations which can be inherited arise either from new combinations of the 'genes' (heredity factors in the parent cells) or from changes occurring in the 'genes' themselves. Darwin did not claim that natural selection was the sole cause of evolution, but that it was the main one. It would go far to explain how the innumerable species of living creatures could have evolved from one original form of life, which was perhaps a single cell. It would also explain the close resemblances between plants and animals which enable them to be classified into families, the resemblances between the human arm, the forelegs of animals, and the wings of birds, and the resemblances between living and extinct species. Finally, it would explain the descent of man himself from early human types and from a still earlier ape-like ancestor.

Effect of Darwin's theory—on science—

The idea of evolution soon dominated the whole world of science, and invaded other fields of thought with startling results. It gave tremendous confidence to scientists, for it now appeared that the world of living things operated under unchanging laws just as surely as inanimate matter. Such was Darwin's triumph that some over-confident scientists were assured that by sustained research they would soon be able to explain the workings of the whole universe, and reduce the human mind itself to a matter of molecules. Their confidence decreased with their progress, however, and biologists today are by no means agreed that life will ever be explained entirely in terms of physics and chemistry.

—and religion

Darwin's teaching brought on a furious battle between the champions of science and of religion, from which Darwin himself kept aloof, leaving the argument to Thomas Henry Huxley, who called himself 'Darwin's bulldog'. Many religious leaders felt that the authority of the Bible was being undermined, as indeed it was so long as they stood upon a literal interpretation of Genesis.[1] But on more general grounds they attacked natural selection

[1] In desperation some religious writers endeavoured to discredit the evidence of the fossilized remains of prehistoric animals by asserting that

as a godless doctrine, for it seemed to reduce all Nature to a soulless mechanism, in which Man figured only as a superior animal. Creation meant only the survival of the fittest, and there was no place in it for love or pity or nobility. On a longer and calmer view, however, the conflict seemed capable of being resolved, and most religious thinkers today are quite ready to accept the findings of science.

Students of human problems drew varying lessons from the teaching of evolution. To some it justified a belief in continuing and inevitable progress, while others condemned measures of social reform as an interference with Nature's law of the survival of the fittest.

3 Medical Science

There is no aspect of the nation's life in which the conditions of the late eighteenth and mid-twentieth centuries present such a contrast as in the practice of medicine and the organization of public health. No accurate figures are on record for the former period, but the death rate, even apart from bad epidemics, was terribly high. Of the large number of infants commonly brought into the world by the mothers of those days, a high proportion, sometimes half or more, died before reaching maturity, for infants were always the readiest victims of bad conditions. *Disease and mortality*

A sharp decline in the death rate was achieved during the latter half of the eighteenth century. While the causes are difficult to establish, land drainage, the disappearance of scurvy, the conquest of smallpox, the increased provision of hospitals and the abandonment of the practice of binding new-born infants in swaddling clothes doubtless all contributed. Some improvement in the general standard of living probably had the most effect. Yet the shocking overcrowding in towns and the lack of water-supply and sanitation for long continued to foster and spread disease. There were constant outbreaks of typhoid, and the dreaded cholera visited England four times between 1830 and 1870. Moreover, throughout most of the nineteenth century the risks of childbirth remained great for both mother and infant,

these had been placed beneath the soil by God to test (or by the Devil to destroy) man's faith in the Bible.

and many children grew up rickety and unhealthy through malnutrition.

The improvement of health depended much upon housing and public health reform,[1] but medical discovery also played a great part. The eighteenth century witnessed steady progress in anatomy and physiology, particularly in London, under the great teacher John Hunter, and at Edinburgh University. Indeed, the increased interest in dissection sent up the demand for corpses to such an extent that body-snatching from graveyards became a most profitable occupation. In the early nineteeth century the Irishmen Burke and Hare improved on this practice; they supplied the medical school at Edinburgh by a series of thirty-two murders, for which Burke—but not Hare, who turned King's Evidence—was duly hanged.

Jenner,
1749–1823

One of the many famous pupils of John Hunter was Edward Jenner, to whom was due the victory over the dangerous and widespread disease of smallpox. Inoculation, i.e. producing the disease in a mild form so that the patient would be immune to further infection, had already been practised with some success. Jenner, working as a country doctor, found that dairymaids infected with the very mild disease of cowpox were proof against

Vaccination,
1796

smallpox. He experimented with vaccine, a preparation of pus from a cowpox patient, and found that it gave immunity against smallpox. The adoption of his method, which he freely made known, diminished smallpox in many countries, and led to similar methods of dealing with other diseases.

Pasteur,
1822–1895

The most important discoveries along these lines were made by the French biologist Pasteur and the Prussian doctor Koch. Pasteur showed that microbes are present in the air in great quantity and variety. Koch identified the microbes which cause anthrax, tuberculosis and cholera, and Pasteur followed this up by achieving prevention and cure, which he did first with anthrax and then with hydrophobia by methods of inoculation. In 1896 Sir Almroth Wright first inoculated against typhoid, a precaution which had notable results in the war of 1914–18.

Anaesthetics

Pasteur's discoveries were to revolutionize surgery, but before this was brought about an immense boon was conferred on suffering humanity by the discovery of anaesthetics. Humphry Davy had tried nitrous oxide on himself in 1799, and a young English doctor, Henry Hickman, had tried to draw attention to the possibilities of anaesthesia in 1824, but it was first successfully prac-

[1] See Chapters 13 and 15.

tised in the United States in 1842 and in England by Robert Liston in 1846. The following year Dr J. Y. Simpson of Edinburgh discovered the use of chloroform, which was effective for a longer period, so that operations of more intricacy and boldness could be undertaken.

The Cow Pock __ or __ the Wonderful Effects of the New Inoculation ! __ Vide *the Publications of ye Anti Vaccine Society*

(Gillray, 1802, from a print in the British Museum)

A satire on the more absurd arguments of Dr Jenner's opponents. Jenner is seen at work in the Smallpox and Inoculation Hospital at St Pancras. As soon as his patients are vaccinated they sprout cows from all parts of their bodies.

The horrors avoided by the use of anaesthetics were more painful but less fatal than those successfully attacked by Joseph Lister. Surgical operations before Lister resulted in a mortality rate of never less than 25 per cent, being invariably followed by sepsis— the putrefaction or 'going bad' of the wound, due to the complete lack of cleanliness in hospitals. The stench of a surgical ward was revolting. There had been a few surgeons, regarded as cranks, who insisted on cleanliness without knowing why, but the normal

Lister, 1827-1912

practice was for a surgeon to put on an old bloodstained coat which he kept for the operating theatre, with a bunch of silk ligatures threaded through the button-hole, and to set to work without any precautions whatever. One surgeon ruefully admitted that 'an abdominal operation should be classed among the methods of the executioner'.

As Professor of Surgery at Glasgow—where he worked in the Royal Infirmary, built over an old cholera burial-ground—Joseph Lister came to suspect that the infection of wounds was due to something carried by the air. His ideas were confirmed when he read of Pasteur's discoveries about the activity of microbes in fermentation and putrefaction, and he therefore determined to destroy the microbes by a generous use of carbolic acid. Everything which touched a wound was first treated with this antiseptic, which was also sprayed into the air. Though he had to face contention and ridicule before he could get his ideas accepted, Lister eventually triumphed through the proven superiority of his methods—for his patients' wounds did not turn septic, and few of them died. This conquest of sepsis made possible many types of surgery which could not have been attempted under the old conditions. But the discovery of improved methods in the wards and operating theatres would have had little effect without the transformation of nursing from being the resort of the ignorant and decrepit to the status of a highly-qualified profession—a change brought about by the splendid example and the organizing ability of Florence Nightingale.[1]

One of the greatest victories over disease was won by the researches of Sir Ronald Ross. Malaria, a scourge afflicting a large proportion of people who dwell in hot climates, had in olden days been attributed, as its name denotes, to 'bad air'. Ross found that it was caused by a parasite, and traced this parasite to the stomach of the anopheles mosquito. Malarial fever could then be overcome both by destroying the breeding-places of the insect—a discovery that incidentally made possible the construction of the Panama Canal—and by the use of drugs and other precautions on the part of possible victims. A later discovery showed that the typhus bacillus similarly finds a host in lice.

The greatest medical advances during the twentieth century have been in radiology and the discovery of new drugs. In 1895 the German scientist Röntgen found X-rays—the invisible rays emitted from a cathode in a vacuum tube. Soon afterwards the

Antiseptics, 1865

Nursing

Ross and malaria, 1897

Radiology

[1] See pages 169–71.

Frenchman Becquerel established the fact of radiation from uranium salts, and Marie Curie found radiation from the element thorium. Then she and her husband succeeded in isolating an element which they named radium, so highly radio-active that it Radium, 1898 would destroy living tissue by its radiations, and could be used against malignant growths in the human body. The penetrating power of X-rays was also a priceless asset to surgery through their use in photography.

Drugs recently discovered have proved more powerful allies of New drugs— the blood in its fight against invading microbes than anything previously known. Sir Alexander Fleming discovered penicillin penicillin, 1928— through a brilliantly exploited accident of the laboratory, arising when the spores of a natural mould alighted on a culture of microbes which then failed to grow. Penicillin, which the chemists can now synthesize, has been of special value in the treatment of pneumonia, septicaemia and meningitis. Before penicillin was developed as a therapeutic agent, however, the complicated substances known as the sulphonamide group were produced by sulphonamides, synthesis in the laboratory. These are effective against many 1935 organisms, for example those of pneumonia and bacillary dysentery, and the organisms commonly infecting wounds and burns.

The results of medical discovery are evident today in the increased attention to preventive medicine and public health, the rising standards of personal hygiene, and the continuing decline of the death rate. Thanks to Lister, people now understand the importance of preventing infection by proper sanitation, and this has been provided in great cities by big engineering projects for water supply and sewage disposal.

Most impressive of all has been the saving of life by the medical Medicine in war services during war. The Royal Army Medical Corps was founded in 1898, and as a result of its work the two World Wars have been the first in history in which disease has not claimed more victims than the enemy. Among the recent triumphs of rescue and healing are the victory over tropical diseases, enabling armies to fight in malaria-infested country, the use of blood transfusion on a very large scale, the wonderful successes of orthopaedic and plastic surgery, and the efficacy of penicillin in the healing of wounds. In some campaigns of the Second World War the proportion of wounded men in the British Army who succumbed to their wounds was reduced to 4 per cent, a figure which in any previous conflict would have seemed miraculous.

4 Recent Advances in Science

The applications of science to everyday life are now innumerable. Discoveries made without thought of practical purpose have had the most revolutionary effects. Chemistry, for instance, is widely used not only as the basis of a great new industry, but in the metal, textile, building and fuel industries, and in medicine. Its most fundamental use is to keep us alive, for the world's food supply depends on it. Examples are seen in the use of fertilizers (in which the pioneer work was done by Gilbert and Lawes at the Rothamsted experimental farm) and in cold storage, which is based on Faraday's experiments on the liquefaction of gases. Chemistry not only augments our food supply, but teaches us how to make the most of it, for on it is based the new science of dietetics, now widely studied and applied.

But though the ordinary person is more and more affected by science, he finds it less and less comprehensible. Even the trained scientist is equipped only to deal with problems in his own particular field. It is clear, nevertheless, that the first place among the sciences has been recaptured by physics, partly as a result of researches into the structure of the atom, partly through fresh discoveries about the laws governing the movements of the heavenly bodies and the transmission of light and energy.

A great pioneer in this sphere of science was Clerk Maxwell. Working from Faraday's results, Maxwell found mathematically that electromagnetic radiation travels with the same speed as light. From this he deduced that light consists of a wave-motion, and that light waves are in fact electromagnetic waves. Later experiments showed that electromagnetic waves conformed to the behaviour previously observed in light waves. From Maxwell's discoveries grew the conception of a field of physical activity pervading all space. On the practical side his results were an important step towards radio-telegraphy, television and radar.

To reinforce the speculations of the physicists about the nature of matter came the discoveries about radiation started in France by Becquerel and Marie Curie. It was found in fact that physics must supply the key to the fundamental mysteries of chemistry. The chief work here was done by Sir J. J. Thomson, working on ordinary substances, and Lord Rutherford, who examined radio-active substances. The latter found that radiation

could consist of two types of particles and also of rays, similar to
X-rays, but of shorter wavelength and such penetrating power
that they would go through two feet of lead. He supposed, as
was afterwards proved, that the atoms of radio-active substances
break up of their own accord, leaving behind new substances of
different chemical properties. Thomson found that the particles
passing through a cathode tube, which he called electrons, were
charged with negative electricity, and he succeeded in measuring
their velocity and mass. Before long it was shown that all the
problems of chemistry were concerned with the structure of the
atom. The practical results of Thomson's work with vacuum
tubes included photo-electric cells, fluorescent lighting and elec-
tronic valves, upon which were based new industries such as
radio, television and sound films.

Rutherford concluded from his own and Thomson's results
that an atom consisted of a positive centre or nucleus, called a
proton, with negative electrons of extremely small mass revolving
round it—that the atom was in fact a miniature solar system.[1] In
radio-active substances some of the electrons and particles from
the nucleus break away, leaving behind at last a different kind
of atom and therefore a different substance. For example, radium
changes through several phases until finally it becomes lead. It
was now proved that a single basis exists for all matter, and the
table of atomic weights discovered by Dalton was at last explained.
The lightest element, hydrogen, consists of a proton and one
electron; the succeeding elements in the table have increasing
numbers of protons and electrons. Uranium, the heaviest occurring in nature, has ninety-two.

In the case of one type of uranium (of atomic weight 235) the
nucleus of the atom can itself be split. The energy it contains is
far greater than that of electrons, and when division takes place
three particles called neutrons are released, which on meeting
another atom divide it in its turn so that six neutrons become
active. If the lump of uranium is of less than a certain size, the
neutrons escape into the air without meeting other atoms, but
once this critical size is passed, a chain reaction takes place, count-
less millions of nuclei being split simultaneously. This was the
principle of the atomic bomb detonated over the Japanese town

Discovery of
electrons, 1897

Structure of the
atom

The uranium
bomb, 1945

[1] This description is now considered much too simple, and the atom is
sometimes described as a system not of particles but of waves, whose
behaviour can be indicated only by mathematical equations. Matter may
thus be conceived as one aspect of energy.

of Hiroshima in August 1945. Fifty years after the initial discoveries of Thomson and Rutherford, the atomic age had begun.

The hydrogen bomb, 1954

It was not long before the uranium bomb, itself terrifyingly destructive, was outclassed by the invention of the hydrogen bomb, based on the principle of fusion instead of fission of atoms. This is so powerful that one aircraft can carry a load of explosive power greater than that of all the bombs dropped in the Second World War. A state equipped with these weapons, against which no defence has been devised, can ensure the utter destruction of the main centres of population of an enemy country, however large. There is the attendant danger of the 'fall-out' of radioactive particles which might put an end to organic life over the whole surface of the earth On the other hand discoveries in

Peaceful uses of atomic power

atomic science have greatly assisted research in medicine and have revealed a new and inexhaustible source of industrial power. The world's first power station to use nuclear fuel began to operate at Calder Hall in Cumberland in 1956. Science has thus presented man with the power either of total self-destruction or of the control of his environment to a degree never before imagined.

Astronomy

The success of the physicists in unravelling the mysteries of atoms and electrons, the most minute forms of matter, has been rivalled by that of the astronomers in explaining the nature of the universe and charting events occurring in incredibly distant galaxies. Various facts that would not fit in with Newton's laws

Theory of relativity, 1905

were satisfactorily resolved by Einstein's theory of relativity, which, through its manifold applications, offers the prospect that the phenomena of light, electromagnetism, gravitation and the atom may all be explained by one system of laws.

The British contribution to science has been maintained during the twentieth century. At Jodrell Bank in Cheshire, for example, has been constructed the world's largest radio telescope, which has penetrated much farther into space than any visual telescope can do, and has been the most potent instrument ever made for solving the riddles of the universe. British scientists have also

Molecular biology

been prominent in the new field of molecular biology, which investigates the behaviour of bacteria and of the cells of the human body, and particularly the chemical basis of heredity.[1] Its discoveries may promote the cure of diseases so far unconquered, and may enable man not only to solve the mystery of life's origins, but to control the evolution of the race by determining

[1] F. Crick and M. Wilkins shared a Nobel Prize for work in this field in 1962.

the characteristics of future generations. As the men of the twentieth century not only transform their earthly environment, but hurtle through space in rocket-propelled capsules, harness the fearful power of the atom, and probe the secrets of their own bodies and minds, they may well crave the wisdom to use their knowledge aright.

24. The Development of Communications

1 Turnpikes and Coaches

The old roads Until the latter part of the eighteenth century the sole means by which passengers or goods could be carried any considerable distance overland was on horseback, or in a horse-drawn vehicle. Since the roads were chiefly distinguished by enormous pot-holes, ruts two feet deep in summer and almost impassable mud in winter, such travel was neither speedy, nor safe, nor comfortable.

The need for improvement The state of the roads did not matter so much when towns and villages were largely self-sufficient. With the growth of trade and industry in the eighteenth century, however, better transport facilities became essential. Equally, an improvement in communications would in turn lead to a still further growth of trade.

Hindrances to progress For a long while no progress was made, partly because no satisfactory method of financing road construction was hit upon, partly because the science of road building was forgotten. In general, each parish was supposed to maintain the roads within its own boundaries, but this naturally led to very little being done; for the local inhabitants would see no point either in working themselves, or in engaging qualified engineers at great expense, to construct a fine stretch of highway through their parish merely for the pleasure of watching coaches dash along it on the way to London. The eighteenth-century solution to this difficulty was the widespread extension of a development which first appeared in 1663—the Turnpike Trust, a board of gentlemen who secured permission from Parliament to build a road and levy tolls for its use.

The Turnpike Trusts The turnpike system had certain disadvantages, including the wrath of the local populace at having to pay for taking their carts along routes they had used freely for generations. This indignation usually expressed itself in acts of rustic simplicity, such as battering down the toll gates at night, or murdering the gatekeeper. Often, however, the Turnpike Trust produced great improvements, because the Trustees were in a position, if they

336

cared, to employ engineers skilled in road construction. Certainly skilled engineers were needed, for no new hard roads had been built since the days of the Roman occupation.

A few details of the work of two of the road-makers employed by the Turnpike Trusts in the late eighteenth century will illustrate the progress that was made. Thomas Telford, the son of a Scottish shepherd, though of humble birth, was a natural genius. Trained as a stone-mason, he became the public surveyor of Shropshire, in which position he showed great skill in building roads and bridges. This led to work in opening up the wild countryside of Scotland, where he built some twelve hundred bridges and nearly a thousand miles of good road. He also transformed the London–Holyhead road, amalgamating various Turnpike Trusts, improving the Welsh section out of all recognition, and crowning his work by the elegant suspension bridge over the Menai Straits. His road-making methods included a hard foundation, a camber and an adequate system of drainage to the sides. Thomas Telford, 1757–1834

An equally great road-maker was John McAdam, a Scottish gentleman whose work in the Bristol area first earned him fame. He built up his roads to a good surface by means of successive layers of broken stones, each composed of smaller stones than the one beneath, and pressed down by the passing traffic—the origin of the word 'macadamized'. John McAdam, 1756–1836

The work of these two men, and of the many others engaged on the same task, was such that by 1830 the country boasted some 22,000 miles of good hard road, whereas a hundred years before there had been almost none. Along these roads there now proceeded reasonably regular and reliable services of coaches and waggons. In 1730 there were few roads on which a coach could travel at four miles an hour, and the quickest method of transport, apart from on horseback, was on foot. Yet by 1784 it was possible to begin the carriage of mail by coach, and before the end of the century nearly four hundred towns were getting a daily post, brought by coaches travelling at an average speed of six miles an hour. By 1830 average speed had increased to nine miles an hour. Mail-coaches

The effect of the new roads can be seen in the times taken for the same journey at different dates. In 1754 a coach journey from Edinburgh to London lasted from eight to ten days; in 1836 it took about forty-five hours. From Manchester to London at the earlier date occupied three days of a traveller's time; in 1836 he could reach the capital in nineteen hours.

Travelling by coach, however, never became either cheap or

comfortable. At the beginning of the nineteenth century the fare on the mail-coach from Edinburgh to London was 3d.–5d. a mile outside, according to the seat occupied, and 5d.–10d. a mile inside. The degree of comfort can best be gauged from some of the descriptions of coach travel in the novels of Charles Dickens and George Eliot. When the railways in the 1830s revealed their wonderful possibilities of speedy, cheap, safe and comfortable transport, it was only a matter of time before the coach was completely outmoded. Wherever the railways spread, the long-distance coach disappeared, though private and public horse carriages continued to serve local needs until the days of the motor-car.

The effect of the railways

2 Canals

The second half of the eighteenth century saw the development not only of the roads, but of an alternative for goods transport in the form of the canals.

Abroad several countries already possessed good canal systems, but in Britain even the main rivers had been so neglected that they were usually navigable for only a few miles from the mouth. The first essential was thus to improve the rivers, which involved cutting fresh channels and making short cuts across wide loops. From this to canal construction in general was an easy and inevitable step.

The first modern canal in Great Britain was built in 1751 by developing an existing stream, the Sankey Brook, between St Helens and Warrington. The most spectacular of the early canals, however, was the 'Bridgewater' Canal between Worsley and Manchester, opened in 1761. The Duke of Bridgewater, owner of the Worsley collieries, was anxious to cut the very high cost of road transport to Manchester, some seven or eight miles away. He employed James Brindley, a Derbyshire millwright of little education but great natural and mechanical genius, to cut a canal. The job was formidable, since it had to begin inside a hill at Worsley, near the coal seams, and traverse the River Irwell and a large bog before it could reach Manchester. These difficulties Brindley overcame triumphantly, taking the canal over the marshes by means of embankments, and over the Irwell by means of a great aqueduct at Barton. The result was the reduction of transport costs to such a point that the price of coal in Manchester was halved.

The Bridgewater Canal, 1761

James Brindley

The success of this great venture encouraged further construction. In 1766, the Duke and his engineer joined a project to link the Mersey with the Trent, a scheme already promoted by other industrialists and landowners. Among these was Josiah Wedgwood, the great Staffordshire potter, who was anxious to secure coal from the north cheaply and at the same time to open up a

(*G. Swertner, from Aiken's 'Description of the Country Round Manchester'*)

BARTON BRIDGE IN 1795

The Bridgewater Canal at Barton, Lancashire, at the point where it crosses the River Irwell.

smoother means of transport for his fragile wares than that afforded by eighteenth-century roads.

The 'Grand Trunk' Canal, as it came to be called, between Mersey and Trent, was finished in 1777, some years after Brindley's death. The engineering problem to be solved with the limited equipment of the times included five tunnels through hills and five aqueducts. Harecastle Hill was the worst obstacle, involving an ascent of 395 feet by a series of thirty-five locks, a

The Grand Trunk Canal, 1777

tunnel of $1\frac{3}{4}$ miles and a further series of forty locks to accomplish the descent of 288 feet the other side. Tunnels through hills of this nature frequently had no towpath and were so low that the bargee had to win through to the other end by lying on his back and pushing with his feet against the roof. But all difficulties of this kind were overcome, and water transport between the great centres of Lancashire and the Midlands was finally available at a quarter the cost of road transport. Some of the industries which particularly benefited as a result, gaining a national market and a national reputation, were Lancashire textiles, Midland hardware, Staffordshire potteries and Burton beers.

Other ambitious projects followed, until by 1820 the country possessed a great network of canals covering the majority of the

Other canals main trade centres. The Grand Junction Canal (linking the Thames with the Trent) and the Leeds–Liverpool Canal were two routes of particular importance. Another great canal, the Caledonian, constructed under Telford's direction between 1804 and 1822, was built with a strategical purpose as well as an economic: it was wide enough to take the warships of the time, which could thus be transferred rapidly between east and west coasts without sailing round the north of Scotland.

Canal-mania' The genuine need for these canals, and their great commercial success, unfortunately caused a wave of speculation. Prices of canal-shares soared, and the 1790s witnessed a bout of 'canal-mania'. In 1792, for instance, a £100 share in the Birmingham–Fazeley Canal sold for no less than £1,170. This sort of atmosphere encouraged promoters to put up schemes for the construction of canals from anywhere to anywhere regardless of economic justification. Much wasteful construction and unsound finance thus marked the canal era, and these proved an additional handicap when the canals had to meet the competition of the railways.

The effect of the railways The birth of the railways marked the end of canal construction in Great Britain, except for the great Manchester Ship Canal (1894), a different type of venture. Big superiority in speed was naturally the main reason for the rapid victory of the railways. One has only to think of Harecastle Hill, with its seventy-five locks, to realize how slow canal transport could be. The average speed of goods transport on canals was about three miles per hour; the average speed on the railways in the mid-nineteenth century was not much below that of today.

Outdated by the railways, the canals languished yet further

when bought up by railway companies which merely intended to neglect them. Nevertheless they have still a useful part to play in our national transport system—besides affording much innocent enjoyment to anglers of all ages.

3 Railways

Both the main elements in railway development—the rails and the locomotives—originated in collieries.

Railroads and locomotives in collieries

By the beginning of the seventeenth century wooden rails along which animals drew trucks were in use in a few collieries, and from these to iron-plated or iron rails was a natural step. Outside the collieries, railroads were also built from time to time, either to link up stretches of canal, or, as in the case of the Surrey railroad (1804), to provide a passage for the usual horse-drawn public waggons. The rails used in all these early systems were flanged.

The second main element in railway development, the steam locomotive, was an application of Watt's steam-engine. The first locomotive, 'Uncle Dick's Puffer', was constructed by Richard Trevithick in 1804. Its possibilities for use in collieries, where the roads and the coal were to hand, were obvious, and by 1820 the use of locomotives in connection with coal-mining was not uncommon. The best remembered include Blackett's 'Puffing Billy' (now in the Science Museum, South Kensington) and George Stephenson's 'Blücher'.

The first public railway on which steam locomotives were used was that between Stockton and Darlington, opened in 1825.[1] The locomotives, however, did not run over the whole of its length. One extremity of the route, where there was a deep ravine, was covered by means of stationary engines and ropes; and over the rest of the route for many years horses supplied an additional means of traction.

The Stockton-Darlington Railway, 1825

Though the opening of the Stockton and Darlington Railway marked the beginning of a new epoch, it was not until 1830, when the Liverpool and Manchester Railway was opened, that the full possibilites of the new means of transport became widely appreciated. Public attention had been attracted by a competition for

The Liverpool-Manchester Railway, 1830

[1] The first public line opened in Scotland was the Monkland and Kirkintilloch Railway, 1826, with steam and horse traction; in Ireland, the Dublin to Kingstown Railway, 1834.

M.B.—M

locomotives held at Rainhill,[1] and by Stephenson's boldness in taking the track over the treacherous bog of Chat Moss; and it was attracted still more when Huskisson was knocked down by a passing locomotive at the opening ceremony. Even this, however, only served to demonstrate the powers of Stephenson's engine, for the fatally injured statesman was rushed to Eccles Hospital at a speed of forty miles per hour.

Other railways Within a very short time the success of the Liverpool and Manchester Railway led to the growth of tracks all over the country. In 1833 the Great Western Railway was begun, built to a broad gauge of 7 feet o¼ inch by the great engineer I. K. Brunel. Eight years later through trains were running between London and Bristol. Men of enterprise now hastened to plan lines for their own localities, so that very soon over a thousand companies were operating stretches of one length or another. Co-ordination in laying tracks and running trains, however, was very difficult to achieve with so many authorities, and the long-distance passenger was expected to exhibit all those qualities of strength and endurance which were so marked, and apparently so much needed, in the Victorian era.

Amalgamations of the 1840s With the growth of the railways in the 1840s, amalgamation of companies became common. Though it was usually undertaken entirely from financial motives, and though it led to an outbreak of 'railway-mania' in 1846 comparable with the earlier 'canal-mania', on the whole it served the national interest—for Parliament safeguarded the public by controlling rates and fares. Well-known companies formed by amalgamation in the 1840s included the Midland, the London and North-Western, the London Brighton and South Coast, and the Lancashire and Yorkshire Railways. Best known of all 'amalgamators' was George Hudson, 'the Railway King', a linen draper who took to railway finance in a big way, built up the Midland Railway, and tried—unsuccessfully —to monopolize traffic between London and the north.

Route mileage The growth of British railways may be seen in the figures for mileage of route. In 1830 there were but 69 miles in the country; by 1840, 1,857 miles; by 1850, 6,621 miles; by 1860, 10,433 miles; and by 1870, 15,557 miles. After this, development was slower, and never again were 5,000 miles of route opened in ten years.

The growth of the railways was more than a matter of laying

[1] This was won by Stephenson's 'Rocket', which is also in the Science Museum, South Kensington.

down fresh stretches of track. Important technical developments were constantly occurring. In the interests of safety and punctuality a more efficient method of signalling was required than relays of men placed along the line to wave flags by day, flash lamps by night, or shout in fog; it was supplied by the develop- *Technical improvements*

(Leech, 1845, reproduced by permission of the Proprietors of 'Punch')

THE RAILWAY JUGGERNAUT OF 1845

'Railway-mania.' Indian religious fanatics sacrifice themselves beneath the wheels of the Juggernaut; British investors sacrifice their fortunes in buying railway shares at inflated figures.

ment in the 1840s of the wooden 'semaphore', or signal-post, and the electric telegraph. Nor was increase in comfort neglected; the open or semi-open carriages were gradually abandoned, and in the latter part of the century refinements such as corridor-coaches, sleeping-coaches, complete corridor trains and dining-cars began to appear.[1]

[1] The accident rate in 1962 was one for every 50 million passengers carried.

'Standard gauge'   Further simplification of the railway system was also achieved, though more slowly than in the 1840s. After a prolonged 'battle of the gauges', the Great Western finally decided to abandon Brunel's specification, and by 1892 the last of the broad-gauge

The amalgamations of 1921–1922   track was replaced by 'standard' gauge. Then in 1921–22 followed a fresh series of amalgamations, from which emerged the L.M.S., the L.N.E.R., the G.W.R. and the Southern Railway.

Underground railways and electrification   Towards the end of the nineteenth century came the growth of underground railways and electrification. The first railway to run underground for any part of its length in a city was the Metropolitan (1863). The first deep 'tube' in London opened in 1884—a very smoky affair, for steam engines were used. Six years later the first electric 'tube' opened—the City and South London Railway. After this, fresh lines were rapidly developed. London and Glasgow are as yet the only British cities to boast underground railway systems, though Liverpool has a line beneath the Mersey. The Southern Railway pioneered main-line electrification, and its lead is now being followed by the Midland and Eastern Regions.

Nationalization   The railways were nationalized in 1948, and are now the property of the State. During the 1950s they operated 19,000 miles of route (51,000 miles of single track including sidings) and employed over 600,000 people. With the growing use of road transport, however, traffic was steadily reduced, until in 1962 the railways were making a loss of £87 million a year. A drastic

The Beeching Plan, 1963   reorganization was therefore planned; it was realized that the railways must specialize in freight traffic, long-distance passenger runs, and the daily movement of commuters. While a large investment was to be made in improving the capacity of the railway to deal with suitable traffic, it was proposed to close 5,000 route-miles of unprofitable lines and 2,363 stations—a measure which would remove a familiar and not unloved feature from large regions of the British countryside

4 Modern Roads and Motor-Cars

As the network of railways spread over the countryside the old coaching trade died away, and the roads fell once again into neglect. The Turnpike Companies ceased to pay, the roads were 'de-turnpiked', and the parishes to whose care they reverted spent little on them. Yet before very long Britain was again in need of an efficient road system, as the motor-car developed from a perilous sporting luxury into a perilous unsporting necessity.

At the beginning of the nineteenth century some effort had been made to run steam-cars on the public highways, but the development of such vehicles had been limited by their weight, the damage they did to road surfaces, and the high tolls that Turnpike Companies naturally exacted from them. Railways thus seemed, on the whole, a much better idea; and the railway companies, who thought this very strongly, acted in combination with popular concern for the safety of life and limb to secure the passage in 1865 of a law designed to make the use of steam-cars almost impossible. This laid down that a mechanically propelled vehicle must not travel at more than five miles an hour on roads in the country, or two miles an hour in the towns; while each vehicle had to be attended by three men, one of whom was to precede it on foot bearing a red flag. No more successful regulation could have been devised to limit speed. The steam-car thus faded from the English countryside, to pursue a more fruitful development in India, where life, it seemed, was less precious.

Steam-cars

The 'Red Flag' Act, 1865

If the steam-car came to little, a very different result attended the birth of the motor-car. In 1884 the German, Gottlieb Daimler, applied an internal combustion petrol engine to wheels, with consequences that within fifty years transformed social life. At first, because of the restrictive laws in Britain, the development of the motor-car was pursued largely by the Germans and the French, and it was not until 1895 that the first specimen appeared on the British side of the Channel. The following year, by a 'Locomotives' Act, the 'red flag' restriction was withdrawn, and a speed limit of twelve miles an hour substituted—an event which was celebrated by a special 'emancipation run' from London to Brighton.[1] Progress was now possible, and the manufacture of cars began in England—the Lanchester being the first. Though Britain's contribution towards the initial development of the motor-car was thus small, she had earlier been responsible for a great invention without which it would be difficult to think of motor-cars—John Boyd Dunlop's pneumatic tyre (1888).

The 'Locomotives Act, 1896 (12 m.p.h.)

The first decade of the new century saw great improvements

[1] The anniversary of this event is still celebrated by a vintage car run from London to Brighton.

The Motor-Car
Act, 1903
(20 m.p.h.)

Taxation
in reliability and speed, the development of public motor transport,[1] the raising of the speed limit to twenty miles an hour, and
the compulsory registration and licensing of cars. In 1910 motor
taxation was first imposed, and, like most other taxation, it has
not grown less with the passage of the years. In 1920 a 'Road
Fund' was created, into which motor taxation was paid (at first
wholly, later only in part), so that the newly created Ministry of
Transport could make grants to County and Borough Councils
for road-building. By the County Councils Act of 1888, the
Councils had taken over responsibility for roads from the
parishes.

The First World War gave a great impetus to the progress of
motor transport, and with the return of peace in 1919 a vast
growth in private motoring was bound to occur. The popular
need was met, and in turn stimulated, by the development of
Mass motoring mass-produced cars, cheap, comfortable and reliable. The pioneer
of mass production in motor-cars was Henry Ford of Detroit; in
England his most successful emulator was W. R. Morris,[2] who
soon became the richest man in the country.

The growth of motoring and motor transport, together with
the growing popularity, from the 1880s onwards, of that very
important invention the 'safety' bicycle, made a great expansion
of the British road system essential. It also brought about a
demand for the abolition of the long-disregarded speed limit of
The Road
Traffic Act, 1930
(abolition of
speed limit) twenty miles an hour, and in 1930 the Road Traffic Act abolished
the general speed limit. But the number of people injured on the
roads, already large, mounted steadily, and before long a restriction to thirty miles an hour in 'built-up areas' was imposed. By
1936 something like £60 million was being spent annually on the
roads, and this sum steadily increased. In 1959 the first of a
system of motorways, to cost £147 million in four years, was
opened.

But despite road improvements the slaughter on the roads goes
on. In a normal year it now amounts to over 6,500 persons killed
and nearly 350,000 injured. Alarmingly enough, road transport
has not yet reached its peak. Its possibilities for the future may be
realized from its growth in the past. In 1895 there was one motor
vehicle in this country; in 1939, nearly three million; in 1962

[1] In 1906 the company controlling the largest number of horse-buses
in the country, the London General Omnibus Company, decided to spend
£1,000,000 on motor-buses.
[2] W. R. Morris was created Lord Nuffield in 1934, after unparalleled
benefactions to charitable, educational, medical and welfare purposes.

10 million. It does not need a very vivid imagination to picture what vast changes this development has brought in its train, how greatly it has standardized the pattern of life throughout the country, and what immense problems of traffic control and town planning it will pose in the future.

5 Shipping

Just as the growth of internal trade was partly the cause, partly the result of roads, canals and railways, so the growth of external trade was bound up with the development of shipping.

From the fifteenth century onwards there had been steady progress in shipping and overseas trade, and the great Tudor seamen —traders all—opened up many new markets. The acquisition of colonies in the seventeenth century was a further stimulus, while English shipping was carefully fostered by the Navigation Acts. In the early eighteenth century, the compulsory registration of vessels, the growth of marine insurance at Lloyd's, and the invention of the sextant and the chronometer, all helped to establish a regular shipping industry. *Early progress*

Much more was needed, however, before British shipping could carry the volume of trade made possible by the Industrial Revolution. Apart from the defects of the ships themselves, there were no proper facilities either for loading and unloading, or for ensuring safety at sea. Fortunately, the development of the steam-engine made excavation an easier job, and after a great spell of activity in London in the early nineteenth century British docking facilities gradually became more adequate. The first half of the nineteenth century also saw the construction of many more lighthouses and the development of a regular lifeboat organization; other important steps towards greater safety, such as the Plimsoll Line, followed later.[1] At the same time British shipbuilders were spurred to improve on their traditional models by increased foreign competition, particularly when the monopolies of the East India Company were thrown open and the old Navigation Laws were repealed. *Docking and safety facilities*

The broad development of shipbuilding may be seen from the fact that in 1800 the world depended on wooden sailing vessels and in 1900 on steel steamers. The change, however, was not as

[1] See pages 191–2.

simple or as direct as this comparison suggests, since the period witnessed not only the birth of the steam-boat but also the transformation of the sailing vessel.

The development of sailing vessels

Sailing vessels of the latter part of the eighteenth century were small and bulky; 1,500 tons at the largest, their length was only four times their breadth. They were extremely heavy, for their wooden walls were some two feet thick, and they often carried a large armament to cope with pirates and privateers, or hostile warships. In consequence, they were also extremely slow—even a good 'East Indiaman' would average only fifty miles a day—as well as uncomfortable and unhealthy. Soon after the turn of the century, however, the United States began to build sailing ships of much greater length in proportion to breadth. The speed of these vessels threatened to put British shipbuilders out of business, and from about 1850 onwards American ideas were adopted in Britain.

Since iron hulls had by now proved a success for steamers, British sailing vessels of this period were usually built of iron, or were of composite construction. The fastest type, the clipper,

Clippers

was first introduced by the Americans in the 1840s, and a few years later was copied in England. It was used especially to race the new season's tea crop home from China—once in as little as ninety-one days.

The development of steamships

All the progress in sailing ships, however, could not stay the triumphant course of steam. The first successful use of the steam-engine adapted to drive a vessel was in 1802, when a tug named the *Charlotte Dundas* ran on the Forth and Clyde Canal. The next advance was made in the United States, where paddle-steamers were built for the rivers and lakes; and it was in imitation of these that Henry Bell built his *Comet* in 1812. It carried passengers in the mouth of the Clyde. Other paddle-steamers quickly followed; a cross-Channel service was started in 1816, and in 1819 an auxiliary steam-engine helped a sailing vessel to cross the Atlantic.

Iron vessels

By now iron barges had been successfully constructed, and in 1825 an iron paddle-steamer was to be seen on the Shannon Then—in spite of the disbelievers—came iron steamships for ocean journeys. In 1838 two iron paddle-steamers, the *Sirius* and Brunel's *Great Western*—both carrying auxiliary sail—made passages to New York in less than eighteen days.

From this point onwards the final victory clearly lay with steam, in spite of the sailing developments of 1840 to 1860. The great advantage of steam was its certainty, for though a sailing vessel might on occasion prove quicker than a steamship, it was much more likely to lose days of precious time by lying becalmed or having to run before storms. At first steamship travel was more expensive, but costs were gradually reduced by various inventions which economized fuel. In 1839 the first screw-steamer demonstrated that it was much more efficient than the paddle-steamer for ocean voyages, where deep troughs were liable to find the paddles beating the air instead of the water. Double and multiple screws followed in course of time. Even more important was the invention of the expansion engine in 1854 by John Elder. *The expansion engine* This incorporated a second and larger cylinder, which was filled and had its piston driven by the expansion of steam which had passed through the first and smaller cylinder at high pressure. By 1874 the expansion principle was still further developed, when it was found that a third engine could be worked by the same steam. The economy in fuel achieved by these inventions meant a double decrease in rates for freight and passengers, for not only was the ship's fuel bill less costly, but much of the storage space previously devoted to fuel could now be occupied by valuable cargo.

Thus it came about that steam superseded sail, just as iron, *The triumph of* and later, steel, superseded wood. By 1870, 75 per cent of British *steam* tonnage was steam-driven, and 83 per cent was constructed of iron—a proportion far in advance of other mercantile marines.

There were, of course, many other important features of *Other developments* Britain's shipping progress in the nineteenth century. Great shipping lines, such as the Cunard, began to spring up in the 1840s. Technical inventions proceeded rapidly, and specialized ships developed—tankers, ice-breakers, refrigerator-ships, steam-trawlers, train-ferries and so on. In 1897 the first marine turbine *Turbines* opened up new possibilities of speed and comfort. Electric and motor ships developed, while oil superseded coal whenever speed and rapidity of refuelling were essential.[1] In 1945 about a third of British mercantile tonnage burned oil. *Oil-fuelling*

The extent of all these developments may be summed up in a few statistics. In regard to size, the largest British merchant vessel in 1800 was about 1,500 tons, in 1939, 85,000 tons—though most cargo-boats are still less than 6,000 tons. In regard to speed, the

---

[1] These qualities are so essential for naval vessels that just before the First World War it was decided to adopt oil as the general fuel throughout the British Navy, though there was coal at home and oil had to be imported.

record crossing of the Atlantic came down from fourteen days in 1840 to the *Queen Mary*'s three days twenty-one hours in 1938. In regard to volume of shipping, the ocean tonnages cleared in British ports rose from 700,000 tons in 1770 to 92,000,000 in 1938[1]—a figure which by itself indicates how much Britain came to depend on overseas trade for her very existence.

6 Air Transport

Though the idea of travelling through the air has a very long history behind it, the translation of the idea into practical achievement was delayed for many centuries.

Balloons

The conquest of the air really began in 1783, when a balloon constructed by the brothers Montgolfier made its first voyage. Balloons, however, were too much at the mercy of the elements to have any value for transport purposes. The logical development was, of course, a 'balloon' with an engine, and much progress was made with airships from 1900 onwards. Both sides used them during the First World War, and in 1919 the British R34 crossed the Atlantic in both directions. But a series of disasters then occurred, and after the loss of the R101 in 1930 no further airships were built in Great Britain.

Airships

Aeroplanes

Regular controlled flight was the achievement of 'heavier-than-air' machines. The steam-engines on which these at first relied for power were too heavy, but in the last decade of the nineteenth century the way to success was opened up through the development of the petrol-engine and the study of gliding. In 1903 the Americans Wilbur and Orville Wright made the first flights in a heavier-than-air machine—driven by a petrol-engine of twelve horsepower. The longest flight was only of fifty-nine seconds' duration, and covered barely half a mile, but, in Orville Wright's words, 'the age of the flying machine had come at last'.

The first aero-
plane flight, 1903

At first Britain was slow to realize the significance of the Wrights' achievement, and it was not till five years later that S. F. Cody made the first power-driven flight in England—remaining airborne for half-an-hour at Farnborough. Public interest was then stimulated by the *Daily Mail* prizes—though the £1,000 offered in 1909 for the first flight across the Channel, and the £10,000 offered in 1910 for the fastest time from London to

[1] Some 62,000,000 tons of coastwise traffic also departed from British ports in 1938.

Manchester, were both carried off by Frenchmen—Blériot and Paulhan respectively.

By 1911 aviation in England was ceasing to be purely the sport of wealthy or eccentric individuals, and a recognized industry was developing. Moreover, its use for military and naval purposes was apparent, and in 1912 the Royal Flying Corps was formed. The Naval Wing of this soon separated off as the Royal Naval Air Service, and when war came in 1914 aeroplanes, seaplanes and airships all participated from the start. *The R.F.C. and R.N.A.S.*

The First World War promoted a hothouse growth in aviation. Though aircraft were at first used mainly for reconnaissance, specialist types soon developed for fighting and bombing. Performances leapt ahead—a BE2 of 1914 was capable of only 80 miles an hour, with a ceiling of 8,000 feet, but the DH9A of 1918 could travel nearly three times as fast and climb nearly four times as high—and by the end of the war the Royal Air Force, formed by the amalgamation of the Royal Flying Corps and the Royal Naval Air Service, had on charge over 20,000 aeroplanes. *The First World War*

The first regular daily passenger air service in the world— from London to Paris—began in 1919. This and other pioneer ventures achieved a very high degree of reliability, and the seventeen forced landings reputedly made by one pilot between London and Paris on a single trip were not at all representative of normal standards. But fares were very dear and foreign competitors, heavily subsidized by their governments, soon captured the 'market'. In 1923 the Government therefore decided to form and subsidize a single privileged organization, strong enough to withstand foreign competition and to operate imperial as well as European air routes. It was thus that Imperial Airways Limited came into being. *Air services between the wars*

During its fifteen years of existence (1924–39) Imperial Airways did magnificent work in opening up the British Commonwealth. It derived more than purely financial benefit from its close association with the Government, for the R.A.F. frequently 'blazed the trail' over routes which the company then developed and operated. The great imperial routes developed before 1939 were England–Iraq–India–Siam–Malaya–Australia, with a branch line from Bangkok to Hong Kong; and England–Egypt–South Africa, with a branch line across Africa from Khartoum to Lagos. An experimental trans-Atlantic air mail service was also begun just before the war. *Imperial Airways*

The most important single step in the years between the wars

The Empire Air Mail Scheme

was the introduction of the Empire Air Mail Scheme, by which letters were carried at ordinary rates of postage wherever air services linked the Commonwealth. To cope with the new commitment, an entirely new fleet of aircraft was ordered—flying-boats—and by 1938 the scheme was operating over the great trunk routes. At the same time it became the practice also to fly mail to European countries without additional charges.

Technical progress

By 1939 Imperial Airways, which had inherited only 2,000 miles of air route, was operating over 25,000 miles of imperial route alone. Great technical developments in aircraft, represented by the monoplane, metal construction, flaps, the retractable undercarriage, better heating and de-icing apparatus had been incorporated; while on the ground, radio direction-finding stations had been established, and much progress had been made in the organization of airfields and flying control systems. Nevertheless, compared with the Americans Imperial Airways was behind in some respects, such as speed and beam-navigation.

In 1938 the Government decided to merge Imperial Airways with British Airways, a competitor which had grown up by concentrating on European routes. At the outbreak of war aircraft from both companies were placed at the disposal of the Air Ministry, and very soon afterwards the official 'merger' into the

B.O.A.C.

British Overseas Airways Corporation took place.

In spite of all the progress made, the British public between the World Wars much preferred reading about fresh aviation records to indulging in actual travel by aircraft. Of great individual feats there was no lack—feats which had far greater value than that of

The first non-stop Atlantic flight, 1919

merely setting up a fresh sporting record. Thus Alcock and Brown's flight across the North Atlantic in 1919 in a Vickers Vimy bomber[1] opened up possibilities which few till that date had ever contemplated. Successive efforts, usually by R.A.F. personnel but often by private individuals like Sir Alan Cobham or Amy Johnson, established new records, or covered fresh routes.

The Schneider Trophy

The Schneider Trophy for seaplanes was finally won outright by Britain in 1931 at 340 miles per hour, and a member of the winning team a few days later broke the world's speed record at that time by flying at 407·5 miles per hour.[2] It is worth remarking that the descent of the Supermarine Spitfire and the Rolls-Royce

---

[1] The passage was made from St John's, Newfoundland, to Clifden, Co. Galway, in 15 hours 57 minutes at an average speed of 118 m.p.h.
[2] In 1962 it was raised to 1,606 m.p.h.

Merlin engine which saved Britain in 1940 can be traced from the S.6B which won the Schneider Trophy in 1931.

The Second World War again stimulated an enormous development in aviation and the aircraft industry. On the transport side, a routine service was established across both North and South Atlantic, so that it is now possible for a man who has breakfasted in Canada to enjoy a late lunch in Scotland. Australia was brought to within two days' flying distance from the Mother Country. A great route along the entire north coast of Africa was operated with the regularity of a country bus service. Districts far from any recognized transport route, in Africa, in the Middle East, in Burma and South-East Asia, were linked by aircraft carrying vital stores and munitions. Whole armies were landed behind enemy lines, food was dropped for starving populations and arms for resistance leaders, wounded men and prisoners were evacuated—all by air. *Air transport in the Second World War*

All this wartime experience proved invaluable for the development of air transport when peace returned. In particular the new radar navigational aids ensured still higher standards of safety and regularity. The invention of the jet engine by Frank Whittle made possible great increases in speed.[1] Under the pattern established in 1949 by which all British scheduled routes were to be run by two state corporations (British Overseas Airways Corporation and British European Airways) while private firms were confined to charter or taxi traffic, civil aviation expanded prodigiously. In 1937 the main British air lines had between them flown some 28 million passenger-miles; in 1963 the corresponding total was 4,876 million. With amazing rapidity, passenger travel to distant parts became the province of the aeroplane, and long voyages by sea took on the character of a luxury. *Expansion of civil aviation*

7 Telecommunications

Man has always been able to communicate across space faster than he can travel—even if only by shouting. At various times such means of communication have included drums, bells, beacons, smoke-signals, heliographs, flags and pigeons. During the nineteenth century the process of signalling across space was revolutionized by a number of developments connected with

[1] Another British invention, C. S. Cockerell's hovercraft (1959), could be adapted to numerous purposes impossible for orthodox aircraft.

electricity, with consequences which have transformed the modern world.

At the end of the eighteenth century the most advanced form of telecommunication[1] in England was the newly-installed Admiralty signalling-system between London and certain naval ports— Portsmouth, Plymouth, Deal and Yarmouth. Frames each containing six movable shutters were erected at high points along the route, and by turning a given number of the shutters in one direction or the other the operator could make any one of sixty-four different signals. In clear weather it worked very well— the noon-time signal was usually passed to Portsmouth, and acknowledged, within thirty seconds—but its scope was strictly limited, and in fog it was entirely useless. The device was supplemented in the early nineteenth century by the contemporary French system of the semaphore, or signal-post with movable arms, which could indicate different letters of the alphabet.

Electric signals had been sent along wire by various experimenters ever since the early eighteenth century, but it was not until the development of a reliable power unit in the form of the Daniell cell (1836) that electric signalling became commercially practicable. In 1837 two British scientists, Sir Charles Wheatstone and Sir William Cooke, invented the 'needle' telegraph, in which needles (at first five, later two) were deflected by electricity to point to the letters of the alphabet displayed on a board. This was first used on the railway between Euston and Camden Town, and was then installed by the Great Western between Paddington and Slough. Its most sensational triumph came in 1845, when a suspected murderer was seen to board a train at Slough. His description was instantly flashed to Paddington, and when the criminal stepped out of his compartment he found the police all ready to receive him. Electric telegraphs of this kind were soon widely adopted by the railways, where they quickly brought new standards of safety and punctuality.

The first public telegraph company—working in association with the railways—was formed in 1846. By 1851 a cross-Channel cable had been laid. In 1858 the first cable was laid across the Atlantic, but it was burnt out within a month—too great a potential difference had been used to drive the current. A replacement was not laid until 1866, when Brunel's *Great Eastern* triumphed over all difficulties. The invention of a more sensitive receiver— Lord Kelvin's 'siphon recorder'—then enabled lower power to

[1] tele = far.

be used, and cable communication across the Atlantic was thenceforth firmly established. Four years later the first cable from England to India was laid. Unlike the railway telegraph, these did not make use of the 'needle' device, but employed the more efficient system invented by the American Samuel Morse, including his code of dots and dashes. Morse

The numerous private telegraph companies for internal work were taken over by the Post Office in 1870. The Morse system has long since superseded the needle everywhere except on the railways, and in recent years technical efficiency has been greatly increased by inventions such as multiplex telegraphy, high-speed automatic transmission and the teleprinter. Post Office control

The electric telegraph was a great convenience to everyone, from Cabinet Ministers to weekend visitors, who wished to send a message in a hurry. Its general effect on business and social life was not, however, so important as that of the telephone, which was invented in 1875 by Alexander Graham Bell, an American of Scottish descent. The new instruments were soon introduced into England, and private companies began to supply services under licence from the Government. By 1891 the National Telephone Company had absorbed most of its rivals, but from then on the Post Office entered the field, and by 1912 it had taken over the whole of the company's business. At that time there were 700,000 telephones working. Since then the service has been greatly expanded, until there are now over eight million telephones in the Post Office system. The quality of reception has been radically improved, and many new developments, such as automatic exchanges of fantastic ingenuity, have been introduced. *The telephone, 1875 / Post Office control*

If the telegraph astonished our great-grandfathers, and the telephone our grandfathers, our fathers had even greater cause to wonder at the marvels of *wireless* telegraphy and telephony. Four main stages marked the early development of wireless. The possibility of transmitting electric signals over short distances without a wire was appreciated as early as 1850; much of the basic theory of wireless was predicated by Clerk Maxwell in 1867;[1] the German Hertz identified and measured wireless waves in 1888; and before the end of the century the Italian Marconi combined his own contributions with those of several others to bring the new discovery to a practical and commercial stage. Coming in 1896 to England (for the first obvious application would be to communicate with ships) Marconi demonstrated his *Wireless telegraphy in England, 1896*

[1] See page 332.

apparatus successfully on Salisbury Plain before representatives of the Navy, the Army and the Post Office. Communication was achieved over a distance of $1\frac{3}{4}$ miles. Three years later, at the naval manœuvres, two warships 85 miles apart exchanged messages. In 1901 Marconi, at a reception station in Newfoundland, heard the first faint message—the letter S (. . .) several times repeated—flashed across the Atlantic from Cornwall. The age of wireless had arrived.

Public control over the new discovery was soon established by the Wireless Telegraphy Act of 1904, which stated that the installation and working of wireless in Great Britain might only be done under licence from the Postmaster-General. In the same year the possibilities of wireless were greatly increased by Professor J. A. Fleming's invention of the thermionic valve, though other detectors, such as crystals, continued in use. Very soon Marconi's own company established a chain of coastal stations for communication with ships, and in 1909 some of these were taken over by the Post Office. A great network of imperial communication, already **Wireless in the** planned before 1914, was held up by the First World War, **First World** which nevertheless fostered important developments, such as air-**War** to-ground communication and direction-finding stations to locate enemy aircraft and warships from their transmissions.

Imperial wireless In 1919 the idea of an imperial wireless service was taken up **communication** again, but while the first stations were in the course of construction scientists of Marconi's company perfected a vastly superior method of transmission for the purpose. They discovered the astonishing properties of short waves (previously regarded as unsuitable for long-distance work) in conjunction with transmission focused in a certain direction (as opposed to 'floodlighting' the **The 'beam'** whole sky). This new 'beam' system gave far greater ranges with **system** the use of far lower power, and by 1927 'beam' services were working from England to Canada, South Africa and India. They were soon so successful that they threatened to put ordinary cable traffic out of business. But the cables, which give secrecy, are very important in time of war, so in 1929 the Government allowed the 'cable' interests to strengthen their positions by amalgamating with some of the imperial beam stations to form the company known as Cable & Wireless Ltd.[1] In addition to the 'beam stations', an enormous high-powered station was built at Rugby in the 1920s. Its transmissions can be received in any part of the world.

[1] This is now under state ownership. See page 299.

Wireless telegraphy brought untold benefits to shipping, revo- lutionized the conduct of war and linked up the most distant parts of the globe. Its cousin, radio-telephony, or the wireless transmission of speech, was soon to invade the home. Good results were achieved over short distances in 1913 by C. S. Franklin, but during the First World War the Government concentrated on the development of wireless telegraphy, which was then more advanced. Great progress was made in America, however, and by 1919 broadcast speech had been transmitted across the Atlantic. Then followed a welter of 'private' broadcasting until in 1922 all the main competing interests in Britain were merged into the British Broadcasting Company—later to become the British Broadcasting Corporation. The excitement with which its first programmes were picked up on home-made sets, the impatience to take one's turn at the headphones, the exasperation when the 'cat's whisker' found only a 'dud' spot on the crystal, were memorable experiences in most families. Since then broadcasting has become part of everyone's life, while other functions of radio-telephony—trans-Atlantic telephone communication, or the control of aircraft, for example—have become increasingly important.

Continuous visual telecommunication, in the form of radar and television, took practical shape during the 1930s. The first use of radar, where the greatest name was that of Sir J. Watson Watt, was in detecting aircraft from the ground, and from this many other applications were developed during the war. In television, a notable pioneer was J. L. Baird, though his system did not survive the early days. The B.B.C.'s television service was started in 1936, suspended during the war, and resumed in 1946, since when the B.B.C. and commercial television (introduced in 1954) have turned the British into a nation of viewers. How far this proves to be a benefit must depend on the quality of the programmes and the extent of the individual's addiction.

25. Industry and Trade, 1850-1964

1 Industrial and Commercial Expansion, 1850–1873

Industry in 1850 Despite the rapid progress made during the period of the Industrial Revolution, by modern standards industry in the mid-nineteenth century was still on a modest scale. The steel age had not yet begun, the network of railways was incomplete, and business concerns were usually in the hands of one master or a few partners. Working conditions were hard, and there was not yet such a plenty of goods that the poorer classes could enjoy any notable improvement in their standard of living.

The adoption of free trade Both the total and the distribution of the nation's wealth stood to benefit by a change in financial policy—the adoption of free trade. It was with the complete approval of British manufacturers that first Huskisson, then Peel, and finally Gladstone hacked away at the tangle of tariffs[1] until by 1860 duties on manufactures had disappeared, and the only customs charges were those on the widely consumed 'luxuries'—tea, spirits and tobacco—and these were retained solely to bring in revenue. Thus did Britain open her ports to the world's goods and proclaim her complete faith in the gospel of Cobden, Bright and the 'Manchester School' of economic thought, for whom Free Trade was the way not only to universal prosperity but also to the brotherhood of peoples and world peace.

The Great Exhibition, 1851 The most notable expression of this confident and optimistic doctrine was the Great Exhibition, conceived by the Prince Consort as a demonstration of what peace, progress and prosperity were doing for mankind. As the result of his tireless efforts, and after a long discussion of rival plans, a site in Hyde Park was chosen and a huge structure of iron and glass erected, so tall that lofty trees were enclosed within the building. The designer was Joseph Paxton, once an under-gardener on the Duke of Devonshire's estate, who had come to specialize in the

---

[1] See pages, 98–9, 129, 137, 157–8.

(Cruikshank, 1851, from a print in the British Museum)

A humorous tribute to the success of the Great Exhibition. London's Regent Circus (now Piccadilly Circus) and Piccadilly, leading to the site of the Exhibition in Hyde Park, are jammed tight; Manchester's main thoroughfare, Market Street, is utterly deserted.

construction of large conservatories. Here, in the Crystal Palace, as it was called, were gathered products of all kinds from the world over—raw materials, works of art, machinery. The six million visitors who toured the Exhibition saw ranged before them the amazing fruits of a new era of specialized production and world trade, in which Britain dwarfed all comers by virtue of her supremacy on the seas and her lead in invention. By the time the Crystal Palace was dismantled and removed to Sydenham for re-erection, the Great Exhibition had made a profit of £160,000, which was used to buy the land on which the South Kensington Museums and Colleges were built. The whole enterprise was a resounding success and a personal triumph for Prince Albert, in token of which his statue in Kensington Gardens shows him holding a catalogue of the Exhibition.

The Exhibition well represented the spirit of the age, with its belief in unceasing progress and boundless prosperity, but the biggest triumphs of invention and mechanization were still to come. It was the latter half of the century that witnessed the

Steel production first large-scale production of steel, the rise of really big industrial concerns and the final triumph of the factory system.

Most important, perhaps, was the change in the metal industries, which, unlike textiles, underwent what was almost a

Bessemer's converter, 1856 second revolution. This took place when Henry Bessemer solved the problem of producing steel in large quantities, for hitherto it had been made only in small clay crucibles. Bessemer's method was to blow air through a mass of molten iron contained in a huge vessel called a converter. The air burnt out the carbon and other impurities which are present in pig-iron (the product of the blast furnaces) and in cast-iron. If the process was carried to its conclusion the result was wrought-iron, in quantities that the old puddling process could never attempt, but if interrupted before all the carbon had been burnt out the process gave 'mild' steel.[1] It was successful, however, only with non-phosphoric iron ores.

Siemens's open-hearth process, 1866 Bessemer's method was in time largely replaced by William Siemens's process, in which much greater heat is obtained by making the outgoing gases pre-heat incoming gaseous fuel. Pig-iron is heated on the furnace bottom and kept in a molten state while all the processes of steel-making are performed.

A further stride was achieved when it was possible to use a Bessemer converter for iron-ore containing phosphorus. The necessary discovery was made by Sidney Thomas, a young

[1] Mild as distinguished from the hard steel used for tools.

London police-court clerk who used to carry out chemical experiments in his bedroom. After many attempts he found a type of brick for lining the converter which would absorb the phosphoric

Gilchrist-Thomas process, 1879

(Gustave Doré, 1872, from Blanchard Jerrold's 'London')

OVER LONDON BY RAIL

The rapid spread of grim, soulless houses, soon to become dreary slums, was one of the worst features of Victorian Britain. This engraving shows the view from an elevated stretch of railway in Central London, as seen by a French artist.

acid produced by combustion. By 1879 this process was tested by his cousin, P. C. Gilchrist, a works chemist, and its efficacy proved. The triumph of steel was now assured. Being more durable than iron, it supplanted the latter as the material for rails, boilers, bridges and ships. Machines of great accuracy were now used for a vast number of manufacturing processes, and machine-tool making became an important trade.

By 1870 the increased output of steel, the continued growth

of the factory system, the building of large cargo steamers, the first railway line across the American continent and the laying of ocean cables had all helped to link the countries of the world **Expansion of** and to expand their trade to a scale which made the achievements **trade** of 1850 look puny. Britain was still well in the lead as an industrial and commercial power, and the trade of the British Empire was greater than that of France, Germany, Italy and the United States combined. It was trade, moreover, that brought in a higher reward for the work done, for Britain exported a high proportion of finished goods, while the U.S.A., for example, was mainly selling raw materials. Notable among British exports were Lancashire cotton goods, Yorkshire woollens, Staffordshire pottery, Sheffield steel, Birmingham hardware—and coal.[1]

Condition of By 1870, too, the wage-earners, or rather the more highly **wage-earners** skilled workers, were enjoying a higher standard of living. Their wage-rates had gone up by 50 per cent since 1850, which meant a 10 per cent improvement even after allowing for the general rise in prices, and a million 'small savers' had accounts with the Post Office Savings Bank. Even the poor could now buy things like matches, soap and paraffin oil, while local authorities were providing better sanitation, paving and lighting, and were in some cities undertaking slum clearance schemes. At the same time hours of work were somewhat reduced, and the custom of the Saturday half-holiday was soon to appear. Britain's increasing wealth was beginning to bring some advantage to the masses, and the new industrial towns were not quite the grim prisons they had been in the previous half-century. Most of the rewards of increased production, however, went not to the workers but to the employers or shareholders, who did not spend much of these growing profits, but invested them again. This new capital they employed abroad as well as at home; by 1900 there were nearly £2,000 million of British capital invested overseas, and by 1914 twice that amount. This latter sum brought in as yearly dividends at least £200 million, enabling Britain to buy from abroad even more than she sold.

2 British Trade in Difficulties

During the last quarter of the nineteenth century British trade began to encounter difficulties. There were frequent commercial

[1] By 1913 coal accounted for three-quarters of the total *weight* of British exports.

crises, and in 1873 a steady fall in prices set in that continued till 1896, a period sometimes called 'the Great Depression'. The skilled wage-earners did not suffer while they were in work, for their wages remained about the same or improved slightly, and owing to the fall in prices they could buy more goods. There was, however, an increase in unemployment—a sinister word that·

'The Great Depression', 1873–1896

(Tenniel, 1896, reproduced by permission of the Proprietors of 'Punch')

CAUGHT NAPPING

'There was an old lady as I've heard tell, she went to market her goods for to sell

She went to market on a market day and she fell asleep on the world's highway

By came a pedlar—German—and stout, and he cut her petticoats all round about.'

Towards the end of the nineteenth century British traders, many of whom had lost their grandfathers' spirit of enterprise and determination to keep abreast of the times, found themselves increasingly undersold by German competitors.

dates from 1888. And the unskilled workers, who accounted for more than half the urban population, were in an unenviable condition, whether in work or out.

Some industries were making progress, but in others Britain lost the lead in production which she had enjoyed for the best part of a hundred years. Now, instead of British industry having the field to itself, the United States of America and Germany were shutting out British products by means of high tariffs, were challenging Britain's hold on foreign markets and were even contriving to sell their goods in Britain cheaper than the native wares. It was little comfort to know that many of their products were made by machinery imported from Britain. The enterprise, adaptability and technical skill which might have kept Britain ahead of her rivals were often lacking. British industry and commerce continued to expand, but the days of easy success were gone for ever, and with them the unquestioned belief in free trade. A 'Fair Trade' agitation arose, to demand that when other states shut out British goods, Britain should exclude theirs. However, the first serious political movement in this direction was defeated by the verdict of the 1906 election.[1]

After the turn of the century trade conditions improved and employment was fairly steady. But from 1900 to 1914 wages barely kept up with prices, a cause of the unprecedented industrial strife of the period and a sign of deep-seated weaknesses in British industry. Too little capital and too little effort were being put into home production. Business men, grown used to Britain's easy supremacy, worked less hard and neglected new processes. There was little enthusiasm for new machinery—coal-cutting machines, for example, were widely used in America before they were introduced into British mines—or indeed for investing in machinery at all. British wealth was invested abroad much more freely than at home, because it brought easier profits—in the expanding Dominions, the United States, South America, even Japan. So productivity (output per worker) in Britain remained low. The one exception was shipbuilding; nearly half the merchant shipping on the oceans of the world was British-built; all rivals were left far behind.

Until the First World War brought prosperity to British farming, it made little progress towards recovery from the great depression of the 1870s.[2] Indeed wheat prices sank lower than ever in 1894–95, and the area of wheat-growing land diminished still further, as did the number of farm workers. Neither the establishment of the Board of Agriculture in 1889 nor anything else relieved the general gloom. After 1900 some farmers found a way out by raising beef cattle, or by the dairy-farming and market-gardening which would likewise feed the ever-increasing town populations. Real prosperity, however, could come only by

Low productivity

Farming in difficulties

[1] See pages 225–6. [2] See page 202.

the exclusion of supplies from abroad. Since the Government would not bring this about by means of tariffs, it could only happen through war.

These adverse trends in agriculture and industry reacted *Poverty* severely on the condition of the people. Of 12,000 men who volunteered in Manchester for the South African War, only 1,200 were found to be thoroughly fit for service. S. B. Rowntree's house-to-house investigation in York about the same time revealed that 28 per cent of the population could not afford the food that was necessary for a man doing moderate work, taking as the standard a less generous diet than that of the York workhouse. The figure was shown to apply to the country in general. The groups worst affected were the unemployed, the unskilled workers —a bricklayer's labourer, for example, earned 19s. compared with the bricklayer's 38s. a week—and the 'sweated' workers in the clothing and other industries, who, unprotected by trade unions, or by law until 1909,[1] received less than a subsistence wage. More people than ever found a remedy in emigration; $1\frac{1}{2}$ million went abroad, over half of them to the Dominions, in the first ten years of the new century.

The plight of those who remained at home received much attention from the more fortunate sections of the nation, especially the growing professional classes whose work often brought them into contact with social problems. The state of the urban poor was much studied and much publicized, for example in the novels of Walter Besant and the plays of Bernard Shaw. This attitude stood in sharp contrast to the behaviour of most *Extravagance* contemporary people of fashion; the Edwardian age was one of great extravagance in clothes, food, and every form of luxury on the part of the wealthier classes. The masses had as their consolations the watching of organized sport, highly developed from about 1870,[2] the reading of cheap newspapers, beginning with Alfred Harmsworth's *Daily Mail* in 1896, and the drinking of cheap beer. But their housing, nutrition and health left much to be desired.

The difficulties of British trade after the First World War[3] were thus rooted in conditions that existed before it, but were severely increased by the disturbance of the war itself and its aftermath. A short boom followed the conclusion of hostilities in

[1] See page 227.
[2] The Football League was founded in 1888.
[3] See page 263.

The great slump, 1920-1936 1918, but a slump soon ensued. After 1922 there was some recovery, but by 1930 the shrinkage of trade was world-wide, and defeated all attempts at a general cure, including an international economic conference held in 1933. In Britain unemployment was the worst ever known; there was only one year in the period 1920-1936 when the proportion of workers unemployed was less than ten per cent.

New industries   The loss of markets overseas was partly offset by the rise of new industries at home. From the turn of the century onwards the development of electrical power, though slow and expensive in Britain compared with Germany and America, brought results hardly less striking than those which followed upon Watt's steam-engine. Especially useful for engineering of all kinds, and easily transmitted by cables, electricity freed industry from its bondage to the coalfields, though not from its ultimate dependence upon coal. As one consequence of this, light industry once more found a home in the south of England, attracted by London, the biggest market for many kinds of goods. Typical twentieth-century developments of this nature were the gramophone[1] and radio industries, as well as the production of electrical apparatus for the home.[2] Besides these new light industries, great new enterprises grew up for the production of artificial silk, motor-cars, aeroplanes, chemicals and armaments.

Nevertheless the period between the wars was full of struggle and anxiety. It was inevitable that to meet difficulties on so great a scale people should look to the Government, whether their views

Policy of protection and imperial preference, 1932 · were Conservative or Socialist—or even Liberal. The National Government of 1931-35 resorted to a general system of protection, thus reversing the trade policy of nearly a century, while making arrangements at the Imperial Economic Conference at Ottawa to increase the proportion of Britain's trade that was carried on with countries of the Empire.[3]

State control   During the 1930s Conservative ministries took over for the state royalties on coal (of course compensating the former owners) and virtually nationalized all airways and London's transport, using for these the new device of state-controlled corporations, run by nominated boards and finally, but not directly,

[1] The parent invention of the phonograph was made by Edison, an American, in 1876.
[2] Swan, an Englishman, invented the carbon filament lamp in 1860 and the incandescent electric lamp in 1878, but electric lighting in the British home was confined to the houses of the fairly well-to-do until after the war of 1914-18.   [3] See page 274.

supervised by Parliament. Government aid to agriculture assumed such varied forms as to bewilder the consumer, if not the farmer. Different crops were encouraged by subsidies or tariffs, by marketing boards, which offered stable prices, or by quotas, which fixed the percentage of total imports that each foreign supplier could send in. Agricultural output increased by one-sixth, wheat by a half, but at a cost to the taxpayer of about £100 million a year.

How far the partial revival of trade was due to government action is doubtful, though Britain's relatively swift recovery suggests that the adoption at last of protection was sound policy. At the same time it was a period of low prices, which meant that those who were in employment—the large majority—could buy more. It was the industries supplying everyday consumer needs, and the service and distribution industries, that flourished. Electricity supply, for example, expanded steadily, and the other new industries continued to do well. There was much activity in housing, and after 1936 a boom in armaments. A basic factor in all this was the change in Britain's favour of the terms of trade— her imports, especially of raw materials, were priced at lower levels than her exports. In so far as this cheapness of raw materials was due to the depression, the slump was curing itself.

The great slump did not pass without leaving its mark on the British people. During the thirties conditions remained wretched for the unemployed, and the difference between the poorer and more comfortable sections of the community was very wide; the infant death rate, for example, though generally much lower, was still over one-tenth in poor families, and worse in the depressed areas. The thirties accordingly saw a movement of population southward as people left the centres of heavy industry and textile manufacture in the North and Midlands to seek work in the more fortunate South, especially London. In the growing towns of Southern England working-class people found opportunities in the new industries, and in their housing and general way of life lived more like the middle class which had previously enjoyed most of the benefits of British prosperity. So the contrast grew sharper between the comfortable South and the often bleak North, the centre of the flourishing industries of the nineteenth century.

The Second World War put an end to unemployment, and required a mobilization of the nation's man-power—and woman-power—more thorough than anything previously attempted.

Conscription and rationing were introduced at the outset. The Government's control of men and materials ensured that only those things would be produced that were strictly necessary for the war effort. Everything was as carefully calculated as the number of calories in the citizen's diet that would keep him in a satisfactory state of health and activity. The return to conditions of peace was managed with similar care and thoroughness. Men passed smoothly, though not quickly, from service into civilian life; there was no unemployment and no major stoppage in industry.

Post-war difficulties—

In the immediate post-war years, production was of course hindered by shortage of materials. Little new industrial plant was built because of the immense demand for housing; nearly four

—shortages

million houses had been destroyed or damaged by enemy action, 1,800,000 of them in London alone; 500,000 more were needed to replace the worst of the slums. During the six years of war the country had consumed less than four years' normal supply of clothing, less than three years' of household goods, and had been living on an uninteresting and barely adequate diet; there was an unsatisfied demand for every kind of consumer goods. But more essential was the equipment of industry so that more things of all kinds could be produced. The answer to many of these needs could be found in imports—if Britain could afford to pay for them. This was the central problem: no release from wartime stringency and no expansion of production without larger imports; no increase of imports unless there were more exports to pay for them—it was estimated that an increase of three-quarters above the pre-war level would be needed. But

—slowly expanding exports

Britain's trade was in fact expanding more slowly than that of other countries, many of which were developing their own manufactures and had less need of British goods. The old method of filling the gap—the use of income from British investments abroad—was hardly available; £1,000 million of these assets had been sold during the war to pay for indispensable supplies.

—debts

Worse than that, huge debts had been incurred, and Britain was in debt to the tune of £13,000 million. The main problem was to find dollars to pay for goods which only the New World could supply, a loan from the U.S.A. and Canada of £1,300 million in 1947 was soon spent.

Fuel crisis, 1947

All these difficulties were acutely worsened by an unprecedented fuel crisis in the early months of 1947, when the country was unkindly stricken by the severest winter since 1881.

Neither the mines nor the power stations could meet the demand; power cuts interrupted production; 2,300,000 men were out of work, and £200 million worth of exports lost. The trade deficit totalled £600 million in the year; the dollar deficit rose to 150 million dollars a month. When the fuel crisis was over things improved somewhat, but the other difficulties persisted, and forced the Government in 1949 to devalue the pound sterling, which became worth 2.80 instead of 4.03 dollars. The effect, as in 1931,[1] was to ease the situation considerably for the moment, because foreigners now found British goods much cheaper to buy, and exports enjoyed a boom. By 1951, however, the war in Korea was causing a world-wide rise in prices, particularly of raw materials, which meant for Britain an adverse change in the terms of trade. This combined with a growing demand for goods at home and increased expenditure on armaments to produce another balance of payments crisis. It was ruefully remarked that these seemed to occur in each odd-numbered year. Every year, however, odd or even, saw a rise in prices; the fall in the value of money seemed impossible to check.

Devaluation, 1949

The failure was not due to lack of governmental powers. So tight was the trade position that some rationing of food was retained until 1954, nine years after the end of the war; clothes were de-rationed in 1949 and soap in 1950, but—of more concern to the young—sweets not finally until 1953. The use of foreign currency for tourist travel was restricted, and in 1947 temporarily stopped altogether. Income tax, maintained at nearly its war-time level, absorbed a large proportion of individual wealth, some of it to be redistributed in social benefits. In purchase tax, first imposed during the war, the Government had a most comprehensive and flexible means of control, for it could be applied at different rates and at different times to any range of goods. Tariff rates could be similarly adjusted, and the pre-war apparatus of farm subsidies, quotas, and agricultural marketing schemes was still intact. Another powerful instrument of control was the bank rate. This could be raised or lowered by the Bank of England, acting under the direction of the Treasury, thus making money dear to borrow, so as to restrict enterprise, or cheap to borrow, so as to stimulate industrial activity. Still more drastic was the power, used only in real emergency, of course, to alter the value of the pound sterling in terms of foreign currencies, as was done in 1949.

Government regulation

[1] See page 274.

Nationalization

The Labour ministry which achieved office—and for the first time with real power—in 1945[1] was not satisfied with indirect controls, however strong. It introduced a whole programme of measures of nationalization, bringing the Bank of England, the coal mines, the electricity and gas industries, railways, canals, road haulage, and the iron and steel industry under the ownership of the state. The last two of these were later restored to private ownership, in whole or in part, by the Conservatives, but even they accepted some element of nationalization as inevitable. The age of planning had arrived; private enterprise and unregulated competition, great as their triumphs had been in the nineteenth century, could no longer satisfy the needs of the community. The Government had come not only to provide for the welfare of the population by education and health services on a national scale; it attempted also to maintain full employment by controlling the use of capital, and to· regulate the movement of the population by controlling the use of land.[2] The results were often unwelcome to the owners of land and capital, to the trade unions and to the ordinary citizen. Planning and freedom, security and enterprise, did not readily go hand in hand.

The 1950s: difficulties persist

The economic troubles of the 1940s became much less acute in the 1950s, but they did not disappear. There was some improvement in the terms of trade and some increase in production. But with nearly the whole working population employed, and wages rising faster than production, imports persistently rose faster than exports. Internally, the value of money continued to fall, so that a pound saved in 1947 would buy only 12s. 6d. worth of goods ten years later. Externally, the failure to balance trade caused continued payments difficulties. The Government intervened with some effect, in 1955 introducing a second budget in October to raise purchase taxes, a remedy applied again in the budget of 1961, with the addition of a 'wages pause' for all employed in the public service. In 1962 the Government took a longer step in economic planning than Conservatives had hitherto

N.E.D.C. and N.I.C.

been willing to contemplate. A National Economic Development Council, composed of experts, was set up to plan investment and financial policy, and a National Incomes Commission to adjudicate on wage and salary claims in the light of the national interest. The co-operation of business with the former and of the trade unions with the latter were, however, matters of some doubt.

[1] See page 298.
[2] A notable example was the New Towns Act of 1946.

In the international field difficult decisions were taken. The Government had at first decided to remain aloof from the customs union formed in 1960 by six countries of Western Europe—France, West Germany, Italy, and the Benelux group. The members of this European Economic Community were to remove all customs duties on each other's products while maintaining a common tariff, and a fairly high one, on goods from outside. British membership of such a group seemed likely to do serious damage to trade within the Commonwealth. Instead Britain gave a lead to six other European countries—Sweden, Norway, Denmark, Switzerland, Austria and Portugal—in forming the European Free Trade Association, whose members would similarly remove, step by step, duties on each other's goods, but would have a free hand in regulating their trade with countries outside, Britain thus being left free to maintain preferences for Commonwealth products. In 1962, however, the Government changed its mind.[1] Trade with Europe and North America was increasing fast, while trade in the Commonwealth was growing very slowly. It seemed that more profit could be gained by going into Europe than by staying out. The Government therefore applied to join the E.E.C. Long and hard bargaining followed in the attempt to reconcile Britain's membership with Commonwealth interests. All was in vain, however, for France, in opposition to the wishes of her partners, vetoed British membership, fearing perhaps the political rather than the commercial consequences.

E.E.C., 1960

E.F.T.A., 1960

Britain rejected by E.E.C., 1963

It was during the 1950s that Britain began to be conscious of a development that was likely to do more to change people's lives than all the plans of the Government—the coming of automation, i.e. the control of machines by machines. Here was the promise—or the threat—of a second industrial revolution that might have even more immense consequences than the first.

Automation

[1] See page 320.

26. Religious Opinion

The most important Christian bodies in England in the late eighteenth and early nineteenth centuries were the Church of England and the Methodists. The large majority of Anglican clergy were thoroughly imbued with the eighteenth-century temper, in the light of which 'enthusiasm' of any kind was to be avoided, and religion was reduced to a code of rules of good, kind and enlightened behaviour. Moreover, in outlook, the bishops and a large proportion of the parish clergy were one with the landed class from which they had sprung, and which they considered divinely appointed to rule the earth and enjoy its blessings. This intention of Providence they were fully prepared to assist by drawing income from as many benefices as possible, while delegating the actual work to poorly paid curates. At the end of the eighteenth century more than a half of Church livings were without a resident clergyman. Many of the clergy were also shamefully unlearned and some set a poor example in their daily lives—the 'squarsons', for whom religion came a bad third to farming and fox-hunting.

It was against these shortcomings of the Established Church that John Wesley's Methodists had protested, by going out among the common people and acting on the Christian doctrine that every man has a soul to save. Their activity was greatest in the new factory towns and the mining districts, where often there were no churches and no parsons; and they did not scorn converts from the dregs of the population. Moreover, the poor man, who in the parish church was reminded only to keep his lowly station and to count its blessings, found that he could share actively in the life of the Methodist Chapel, helping to choose the minister and manage the congregation's affairs. There he could find refuge from the injustice, tragedy and hopelessness of the hard world in which he lived; and there he learnt that the greater his patience and courage in enduring suffering in this world, the greater his reward in the life to come. The effect of

Methodism on the poor was thus not only to stress the importance of saving their souls, but also to divert them from the pursuit of worldly betterment. 'The Methodist movement was a call not for citizens, but for saints', and in spite of their practical training in democracy, Methodists seldom made reformers. The Radicals counted them as enemies, and it may be true that in critical times Methodism helped to save England from revolution by its steadying and soothing influence on many of the natural leaders of the working class.

The other Nonconformist sects of this period were older than Other sects

You shall find him as tender as a chicken, master

That's right, Cook, turn the rascal well, gun him a Negro flagellum.

(*Anon., 1784, from a print in the British Museum*)

THE PARSON'S PIG

A satire on the worldliness—in this case, gluttony—of the eighteenth-century clergy. The parson's negro cook (in devil's form to denote temptation) beats a young tithe-pig to make tender eating for his master.

Methodism but had less influence. From the Puritans of the seventeenth century were descended the Presbyterians, the Baptists, the Congregationalists and the Unitarians, while throughout England were small groups of the Society of Friends, or Quakers. Nearly all these had been free to worship in their own ways since Religious liberty the Toleration Act of 1689, and free in practice to exercise their political rights, for every year since 1727 an Act had been passed excusing them from any penalties they had incurred by sitting in Parliament or on borough corporations in contravention of the Test and Corporation Acts.[1]

[1] The Test and Corporation Acts were repealed in 1828: see page 104.

M.B.—N

Less fortunate were the Roman Catholics. Liable to persecution till 1791 for the mere practice of their faith, they did not gain political equality with Protestants until the passing of the Catholic Relief Act in 1829.[1] Only then, after 150 years of humiliation, were Catholics at last permitted to vote, to sit in Parliament, and to hold almost any office under the Crown.

The Evangelical Movement

Not all the followers of John Wesley had left the Church of England; indeed, none of them need have done so if the bishops had known their business. Those who carried on his tradition within the Church were called Evangelicals. Like the Methodists the Evangelicals had an intensely personal faith, expressed in strict standards of conduct and overflowing good works. The movement had many followers among the rich, some of whom felt the horrors of the French Revolution to be a warning against irreligion and thoughtless living. Evangelical religion inspired the two great social reformers Wilberforce and Shaftesbury. In each case the lifelong pursuit of a cause was due first to belief in a divine summons to duty, only secondly to love of mankind.

Social reform

'The Clapham Sect'

Wilberforce was the leading member of 'the Clapham Sect', a group of Evangelicals who used to meet in the homes of some of their number by Clapham Common. They stressed the importance of the Sabbath and helped to bring about the decline of duelling and brutal sports like cock-fighting. Their great triumph was the abolition of the slave-trade.[2] The Evangelicals put new life into missionary work abroad, and throughout the nineteenth century they were in the forefront of educational advance, prison reform and the protection of factory children. Shaftesbury, like Wilberforce, sacrificed the prospect of a great political career to devote his whole life to humanitarian causes, and many leading men throughout the Empire were similarly inspired.[3]

*   *   *   *   *

Whig reform of the Church of England

The Whig governments of the 1830s directed some of their reforming enthusiasm to the removal of abuses in the Church of England.[4] Clergy were forbidden to hold more than two livings at once, and the incomes of the richest bishoprics were cut down in order to provide more money for poor parishes. These changes were for the good of the Church, but they showed up the Church's subjection to the State. This was made even

[1] See page 106.   [2] See page 59.
[3] For Shaftesbury's work in social reform, see pages 131–2, 150–4.
[4] See page 126.

clearer in 1833 when some Irish bishoprics were suppressed against the wishes of the whole bench of bishops.

It was at this point that certain young men of Oxford began to put forward new ideas about the Church and its position in the nation's life. The three leaders, John Keble, John Henry Newman and Edward Pusey were all fellows of Oriel College. These men, aghast at what seemed to them the lack of holiness in the Church as well as in the nation at large, and believing that the Church was passing under the command of a scarcely Christian Government, determined to proclaim the supreme importance of the Church as a body ordained and inspired by God. They demanded complete freedom for the Church and unquestioning obedience to its teachings, while to make the Church worthy of their claims they showed an intense earnestness about its sacraments, creeds and ritual. They published their ideas in a series of *Tracts for the Times*, which struck clergy and laymen alike with a force unknown since the seventeenth century. *The Oxford Movement*

Tracts for the Times

The nineteenth-century Englishman was usually quick to detect anything that resembled 'Popery', and it was soon remarked that the teaching of the 'Tractarians' about the majesty of the Church and the high office of the priest savoured of the Church of Rome rather than the Church of England. This suggestion Newman and his friends were anxious to rebut, and in *Tract No. 90* Newman argued that the Thirty-nine Articles[1] which summarize the doctrine of the Church of England could be interpreted in a Catholic way. In other words, the Church of England had remained, in spite of the Reformation, a part of the living universal Catholic Church, and therefore one could be a Catholic without being a member of the Roman Church. *Tract 90* aroused a storm of angry condemnation which obliged Newman to give up his position as Vicar of St Mary's, Oxford, and his fellowship of Oriel. *Tract 90, 1841*

For the moment Newman had convinced himself that he could remain a loyal member of the Church of England. But the conviction did not last very long. Four years later he gave up Anglican orders and entered the Roman Catholic Church, whither he was followed by many whom his earlier teaching had inspired. It seemed to be true after all that those who longed to rest their faith upon the secure foundation of an infallible Church must find what they sought in Rome. In due course Newman became a Cardinal. *Newman goes over to Rome, 1845*

[1] They are printed in the Book of Common Prayer.

Influence of the
Oxford
Movement

Not all the Tractarians went over to Rome, and the example of these young men of Oxford, who fasted, did penance and confessed their sins, spread throughout the Church of England. Their followers, called 'High Churchmen' or later 'Anglo-Catholics', claimed a high place for the Church in the national life, and insisted on dignified observance of its rites. They went far to transform the Church of England by their devotion, of which their hymns remind us. People would no longer place their hats on the altar or their umbrellas in the font, nor were candidates for ordination examined during a few moments snatched from watching a cricket match. On the other hand, emphasis upon ritual caused many protests and even riots against 'Romish' practices, and the gap between High and Low Churchmen was widened.

*   *   *   *   *

The Scottish
Presbyterians

During the nineteenth century the Nonconformist bodies more than held their own with the Church of England, while in Scotland, of course, the Presbyterians predominated. The Presbyterian Church of Scotland, by law established, was not without its troubles. A large body of ministers, led by Thomas Chalmers, broke away in 1843 to form the Free Church of Scotland—free, having shaken off State control, to take the path of reform on which the dissident ministers had determined, but bereft of the endowments which had maintained them in their livings. The two Churches were reunited at length in 1929, by which time the Church of Scotland had severed its connection with the State. The Anglican Church in Wales had not to wait so long for this change, being disestablished by an Act of Parliament in 1914.[1] Only a small minority in the Church of England would have had it follow these examples, and the Church continued to enjoy the advantages, in status and finance, of its established position.

Nonconformist
influence

The remaining legal handicaps of the Nonconformists were removed by their Liberal champions, as for example when Gladstone caused compulsory Church Rates to be abolished in 1868, and when all positions in the universities of Oxford and Cambridge were opened to them in 1871. The influence of the great number of Nonconformist voters, mostly of the middle class, can be seen in almost every political event of the period, and provided the Liberal Party with its most sure and solid

[1] See page 232.

support; while no statesman on either side could afford to neglect the famous 'Nonconformist conscience'.

The one religious enterprise of the nineteenth century compar- The Salvation able with George Fox's founding of the Quakers in the seven- Army, 1877 teenth, and Wesley's launching of Methodism in the eighteenth, was the creation of the Salvation Army by William Booth. Having already toiled for thirteen years in the East End of London, Booth set out to win souls for Christ in a new way. The Christian fights perpetually against evil: Booth decided to bring the point home by stretching the military metaphor. Avoiding intellectual refinements, he resorted to any methods that would appeal to the coarsened and outcast people among whom he worked—fiery preaching at street corners, uniforms, brass bands, and hymns set to popular melodies. 'Why', he asked, 'should the Devil have all the best tunes?' In 1890, impressed by the crying need for social work in the slums and for the homeless, Booth wrote *In Darkest England, and the Way Out.* and set himself to raise £100,000 for his work. He succeeded, and the Army's missionary activity was later extended to all parts of the world.

Some progress has been made towards the ideal of Christian Christian unity, at least among the Protestant bodies. The two branches of reunion the Baptists, 'General' and 'Particular', came together in 1891, and the three sects into which Methodism had split reunited in 1932, composing the largest of all the Free Churches. In 1892 the first Congress of all the Free Churches was held; this became an annual event, and a Free Church Council was set up. During the twentieth century attempts have been made to bring about a reunion of the Free Churches with the Church of England. Differences of belief are not very wide, but the Anglican insistence on the position of the bishops has been a great obstacle.

*   *   *   *   *

Victorian England has been described as, 'among highly Victorian civilized communities, one of the most religious the world has religion known'. The evidence for this may be seen in the careers of men like Shaftesbury, Gladstone, Gordon and Livingstone, in the tone of the public schools after Arnold, and in the social customs of the period. Notable among these was the strictness of Sunday observance, which obtained in all classes except the poorest. Places of business and entertainment were closed, all unnecessary household tasks were avoided, games and light reading were taboo, and serious doubts would be entertained about travel or even the purchase of a newspaper on the Sabbath.[1] Attendance at church was regular, often three times in the day, for all who claimed to be respectable citizens, so that in the course of ten years a churchgoer might well hear a thousand sermons (not perhaps all fresh). Low Churchmen and Nonconformists of nearly every sect frowned upon most public pleasures and looked upon the theatre as the house of Satan. One result was, of course, to create a good deal of unnecessary gloom, especially for young people. Another was to cultivate hypocrisy, since a man of the middle class would have to seem religious to stand well in the eyes of his neighbours. At the same time there were a great many people in all walks of life who were led by their religion into a decent way of living and a constant effort to put duty before pleasure, and these in their fashion were the salt of Victorian England, in business, politics and empire-building no less than in family life.

Criticism of
religion There was one danger to religion that none of the Churches was prepared to meet—the development of liberal and rationalist thought, tremendously reinforced after the middle of the nineteenth century by the discoveries of science. The generally accepted beliefs were attacked from three sides: by those like Bentham who disbelieved in revealed religion altogether, by those who rejected the Scriptures where they were contradicted by the new revelations of science,[2] and by those who followed the German scholars in a detailed examination of the Bible itself to find out when and by whom its various books were written. As a result of these criticisms the faith of many was shaken, first among the learned, but in time among numbers of the lesser folk, who began to query stories and incidents in the Bible in a way they would never previously have dreamed of doing. Those who believed in the literal interpretation of the Bible had either to change their ground or admit defeat. A change of ground was reasonable, for the new teaching did not lessen the worth of the Bible as a religious book, but many devout people thought that all was lost if they admitted that the walls of Jericho might not have fallen at the seventh blast of the trumpet, or that the making of the universe might have occupied more than six days.

Other changes too were loosening the hold of the Church, so

---

[1] Faraday, the great scientist, who belonged to a very narrow sect, was expelled from it because he obeyed the Queen's command to dine at Windsor on a Sunday, thus missing service.

[2] See page 326.

that after 1870 the pews began to empty, the observance of Sunday became less strict, the custom of family prayers declined, and the number of young men preparing themselves for the Church diminished. The chief cause of the decline was probably the increase of comfort, with the later advent of the cinema and broadcasting and the extensive spread of outdoor sports, which gave people other things to think about on the weekly day of rest. Improved facilities for travel, especially the motor-car, affected churchgoing most of all.

The exception to the general weakening of religion was found in the Roman Catholic Church, which considerably increased the number of its adherents in Britain from the latter part of the nineteenth century onwards, though mainly because of immigration from Ireland. The Protestant Churches, by contrast, could present no agreed summary of Christian doctrine, and with the spread of education there were many people with enough learning to doubt religion, but no means of finding a bedrock of firm belief. The two World Wars, with their spectacle of evil and bloodshed on so enormous a scale, shook the faith of many. In general, the people of England now, while still imbued with many notions of Christian origin, are only vaguely Christian in belief and can no longer be described as a religious people. A Church of England report in 1945 called for a repetition at home of the great missionary efforts which had gained millions of new adherents for the Christian Churches in foreign lands. It was aptly entitled *Towards the Conversion of England*.

It was still possible, however, for the New English Bible to be the best seller of 1961, and for the opening of the rebuilt Coventry Cathedral, designed and adorned by the foremost artists of the time, to be a major national event of 1962. And under the pressure of forces hostile to religion the Christian Churches showed further signs of drawing together. There were conversations aimed at the reunion of the Methodists with the Church of England, and in 1960 the Archbishop of Canterbury—the first holder of the office to do so—visited the Pope.

27. The Advance of Education

1 Primary Education in the Nineteenth Century

Neglect in 1800 At the opening of the nineteenth century, though there had been a school in every Scottish village for a hundred years or more, England lacked even the beginnings of a system of primary education. The religious charity schools were few in number, and the local 'dame schools' usually served little better purpose than child-minding. The need of schooling for the mass of the people was realized by few; indeed to the ruling class it seemed likely to spread dangerous notions, while employers feared discontent among the workpeople on whose cheap and docile labour their profits depended.

During the nineteenth century, however, the idea gained ground that an uneducated and uncivilized working class might be more dangerous than one which had been to school. There **Factors making** were three powerful factors in its favour. The first was the desire **for change** to instruct the poor in religion, for which purpose they should be able to read the Bible. The second was the growing need in business for people who could read and write, and for some with a technical training. The third arose from the granting of political power to working-class people; as Robert Lowe, a leading Liberal, said in 1867, 'We must educate our masters.'

Bell and The beginnings of a widespread primary education system in **Lancaster—'the** England—unless one counts the Sunday schools started by **monitorial** Raikes of Gloucester in 1780—are to be found in the schools set **system'** up in rivalry in 1798 by Andrew Bell, a Church of England clergyman, and Joseph Lancaster, a Quaker, in London. Both used the older children as monitors to teach the juniors. Bell said, 'Give me twenty-four pupils today, and I will give you twenty-four teachers tomorrow.' This 'monitorial system' had the merit **The Voluntary** of economizing in teachers and in money—one teacher could **Societies—** manage several hundred children at a cost of seven shillings a year per child! Lancaster's supporters, mainly Nonconformists, **—British and** founded in 1808 a society to spread education by his methods, **Foreign** later called the British and Foreign Society, while the bishops of the Church of England, in alarm, helped Bell to organize the

'National Society for the Education of the Poor in the Principles —National
of the Established Church'. The latter soon became much the
richer of the two societies, and founded 3,000 schools in its
first twenty years.

Unfortunately this religious rivalry, while beneficial in Rivalry of
establishing a considerable number of schools, bedevilled educa- Anglicans and
tional progress in England throughout a century. The partisans Nonconformists
of Anglicanism and Nonconformity preferred to see children
not educated at all rather than see them educated by their rivals.
Every step proposed by the State for increasing the provision of
education was resisted by one section or the other—or both—as
a weakening of its own schools. Proposals to set up schools at

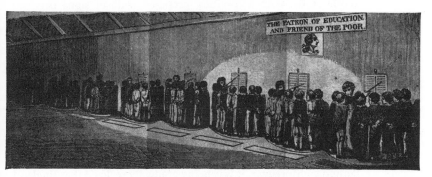

THE PATRON OF EDUCATION
AND FRIEND OF THE POOR

(Early 19th century, reproduced by permission of 'The Times')

THE LANCASTERIAN SYSTEM

Education on the cheap. The older boys, or monitors, teach the younger ones.

government expense thus failed, but in 1833 Parliament ventured The first
on the first grant of public money for education—a sum of education grant,
£20,000, which was to be spent by the two religious societies. 1833
The precise importance of education in the national budget at
this time may perhaps be gauged from the £50,000 granted by
Parliament in the same year for the improvement of the royal
stables. In 1839, when the education grant was increased to
£30,000, a Special Committee of the Privy Council was formed
to supervise the spending of the money, and inspectors were
appointed to visit the schools. By 1858 the Government grant had
swollen to £900,000; but only one-tenth of the children in the
schools were proficient in 'the three R's' (reading, 'riting,
'rithmetic) which were their subjects of study.

At this stage an Education Department of the Privy Council was set up. In 1862 its head, Robert Lowe, introduced by way of improvement a system of 'payment by results'. This meant that the grant paid by the Government to school managers would depend mainly on the performance of the children at each stage of their school career in an examination conducted by Her Majesty's Inspectors. Naturally the system encouraged soulless drilling, parrot-like learning by heart and even downright trickery —anything so long as the maximum number of pupils reached the required 'standard' on the dreaded day. The detection of a book held upside down by a pupil who had learned his reading test by heart was not usually beyond the Inspector, but more subtle ruses, with a carefully prepared code of signs between teacher and pupils, might well defeat him. 'Payment by results' made for efficiency of a sort and more careful attention to backward pupils, but before it came to an end in 1897 it made school life a wearisome burden and a hated memory for hundreds of thousands of hapless youngsters.

'Payment by results'

By 1870 few were prepared to deny the value of rudimentary education for the poor, and yet there were over 10,000 parishes without a school. Again in the words of Robert Lowe, 'the lower classes ought to be educated to discharge the duties cast upon them'. The Parliamentary Reform of 1867 had increased these duties by giving the vote to working-class householders in the boroughs. Moreover, it was being gradually realized that England was far behind many other countries in education, and that her industrial position, and even her national security, might be endangered if she continued to allow half her children to remain unschooled.

Change of opinion by 1870

The Education Act of 1870, introduced by W. E. Forster during Gladstone's first Ministry, was concerned only with primary education for the poor. And it did not attempt to supplant the religious societies, whose schools, 20,000 in number, supplied the needs of many areas. Where schools were lacking, however, they were now to be built and maintained, with money levied by a special rate, by specially elected local boards. Parents were excused fees if unable to afford them, and so every child had the opportunity to attend school. It was left to each board to decide whether attendance should be made compulsory. In an attempt to avoid religious difficulties, the Act laid down that no religious teaching distinctive of any particular denomination might be given in board schools, and that in all schools a child

The Forster Act, 1870

might be withdrawn from Scripture lessons at the parent's wish. The religious bodies were not placated, however; the Church of England objected to the board schools as almost pagan institutions, while the Nonconformists bitterly complained of the continued and enlarged State aid to the Societies' schools—by far the majority of which gave religious teaching according to the doctrines of the Church of England.

(*Tenniel, 1853, reproduced by permission of the Proprietors of 'Punch'*)

WHO SHALL EDUCATE? *or,* OUR BABES IN THE WOOD
Churchman and Nonconformist battle for the right to educate the two babes (the young—who meanwhile go largely uneducated).

After 1876 the question of compulsory attendance was no longer left to the local school board, for an Act of Disraeli's Ministry in that year penalized parents who kept their children away from school without official 'exemption'. Four years later Gladstone's Government made attendance compulsory everywhere up to an age, not above thirteen, to be fixed by each board. In 1891 a new kind of government grant introduced by Salisbury's Ministry made education free in almost all primary schools.

Later Acts, 1876, 1880 and 1891

The new schools There was much opposition at first from parents to obligatory school attendance, and teachers often found their new charges rough, unclean, unruly and ill-nourished, and incapable of attention. Discipline was harsh, punishment frequent, and relations between teacher and pupil often hostile; indeed, teachers sometimes found it inadvisable to go home alone. There was soon, however, a notable improvement in manners and bearing, which resulted in turn in a more friendly atmosphere in the schools.

2 Secondary and University Education in the Nineteenth Century

Schooling beyond the primary stage was a privilege enjoyed in the early nineteenth century by very few boys, and fewer girls.

Grammar and public schools It could be had either in the old endowed grammar schools, attended mainly by the sons of professional people and tradesmen, or in the few great public boarding schools. There were also private schools, of all grades of efficiency—or none: Dotheboys Hall in *Nicholas Nickleby* was no figment of Dickens's imagination.

Low standard of grammar schools Both the grammar and the public schools charged fees, but most gave a poor return for the money. The grammar schools kept to a most narrow curriculum, innocent of any teaching in modern languages or science, or even of a proper study of English. Half of them taught Latin grammar, but seldom any Greek; the rest rose hardly above the level of a primary school. After 1870 a marked improvement took place, partly through the public demand for a more efficient and 'modern' education, and partly through the complete overhaul carried out by the Commission for the Endowed Schools.

Degraded condition of public schools The condition of the public schools[1] was not much better on the intellectual side, and alarmingly bad in most other respects. The schools were understaffed, and the boys were left largely to their own devices outside the classroom,[2] except that they were punished for their misdeeds by savage floggings. There was an

[1] The great public schools in 1800, Eton, Winchester, Westminster, Charterhouse, St Paul's, Merchant Taylors', Harrow, Rugby, Shrewsbury and Christ's Hospital, were all of ancient foundation.
[2] If the Duke of Wellington said that the battle of Waterloo was won on the playing-fields of Eton, he was referring not to organized games but to unorganized fights.

unceasing state of war between boys and masters, which developed on occasion into downright rebellion. In 1818 a revolt at Winchester College was quelled by two companies of troops with fixed bayonets.

It was a small number of exceptional headmasters who raised the public schools from this slough of degradation, physical cruelty and mental drudgery. Arnold of Rugby won the respect of his boys by his personality, and raised the tone of the school through the prefects, whom he inspired with his own ideal of 'a Christian gentleman'. Butler of Shrewsbury introduced modern subjects. Thring of Uppingham tried better-furnished classrooms with good pictures on the walls, stressed manual instruction, and gave thought to the less bright boys. The example set by these men soon took effect, and helped to provide standards for the many new schools which were founded in the middle years of the century.[1] The public schools continued to cater for the well-to-do, and clung to a code of behaviour which was designed for a ruling class, but they improved out of all knowledge in the course of the century.

Reform in the universities came later than in the public schools, for government action was required. In the earlier part of the nineteenth century there were only the two ancient and expensive universities of Oxford and Cambridge, where it was impossible to take a degree if not a member of the Church of England. Teaching facilities were badly organized, and fellows of colleges usually idle and incompetent. By the middle of the century some improvement could be seen, and both universities began to provide for the study of science. But meanwhile Lord Brougham[2] and a number of Radicals had founded University College, London, in order to provide university education without any religious test. The Anglicans replied by founding King's College, and the two together became London University by Act of Parliament in 1836. Durham University dates from 1832, but no other university was founded until Owen's College became the Victoria University of Manchester in 1880. After an interval of twenty years there were established in rapid succession Birmingham, Liverpool, Leeds, Sheffield and Bristol. The new civic universities (or 'Redbrick', as they were less respectfully

Marginal notes:
- Reforming head-masters, 1830–1870—
- Arnold
- Butler
- Thring
- Slumbers of Oxford and Cambridge
- University College, London, 1828
- London University, 1836
- Civic universities, 1900–1909

---

[1] The majority of the well-known public boarding schools of today were founded in the mid-nineteenth century. Foundations of this period included Bradfield, Cheltenham, Clifton, Haileybury, Malvern, Marlborough, Radley and Wellington. [2] See page 96 n.

called) shared certain characteristics: they were endowed by and situated in large industrial cities, and served the main occupations of these centres by developing strong technological departments. Moreover, unlike Oxford and Cambridge, the new foundations were non-residential and inexpensive, and provided no religious teaching. Wales gained its University in 1893 by the federation of three university colleges, to which a fourth was later added. Scotland had again been well ahead, for the universities of St Andrew's, Glasgow, Aberdeen and Edinburgh had all been founded before the end of the sixteenth century.

Reform of Oxford and Cambridge

The reform of the two ancient universities of England was undertaken by Gladstone's first Ministry. By the Universities Tests Act of 1871 university posts were thrown open to men of all religious persuasions, and a later Act made possible a better use of college endowments and the provision of teaching in modern subjects. As a result of these changes Oxford and Cambridge were fitted to play once more a worthy part in the national life.

Adult education outside the universities was to be had at the Mechanics Institutes, the first of which was opened in London by Dr Birkbeck (1826). From the 1880s there were also polytechnics, a growing number of evening schools (particularly in commercial subjects), and 'university extension' lectures given by university teachers to non-members of a university.

Higher education of girls

The higher education of girls was almost entirely neglected until the middle of the nineteenth century, except that wealthy people engaged governesses to teach their daughters at home. People then saw no point in educating girls, except to teach them 'accomplishments' such as music and deportment which might improve their chances in the marriage market. However, Queen's College, London, which was opened in 1848 largely to train governesses, provided the first approach to university education for women. Two of its students launched the pioneer girls' schools of this period, Miss Buss when she founded the North London Collegiate School in 1850, and Miss Beale when she became head of the Cheltenham Ladies' College in 1858.[1] The

---

[1] A schoolmaster once had to show these distinguished ladies round Clifton College. When his task was completed, he received from a colleague a note containing the immortal lines,

> Miss Buss and Miss Beale
> Cupid's darts do not feel:
> How different from us,
> Miss Beale and Miss Buss.

former became the model for a number of girls' public schools, governed by a trust, while many new girls' schools came into being when educational endowments were overhauled to make their funds available for girls as well as boys. To meet the difficulty of finding teachers for these schools, women's colleges were opened in the 1870s at both Oxford and Cambridge, their members being allowed to attend lectures and sit for examinations, but not until much later to take degrees Women at the universities

3 Developments of the Twentieth Century

Britain faced the twentieth century still lacking a complete and unified system of education. The Act of 1870 had left—had even widened—two deep rifts, one dividing State schools from those belonging to the churches, and one separating free elementary education for the poor from more advanced schooling for those who could pay. Weaknesses of the educational system

Attention was drawn to the second of these deficiencies by a judgement of the courts delivered in 1900, which pronounced it to be illegal for school boards to spend ratepayers' money on anything but elementary education. Technical classes had been provided since 1889 by the County Councils, but the higher grade schools set up by some boards had now to be stopped. Something, however, had to take their place; and the problem was tackled in a Bill introduced in 1902 by Balfour, the Conservative Prime Minister.

The Balfour Act made secondary education the concern of the State as the Forster Act had made elementary education. But it tidied up the latter as well. The numerous school boards set up in 1870 were swept away, and the County Councils were now given charge of the elementary schools.[1] They were also to run secondary schools on the local rates with the aid of a government grant. The schools provided by the religious societies were for the first time brought under public control and raised to the same level of efficiency as the rest, for while the societies met all building expenses (and still appointed the teachers), the councils met all other expenses from the rates. This angered the Nonconformists, who liked the board schools (now to be 'council schools') with their undenominational teaching of religion, and The Balfour Act, 1902

---

[1] Boroughs with a population of over 10,000 managed their own elementary schools.

were exasperated by the further help given to the church schools. Some Nonconformist leaders refused to pay their rates by way of protest, and in Parliament the Liberal opposition fought tooth and nail against the Act.

It was nevertheless enforced firmly and with success. It had the merit of bringing all types of education under the control of the local authorities, who worked in partnership with the State. **New secondary schools** The councils were soon busy building new secondary schools, as well as helping the old grammar schools with grants. The main drawback was that elementary and secondary schools were still planned to provide two different kinds of education for two different sets of children, instead of being successive stages in school life. This was partly remedied, from 1907, when all secondary schools receiving public money were required to give at least 25 per cent of their places free to scholars chosen from the elementary schools. Thus was begun the educational ladder by which a boy or girl might in favourable circumstances climb from elementary school to university. In twenty years numbers in secondary schools rose from 30,000 to 200,000, and many of these received a training comparable to that of the better grammar schools.

Meanwhile the elementary schools were improving, especially **Social services in the schools** in the towns. In 1908 social services were introduced, in the shape of school meals and medical examinations. Margaret McMillan broke new ground by opening in Deptford the first nursery school for children under five, for many children were found to be suffering from preventable physical defects when they first came to school. One achievement partly due to the elementary schools is the marked difference between the shocking amount of disease and dirt reported by the doctors in 1908 and the much improved conditions which obtain today.

The large majority of children who did not win places in secondary schools were still denied a fair start, however. The Act drafted by H. A. L. Fisher in 1918 attempted reforms, but these were smothered by post-war difficulties. Thus it was left for the Second World War to spur the country on to the advance which had long been recognized as necessary. The Act introduced **The Butler Act, 1944** by R. A. Butler recognized that education was incomplete without the secondary stage, and that this should be provided free for all children. Leaving the primary school at eleven, **—secondary education for all** children would receive their secondary education to the age of fifteen in a school which, it was at first intended, should be either grammar, with an academic curriculum, 'modern', with a practical bias, or—where such schools were provided—technical. The selection of children at eleven for different types of schools came under criticism on both social and educational grounds, and some local education authorities, notably the London County Council, then under Labour Party control, preferred 'comprehensive' schools. These were large, some over 2,000, had an unselected entry, provided all kinds of courses, and were usually handsomely housed and equipped in buildings costing some £750,000 each. The Butler Act declared that the leaving age should later be raised to sixteen, a decision finally made in 1964 to take effect in 1971. Meanwhile those leaving at fifteen were to have further part-time education till they were eighteen—a scheme which always came last in the list of financial priorities and so had little effect. The amount of money spent on education—and the amount of attention it received in Parliament and the Press—greatly increased, but persistent shortages of teachers and buildings kept many classes in both primary and secondary schools above the regulation size.

Reform extended even to the examination system, though the new General Certificate of Education differed little (except that it could be obtained by passing in one or two subjects only) from the old School and Higher School Certificates. It was also decided to establish a new Certificate of Secondary Education for those children who found G.C.E. standards too high or its syllabuses too academic; the majority of children would thus for the first time be brought within the system of public examinations. *G.C.E., 1951* *C.S.E., 1965*

The universities too had their share of public money and attention. In 1964 their affairs were placed for the first time in the care of the Government, a Minister of State for Higher Education and Science being responsible at least for their finances. Meanwhile their numbers and size greatly increased: in 1939 there were in England and Wales twelve universities and five university colleges with 50,000 students; in 1963 there were twenty-two with 113,000. In that year a committee headed by Lord Robbins proposed, at a cost of £1,420 million, a great expansion of higher education. Many universities were to be enlarged and six new ones created, so as to increase the number of places to 350,000 by 1980. *University expansion* *Robbins Report, 1963*

28. The British in India

1 Company and Crown in India

'Trade follows the Flag' was a popular dictum of nineteenth-century Imperialism. But the Flag may also follow Trade, as the history of British rule in India amply proves.

The East India Company
The East India Company, which enjoyed the monopoly of British trade with India, was formed in 1599. By the mid-eighteenth century, it had become far more than a commercial concern. To secure its trading privileges and depots against the French, the Company found itself concluding alliances with native rulers, waging war on a considerable scale, and acquiring extensive territories—thanks largely to the initiative of its ambitious servant, Robert Clive. Developments of this kind, which gave the Company power over millions of Indians, could not be ignored by the Government at home.

The Regulating Act, 1773

Warren Hastings, 1774-1785
To bring these political activities under some form of control, North's Ministry in 1773 introduced a Regulating Act, which laid down, among other things, that the Governor-General should be assisted—or checked—by a Council of four nominated by the Government and the Company. To Warren Hastings, as Governor-General from 1774 to 1785, fell the duty of trying out the new system. The territories of the Company at this time comprised Bengal, the Circars (a strip on the eastern coast of the Deccan), Madras with a small surrounding region, and the port of Bombay. It was the glory of Hastings not only to build up an efficient administration in the great region of Bengal, but to preserve these scattered and extensive territories during the American War of Independence. He did this without any assistance from home, and against the attacks of the greatest native powers of India in alliance with the French. His reward was impeachment and the longest trial in English history.[1]

The experiences of Hastings proved that the arrangements of the Regulating Act could ensure neither effective political control by the Government nor efficient collaboration between the Governor-General and the Council. The problem therefore faced

[1] See page 30.

Pitt when he became Prime Minister. His solution—the India Act of 1784—lasted until the Mutiny in 1857.

Pitt's India Act set up a dual control by the Crown and the Company, the Crown being the more powerful, if often the less active, partner. Despatches and instructions with any political bearing were to be supervised by a Governmental Board of Control in London; after 1812 its President was always a Cabinet Minister—the forerunner of the Secretary of State for India. The consent of this Board was necessary for the higher appointments made by the Company—the Governor-General, the Governors, and the Commander-in-Chief of the Company's forces. On the other hand the Governor-General, who was also Governor of Bengal, was strengthened for his tasks by being empowered to overrule his Council and by being granted fuller authority over the Governors of Madras and Bombay. Somewhat optimistically, the Act also prohibited the Company from making alliances with Indian states or taking part in Indian politics.

Pitt's India Act, 1784

The first Governor-General to wield the increased powers conferred by the India Act was Lord Cornwallis, the unfortunate commander who had surrendered to Washington at Yorktown. A man of fine character, he made a determined onslaught on every kind of corruption, even refusing the frequent requests of the Prince Regent to place his dissolute young friends in well-salaried posts.

Cornwallis, 1786–1793

Cornwallis did his best to avoid both alliances and conflicts, but when the barbarous Tipu, Sultan of Mysore, son of Haidar Ali, forced war on the British in 1790, Cornwallis defeated him with the aid of the other two major native powers, the Nizam of Hyderabad and the warlike chieftains who were leagued together in the Maratha Confederacy. All the once great native states were now defeated enemies or dependent allies. Yet the British were soon to face a situation almost as critical as that which Hastings had overcome; it was Richard Wellesley[1] who brought them through it with not only an Empire in India but an Empire of India.

The third Mysore War, 1790–1792

As the Company, under Pitt's Act, was standing aloof from Indian politics, native rulers had been seeking security by getting French officers to organize their armies. Danger from this source was all the greater after 1793, when Britain and France were at war. Soon Tipu of Mysore, an implacable enemy of the British, was referred to in Paris as 'Citoyen Tipou', and was negotiating

[1] Elder brother of Arthur Wellesley, later Duke of Wellington. Richard Wellesley, Earl of Mornington, became the Marquess Wellesley in 1799.

an alliance with French agents. Moreover, by 1798 Napoleon was in Egypt, entertaining visions of marching thence to India, as Alexander had done. Wellesley took rapid measures. He renewed the alliance with the Nizam, and won over the strongest of the Maratha rulers. Having thus isolated Tipu, he accused him of plotting with the French and gave him the choice of surrendering the greater part of his remaining lands and paying a huge indemnity—or war. Though outmatched by his enemies, Tipu chose war. At Seringapatam he was killed, his court and treasure captured, his army destroyed. Not all the commanders showed the abstinence of the Governor-General, who refused the £100,000 offered him as prize-money.

Seringapatam was as important a victory as Plassey. Clive's victory had placed Great Britain among the foremost powers of India; now she was easily the first. The Company took all the lands of Mysore on the west coast, and a belt linking them with Madras; other parts of Tipu's territory went to the Nizam of Hyderabad. In what remained of Mysore the former Hindu dynasty was restored, the terms of restoration in this case becoming the model for many 'subsidiary alliances' forced by Wellesley on Indian potentates. The ruler promised to have no relations with other powers except with the Company's approval; at his court he had an English Resident who was constantly consulted; and his power was maintained and his territory protected by a force of Company troops for which he usually paid by giving up some of his land. Indeed, as Warren Hastings had confessed, a British alliance was dreaded by the Indian powers as much as British enmity, because of the humiliations and exactions it involved. The system brought hatred upon the puppet prince, and often made the British responsible for the misgovernment of a ruler who without their aid would have been deservedly overthrown.

The Marathas, whose lightly-armed horsemen had long terrorized vast districts of India, found their scope for pillage much reduced by the British conquests, and their distrust of Wellesley's plans led inevitably to war. Four armies invaded the Maratha lands, and found the enemy's French-trained troops far from formidable, except at Assaye, where Arthur Wellesley s army fought against odds of 8–1 and paid for its victory with over 2,000 dead. By 1805 all but one of the Maratha princes were defeated, and had to cede lands to the Company and accept 'subsidiary' treaties.

Wellesley, 1798–1805

Seringapatam, 1799

'Subsidiary alliances'

Second Maratha War, 1803–1805

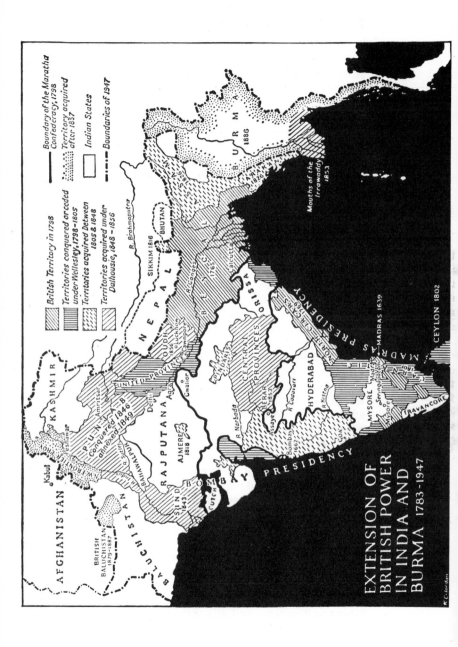

EXTENSION OF
BRITISH POWER
IN INDIA AND
BURMA 1783–1947

Key:

Boundary of the Maratha Confederacy, 1798
Territory acquired after 1857
Indian States
Boundaries of 1947

British Territory in 1798
Territories conquered or ceded under Wellesley, 1798–1805
Territories acquired Between 1805 & 1848
Territories acquired under Dalhousie, 1848–1856

AFGHANISTAN
Kabul
BALUCHISTAN
BRITISH BALUCHISTAN 1879–1887
KASHMIR
Peshawar
NORTH WEST FRONTIER
Amritsar
P·U·N·J·A·B Conquered 1846 annexed 1849
SIND 1843
Delhi
BAHAWALPUR
RAJPUTANA
AJMERE 1818
CUTCH
BOMBAY
BOMBAY 1662
NEPAL
UNITED PROVINCES
OUDH 1856
Lucknow
Cawnpore
Agra
Gwalior
SIKKIM 1816
BHUTAN
R. Brahmaputra
R. Ganges
BENGAL 1765
BURMA 1886
ARAKAN 1826
PINDARIS
CENTRAL PROVINCES
BERAR 1853
ORISSA
R. Narbada
R. Godavari
R. Krisna
HYDERABAD
MYSORE
Seringapatam
Mysore 1799
GOA
NORTHERN CIRCARS
MADRAS 1639
MADRAS PRESIDENCY
TRAVANCORE
Mouths of the Irrawaddy 1853
CEYLON 1802

PRESIDENCY

British power in
India, 1805

By this time the Directors were finding Wellesley too expensive a Governor-General and recalled him to England, but he had already extended the power of the British to the point where they found themselves responsible for the peace and order of all India. French influence was ended for ever, and the Mogul Emperor had passed under the Company's control. No strong independent power remained south-east of the Indus and Sutlej, where the Rajput rulers were seeking British protection. Wellesley had acted convincingly on his own belief that 'no greater blessing can be conferred on the native inhabitants of India than the extension of the British authority, influence, and power'

There was, however, no basis for settled peace. Wellesley had left the British frontier very ragged, with no natural boundaries to assist defence. The savage Pindari tribes, who enjoyed the protection of the Marathas, terrorized large areas of Central India and even raided British territory. Such were their cruelties that whole villages committed suicide to escape them. Everywhere beyond the British boundaries were Indian states for whose governments no description could be too bad; their conquest would be easy to accomplish and easy to justify.

Marquess of
Hastings,
1813–1823

Nepal War,
1814–1816

All these problems were attacked between 1813 and 1819 while the Marquess of Hastings was Governor-General. In 1814 boundary disputes and raids brought on a war with Nepal which turned out very differently from most affairs of the kind. The Gurkhas proved doughty fighters, and inflicted many defeats on the British. Finally the Maharajah had to give up some territory and receive a Resident, but he was subsequently left alone. He allowed his subjects to join the British forces, in which 'Johnny Gurk' won a fine reputation.

Pindari War
and third
Maratha War,
1816–1819

Next Hastings turned upon the Pindaris. Large forces were prepared and humiliating terms of alliance were dictated to the Marathas. They could not believe that all these preparations were aimed at the Pindaris only. They were right; the army was itching for a final settlement with the Marathas themselves, who richly merited their approaching fate. Even their military qualities now made a poor showing, for most of the battles were won by the British forces—mainly native troops with British officers—against heavy odds. By 1810 the Maratha fortresses had fallen and their capitals were occupied. Those rulers not deposed had to give up part of their lands and their powers, and the Marathas ceased to be a force in India. British territory was increased by large areas of the Western Deccan, with a belt linking Bombay with the Ganges. The Rajput states came under British protection, and all India except the Punjab and Sind was now controlled directly or indirectly by the British. The conquest of India was almost complete.

The great expansion of British power which ended in 1819 was succeeded by a period of intense reforming activity under the Governor-Generalship of Lord William Cavendish-Bentinck. The impulse to reform arose partly from a religious motive—the Evangelical sense of a mission to improve the lot of man—and partly from the pride of men who believed they represented a higher civilization. Well might they think so when confronted by some Indian practices of that time.

Bentinck, 1828–1835

The most shocking of these customs was suttee—the burning alive of a widow on her husband's funeral pyre. The practice had of course a religious basis, but the Hindu law of inheritance also helped to maintain it in favour with heirs. In some parts of India other kinds of human sacrifice were practised, and the killing of female infants was far from uncommon. In Bengal and elsewhere were found the criminals called Thugs, a hereditary caste who claimed the protection of the Hindu goddess Kali. They were more feared because they—religiously—murdered their victims before robbing them; and since they were capable of terrorizing whole districts it was found most difficult to secure witnesses against them. Bentinck, a Whig with strong humanitarian convictions, determined to suppress these evils, which his predecessors had tolerated—either because they thought it more discreet, or because they were too busy with war. Bentinck did not complete the task. The evils persisted in territory outside British control—in 1839 for instance, at the funeral of Ranjit Singh, 'Lion of the Punjab', four widows and seven dancing girls were sacrificed. Cases of suttee have even occurred during the present century; but great progress was nevertheless made, especially in exterminating the Thugs. Some Indians too had pressed for these humane measures, yet in fact they were seen as an imposition of Western standards and values.

Suttee and thuggee

At the same time Englishmen were thinking constructively about the future of India. An enlightened Governor of Madras wrote in 1824 that the British should rule India 'until the natives shall have abandoned most of their prejudices, and become sufficiently enlightened to frame a regular government for themselves, and to conduct and preserve it'. Something of this forward-looking spirit is to be seen in the Act of 1833. The Company had

India Act of
1833

lost its monopoly of trade with India in 1813, and while still in name a commercial body, was in fact mainly a political one. It was now forbidden to trade at all, though £630,000 was set aside from Indian revenues to compensate the shareholders for lost profits. India was to have a defined and uniform system of law, drawn up with due regard to 'the rights, feelings, and peculiar usages of the Indian people'. The Act contained the well-intentioned statement: 'The interests of the native subjects are to be consulted in preference to those of Europeans whenever the two come in conflict.'

Education in
English

More important than anything in the Act were the developments in education which began at this time. An enquiry was undertaken by the historian Macaulay, just appointed the first Legal Member of the Governor-General's Council, to decide whether instruction should be given in the classical languages of India—Sanskrit, Arabic and Persian—or in English, for the languages in everyday use were too numerous (about 150) and too limited. Macaulay came down heavily on the side of English, saying that 'a single shelf of a good European library is worth the whole literature of India and Arabia'—an opinion characteristic of the sublime confidence of the British in Western cultural superiority. His idea was that a select number of Indians would be instructed in Western learning, and then gradually influence the rest. What in fact happened was the development of higher education for a small number of Indians of the land-owning and professional classes, who learnt through the English tongue the political and scientific ideas of nineteenth-century Europe. They gained not only a language in which educated Indians could communicate with one another, but Western notions which were to transform the upper ranks of Indian society and make them impatient of British tutelage. The invasion of the Indian mind wrought changes as striking as the invasion of Indian territory.

*　　*　　*　　*　　*

The North-
West Frontier

Twenty years of comparative peace from 1819 to 1839 were followed by ten years of war, brought on in North-Western India by frontier problems and British fears of Russia. In the north-west remained two independent powers, the Amirs of Sind and the Sikhs; beyond was the barrier country of Afghanistan, its relations with India as yet unsettled. Beyond that again was Turkestan, which the Russians were approaching in the latest stage of their expansion in Asia. Lord Auckland, the new

Governor-General, was determined that Russian influence should not penetrate Afghanistan. Instead of securing the friendship of that country, however, he decided that it must become a vassal state, and so brought about one of the most disastrous and disgraceful episodes in British history. ^{Auckland, 1836–1842}

Auckland's plan was to depose Dost Mohammed, the popular Amir of Afghanistan, and put in his place Shah Suja, an exile who had lost the throne in 1809. An army escorted Shah Suja to Kabul—his entry was 'like a funeral procession'—and he was installed as Amir with a British Resident to guide him. If anything could have increased Shah Suja's unpopularity it was his obvious dependence on British support, and in 1841 there was a general rising of the tribes in favour of Dost Mohammed. Several of the British in Kabul were murdered; and the Resident's troops, evacuating under treaty, were butchered by the hillmen as they struggled through winter snows towards the Khyber Pass—one man out of 15,000 got through to meet the relieving force at Jalalabad. This force, which had been despatched by the new Governor-General, Lord Ellenborough, advanced to Kabul, sacked it and withdrew—after which Dost Mohammed duly returned to his throne. An army had been destroyed, £15,000,000 had been thrown away that could have been well spent in India, and none of the ill-conceived objectives of the enterprise had been gained.

The Afghan War was followed by the annexation of Sind. The Amir was assumed on the flimsiest grounds to be guilty of treachery against the British, and Sir Charles Napier, Ellenborough's representative, commented in his diary, 'We have no right to seize Sind, but we shall do so, and a very advantageous, useful, humane piece of rascality it will be'. Well might *Punch* summarize his achievement in the word 'Peccavi' ('I have sinned'). Napier won two battles, in which 'the ferocity on both sides was unbounded, the carnage horrible', and Sind was annexed. Napier justified his forecast by his rule in Sind, making war of a better kind on slavery, suttee, and many other barbarities.

A second consequence of the Afghan War was the conquest of the Punjab. The Sikhs, a strict and warlike Hindu sect, feared the designs of the British, and provoked war by attacking across the Sutlej. They fought with fanatical courage and the British at first barely avoided defeat; but ultimately the Sikhs were driven back across the river and defeated with heavy losses. The

Marginal notes:
- First Afghan War, 1839–1842
- Ellenborough, 1842–1844
- Annexation of Sind, 1843
- The Punjab
- First Sikh War, 1845–1846

Sikhs lost by the peace treaty all their lands south-east of the Sutlej; and because they could pay no indemnity, they had to give up the country of Kashmir—whose people, mainly Mohammedans, were entrusted by the British to a Hindu ruler. A second war, following upon a revolt of the Sikh lords, resulted in the outright annexation of the Punjab. British power now enclosed the valley of the Indus and stretched to the great mountain barriers which are the natural frontiers of the sub-continent.

Second Sikh War, 1848–1849

The government of the Punjab was entrusted to two remarkable brothers, Henry and John Lawrence, who worked unceasingly for the welfare of the people, halving the peasants' tax burden and setting up fair courts of justice. When the storm of the Mutiny broke over India soon afterwards, the Punjab, thanks to their labours, gave decisive help to the British.

Burmese Wars, 1824–1826 and 1852

Responsibility for India's frontiers involved the British in wars against Burma as well as in the north-west. Burmese attacks on Assam were punished in 1826, after two years of warfare, by the annexation of the coastal strip. Twenty-six years later, Southern Burma was also taken.

Dalhousie, 1848–1856

The annexations of the Punjab and Southern Burma were the work of Lord Dalhousie, who proved himself one of the most masterful and acquisitive of India's rulers. His maxim was that 'the British Government is bound not to put aside or neglect such rightful opportunities of acquiring territory as may present themselves'. The opportunities came, apart from conquest, when Indian rulers died without heirs, though Hindu custom allowed a ruler to adopt an heir with the consent of the superior power.

Doctrine of lapse

This consent was now refused in one case after another, and in this way several important states fell into British hands. In 1856 Oudh was annexed for a different reason—the utter viciousness of its government, which would have justified its annexation at any time since Plassey; when the people of neighbouring districts heard cannon-fire in Oudh they knew the King was collecting his taxes. But the step was not entirely wise; for it seemed that whether Indians fought, like the Sikhs, or slavishly submitted, like the King of Oudh, the end was the same.

Annexation of Oudh

Westernization

The doubts and fears aroused by the annexations were intensified by the rest of Dalhousie's activities. He was filled with a burning zeal to stamp out misgovernment and drive India along the path of progress. He planned first-rate roads, especially the Grand Trunk road from Calcutta to Peshawar; irrigation canals were dug, new harbours built, coal and iron mines opened up.

A cheap postal service was started, and plans made for a comprehensive system of education. Steps were taken to conserve the forests and improve every branch of agriculture. The telegraph was introduced, and the energy of the West appeared in its most striking form with the building of the first railways, a project close to Dalhousie's heart. This restless activity affected all classes, and sowed disquiet and fear in Indian minds. The results were apparent within a year of Dalhousie's retirement—in the great Indian Mutiny.

2 The Indian Mutiny

The Mutiny was mainly a revolt of the sepoys—native troops in the employ of the Company. But the mutineers, who had been in a bad state of discipline for some time, were giving expression to more than purely military discontents.

Causes of the Mutiny, 1857—

The Bengal sepoys—many of them high-caste Hindus—resented a proposal to form new regiments from Gurkhas, Sikhs and Punjab Muslims; and they equally objected to the regulation of 1856 which required recruits to serve overseas if necessary—for a Hindu might lose caste by travelling in a crowded troopship. The sepoys from Oudh resented the annexation of their kingdom, the treatment of their King, and the loss of army privileges when they ceased to belong to an Indian state. And all the sepoys, one way or another, resented the new cartridges.

—Proposals for new regiments and overseas service—

When the new Enfield rifle was introduced, the soldier had to bite the cartridge from the clip in loading his rifle. The rumour spread that the cartridges were greased with animal fat; if it was beef fat it would be sacrilege for the Hindu, to whom the cow was a a sacred animal; if it was lard it would defile the Mohammedan, to whom the pig was unclean. The rumour was true of some of the cartridges issued, but the issue was stopped upon the first complaints. Subsequent denials were not believed by the sepoys; several incidents occurred, and two regiments were disbanded before a third, already insubordinate, was ordered to use the hated cartridges. When eighty-five troopers were sentenced in May 1857 to ten years' imprisonment for disobedience the outbreak began in earnest.

—Greased cartridges—

The sepoys were thus stirred by religious and political grievances as well as the discontents of rankers. The Mutiny cannot

—Dalhousie's innovations

be understood without the background of Dalhousie's 'westerniz-ing' policy and the upsetting of Indian life and custom it involved. Indeed, in the light of this it is astonishing that the Mutiny did not receive wider support. Dalhousie had dispossessed many landowners and petty rulers, and the privileged classes in general saw their chances of exploiting their fellows disappearing. The rigid rules of the ingrained caste system were threatened, for example by railway carriages in which members of all castes must sit together. It was said that these attacks on caste were part of a planned campaign by which the Government would force Christianity on the country. The Muslims, on the other hand, once a ruling sect in India, felt that their position had been steadily weakened ever since the British had come. India was being jerked out of its ancient grooves, and did not like it.

The Mutiny might have been a dangerous rising. In fact it was much less dangerous than its dramatic happenings make it appear. The region later called the United Provinces was the centre of the disurbance, which spread to Central India, but over most of the country life went on as usual. Yet the situa-tion looked ugly enough at the outset. Some of the British troops normally in India were in Afghanistan, some were on their way to Burma, and some had not yet returned from the Crimean War, when three sepoy regiments at Meerut murdered their officers, released the men imprisoned for refusing to use the new cart-ridges, and marched on Delhi. Joined there by others, they took possession of the city, and proclaimed the old Mogul King of Delhi once more Emperor of India. Then they did nothing for three weeks—a valuable respite for the British, whose total forces in India numbered only 40,000 as against 230,000 sepoys.

In the Delhi–Cawnpore region the revolt was general. There was nothing for the British to do but to hold on where possible with the tiny garrisons available, and await relief. And slowly— for transport was very scarce—relief came; not only from Calcutta but from the recently conquered North-West, which might have been expected to throw its forces eagerly on the rebel side. Instead, John Lawrence was able to raise Sikh levies to fight for the British and, with Dost Mohammed and his Afghans remain-ing quiet, to organize the Punjab as a second British base. Thence John Nicholson, an inspiring leader, marched to reinforce the 5,000 who had been holding the Ridge outside Delhi against the onslaughts of 30,000 sepoys through the scorching heat of June and July. On arrival he urged that the walled city should be

Course of the Mutiny

Delhi

attacked; on 14 September an entry was made, Nicholson being mortally wounded, and after six days' fighting the city was recovered. Though many of the citizens were known to be friendly the troops committed wholesale massacre, in the same way as the sepoys in their moment of triumph had murdered all the Europeans they could find. Thus one of the main centres of rebellion was put out of action. If help from the Punjab had failed, and the forces on the Ridge had been overcome, the whole of North India might well have been lost.

Meanwhile at Cawnpore the leadership of the mutineers had been assumed by the Nana Sahib, adopted son of a deposed Maratha prince. After a siege of three weeks the small British force was compelled by hunger and thirst to negotiate a surrender on 27 June. Nevertheless, the men were massacred, and when Havelock's relieving force arrived from Allahabad, they discovered an atrocity which was long remembered above all other horrors of the Mutiny. The Nana Sahib had two days earlier ordered the death of two hundred and eleven women and children who were his captives. The sepoys had refused, but five of his palace servants were found to do the work of butchery; they had hacked the bodies to pieces and thrown them down a well. This crime was held to justify any retaliation the Government troops might inflict. *Cawnpore*

In Lucknow, forty miles away, a thousand British troops and 700 sepoys were holding out against 60,000 Indians, though Sir Henry Lawrence, the Resident in Oudh, had been killed. They were relieved by Havelock on 25 September, and this success, coming soon after the fall of Delhi, meant that the Mutiny had failed; though the British forces in Lucknow were besieged and relieved twice more before their ordeals ended. *Lucknow*

If the Mutiny had thrown up competent leaders the whole area between the Sutlej and Narbada rivers could have been overrun, and the movement might have flared into a war of independence. Instead, the risings in different centres took their course without any general plan, and although Delhi was so promptly seized no rebel government was set up. The mutineers even failed to cut the new telegraph wires which were almost the only means of communication open to the British. The heroism of small bodies of British, soldiers and civilians, was not matched by the rebels; Indian honours went rather to the loyal sepoys, Sikhs, and Gurkhas who fought, outnumbered, for the Europeans. *Failure of the Mutiny*

With the end of military operations a clamour for wholesale
revenge arose in both Britain and India. It was wisely resisted
by the Governor-General, Lord Canning—'Clemency' Canning
as he was afterwards called—but the breach of all rules of war
by both sides and the ruthless punishment of the rebels under
martial law before peace was proclaimed had already done irrepar-
able harm. Racial hatred was thus the worst legacy of the Mutiny
and a lasting one. Many of the British, unable to forget the
unexpected attacks and the slaughter of women and children, now
regarded Indians with distrust and contempt, and were determined to keep them out of responsible positions, thus perpetuat-
ing one of the grievances that caused the outbreak.

In regard to the westernizing policy, however, the Mutiny
taught a lesson: the British no longer believed that European
ways could quickly bring happiness to India, and were careful
to avoid changes which would arouse Indian prejudices. There
were no more annexations of Indian states—700 of which still
survived. On the other hand the Indians now felt that the British,
efficient and aloof, were there to stay.

After the Mutiny, changes were inevitable. The obvious precautions were taken in the Army. The Crown took over the
Company's troops, the artillery was manned by Europeans, and
in other branches their proportion was raised to one-third. The
East India Company was abolished—a fate it had hardly deserved
—but its passing made little difference, for since 1853 the higher
posts in the Indian Civil Service had been filled by competitive
examination and not by the Company's patronage. Henceforward, instead of the Governor-General there was the Viceroy,
the direct representative of the Crown; though with the invention
of the telegraph he was under stricter control by the Secretary of
State. So ended the long and strange history of 'John Company',
first a trading venture, then a sovereign power, and finally an
agent, more and more controlled, of the Crown.

3 Modern India

For almost twenty years, since the opening of the First Afghan
War, India had suffered strife and terror. Now, from 1858, began
a period of calm, broken, however, by the last important war
fought upon India's frontiers.

The North-West Frontier was a constant worry, partly because of the restless hillmen beyond the valleys of the Punjab, and The North-West Frontier again partly because of Russia's advance towards Afghanistan as she subdued the tribes of the barbarous region between the Caspian Sea and China. The frontier problem took on a new urgency in 1876–78 when Britain and Russia came so near to blows in the Balkan crisis.[1] Disraeli's solution was to meet the Russian advance half-way by getting Afghanistan under British control—the 'forward policy' which had proved so disastrous when tried by Lord Auckland forty years earlier.[2]

Lord Lytton, the Viceroy, having first outflanked Afghanistan Lytton, 1876–1880 by making Baluchistan a protectorate, demanded that a British mission should be received in Kabul. He followed this demand, when the Amir hesitated, by the despatch of three armies against the capital. The Amir fled, and his son accepted a treaty by which Afghanistan must receive British protection, conduct its foreign policy under British supervision, accept a British Resident at Kabul, and amend the frontier so as to give the British control of the passes. Having thus reduced Afghanistan to a vassal state, Lytton congratulated himself on saving the Amir from 'alliance with the ambitious, energetic and not over-scrupulous' government of Russia.

But the Amir's subjects did not appreciate their good fortune. Second Afghan War, 1879–1881 Trouble began in his army and flared into general rebellion; the Resident was murdered, and the Amir fled into the British camp. General Sir Frederick Roberts reoccupied Kabul, hanged many rebels and burned their villages, and rescued a force at Kandahar after a famous march of 313 miles through the mountains in twenty-three days. His troops then left the country, and Lytton was replaced and his policy reversed by Gladstone. It was a pity that two wars were needed to teach the lesson summed up in Roberts's verdict: 'The less the Afghans see of us, the less they will dislike us.'

Only once after 1880 was there difficulty with the Afghans, when they committed aggression in 1919. But the frontier region was long a scene of trouble, for there were still on the Indian side a million and a half Muslim tribesmen whose land was too barren to occupy them as whole-time farmers, who prized a rifle more than a wife, and who could always be stirred by a summons to a holy war.

The last of the wars to extend India's frontiers came in 1885, Complete annexation of Burma, 1886 and resulted in the annexation of the rest of Burma. The new

[1] See page 195.   [2] See page 397.

King of Upper Burma, who had secured his position on the throne by murdering eighty of his relatives, had imposed handicaps on British trade, and the British were anxious to forestall the French, who were growing very active in that region.

★   ★   ★   ★   ★

Condition of the people

After the Mutiny the government of India settled down into a steady routine which was very efficient up to a point, but gave no scope for the growing desire of Indians to run their own country. Even by 1915, no more than 5 per cent of the higher civil service posts were filled by Indians. The typical British administrator was the District Officer, who often had charge of an area the size of Norfolk and a population as big as New Zealand's. He spent much of his time in touring his district[1] and was looked to for help in time of flood, famine and other disasters. But it was too much to expect of 5,000 British officials that they should create happiness and prosperity in a country of nearly 300 million people (in 1900), most of them illiterate peasants living in India's 500,000 villages on the lowest possible standard, and many of them hopelessly sunk in debt. In the more peaceful conditions produced by British rule the population rapidly increased, and came to press hard upon the country's food output. There were terrible famines, one of which caused between 5 and 6 million deaths in 1877. Plague was brought to India in 1896, and in six years carried off over a million people; the influenza epidemic which swept the world in 1918 killed 8 million Indians.

Curzon, 1899-1905

The bureaucratic government of India was seen at its best under that supremely energetic Viceroy, Lord Curzon, who stirred up every department of the administration. He gave India a first-rate police force, prepared vast irrigation schemes and helped the peasantry in many ways, especially by setting up co-operative societies to furnish credit on fair terms—perhaps the most promising solution of India's agrarian problems.

Nationalist movement

Meanwhile the desire for self-government had been strongly aroused in educated Indians by their contact with Western culture. This first declared itself in the formation of the Indian National Congress—an organization started largely by the efforts of an Englishman, Allan Hume, retired from the Indian Civil Service. For a long time its members favoured the spread of Western civilization and believed in the necessity of British rule,

National Congress, 1885

[1] It was reckoned, however, that even when British rule ended most of the people of India had never seen a European.

asking simply for the liberties which Britain had fostered in her white Dominions—though outside the Congress appeared extremists who were opposed to the British connection entirely. All this nationalist feeling was reinforced by economic discontents. India's imports cost more than her exports, which were mainly of raw materials sold with little profit to the producer. The growing industries were largely in European hands and there was much complaint of 'the drain' of India's wealth represented by the profits on British capital invested in railways and other big undertakings.

Only the most cautious steps towards self-government were taken in the nineteenth century. Before the end of the century Indians—either selected or elected—were included in the legislative councils of the Viceroy and the provincial governors, but usually they could be outvoted by the official members (corresponding to ministers in England), and each governor could make laws by himself if he thought it necessary to do so. An important departure was made in 1909 by the Morley-Minto reforms, so called after the Secretary of State and Viceroy who inaugurated them. The provincial legislative councils were now to have an Indian majority, elected indirectly, and the Imperial Legislative Council was to have a large proportion, though not a majority, of elected members. Morley made it clear that this change was not meant to give India real parliamentary government, for which he thought the country quite unqualified. The new bodies would be for consultation rather than legislation, and they could not, of course, control the executive; so they made the most of the one function allowed to them—criticism. *Beginnings of self-government*

Morley-Minto reforms, 1909

Events outside India helped to fan the nationalist movement—notably the Japanese victory over Russia in 1905, and the humiliating treatment of Indians who emigrated to South Africa. The war of 1914–18 produced an outburst of loyal enthusiasm and India played a worthy part, contributing 800,000 combatant troops. But when the war was over, the one idea of officials seemed to be to return to normal, and hopes of self-government were disappointed. *India and the First World War*

The Government in England, however, realized that a further advance was required, and E. S. Montagu, Secretary of State, went to India to consult with Lord Chelmsford (Viceroy, 1916–21). The result was the India Act of 1919, whereby there was to be an elected majority in the central Legislative Assembly as well as in the provincial legislatures. In the provinces certain *Montagu-Chelmsford reforms ('diarchy'), 1919* 'transferred' subjects—health, education, agriculture—would be in charge of ministers responsible to the legislatures; but law, police and finance were 'reserved' subjects, handled by officials who were not answerable to the elected representatives. This ingenious division of government into responsible and irresponsible sections was called 'diarchy'. It was India's first taste of real parliamentary government, but it was such an obvious half-loaf that she was sure to ask for more.

Diarchy had little success; Congress—in which the extremists now had a majority—condemned the whole plan and boycotted the elections. There were widespread disorders and occasional terrorist crimes. Racial hatred was embittered by a massacre at Amritsar in 1919, when General Dyer, after Europeans had been murdered in the town, ordered troops to fire on a packed crowd of Indians who had assembled in defiance of his prohibition; 379 were killed and 1,200 wounded.

The Amritsar massacre, 1919

The leader of Indian nationalism in this period of ferment was Mahatma Gandhi, once a moderate, who first appeared as a champion of the Indian cause in South Africa. In 1918 he became a Nationalist, and threw himself into the campaign for self-government. Belonging to one of the lower Hindu castes, he could readily win followers from the humbler classes, and he impressed his ideas upon his countrymen by his character, especially by the simplicity and asceticism of his way of life. Though a shrewd negotiator and a skilful propagandist, Gandhi based his campaigns on religious ideas. His plan was to force further reforms from the Government by 'non-violent non-co-operation'—a strike on the part of officials and professional workers, and a boycott of British goods.

Gandhi, 1869–1948

Gandhi's campaign, despite his teaching, led to frequent disorders, but a new hope arose when Lord Irwin[1] established friendly relations with Gandhi and implanted the idea that India's future should be settled by conference between British and Indians on equal terms. Accordingly a Round Table Conference met in London to work out the means whereby India should attain 'dominion status'. But the phrase was not properly defined, and when Congress was refused a guarantee of immediate self-government, it declared for full independence, boycotted the Conference and renewed the campaign of civil disobedience.

Irwin, 1926–1931 Viceroy

A new India Act was eventually passed in 1935, but it showed few traces of Indian influence, and savoured little of 'dominion

India Act, 1935

[1] Later Lord Halifax.

status'. It made some notable steps forward, however. Diarchy was abolished in the provinces, whose governments now became fully responsible, but was introduced at the centre, where the Viceroy was to control foreign affairs and finance, while other matters were to be in the hands of responsible ministers. With the introduction of parliamentary government at the centre went another ambitious proposal: that the government of India should become a federal one in which should be included not only the provinces of British India, but also the purely Indian states.

From 1937 to 1939 responsible government in the provinces was tried with some success, with Congress Party ministries in seven provinces. But they resigned in 1939 in protest against the Viceroy's declaration of war without consulting Indians, and the governors of those provinces had to take charge. The other feature of the Act, the setting up of a federal government, was held up by two difficulties which were unsolved when war broke out in 1939 —the framing of terms acceptable to the princes, and the opposition between Hindus and Muslims. The Muslims had never admitted the claim of Congress to speak for all Indians, and now, under the leadership of M. A. Jinnah, evolved a plan for a separate and independent Muslim state in India, called Pakistan. Thus deadlock prevailed at the opening of a war which was to come to India's very gates. *Hindus and Muslims*

During the war the demand for independence, on the one hand, grew stronger; the British, on the other hand, refused to consider granting it until the war was over. When Sir Stafford Cripps visited India in 1942 with new proposals agreed by the Cabinet, Gandhi described them as 'a post-dated cheque on a crashing bank'—the Japanese forces were overrunning Burma at the time and soon reached India's eastern frontier. The proposals were withdrawn, and Gandhi launched another civil disobedience campaign, which led to the imprisonment of himself and several other Indian leaders. There was a good deal of disturbance, but the Viceroy, Lord Linlithgow (1936–43), handled it firmly and neither production nor recruiting was seriously affected. *India demands self-rule* *Linlithgow, 1936–1943*

By the time the war was over and Cripps went to India again in 1946 the rift between Hindus and Muslims was wider than ever, and each suspected the British of favouring the rival group. There was a deadlock which Lord Wavell (Viceroy from 1943 to 1947) could do nothing to resolve. It was broken only when the British Labour Government announced that it would hand over power not later than June 1948 to whatever authorities were then *Wavell, 1943–1947* ready to receive it, and sent out Lord Mountbatten as Viceroy to prepare for this event.

Mountbatten, 1947

Mountbatten at once accepted partition as inevitable, and advanced the day of independence to 15 August 1947. This gave him nine weeks in which to divide the sub-continent, the army

Independence of India and Pakistan, 1947

and the civil service, and to arrange the transfer of power. By a remarkable blend of determination and personal charm he succeeded, remaining for a short time as the first Governor-General of an independent India, Jinnah filling the same office in the state of Pakistan. Unfortunately, sanguinary episodes marred the partition. Violence broke out on a scale quite unforeseen, especially in the Punjab, where the Sikhs were enraged by the rejection of their special claims to self-rule. Muslims were massacred in vast numbers; where they were in the majority they retaliated upon the Hindus. The total of deaths was not less than 200,000, and may have been over half a million. Immense crowds of refugees, fearful of a similar fate, poured across the new frontier in both directions, imposing a baffling problem on the newly-established governments. Four-and-a-half million Hindus fled from Pakistan to India, six million Muslims from India to Pakistan. There was also an outbreak of violence in predominantly Muslim Kashmir, which was invaded by neighbouring Muslim warriors to prevent its Indian ruler from taking it over; the Indian army intervened, and the outcome was an uneasy truce which was to last, since every attempt at agreement failed, for many years. These episodes might suggest that Britain's departure from India was over-hasty.

Death of Gandhi, 1948

Gandhi did not long survive the achievement of independence, to which he had contributed so much. Tireless to the end in trying to appease Hindu-Muslim violence, he was assassinated in 1948 by one of the extremist Hindus to whom moderation was irreligious. Always a prophet of non-violence, he was looked upon by most Hindus, and by many others, as a saint. When he was the leader of millions he still went about on foot and lived a life of the strictest self-denial, associating himself with the poor and disinherited. He allowed circumstances sometimes to change his policy, but never his moral principles, and was grieved by the failure of his countrymen to live up to his pacifist teaching.

Both India and Pakistan remained within the Commonwealth, but not for long in allegiance to the Crown. First India and then Pakistan decided to adopt a republican form of government, an arrangement which the elasticity of the Commonwealth made possible. They were closely followed into independence by Ceylon and Burma, the latter choosing to end her connection with the Commonwealth at the same time as she achieved self-rule. All four countries, as they faced formidable problems of every kind, but especially economic problems caused by pressure of population, were fortified by ideas of progress and liberty which they inherited from the West, and were assisted by civil services, still in some cases using English as an official language, which had been trained in the days of British rule.

Independence of Ceylon and Burma, 1948

29. The British in Africa

1 South Africa

Cape Colony

The Dutch settlement at the Cape of Good Hope, first taken over by Britain in 1795 and then restored by the Peace of Amiens, was seized in 1806, and retained by the Treaty of Vienna.

When the British took over control, the Colony contained 26,000 whites, 39,000 slaves and some 2 million free Africans, among whom were the peaceful Hottentots, and the Bantu or Kaffirs, warlike tribes who were found in the south-east and dominated much of the interior. To make a bulwark for the Colony against these tribes, the British Government in 1820 sent out, and provided land for, 5,000 settlers, who established themselves in the region of Algoa Bay to form the province of Albany —an early example of planned emigration.

In general, however, South Africa at this time attracted few settlers. Only the missionary societies took much interest in the Colony, and they, in their zeal to protect the African against steady white encroachment, swayed the Government at home against the Dutch—with most unfortunate results. When slavery was abolished throughout the British Empire by the Act of 1833, the Dutch, who had treated their slaves reasonably well, resented the interference and were in many cases cheated of their compensation.

Dutch grievances—

Abolition of slavery, 1833;

Most of the Dutch owned no slaves, however, and the Government's attitude to the hostile tribes was a worse grievance. In 1834 the new province of Albany was invaded by Kaffirs (in the sixth Kaffir war, by Dutch reckoning), who killed many settlers and lifted 120,000 cattle and horses. Sir Benjamin d'Urban, the Governor, drove out the Kaffirs and seized part of their territory, to give the Colony a better frontier. But Lord Glenelg, the Colonial Secretary—of whom someone unkindly said that South African problems caused him many sleepless days—adopted the missionaries' view that the whites had provoked the war. He accordingly revoked the annexation, and recalled d'Urban.

Policy towards Kaffirs: d'Urban in Natal

Experience of this kind convinced many frontier Boers[1]

[1] 'Boer' is the Dutch for farmer.

410

that British citizenship was a blessing they would rather be without. Moreover, they needed fresh grazing land which the Cape region could not provide. Their remedy was heroic. Some thousands of them—but not the majority—set off, with their families and belongings in their ox-waggons, into the unexplored interior, where they could find freedom. From behind laagered waggons they beat off attacks by Matabele and Zulus, and won their way through to their Promised Land. Many of the trekkers at first went into Natal, but when this, too, was again annexed by the British Government in 1843 they left it, and joined the others

The Great
Trek, 1836

British annexation of Natal,
1843

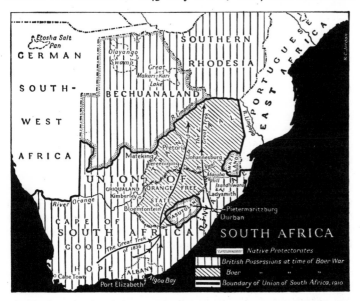

who had trekked across the Orange River or even far beyond the Vaal.

The British Government was not so easily eluded. Anxious to control the dealings of the Boers with the native tribes, in 1848 it annexed the whole region across the Orange River. The move aroused opposition at home as well as among the Boers, and in 1852 it was reversed when the British Government recognized the right of the Transvaal Boers to govern themselves as an independent state. Two years later, by the Convention of Bloemfontein, the Orange Free State gained a similar position.

The opportunity of federation was missed, and there were now

Sand River
Convention,
1852

Convention of
Bloemfontein,
1854

in South Africa two British colonies and two Boer republics, the latter surrounded by African tribes. With these the Boer states, weak though they were, constantly quarrelled and fought. The tribes were championed by British missionaries—the Transvaal President threatened to kill David Livingstone if he caught him —and were protected against the Boers by the Governor of Cape Colony in his other capacity as High Commissioner for all native questions. The High Commissioner often intervened to define the vague frontiers of the Boer republics; when, for instance, diamonds were discovered in a district claimed by both the Griqua tribe and the Orange Free State, the issue was decided in favour of the Griquas, who then made over their rights to the British Government. Compensation to the amount of £90,000 was granted to the Free State—not an expensive outlay for a clear title to the Kimberley diamond fields.

Griqualand and diamonds, 1867

When the Zulus recovered their zest for fighting under their new chieftain, Cetewayo, the Transvaal felt itself to be in danger. Lord Carnarvon, Disraeli's Colonial Secretary, was not displeased to have an excuse to bring the Transvaal again under British control, and thus to advance his favourite project of a South African federation. An experienced Natal administrator, Sir T. Shepstone, was sent to investigate affairs in the Transvaal. He found that the resources of the public treasury amounted to 12s. 6d. The President agreed (on condition that he was allowed to make a public protest) to come again under British rule for the sake of British protection, and Shepstone declared the Transvaal to be once more annexed to the Crown. But many Boers in fact objected to the loss of their independence, and they regretted it all the more when the menace to their safety was removed by a British campaign against the ferocious Zulus. This began with a disaster at Isandhlwana, where an ill-defended camp was wiped out by the Zulu spearmen, but ended in complete triumph at Ulundi.

Transvaal re-annexed, 1877

Zulu War, 1879

Disraeli was hotly attacked by Gladstone for sanctioning this 'forward' policy. The Boers therefore expected a reversal of it when the Liberal leader came into power in 1880. But the Liberals were hesitant, and the Boers impatiently declared the independence of 'the South African Republic' (the Transvaal). When an inadequate force advanced from Natal to compel their obedience, they defeated it at Majuba Hill. Gladstone's Government then gave way, rather than undertake a difficult war with an uneasy conscience, and the Transvaal was granted self-government under the suzerainty of the British Crown.

First Boer War: Majuba Hill, 1881

The Pretoria Convention, 1881

This example of Liberal moderation was soon forgotten, however, in a burst of imperialist expansion which changed the face of South Africa. To the north of Griqualand (West), the diamond area, lay Bechuanaland. The habitable part of it formed a corridor between the Kalahari desert on the west and the Boer republic on the east, and provided the only route by which Cape Colony could reach out to the north. The Boers, the Portuguese and the Germans (newly arrived in South-West Africa) were all casting eager eyes upon this region, so the British Government annexed it in 1885.

Annexation of Bechuanaland, 1885

Further north again was Matabeleland, ruled by King Lobengula from his kraal in Bulawayo. The extension of British power into his vast and barbarous hinterland was the work of one man, Cecil Rhodes. 'My North', he called it.

Matabeleland: Cecil Rhodes

Coming to Africa at the age of seventeen for the sake of his health, Rhodes had made a fortune at the Kimberley diamond-diggings, taken a degree at Oxford, and entered the Cape Parliament, all by the time he was twenty-seven. In another ten years he had become Prime Minister of the Cape and managing director of the South Africa Company, and had amalgamated all the Kimberley mines into the de Beers Company, thus bringing nine-tenths of the world's output of diamonds under his control. Characteristically, he stipulated that the surplus profits of de Beers should be devoted to empire-building; for the passion of his life was the extension of British power.

Foremost in Rhodes's dreams was an all-British railway from the Cape to Cairo. The first step in this great plan was to gain control of the vast region of 750,000 square miles between the Limpopo and the Zambesi which was ruled by Lobengula. Rhodes could not get the Government to annex it, but he contrived to make a treaty in which Lobengula granted rights to extract any minerals that might be found in his dominions. To exploit these rights the British South Africa Company was formed, with a government charter which granted privileges of administration. When war broke out between the Company's settlers and the Matabele, spears and courage availed little against Maxim machine-guns. On the defeat of the Matabele, 200,000 of their cattle were distributed among the Company's victorious volunteers. After a second outbreak had been crushed Matabeleland was taken over by the Company and renamed Rhodesia. Rhodes could now claim to have ended the rule of barbarism south of the Zambesi. He could also point to a sharp and welcome

British South Africa Company, 1889

Matabele Wars, 1893 and 1896

Rhodesia

rise in the shares of the Company, which had spent heavily in developing the new territory and had so far made no profit.

The Transvaal: the Rand gold-field, 1886

The creation of Rhodesia shut in the Boers on the north, while British control of Bechuanaland hemmed them in on the west. But still more galling for the Boers were the consequences of the discovery of gold in the Transvaal in 1886. The Boers took no part themselves in exploiting the Rand goldfield; they preferred the old life of the veld to the bustle and turmoil of the mushroom city of Johannesburg. Hating the intrusion of these 'Uitlanders',

Uitlanders

mostly British, who came flocking in to 'get rich quick', the Boers did everything they could to hinder and to fleece them. Freight charges on the inadequate railways were absurdly high. A monopoly was set up to sell dynamite for the mines at an exorbitant price. The law courts used only Dutch and virtually no education was provided in the English tongue. British citizenship must be given up; ten years' residence was required for the franchise; and meanwhile the Uitlanders, who soon outnumbered the whole Boer population of the Transvaal and paid nine-tenths of the state's taxes, had to be content with 'second-class citizenship'.

Kruger and Rhodes

The Boer attitude was worthily represented by the President of the Transvaal Republic. Paul Kruger, a man of little education, came of farming stock and had taken part as a boy of ten in the Great Trek. He hated everything new and everything foreign. His reply to the Uitlanders' grievances was simple: 'This is my country, these are my laws. Those who do not like my laws can leave my country.' This attitude was intolerable to Rhodes, alike as empire-builder and as a large shareholder in Rand gold. These ignorant farmers with their dog-in-the-manger behaviour stood in the way of all his schemes.

Rhodes's solution was a rising in Johannesburg, for which he supplied the weapons, and a simultaneous attack upon the Transvaal from the outside. The Company mustered armed railway 'police' in Bechuanaland at the most convenient point on

The Jameson Raid, 1895

the Transvaal's western border, and L. S. Jameson led them into the Transvaal in the last days of 1895. Everything in the scheme was Rhodes's work, except the timing. He vainly tried to stop Jameson when he found that the plotters in Johannesburg had cooled off and were nowhere near ready. The raid was a dismal failure. Jameson's band of fewer than 500 was surrounded and taken prisoner; the leaders were handed over to the British authorities, tried in London, and sentenced to terms of imprisonment not exceeding fifteen months. The unfortunate results of this desperate and unscrupulous venture were to strengthen the hold of Kruger on the Transvaal, to destroy that of Rhodes on Cape Colony, and to worsen relations between British and Boers. For the Cape Boers would never trust Rhodes again, and without their support he had to resign the position of Prime Minister. The Boers suspected too that Joseph Chamberlain, the keenly imperialist Colonial Secretary in London, was an accomplice in the crime, as indeed he was. Disgrace of Rhodes

During the next few years there were negotiations with Kruger to improve the position of the Uitlanders, but on the British side Sir Alfred Milner, Governor at the Cape, was dictatorial, while Kruger hardly admitted that the British had any right to intervene. A petition to the Queen from 22,000 Uitlanders complaining that 'the condition of your Majesty's subjects in this state has become well-nigh intolerable' served its intended purpose of stiffening the British Government's attitude. Moreover, the British Press and public seemed positively to desire war. On both sides counsels of moderation were ignored, and troops were moved in preparation for the final argument. The Boers would have been foolish to await the arrival of British reinforcements; they sent an ultimatum demanding the removal of forces from their frontiers, and on its rejection declared war, the Orange Free State joining the Transvaal. The attitude of the British Government to the two little Boer republics looked very much like bullying; it even looked like bullying in the interests of stockholders in mining companies—and was so regarded in other countries. Kruger-Milner negotiations Second Boer War, 1899–1902

The British public light-heartedly expected the war to be over in a few weeks, yet the defeat of 50,000 Boers took 450,000 British troops, and before the end cost 22,000 lives and well over £200 million of money. The Boers proved themselves unrivalled as mounted infantry; they were splendid marksmen and adept in the use of ground. They had the great advantage of fighting in familiar country where they could usually find friends. They had plenty of arms, with enough to spare for the Cape Boers, whose aid they expected. Their artillery, recently bought from Krupps of Essen with the ample funds of the Transvaal treasury, was better at first than the British. Apart from its handicaps in these respects, the British Army suffered from the difficulty of supply over a 4,000-mile route, and above all from the lack of any plans for a campaign, for the Army had no general staff to make them. Moreover, since there were fewer than 15,000 British troops in Boer advantages the country at the outbreak of war, the Boers had a good chance of winning before the vast resources of their opponent could be brought to bear.

Boer mistakes   In the first phase of the war, however, Boer strategy was bad. They launched their chief attack against Natal, where the white people were British, instead of against Cape Colony, where there were 30,000 Dutch. Having driven back British forces from their frontiers into the towns of Kimberley, Mafeking and Ladysmith, they wasted precious time in besieging them when they might have pressed on. But the Boers did well enough against the new British forces which were sent out to take the offensive. One army was defeated at Stormberg, another, which tried to relieve Kimberley, was defeated at Magersfontein, and a third of 20,000 men under Sir Redvers Buller, the Commander-in-Chief, was defeated at the Tugela River when advancing on Ladysmith—

'Black Week',
December 1899   all within five days in December 1899—the 'Black Week'. Buller was then replaced by Lord Roberts,[1] with Lord Kitchener as his Chief of Staff.

Roberts's
campaign   This was not the end of the Boer successes, but Roberts soon changed the complexion of affairs. He concentrated his forces instead of dividing them, and deceiving the Boers as to his objective, advanced from the Orange to the Modder River, outflanking and surrounding Cronje's army with his more numerous forces. Other movements brought about the relief of Kimberley and Ladysmith. Mafeking was freed later, having held out under Baden-Powell for 217 days. By March Roberts had Bloemfontein, and by June was in Johannesburg and Pretoria. It is a remarkable fact that the retreating Boers did not attempt to wreck the goldmines. By August 1900 the last of the organized Boer armies was defeated and Kruger had fled. The two republics were annexed once more, and the war seemed to be over.

Guerrilla war,
1900–1902   It was in fact entering on its most difficult phase. The Boers now resorted to the guerrilla mode of warfare which best suited their own and their country's characteristics. The largest British forces, newly raised, were only just reaching South Africa, but even so Kitchener, left in charge by Roberts, had to spend from October 1900 to March 1902 in breaking down the Boer resistance. The whole Boer country was alive with irregular fighters; both Natal and Cape Colony were raided, sometimes in considerable strength. The commandos led by Botha, de Wet, de la Rey and Smuts covered amazing distances, appeared in most un-

[1] Formerly Sir Frederick Roberts—see page 403.

expected places, and slipped out when apparently cornered. Smuts's commando covered 700 miles in five weeks, much of the time lacking food, fodder, boots and ammunition, and came within sight of Port Elizabeth.

Kitchener's painstaking method of defeating the commandos was to build blockhouses to guard the railways—their favourite objective—and to clear the country of all who could aid the guerrillas with food, remounts and information. This involved the destruction of buildings and supplies and the internment of large numbers of civilians in concentration camps. The army administration was not equal to the difficult task of maintaining healthy conditions in these camps, and of 100,000 people interned 20,000 died; in one camp half the children perished. The Liberal opposition in Parliament raised an outcry against 'methods of barbarism', and Chamberlain then saw that conditions were improved.

The guerrillas were at last worn down and the Boers made peace at Vereeniging in 1902. If Britain's reputation had suffered from the events leading to the war, her treatment of the beaten side did much to redeem it. There was to be no punishment of Boer civilians who had taken up arms; the Boers were promised a measure of self-government; and the British made a gift of £3,000,000 to re-stock devastated Boer farms—a unique instance of reparations in reverse. *(Treaty of Vereeniging, 1902)*

A great effort to wipe out the hatred and bitterness of the South African War was made by the new Liberal Government which came into power in 1906. They decided to trust the recently defeated Boers, not merely with an elected parliament, but with fully responsible government.[1] Accordingly in 1907 Boer governments took office in both the states, the Transvaal Prime Minister being Botha, lately Commander-in-Chief, with Smuts, the lawyer turned soldier, as the chief power in his Cabinet. *(Self-government, 1907)*

The Boer states were now on the same level as the British; three years later came the union of all four into one self-governing Dominion. Outside the Union there remained Rhodesia[2] and three native territories under British administration—Bechuanaland, Basutoland and Swaziland. Within the Union three questions especially needed to be handled by a single authority: the *(Union of South Africa, 1910)*

[1] Cape Colony and Natal, the predominantly British colonies, had been granted responsible government earlier.
[2] Southern Rhodesia was granted responsible government in 1923. Northern Rhodesia, until the large majority of Africans took over, had representative but not responsible government.

management of the railways, customs policy, and the treatment of the Africans, who were five times as numerous as the Europeans. The four divisions remained as separate provinces, but there was a national executive at Pretoria, and a national legislature at Cape Town, to which those of the provinces were subordinate. The first Prime Minister of the Union was Botha, and Smuts was his successor.

The Union in the two World Wars

Even these remarkable developments could not completely wipe out the memory of a century's disagreeements. There was a rebellion under de Wet when South Africa entered the war in 1914, but it was easily suppressed, and the country, under Smuts's guidance, made a notable contribution to victory. German South-West Africa was occupied by the Union forces, and the colony was retained after the war under a League of Nations mandate.[1]

The outbreak of a second and even greater conflict in 1939 found some South Africans still strongly against participation in any British cause, but once again the majority felt the other way and the wise counsels of Smuts prevailed. Under his leadership the South African forces, at first tactfully reserved for the defence of the Union, were given a successively wider rôle. Very early the defence of the Union was interpreted as the defence of all Africa—with what credit to the South African troops all the world saw in Egypt, Libya, Abyssinia and Tunisia; and they finally took their share in the fighting in Italy.

In 1948, however, the Nationalist Party, which inherited the Boer tradition, defeated Smuts's United Party at the polls and embarked on a policy, contrary to all trends in other parts of the world, which was to result in breaking South Africa's connection with the Commonwealth. The solution of the native problem was

Apartheid

to be 'apartheid'—the separation of the European and African peoples into distinct communities and areas. This involved the ending of any African or coloured representation in the national parliament, and discrimination against non-Europeans in every sphere of life. When the Nationalist Government proposed in 1961 to declare South Africa a republic, while remaining in the

South Africa leaves the Commonwealth, 1961

Commonwealth, the other members had to be consulted. Strong objections were raised, because of the apartheid policy, not only by the newly independent members like India and Ghana but by Canada too, and South Africa left the Commonwealth.

Meanwhile the British Government had tried to solve the

[1] See page 258.

economic and political problems of the great regions to the north by combining Southern Rhodesia, which was rich and had a substantial European population, with Northern Rhodesia and Nyasaland, which were less developed and mainly African, in the Central African Federation. Politically-minded Africans opposed this from the start as likely to produce European control of the whole area, and when the African majorities gained political rights in Northern Rhodesia and Nyasaland the new Federation broke up. The result was the birth very soon of two more independent African states, renamed respectively Zambia and Malawi, while Southern Rhodesia remained—unreasonable as this seemed to most of its European inhabitants—in the last resort subordinate to the British Parliament.

Central African Federation formed, 1953—

—dissolved, 1964

Zambia and Malawi, 1964

2 Egypt

During the first half of the nineteenth century, the unscrupulous adventurer Mehemet Ali[1] modernized Egypt in such a way as to increase the revenue of the Government, the size of the army and the misery of the people. His successors continued the tradition, but much less efficiently. The Khedive Ismail[2] encouraged de Lesseps to build the Suez Canal (1859–69), but spent recklessly, and by 1875 was bankrupt. It was when Disraeli secured the Khedive's Suez Canal shares—his only asset—that the British Government acquired a direct interest in Egypt for the first time.

Purchase of Suez Canal shares, 1875

The Egyptian Government, however, was still on the rocks, and could only be refloated by a reform of its whole financial system. This was undertaken by an Anglo-French commission, and when Ismail resisted some of their measures, the two governments persuaded the Sultan to depose him in favour of his son Tewfik (1878). Resentment against this interference by foreigners and the economies they enforced, and the general wretchedness of the country, soon produced a revolt. It was led by Arabi Pasha, an army officer. British and French ships were sent to Alexandria as a precaution, but when Arabi's followers began to murder Europeans and to fortify the place, the French ships withdrew and left the British to take action. The fortifications

Anglo-French financial control

Arabi Pasha's revolt, 1881

Withdrawal of France

[1] See pages 143–4.
[2] The Khedive was nominally the viceroy of the Sultan of Turkey but in fact was almost independent.

were bombarded, and a force under Sir Garnet Wolseley which was promptly sent from England neatly defeated Arabi's troops at Tel-el-Kebir.

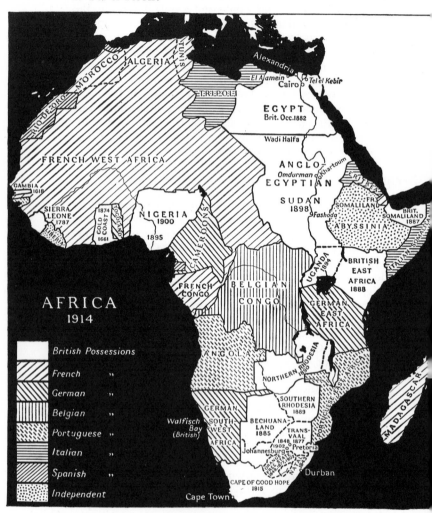

AFRICA
1914

British Possessions
French "
German "
Belgian "
Portuguese "
Italian "
Spanish "
Independent

Through the unexpected retirement of France, the British now found themselves the virtual rulers of Egypt. But for Gladstone's horror of new commitments the Government might well have annexed it outright, for Egypt's position on the route to India was now seen to be vitally important, and its new cotton-fields supplied Lancashire with its finest raw material. Instead, Gladstone contented himself with maintaining a British force in the country as a guarantee of order and obedience to British intentions; and he despatched Sir Evelyn Baring, later Lord Cromer, to Cairo, to begin the overhaul of Egyptian finance and administration. *Occupation of Egypt*

The first problem to assert itself was Egypt's dependency, the Sudan. The government of the country was shockingly bad, and a leader who proclaimed himself as the Mahdi, or Messiah, found it easy to stir the people to revolt, adding religious fervour to their ample discontents. The country was soon overrun by the rebels except for a number of marooned Egyptian garrisons. *The Sudan*

The decision whether to reconquer the Sudan, or to rescue the isolated garrisons and withdraw, now rested upon Gladstone and his Cabinet. They resolved to abandon the country south of Wadi Halfa, and chose General Gordon—who had earlier been employed in the Sudan by the Khedive—to evacuate the garrisons. The choice was scarcely wise. Gordon had proved himself a fine soldier and an inspiring leader, and a policy of retreat was not likely to commend itself to him. When he reached Khartoum he began to devise ways and means of saving the Sudan from the hordes of the Madhi. By the time this policy had been vetoed from London valuable weeks had been lost, and by May 1884 Gordon in Khartoum was cut off by the Mahdi's forces. Only a new expeditionary force could save him.

It was not surprising that Gladstone should resent being compelled by Gordon's plight to send a substantial force to the Sudan—the very thing he had tried to avoid. He therefore postponed action for some time. Only in October did an expedition leave Wadi Halfa; it spent three months fighting its way up to Khartoum, and arrived on 28 January 1885 to find that the place had been stormed and Gordon killed two days before. Nothing did more to damage Gladstone's reputation as a guardian of imperial interests. The Sudan was then evacuated, and left to the tender mercies of the Mahdi's followers. *Death of Gordon, 1885* *Evacuation of Sudan*

In Egypt itself, British efforts, though hampered by the claims of other interested Powers, were more fortunate. Lord Cromer, as 'adviser' to the Egyptian Government, accomplished great reforms. Dams, reservoirs and canals were built by British engineers to conserve and distribute the waters of the Nile—on *Cromer in Egypt, 1883–1907* which the fertility and wealth of Egypt have always depended —to better effect than ever before. In spite of having to provide for the service of the debt, Cromer was able to reduce almost every tax, and with the abolition of forced labour under the whip the lot of the peasantry was much improved. The administration and the courts were purged of corruption and the land-tax was re-assessed on a fair basis. Though a return had to be made to foreign investors on the railways and other developments provided by modern enterprise, the people of the country had some share of the benefits. 'Water and Justice' aptly summarizes the achievements of Cromer's twenty-four years in Egypt.

The conquest of the Sudan

In 1896 Salisbury's Government decided to gain security for Egypt and control of the upper waters of the Nile. A model campaign was directed by Sir Herbert (later Lord) Kitchener, in command of the Egyptian army. He built a railway to supply his forces as he marched into the Sudan, and—with the help of the Maxim gun—defeated the fanatical enemy in every engagement, the last being Omdurman, which gave him Khartoum.

Omdurman, 1898

The Fashoda incident, 1898

On pushing up the Nile to complete his task, Kitchener found at Fashoda Major Marchand, who had marched eastward 2,800 miles to secure the Upper Sudan for France. After exchanges between the two countries that brought them to the brink of war, Marchand's expedition was withdrawn. A joint government by Britain and Egypt was established over the Sudan, but in view of the predominance of the British in Egypt itself the Egyptian share of power was small. The transformation subsequently wrought in the Sudan, which in the preceding years of chaos had been half depopulated, outdid the British achievement in Egypt itself.

The war of 1914–1918; the Nationalist Movement

On the outbreak of war in 1914 the nominal suzerainty of Turkey over Egypt was at last discarded, the ruling Khedive, who was pro-Turkish, was deposed, and his successor eventually took the title of King. But Egypt's claim to some real independence, urged by a growing and vigorous nationalist movement under Zaghlul Pasha, met with no satisfaction until Mussolini began to carry out his plans for a revival of the Roman Empire in Africa. Then the Egyptian leaders lowered their terms, and after fifty-four years the British occupation was at last given a legal basis by the conclusion of a treaty between the two governments. Under this agreement British troops were to remain in Egypt for another twenty years, but were to be largely withdrawn to the Canal Zone. The Egyptians gained control of their own affairs both domestic and foreign, without the former restrictions

The Anglo-Egyptian Treaty of 1936

in favour of foreigners, but the future of the Sudan was left unsettled until the treaty should come up for revision.[1]

The outbreak of war in 1939 deferred the retirement of British troops to the Canal Zone. The Egyptian Government declined to declare war against Germany and Italy, but was generally helpful to the Allied effort. After the country was saved from an Italo-German invasion at El Alamein in 1942 the British forces were for a brief spell positively popular. But after the war the troops were duly withdrawn to the Canal Zone, and in 1956 were evacuated altogether. Thereupon Colonel Nasser, who became a dictator in Egypt about this time, nationalized the Suez Canal. On the failure of Anglo-French military intervention,[2] broken off almost as soon as begun, Britain lost the whole of her stake in Egypt—her shares in the Canal, her base, and a strategic position of great value.

Egypt and the Second World War

British out of Egypt, 1956

3 Tropical Africa

In the history of European activity in tropical Africa pride of place belongs to the explorers. Into a continent unknown except for its coastal regions they pushed their intrepid discoveries in the face of disease and hostile tribes, until by the end of the nineteenth century they had revealed the courses of the great rivers, delineated the lakes and charted the immense forests. They found new sources of wealth for the white man to exploit, and showed up the darkness of a continent many of whose peoples were sunk in superstition and barbarism. British explorers were prominent in every region—on the limits of the Sahara and in the hinterland of the west coast, in discovering the great lakes of the east and the sources of the Nile, and in southern Central Africa.

No journey was more daring than that of Mungo Park, a young Scottish surgeon, who ventured alone in 1795–97 from Gambia to the River Niger, the course of which was then quite unknown, and lost his life in repeating the exploit to make further discoveries. In 1857 the Royal Geographical Society sent Sir Richard Burton, who had achieved fame by penetrating into Mecca disguised as an Arab pilgrim, to search for the great lakes rumoured to lie in the heart of Africa. He was accompanied by J. H. Speke until they separated after reaching Lake Tanganyika, when Speke

Mungo Park, 1771–1806

Sir Richard Burton, 1821–1890

J. H. Speke, 1827–1864

---

[1] The Sudan gained its independence in 1956.
[2] See pages 317–18.

went on to discover Lake Victoria. On a second journey he found the place where the Nile flows from the lake, and following the great river down its course he encountered Sir Samuel Baker, a wealthy sportsman and seeker after adventure who had made his way up the Nile from Egypt. Baker explored the region further and carefully surveyed it.

Sir Samuel Baker, 1821-1893

The crowning achievement was that of David Livingstone, a self-educated Scot who had started work in a cotton-mill at the age of ten. Preparing himself by taking a course in medicine, he offered his services to the London Missionary Society, which had decided to 'go forward to the dark interior' of Africa. Livingstone's first great expedition was made in 1853-56 entirely on foot and without white companions; a handful of faithful Africans accompanied him. Starting from the middle Zambesi he made his way across to the west coast at Loanda and returned to the east coast, discovering the Victoria Falls on his way. He was continually confronted with the slave trade, and made the ending of it the main objective of his life. The reports of this journey made him famous at home and gave the British public its first picture of the mysterious continent. On his second journey of exploration he started from the mouth of the Zambesi, and later, pushing northwards, discovered Lake Nyasa. Finally the Royal Geographical Society, hoping to follow up the work of Speke and Baker, commissioned him to seek a higher source of the Nile beyond Tanganyika, and he set out in 1866. Obstructed by slave-traders, beset by every kind of difficulty, and often desperately ill, he persevered, but discovered in fact the upper waters of the Congo and not those of the Nile. H. M. Stanley led a relief expedition which gave Livingstone a fresh start in 1871, but two years later his last great effort was ended by his death. To him more than any other explorer was due, not merely the discovery of Africa, but the extinction of the slave trade and the penetration of the continent, for good or ill, by Europeans.

David Livingstone, 1813-1873

Livingstone's journeys, 1841-1873

Livingstone's last journey, 1866-1873

At the opening of the nineteenth century the only British possessions in Africa had been on the west coast. They consisted of forts which had been useful for the slave trade, and Sierra Leone, which had by contrast been founded in 1788 as a home for slaves liberated in America. After the neighbouring Danish and Dutch forts had been purchased, British control of this coastal strip was consolidated by the wars against the Ashanti tribes in 1873-74 and 1895-96.

West Africa

British expansion in tropical Africa took place in keen rivalry with other Powers which were trying to meet the needs of Europe's ever-expanding industries by finding outlets for their products and securing supplies of raw materials. That 'the scramble for Africa' passed off without a war was largely due to the Conference of Berlin, which laid down rules for the claiming of territory, prohibiting secret agreements between the countries. The British Government was slow to enter the race, Lord Salisbury being the first Prime Minister to see any value in further tropical possessions. Joseph Chamberlain, taking an imaginative business man's view of their possibilities, chose the post of Colonial Secretary in Salisbury's third Ministry, so that he could attend to Britain's 'undeveloped estates'. *Conference of Berlin, 1884–1885*

The pioneer work was done, however, by chartered companies, as in South Africa. The Royal Niger Company was formed in 1886 to forestall the penetration of the French; it developed the trade of the Lower Niger, and looked after native affairs until the Crown took over Nigeria in 1900. There Lord Lugard, the greatest of Britain's administrators in tropical Africa, developed the system of 'indirect rule', by which the education of the natives in government was based upon their own tribal institutions, and the work of the British officials limited to guidance and supervision. *Nigeria*

The British East Africa Company (1888) not only secured what is now the country of Kenya, but took over Uganda, bordering the Sudan on the south. The rival claims of Britain and Germany in East Africa were settled by a convention in 1890, whereby Germany, in return for the European island of Heligoland, recognized the British claims and surrendered her own ambition of building an East African empire which should include the great lakes and the sources of the Nile. H. M. Stanley called it 'exchanging a trouser-button for a suit of clothes'. Agreements were made by Britain in the same year with Portugal and France, by which the boundaries of all adjoining territories were settled, except for Northern Nigeria, delimited in 1898. *East Africa*

The position by 1900 was such that a gain for one country could only be at the expense of another, and this became a contributory cause of the war of 1914–18. As a result of that war, however, one competitor disappeared from the field, for the German colonies were taken over by Britain, France and the Union of South Africa under League of Nations mandates. *African mandates*

By the end of the Second World War the spread of education and of political ideas among Africans, developments in India and elsewhere, and the upheavals of the war itself had produced a 'wind of change'[1] which blew throughout the continent. Everywhere, except in South Africa and the Portuguese colonies, Africans demanded self-rule, and British governments, whether Labour or Conservative, showed no tendency to resist. In the Gold Coast in 1946 and in Nigeria in 1947 elected members were allowed to outnumber nominated members of the legislatures. In the former colony, soon to be known as Ghana, Kwame Nkrumah was released from gaol, where his leadership of the independence movement had landed him, to become Prime Minister in 1951. Both countries became independent members of the Commonwealth as republics in 1961. The countries of East Africa, in general less sophisticated, soon followed, Uganda in 1962, Kenya and Zanzibar in 1963, though in Kenya the Mau Mau rebellion, a tribal and anti-European outbreak of great savagery, showed how far removed these communities were from the conditions normally thought suitable for parliamentary rule and efficient government. The government of Ghana, moreover, immediately adopted a highly independent, sometimes even pro-Communist line of policy, an indication both of the risks involved in the liberation of former colonies and of the degree to which the Commonwealth was being transformed.

[1] The phrase was used by Harold Macmillan when addressing the South African Parliament in 1960.

30. Canada; Australia; New Zealand; the Changing Commonwealth

1 The British Attitude to Colonies in the Early Nineteenth Century

Possessed of the kind of wisdom that comes after the event, one may be amazed at the short-sightedness of leading British statesmen of the early nineteenth century. Almost without exception they thought that colonies were more a nuisance than a blessing. Yet they too were being wise after the event—or thought they were; for after the loss of the 'old Thirteen' in 1783 it seemed plain that colonies would always revolt as soon as they felt strong enough, and that all the trouble and expense of settling and defending them would be wasted. *Opinion after 1783*

Again, there was little to interest British people of the ruling class in the colonies of that time. They were inhabited mostly by coloured races, people of foreign origin, or poor emigrants. The West Indies had an aristocratic planter class, and were the most profitable of all the colonies, but their prosperity depended on slavery. People who objected to corruption in government had a further complaint, for the colonies provided many of the best opportunities and worst scandals. But the main cry was against useless expenditure without return: 'the public derives no commercial advantage from colonies which it might not have without them', as one writer put it—and that seemed to settle the matter. *Objections to colonies*

After the Napoleonic War, however, a positive interest in the colonies began to revive. The possessions which passed into British hands by the peace settlement of 1815[1] were chiefly of strategic value as bases for the exercise of wider and greater sea power. But as the century wore on, other factors gained influence, foremost among them being the Industrial Revolution. This created an urgent need for great supplies of raw materials, markets to absorb the increased output of goods, and room for emigrants. *Revival of interest*

[1] See page 72.

427

The trade which supplied these needs became, for a time at least, a bond between Britain and the colonies, not a cause of quarrel, as trade had often been in the eighteenth century. Moreover, Britain's complete conversion to free trade policies removed one

(Leech, 1848, reproduced by permission of the Proprietors of 'Punch

HERE AND THERE; *or,* EMIGRATION A REMEDY

In the 'Hungry 'Forties' emigration offered many working men their only chance of decent and happy existence. It was strongly recommended by *Punch* as an alternativ to Chartism or Socialism!

of the chief motives for trying to control the colonies—the exclusion of foreign goods. By 1860 Britain was allowing free trade with all parts of the Empire.

Ideals were at work, however, as well as cash considerations. The humanitarian reformers were not satisfied with the abolition of the slave trade in 1807 and of slavery in 1833; spurred on by the reports of missionaries, they were eager to better the lot of savage and ignorant people everywhere, and if necessary to extend British rule for this purpose. Then the appalling distress at home, it seemed, could be relieved only by emigration when the numbers of the poor were increasing at such an alarming rate.

The men who did most to foster new possibilities of Empire were the 'Radical Imperialists'. Their leading spirit was Edward Gibbon Wakefield, who ruined his prospects of a political career by twice running off with heiresses and consequently spending some time in Newgate Prison. He used his enforced leisure to read everything he could about the colonies, where he hoped later to make good. But his reading served a wider purpose: he realized from it what was wrong in the new colonies where British people were trying to settle—particularly in New South Wales—and worked out a method, which he called 'systematic colonization', for overcoming the principal difficulties. These arose mainly through the early settlers staking claims to large areas of land and then having no labour with which to farm them. The results were a dispersed population without towns or amenities, and a hard and wretched life which respectable and moneyed people would not endure.

Radical Imperialists

Wakefield's scheme was for the Government to take possession of all the land, which should be sold, not given away, to settlers with capital; the proceeds would pay for the passage of new emigrants who would work for wages until they in their turn could afford to take up new land; thus there would always be labour available, and the country would be developed in an orderly way. Wakefield hoped that some people of every class would be transplanted, to make the new colony like a cross-section of Britain. Instead of being despised as rough pioneers the colonists would be respected, and would be worthy of self-government as soon as there were enough of them. Fortunately a number of prominent M.P.s soon became converts to Wakefield's plans, including Edward Buller and Lord Durham, both Radicals in politics and rebels in character.

Wakefield's 'systematic colonization'

Inspired by these ideas, Britain built a new empire in the nineteenth century on the foundations laid by her success in the Napoleonic War. She came, 'in a fit of absence of mind' as far as the Government was concerned, to acquire vast territories suited to white settlement. She peopled them with emigrants,[1]

Britain's imperial achievement

[1] There were 300,000 in the one year 1850. 'Between 1815 and 1872 there passed from the United Kingdom 7,561,285 souls, about a million and a half to Canada, four millions to the United States, one million to Australia, and not quite two hundred thousand elsewhere—an astonishing achievement for the common people, who paid the cost in money, labours,

became the foremost colonizing power, and built up a partnership of nations based on new ideas of freedom and co-operation.

2 Canada

In 1783 the British possessions in North America consisted of Newfoundland; the three maritime colonies of Nova Scotia, Prince Edward Island and New Brunswick; and Quebec, taken from France in 1763.

The loss of the Thirteen Colonies caused a great change in Canada through the immigration of those who had taken the British side in the War of Independence. These 'United Empire Loyalists', to the number of some 50,000, gave Canada its first English-speaking population; some settled in New Brunswick, but most in Ontario. Unlike the French in the neighbouring region, they would not be satisfied without rights of self-government. William Pitt the Younger decided to treat both peoples alike, and in his Canada Act of 1791 created two new governments of Upper Canada (Ontario) and Lower Canada (Quebec). Each had an elected assembly which controlled most of the revenue, but there was also a council nominated by the Governor, who kept to his policy and his chosen advisers whatever the elected assembly might say or do. This was representative but not responsible government, and was said by Edward Buller to be 'like a fire without a chimney', because the assembly obstructed and criticized the Government for all it was worth, these being the only things it could do.

By 1830 there were serious discontents in both Upper and Lower Canada. In the latter the trouble was that a mainly French people, represented by a French Assembly, were ruled by a British Governor who chose British advisers. In Upper Canada there were three main grievances. First, the Governor's Council and all the best posts in government were filled by a small clique of Loyalists who kept all favours to themselves to the detriment of later immigrants. Secondly, great tracts of land were 'clergy reserves', set aside for the upkeep of religious bodies and mostly left waste—a criminal hindrance to the development of a new country. Thirdly, Lower Canada kept an unfairly large share of the customs revenues. The people of both provinces helped

Pitt's Canada Act, 1791

Rebellions, 1837

sorrows, sickness and death.'—Professor J. L. Morison in *The Cambridge History of the British Empire*, Vol. II.

loyally to repel the American invasion in the war of 1812–14,[1] but discontent grew until both broke into rebellion in 1837.

The risings were easily suppressed, and the Government might have treated them lightly. Fortunately the Whig Ministry of Lord Melbourne looked upon them as a symptom of serious trouble, and chose Lord Durham—partly, it must be confessed, to get that turbulent peer out of the way—to go to Canada as Governor-General and investigate the cause. He took with him Buller and Wakefield, and with their assistance he collected material for the Report which was to be the basis of British policy towards the 'white' colonies for the rest of the century.

Durham Report, 1838

Durham hit upon the principle which was essential for the future welfare of the Empire: the colonists must be trusted to manage their own affairs. First, Upper and Lower Canada, divided by Pitt, should be reunited to form one colony, for Durham considered that the French must be subordinated to the British. Then responsible government was to be introduced, i.e. the Governor, like the King in Britain, should rule with the advice of ministers who were supported by the majority in the elected assembly; this assembly would have control of all the revenues, and if the ministers lost its approval for any reason, they must resign. The only matters to be withheld from popular control were defence, external trade, foreign affairs, and the empty lands of the colony. Although these were big exceptions, the change proposed was drastic, so drastic that Russell, Gladstone and many others thought it meant the virtual separation of the colony from the mother country. But whereas the doubters thought self-government for colonists would break up the Empire, Durham and his friends were convinced that nothing else could save it.

Responsible government

The first and more easily swallowed of Durham's proposals was put into effect in the Canada Act of 1840, which merged Upper and Lower Canada into one government, in which the British had a majority, but a moderate one, over the French. The second proposal was adopted to the full when Lord Elgin became Governor-General.[2] Elgin selected a prime minister from the majority party, allowed him to choose his colleagues, and did not use the Governor's veto on acts of the Canadian Parliament unless they affected imperial interests. British and

Canada Act, 1840

Elgin, 1847–1854

[1] See page 65.
[2] He was son-in-law to Lord Durham, as Durham was to Lord Grey of the Reform Bill.

French worked together, both in the Ministry and in opposition, and old difficulties were overcome. The most striking sign of the colony's new position was seen in 1859 when the Canadian Parliament placed a tariff on imported manufactures, including British products, at a time when Britain had adopted almost complete free trade.

Canada and U.S.A.—boundary disputes

Canada's relations with the United States were disturbed by two awkward boundary questions, but both were settled peacefully,[1] and the two countries continued to enjoy the enormous blessing of an undefended frontier. However, the militant mood of the North American states at the time of the Civil War (1861–65) brought new troubles. The U.S. Government put an end to a commercial treaty which had been in force since 1854, and thus struck a shrewd blow at Canadian trade—for Canada's trade routes all ran north and south, linking the country with the U.S.A. and leaving the provinces unconnected with each other. This brought the American ambition to absorb Canada one stage nearer fulfilment; and it was partly to guard against this that the union of all Canada was now planned.

Need for unity of Canada

There were other reasons too. Railways were badly needed to link up the maritime colonies with the rest of the country. Moreover, the racial problem called for a new solution. Emigration from Britain was tipping the balance against the French, who now felt insecure in face of the growing English-speaking majority. There was only one way to reconcile their desire for separate status with the general need for greater unity—federation, the method adopted by the United States in 1789.

British North America Act, 1867—

—Dominion of Canada

So another great experiment in imperial government was launched in 1867 by the British North America Act, based on a scheme which the Canadians had worked out for themselves. Ontario and Quebec were now separated once more, but together with New Brunswick and Nova Scotia[2] handed over many important powers to a new federal government whose capital was finally fixed at Ottawa. The Canadian constitution gave strictly limited powers to the member governments, calling them provinces instead of states, and left all other powers to the federal government. Special safeguards were included to secure the rights of the French-speaking province of Quebec.

Canada now turned her attention to the task of developing the

---

[1] See pages 146–7.
[2] Prince Edward Island came into the federation in 1873: Newfoundland remained a separate Dominion until it became a province of Canada in 1949.

vast western tracts which had thus far been put to little use except The prairie provinces for the fur trade of the Hudson's Bay Company. The Company gave up its control of these regions in 1869 in return for £300,000 compensation. British Columbia, already comparatively well populated with the help of a gold rush to the Fraser River—as in the United States, the westward movement jumped a huge width of prairie which was filled up later—joined the federation in 1871 on condition that a railway should be built to link it with the east. The railway, reaching from Atlantic to Pacific, would be the life-line of the new Canada, but ten years elapsed before its construction was begun. The task required a great deal of Canadian Pacific Railway, 1881–1886 financial help from the Government, which was forthcoming under the guidance of the Conservative Prime Minister, Sir John Macdonald.

Macdonald was also responsible for setting up a high protective tariff, enacted in 1879. This seemed necessary to prevent Canada from being flooded with American goods to the detriment of her own and Britain's industries, which were favoured under the tariff by a lower duty.

Emigration to Canada was stimulated by the improved commu- Immigration nications within the country as well as by improved transatlantic travel. The Grand Trunk Railway and the Canadian Northern Railway followed the Canadian Pacific in spanning the continent. The population increased from nearly 4 million in 1867 to over 7 million in 1911 and nearly 19 million in 1963. With the filling of the prairie lands, Manitoba became a new province in 1870, Alberta and Saskatchewan in 1905; these were the provinces which grew most rapidly in population. The number of immigrants reached the very high total of 400,000 in 1913; a third of them came from the United States, and most of those from Europe were not of British birth.

Generally the oldest Dominion has grown fast. The populated region must always for reasons of climate be limited to the more southerly latitudes, but through the breeding of hardier types of wheat and the discovery of mineral ores this region has been widened. Canada enjoys a large variety of resources, and through the stimulus of two world wars and a considerable influx of U.S. capital has greatly developed her industries. The St Law- St Lawrence Seaway, 1959 rence Seaway, a great and imaginative project enabling ocean-going ships to reach the ports of the Great Lakes, was a joint U.S.–Canadian enterprise. Canada plays an important part in world politics by reason of her growing industrial resources, her traditional links with two European states, and her involvement in both Atlantic and Pacific affairs.

3 Australia

The continent of Australia should have been the scene of the most fortunate of colonial adventures, for it was free from many of the difficulties which beset the other Dominions. Its native people were most primitive and offered hardly any resistance to the white man, it was not troubled by the presence of European rivals to cause wars and racial bitterness, and though vast distances presented problems to the engineer and the statesman, the habitable parts of the continent were not too far from the sea. Yet the history of Australia is the story of a bad start retrieved with difficulty.

Captain Cook

The expedition commanded by Captain James Cook rediscovered Australia in 1770—part of its coastline had been known earlier to the Dutch—and sailed northwards along its eastern coast, which no European had seen before. In 1788 Captain

Transportation
of convicts,
1788-1868

Arthur Phillip arrived at Botany Bay with instructions to annex the whole east coast, in charge of a company of 700 convicts with 200 marines to guard them. This was the British Government's notion of the best way to make use of the new continent which lay at its feet, and the notion died hard. Till 1830 convicts outnumbered free immigrants, and altogether 167,000 were dumped in Australia before the traffic finally came to an end in 1868.

There was nothing to be said for the transportation system, though it was considered a more humane—and less expensive—way of dealing with convicts than imprisoning them in Britain. Conditions on the voyage caused many convicts to die; discipline was maintained by brutal punishments; 'assignment' to a private employer meant virtual slavery; there was no provision for a return passage, and convicts who had served their sentence had little chance of making an honest living in the new country. At times a large proportion of the transported men were political prisoners such as Chartists or Irish agitators whose chief fault was independence of mind. But when Peel reduced the application of the death penalty, sentences of transportation became more numerous and the convicts were of a worse type.

Free
settlement

For a long time the presence of convicts and the length of the voyage deterred emigrants from trying their fortune in Australia. Captain Phillip moved his settlement after a week from Botany

Bay to Sydney, having reconnoitred the site which adjoins one of the world's finest harbours. Free settlers came in only negligible numbers, until first sheep-rearing and later gold-mining held out promise of prosperity. John Macarthur imported merino sheep and reared them successfully (1797). Later a pass was discovered leading across the Blue Mountains to the fine grazing land beyond, and then more settlers arrived. The desire to avoid the convicts of New South Wales and Van Diemen's Land[1] helped to bring about the first settlements in Victoria in 1817. Though Sturt explored the river system of South-Eastern Australia by 1830, and began to probe the vast interior desert, the crossing of the continent was not achieved till 1861.

The founding of South Australia, beginning with the region at the mouth of the Murray River, was an attempt to carry out Gibbon Wakefield's plan of systematic colonization. Previously land had been sold cheaply at 5s. an acre or given away, and there was no labour to work it except that of convicts, because free men preferred to start on their own. Wakefield organized a company to colonize South Australia, Adelaide was founded in 1836, 16,000 people were settled on the principle of selling land at a price not lower than £1 per acre, and the colony made good progress. South Australia, 1836

It was the discovery of gold, 'that great fertilizer of settlement', that gave Australia a substantial population for the first time. It was found in 1851 at Bathurst in New South Wales, and then in richer quantities at Ballarat, Victoria. The rush was unparalleled; sheep were left untended, derelict ships littered the harbours, and Melbourne had two policemen left to uphold law and order. The population of Victoria increased from 70,000 to 333,000 in the five years after 1850, and the population of the whole country, only 400,000 in 1850, reached a million in 1860. Gold

The consequence was an advance towards self-government. New South Wales was allowed a partly elected legislature in 1842; after that things moved fast. An act passed in 1850 at the instance of Lord John Russell gave the Australian colonies permission to frame institutions of their own choice—the surest sign that the daughter-nations were coming of age. Tasmania, South Australia and Victoria, as well as New South Wales, drafted constitutions of a very democratic kind, and these were confirmed by the British Parliament in 1855. The colonies were then launched on responsible government after the Canadian model. Queensland Self-government

---

[1] When transportation to Van Diemen's Land ceased in 1853 the island was renamed Tasmania in an effort to obliterate the past.

gained the same status as the rest in 1859, West Australia in 1890.

Australia took much longer than Canada to achieve unity as a Dominion. The colonies, separated by mountain or desert, went their separate ways, even building railways with different gauges. Each had ample land and access to the sea through a seaport-capital, and until the later years of the century there was no foreign danger to drive home the need for unity. But when the rising sun of Japan appeared on the horizon, and France, Germany and the United States were eagerly seizing their opportunities in the Pacific, and when Australian standards of living were endangered by an influx of Asiatic immigrants, the colonies sank their differences. After many years of negotiation they hammered out a scheme of federation, which left much more power in the hands of the states than was the case in Canada.

Australian politics since the federation was formed have shown interesting features. Australia was among the first countries in the world where the working man tried to build a paradise for his kind by the use of the vote, which is compulsory. Early in the twentieth century many bold measures were enacted—the breaking-up of big landed estates, laws to enforce minimum wages and an eight-hour day, compulsory arbitration of industrial disputes, old age pensions at sixty-five, and state ownership of the railways. These have been accompanied by a 'White Australia' policy, which means the rigid exclusion of non-Europeans in order to maintain a high standard of living. The area of undeveloped fertile land is not large, however, and there can be no denying the difficulty of Australia's position as a neighbour of teeming Pacific countries. Indeed, during the Second World War the danger reached a critical stage, and valiantly as Australian soldiers fought in New Guinea and elsewhere, the Japanese enemy could hardly have been driven from the gates without the great naval and air power of America. The logic of this situation was recognized by the formation in 1951, without the participation of Britain, of the 'Anzus' defence pact by Australia, New Zealand and the United States

Federation: Commonwealth of Australia, 1901

Australia in the twentieth century

Anzus Pact, 1951

4 New Zealand

The first white men to interest themselves in New Zealand were buccaneers, escaped convicts, and unscrupulous traders whose staple wares were firearms and spirits. This was the more to be regretted because the natives of the country, the Maoris, were a noble and likeable race, though overmuch given to fighting. They numbered 100,000 in the North Island, but were very few in the South Island. Missionaries did their best to protect the Maoris from less reputable Europeans, but the British Government took no interest until the New Zealand Association, another of Gibbon Wakefield's ventures, landed 1,200 colonists in 1839. New Zealand Association—first settlement, 1839

Then at last the Governor of New South Wales was told to take the country under his charge. The Treaty of Waitangi was made with a gathering of Maori chiefs, whereby they recognized the sovereignty of the British Crown, and were confirmed in possession of all the lands of New Zealand—only a fraction of which they occupied. This was perhaps a good start, but it left unsettled the terms on which white men could obtain the land they required. Years of confusion followed, in which settlers continued to purchase land on dubious terms, to find their claims challenged later by the tribes. The New Zealand Association disregarded the Treaty, which they described as 'a praiseworthy device for amusing and pacifying savages for the moment'. But the Colonial Office stood by it, and refused to support the settlers' claims against the Maoris even when the latter rebelled. Treaty of Waitangi, 1840

Harmony was restored for a time by Sir George Grey,[1] who so won the trust of the Maoris that they desired him to be made Governor for life. Grey stopped irregular acquisition of land, and at the same time the Crown purchased the whole of the South Island from the Maoris and made large areas available for settlement by the Association, which, however, was bought out and dissolved in 1850. Its final achievement was to establish new settlements in Otago and Canterbury, the first with the co-operation of the Free Church of Scotland, the second in association with the Church of England Society for the Propagation of the Gospel. There were now six distinct settlements; they were given each an elected council, with an elected assembly for the country as a whole. Government was made fully responsible in 1856, so that New Zealand ran the full course from the first organized settlement to complete self-government in little more than a Sir George Grey Responsible government, 1856

[1] Grey had a remarkable and honourable career: he put South Australia on its feet when he was Governor 1841–45, was Governor of New Zealand twice, 1845–53 and 1861–68, of Cape Colony 1854–59, and going later to live in New Zealand was elected to Parliament and became Prime Minister 1877–79. He is not to be confused with the Sir George Grey who as Home Secretary in Russell's ministry introduced the Factory Act of 1850.

quarter of a century. In 1876 the provincial governments were found unnecessary and a single government at Wellington ruled the whole country.

The Maoris

Unfortunately trouble recurred with the Maoris of the North Island in 1860, and a war broke out which dragged on for ten years. The more intractable chiefs resented European encroachment, and even when punished by confiscation of their lands refused to admit defeat. They finally retained about half of the North Island, which was sufficient for their needs after the reduction of their numbers, brought about not so much by war as by the contagion of the white man's diseases. As early as 1867 they were given representation in the New Zealand Parliament. Their numbers and prosperity have since grown, and New Zealand may be considered the most successful of the countries of the Empire in the solution of its native problem.

Recent history

The subsequent history of the country was marked first by difficult years when a return had to be made on the capital lavishly invested in the early developments, and then by a recovery in the early 'nineties which was aided by bold government measures. New Zealand has had a larger dose of Socialism than any other English-speaking nation, and seems to like it. Wealth is comparatively evenly spread, and the people enjoy a high degree of social welfare through state insurance and regulation of industry. At the same time security against external forces has been sought in stiff tariffs and severe restrictions on immigration. The efforts of New Zealand in the two World Wars were, in proportion to her resources, no whit less than those of her sister Dominions.

5 Commonwealth Changes in the Twentieth Century

In the nineteenth century the freedom of the colonies with mainly European populations grew until they became almost independent nations, though strongly united by bonds of sentiment and interest with the mother country. Attempts to create more formal ties found little support. The gatherings of Prime Ministers which began at the time of Queen Victoria's first jubilee in 1887 were regularly renewed, usually at four-year intervals, for the discussions of matters of common interest. The meetings, however, have always been purely consultative, and so no member of the Commonwealth is bound by their conclusions. In the latter part of the

Imperial Conference

nineteenth century there was a movement to introduce Imperial Federation, with a representative Council which should act as a government for the whole Empire, but this proposal met with little favour in the Dominions.

Plans for the closer economic unity of the Empire have had better but only limited success. Whereas in the nineteenth century trade between Britain and the daughter-nations was largely complementary, their raw materials being exchanged for British manufactures, they have become largely industrialized during the twentieth century, and their products are often in competition with those of the mother country. Of the total trade of the Commonwealth one-third is internal, but, despite the imperial preference scheme adopted in 1932,[1] the proportion decreases as the trade of the member countries expands. It remains true, however, that Britain is one of the most important suppliers and one of the most important markets for nearly every Commonwealth country. After 1945, moreover, the British Government laid out considerable sums every year through the Colonial Development Corporation for the benefit of the poorer colonies.

The first attempt to define the new constitutional relationship between Britain and the five self-governing countries of that time, usually called Dominions—Canada, Australia, New Zealand, South Africa, and Newfoundland—was made in the Statute of Westminster, 1931. This was based on the Balfour Declaration, of which the key phrases were: 'autonomous communities within the British Empire, equal in status, in no way subordinate, united in a common allegiance, freely associated'. By the terms of this Statute the British Parliament gave up all claim to legislate for the Dominions, while their own power of legislation was not to be limited in any way; they could repeal British-made laws if they wished. The Dominions signed the peace treaties of 1919 as separate states, and increasingly sent their own diplomats to represent them in foreign capitals. The new status of the Dominions rendered the word 'Empire' inappropriate in reference to them, and 'Commonwealth' was adopted instead, though while a large number of colonies remained dependent only the phrase 'Commonwealth and Empire' could properly represent the facts.

Statute of Westminster, 1931

'British Commonwealth and Empire'

This very mixed and unprecedented collection of countries was at the limit of its extent and the height of its prosperity before the economic crisis of 1931, from which it suffered in common

[1] See page 225 for J. Chamberlain's proposals and page 274 for the Ottawa Conference, 1932.

with the rest of the world. The supreme test of the Second World War proved its cohesion. The dependent countries—including India—were involved in the war by the action of Britain, but the self-governing states, excepting of course Eire, unhesitatingly joined Britain of their own accord and played a full part in the six years' struggle. No better proof could have been given of the reality of unity without coercion.

The period since the war has seen the most rapid and drastic changes in the Commonwealth. The war disturbed the life of every colony, and incidentally provided the spectacle of the temporary defeat of Americans and Europeans by an Asiatic people—the Japanese. In each colony by 1945 there was an educated minority, however small, of people who were conversant with European ideas and methods of government, and who were ready to claim self-rule, sometimes perhaps in their own particular interests but usually with the backing of a majority of their fellow-countrymen.

Independence of the colonies

These claims were not to be denied unless at great expense and probably with bloodshed, and in contradiction of the main principle of colonial rule. For it had always been understood that government by the British was a trust exercised on behalf of native populations—a trust to be surrendered when the people concerned were ready for self-government. If sometimes through natural impatience they claimed independence before they were ready, the choice between efficient rule and freedom was nevertheless for the people themselves to make. Already by 1949 every colony but Somaliland had a legislative assembly of some kind; and in one after another of these colonies elected representatives came to have a voting majority. But this was not enough; full independence, perhaps with a republican form of government, was the aim. In 1957 Ghana achieved independence, in 1960 Nigeria, in 1961 Sierra Leone and Tanganyika, in 1962 Uganda, in 1963 Kenya and Zanzibar, the latter soon to be merged with Tanganyika. In the same year North Borneo and Sarawak joined with Malaya and Singapore, already independent, to form the Malaysian Federation; in the Caribbean, on the other hand, the proposed federation broke up, and Jamaica emerged as one separate state, Trinidad and Tobago as another. In 1964 British rule in Malta came to an end, while Northern Rhodesia (renamed Zambia) and Nyasaland (renamed Malawi) celebrated their independence under African governments. Whereas at the end of the Second World War only 14 per cent of the population of the Commonwealth lived in independent states, 89 per cent did so by 1961, a total of 685 million people.

Independence of course carried with it the right to secede from the Commonwealth altogether. This was the choice of Burma, Somaliland, Sudan and the South Cameroons—and of South Africa. Those new members that remained were Dominions of a different kind from their senior fellows. All had populations mainly of non-European origin; most were poor and very much dependent on outside aid; many comprised tribal societies with hardly the makings of a nation. Some governments, while not repudiating the Commonwealth, were far from pro-British in their attitude. Ghana leant heavily towards Communism, both in its internal arrangements and in its external contacts. Russia and China indeed took a lively interest in these new members of the world family of nations. In the Assembly of the United Nations their numbers, if not their wealth or experience, gave them some weight.

Secession from the Commonwealth

The newly independent members

The result of all these changes is virtually a new Commonwealth, more difficult than ever to define. At its core are the countries formed mainly by settlement from Britain, still bound to her by tradition and common political ways and ideas even if they are conscious of different social ideals. Joined with them now as equal partners are the new nations of Asia and Africa, some endowed with, others lacking, an ancient religious and cultural heritage. All in varying degrees have links with Britain in defence and in trade, through language, law and education, and they join in general consultation on world affairs which they would not share as foreign and unassociated countries. While the links are weak and sometimes intangible, the former imperial connection has more often left a legacy of trust than one of bitterness, and it may be hoped that in a rapidly shrinking world this group of freely associated states may come to find their common interests growing rather than diminishing. Whether they will actually do so, however, is anyone's guess.

The new Commonwealth

Epilogue

By the 1960s the growth of mechanical power and the transfer of political power to the masses had gone far, and the lot of the British people was very different from that of their 18th-century ancestors. All adults might vote, all might aspire to the highest office, all might have the benefit of state-provided education. At home, Britain had become a democracy; overseas, her Empire had evolved into a freely associated Commonwealth. At the same time the power of the machine, controlled by the voice of the people, had abolished many wearisome tasks, shortened hours of work and brought a new wealth of leisure. New opportunities for sport and seaside holidays, deriving from shorter hours and mass transport; better and healthier houses; new comforts and facilities in the home—good water and sanitation, gas, electric light, the telephone; cheap food, furniture and clothing; broadcasting, television, and the films; widely distributed books and newspapers; an increased 'expectation of life' of twenty years—these were but a few of the advantages mechanical progress had brought in its train. In the process, things of value had partly succumbed—diversity and independence of outlook, nearness to nature and nature's beauties, popular belief in religion—but on balance the British people were immeasurably better off, more humane, healthier and happier in 1960 than in 1783.

Yet in many respects the power of the machine had outrun the ability of man to control it. The private motor-car, for instance, had immensely eased the problem of transport; but at the same time it was destroying the amenities of cities and turning peaceful rural beauty spots into litter-strewn popular resorts. With every new invention man had increased his capacity not only for good, but for evil. This was seen above all in the international field. The first great external struggle of the British people during these years, against the France of the French Revolution and Napoleon, had been won at comparatively little cost in British blood. But by the time of the second and third struggles—against the Germany of Kaiser Wilhelm and Hitler—science had 'progressed' sufficiently to take a grimmer toll of broken minds and bodies.

Today the danger is greater still, with new and terrible weapons of destruction in the form of atomic bombs and deadly bacteria, and with a standing challenge to the free world's way of life in the principles of the Communist Revolution, at first proclaimed most stridently by Russia, more recently by China. Against these

"BABY PLAY WITH NICE BALL?"

(*Low, August 1945, reproduced by permission of the 'Evening Standard'*)

A cartoon which appeared the day the second atom-bomb fell on Japan. The modern scientist presents poor little humanity with powers far beyond his infant capacity to control.

perils the infant organization of the United Nations is as yet little safeguard. Conscious that wireless and the aeroplane have annihilated distance, man strives vaguely towards political institutions meet for the new world of science, but still seems unable to escape the legacy of his old hatreds and fears. The message before him, however, is now clear: co-operate—or perish.

Index

445